Human Le

CW01083398

A Sourcebook for Head, Heart, Hands, Health and Habitat

in Lean and Agile Enterprise

John Bicheno

Noel Hennessey

PRODUCTION AND INVENTORY CONTROL, SYSTEMS AND INDUSTRIAL ENGINEERING (PICSIE) BOOKS

BUCKINGHAM, ENGLAND
2022

Other books by John Bicheno

- The Lean Toolbox (5th edition) with Matthias Holweg. (A companion volume to this book)(Versions translated into Swedish, Danish, German, Chinese)
- The Service Systems Toolbox
- The Lean Games and Simulations Book
- Innovative Lean (with Andy Brophy) (About Ideas and Idea Management)
- Six Sigma and The Quality toolbox (with Phil Catherwood)
- Fishbone Flow

Published by:
PICSIE Books
15 Chandos Road
Buckingham, MK18 1AH
United Kingdom

E-mail: bichenojohn@me.com

We have attempted properly to reference the many authors whose works have been drawn on. If we missed some, our apologies. Please let us know. We will rectify in future printing.

Publication date: January 2022
ISBN 978-0-9568307-8-4
British Library Cataloguing-in-Publication Data
A catalogue record for this book is available from the British Library

"It is not the critic who counts; not the man who points out how the strong man stumbles, or where the doer of deeds could have done them better. The credit belongs to the man who is actually in the arena, whose face is marred by dust and sweat and blood; who strives valiantly; who errs, who comes short again and again, because there is no effort without error and shortcoming; but who does actually strive to do the deeds; who knows great enthusiasms, the great devotions; who spends himself in a worthy cause; who at the best knows in the end the triumph of high achievement, and who at the worst, if he fails, at least fails while daring greatly, so that his place shall never be with those cold and timid souls who neither know victory nor defeat."

Theodore Roosevelt
        "Citizenship in a Republic", Speech delivered at the Sorbonne, Paris, on 23 April, 1910

'All you need is Love'

(There's nothing you can do that can't be done..)

 (Title of song by Lennon and McCartney)

Contents

Chapter 1
The Human Dimensions of Lean

To introduce this book we will use eight concepts

1. Head, Heart, Hands, Health, Habitat
2. People, Planet, Prosperity
3. Lean Drivers
4. Shingo Prize Principles
5. Agile Manifesto
6. Complexity
7. Why People and Lean?
8. A House of Lean

Throughout the book we have attempted to take a wider, systems, view of the implications for Human aspects of Lean and Agile – as encapsulated in the eight concepts. Many sections of the book inter-relate. It is just not possible to make each section independent. We have therefore indicated the cross-references, where appropriate.

Readers looking for a quick overview of key insights and learnings contained in the book may wish to start with Chapter 15

1.1 Head, Heart, Hands, Health, Habitat

'Head, Heart, Hands, Health, Habitat' is not derived from a recent book 'Head Hand Heart' by David Goodhart (2020), but is an extension from Wallace Hopp's superb article 'Positive lean: merging the science of efficiency with the psychology of work' (Int. Jnl of Production Research, 56:1-2, 398-413, 2018).

Scientific Management's original focus was 'Hands' – the optimal size of a shovel, the breakdown of work into small timed elements and their construction into the assembly line. The separation of doing from thinking. The legacy of correct method and efficiency remains. Hands was quickly joined by Health, and today it is a fundamental requirement in any enterprise. But Toyota-style Lean rejected the separation of Hands and Health, leading to TPS being referred to as the Thinking People System. Head now means much more than problem 'solving' – today a prime requirement is understanding Psychology – particularly the insights that Behavioural Economics have, and are, bringing. Also, just emerging, insights from Anthropology. And Heart – without heart there can be no meaningful engagement, no meaningful commitment – it's winning hearts and minds. Finally, and crucially, comes Habitat – the environment, the green imperative. 'No man is an island' so the story goes – and today no organisation is an island that can ignore pollution, conservation and climate change. Indeed most try to go beyond the legal requirements to protect and conserve our Habitat.

1.2 People, Planet, Prosperity

People, rather than tools, now stand at the centre of Lean. Not just employees, but also a concern for the wellbeing of everyone connected with the organisation – be they customers, suppliers, neighbours, community – and including their families, their security, and their quality of worklife. Today we are beginning to see 'people first' rather than 'customer first'.

Planet: to build on Habitat just discussed, consider Entropy: the 2nd Law of Thermodynamics - often called the supreme Law of the universe. Everything runs down to a state of maximum entropy. For instance, any heat will dissipate until it reaches the same temperature as its surroundings. Every single activity in the world has to be paid for with entropy. Hot food goes cold, we grow old and wrinkly, organisations disappear, races intermingle, empires fold and buildings degrade. All this is impossible to reverse without expending energy. But energy has to come from somewhere, so there is always a penalty to be paid – by someone, by an organisation, by some country, or by the world. Ultimately, 'There is no free lunch'. If this was not true we could have perpetual motion machines - impossible - which relates to the first Law of Thermodynamics. And Energy is the supreme waste - to which every type of waste can be related. Hence, EVERY activity involves waste - even so-called 'value adding' activities, because EVERY activity involves a penalty of energy loss – a trade-off. So Lean, in the wider sense, should be concerned with reducing Entropy – for Planet's sake!

Prosperity. Once the trio was People, Planet, Profit. No longer! First, not all readers of the book will be concerned with Profit. We hope that there will be readers from non-profits, government, charity, and health sectors. (Certainly Lean and Agile apply in these areas.) This is not to deny the role of Profit. It is vital to sustain, renew, and grow. BUT, Milton Friedman not-withstanding, Corporate Social Responsibility goes well beyond profit. (To be fair, Friedman also noted that there are many circumstances in which an organisation's management may engage in actions that serve the long-run interest of the organisation's owners and that also have an indirect positive social impact.) In August 2019, 200 top CEO's forming the Business Roundtable issued a statement. The purpose of a corporation, they said, should no longer advance only the interests of shareholders. Instead, they said, corporations must also invest in their employees, protect the environment and deal fairly and ethically with their suppliers.

1.3 What is Lean? Aims and Drivers

Lean is ultimately about Customer Satisfaction. However, increasingly, there are two wider requirements: Employee satisfaction and minimisation of Environmental impact. Employee satisfaction is not a direct objective of Lean – rather it is a major (perhaps THE major) facilitator to allow Lean and to foster customer satisfaction.
For some organisations, 'Customers' may include shareholders. Environmental impact would include 'citizenship' with the local community, not just reducing emissions and consuming less resources and energy.

To achieve these outcomes there are four Lean objectives:
- Quality: Meet or exceed customer expectations; reduce rework; 'right first time'.
- Reduce Time Buffers: Requiring customers to wait; non-value added activity time; information delays.
- Reduce Inventory Buffers: Queues of work; safety stock, information.
- Reduce Capacity Buffers: unused capacity, both physical and human, including buffers to allow for process variation.

ALL FOUR are necessary. To omit one would indicate that true Lean is not being pursued. Inter-connections between the four allows mutual reinforcement. A buffer is any quantity above the minimum necessary to achieve Just-in-Time FLOW. Minimum buffers will not be known up front – rather they are a moving target as opportunities are revealed as buffers are reduced. ('Peeling the onion' to quote Dan Jones, or Occam's razor, the problem-solving principle that "Entities should not be multiplied beyond necessity.")
In traditional operations the four outcomes were considered as trade-offs. For example, trade off quality against lead time. Wallace Hopp maintains that there are only three types of buffer, and

they are inter-related – for example, capacity can be traded off against inventory and time. Demand uncertainty means that, traditionally, capacity OR time buffers are needed.

From a Lean perspective, however, there are no trade-offs – the ongoing aim is to reduce ALL buffers AND to improve quality – or at least not to back-track on one to achieve another.

A generic diagram, applicable to both manufacturing and service, is shown below. Each of the elements (Time, Inventory, and Capacity) have buffers that Lean would aim to reduce.

A quote from Mary Parker Follett: 'We should never allow ourselves to be bullied by an either-or. There is often the possibility of something better than either of these two alternatives.'

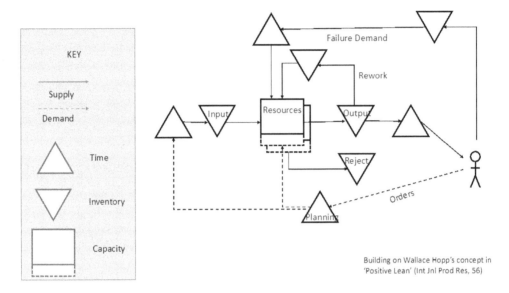

Building on Wallace Hopp's concept in 'Positive Lean' (Int Jnl Prod Res, 56)

Quality is the prime objective, being the requirement to meet or exceed customer expectations. Quality is a moving target as customer expectations change. Improving Quality enables all three buffers to be reduced – 'right first time' reduces stoppages hence reducing time and capacity buffers. Right first time means less rework leading to inventory buffer and time buffer reduction. 'Defects' are here treated widely – not only a rejection during a work process, but also any human activity that fails to meet customer requirements.

Reducing time buffers comes second. As time is reduced quality improves through faster feedback, and inventory and capacity buffers can be reduced through reduced uncertainty. Time buffers include delays in planning, external supply, internal movement, and final delivery – together these activities constitute a huge proportion of total time. (Ohno is reported to have said, 'All we are trying to do is to reduce the time between order and cash'). Reducing inventory buffers – both physical and information - comes next. Reducing inventory buffers reduces time. (Little's Law establishes relationship between inventory, time, and throughput.) Note that the objective is not to eliminate Inventory (impossible!) – but to have just the right amount just in time. Inventory buffers are aligned with Ohno's waste of 'overproduction'. Capacity buffers include both physical and human resources. Some buffer capacity is needed to absorb variation and uncertainty – both demand and process - but as variation and rework is reduced, and as time is reduced, capacity buffers can be reduced. The reduction of Capacity buffers is aligned with the waste of 'overprocessing'. A 'monument' is an over-sized physical capacity resource – best replaced by smaller machines or a cell, thereby reducing the in-built buffer. But, in a similar vein, there are 'human monuments' – oversized and under-used groups where 'work expands to fill the time available' (Parkinson's Law). Some 'bottlenecks' may be overloaded. ('Muri' in Toyota terms). An overload would be a negative buffer – one that has gone too far.

In the Figure below, the interactions between all four objectives are shown. As one is reduced, the opportunity to reduce another becomes apparent. However the interactions between Capacity and Inventory are shown dotted to indicate a traditional trade-off: inventory is increased to allow capacity to be reduced. This should be considered a temporary situation from a Lean perspective, for example to 'level the schedule'.

Note that the interpretation of Lean being aligned with 'The Seven Wastes' is regarded as too restricted a view. In fact, Toyota talks not only about 'muda' (waste), but also about 'muri' (overload or stress), and 'mura' (variation). Ohno discussed not using human potential – what became known as the 'eighth waste' but did not directly list unnecessary physical capacity. Mura and muri are considered to be drivers for reducing the four buffers.

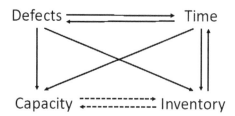

Finally, we strongly believe that Lean is not 'mean' and those organisations (and academics) that have allowed the Lean is Mean phrase to develop simply do not understand, or refuse to understand for their own reasons, the achievements – past, present, and potential.

The Drivers of Lean

Six prime drivers are shown in the Figure below.
Their influence on Lean objectives is shown. Most drivers have a direct influence on the four objectives. Here we will consider a few of the interactions.

Employee Skills: Traditionally skills were wide. Then came the industrial revolution and the Ford system when skills were dramatically narrowed. Today the range of skills is widening due to employees demanding more varied work, product range expansion, and management recognising the opportunities for work flexibility leading to cost reduction and employee retention.

Employee Participation: Participation is a further response to employee demands, but a strong driver is manager realisation as to the 'true experts' and the possibility of employee participation in continuous improvement.

Failure Demand is unnecessary demand resulting from 'not doing something or not doing something right'. The reduction of failure demand has a direct impact on customer quality, and also impacts all three buffers. Failure demand is directly influenced by employee participation coupled with employees' ability to respond appropriately to changing circumstances and demands.

True Demand Understanding. Total demand is apparent demand minus failure demand. Understanding true demand is a requirement for reducing all three types of buffer.

Product Design influences all three buffers through product simplification. Of course, product design has a huge impact on Quality.

Process Design and Wastes. This has been the prime set of activities in implementing Lean, including setup reduction, cell design, kanban, and value stream mapping. Problem solving and kaizen have grown in prominence as employee capabilities are increasingly recognised.

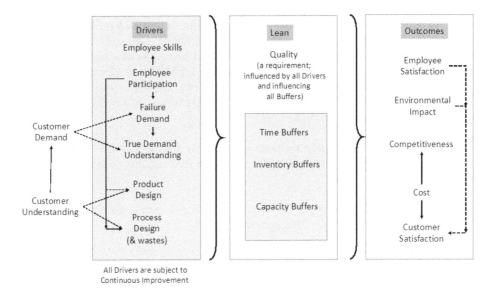

The Lenses of Lean

Wallace Hopp and Mark Spearman offer another valuable perspective that they term 'The Lenses of Lean'. The four lenses are essentially viewpoints about Lean transformation. The Table below shows the lenses with Chapters of this book that are roughly aligned.

Lens	Focus	Key References	Strengths
Process	Waste Elimination	Taylor; Gilbreth; Ohno (Chapters 2, 3)	Identification of internal waste.
Flow	Minimising the cost of inventory, capacity or time. Reduce variation.	Hopp and Spearman; Spear and Bowen (Chapters 3, 8, 9)	Value stream approach. Early Toyota Defect reduction.
Network	Getting the system right. Focus on many interconnected flows.	Shingo Prize; Womack; Queues (Chapters 5, 10)	Provides a big picture view. Simplify flow networks and designs
Organisa tion	Building a foundation of trust to engage employees on the lean journey	Kahneman; Liker (Chapters 7; 11 to 13)	Creates a lean culture; Decision making; Recognise bias

Our experience is that, yes, particular Lean transformations do seem to plump predominantly for one or other of these lenses. Each has risk and opportunity, and different time horizons. Each has important implications for the subject of this book – Human Lean.

The Process Lens may yield short-term results, but sustainability is the issue. A foundation of sand (little human involvement) will not sustain the house. Another danger is creating islands of efficiency, but without being joined up these have little effect on cost or lead-time. A Flow Lens overcomes the islands problem. But who analyses the value streams? If it is only a consultant (internal or external) without people buy-in, the potential will not be gained. Is Lean seen as a project? In both Process and Flow lenses, managerial attitude will be decisive. By contrast, and by definition, the Network lens implies longer-term commitment. Gains can be substantial if wider organisational systems are brought in, but nevertheless a finance-oriented board may lose patience and new management can kill. The Organisation lens is a deliberate medium- or long-term strategy requiring sustained leadership and managerial attention, but offers huge potential. It can be destroyed in the short-term by impatient cost-cutters. Behavioural insights (not associated with earlier versions of Lean) are enabled.

Hopp and Spearman suggest that a contemporary view is a Network lens, guiding a Flow lens, in turn guiding a Process lens, with feedback loops and an over-arching Organisation Lens.

Further Reading.
Hopp, W.J. and Spearman, M.S., The lenses of lean: Visioning the science and practice of efficiency. *Journal of Operations Management*, 2020; 1-17

1.4 Shingo Prize Principles

The 10 Guiding Principles of the Shingo Prize make up a concise set of what contemporary Lean operations practice should involve. They are
- Respect Every Individual
- Lead with Humility
- Seek Perfection
- Embrace Scientific Thinking
- Focus on Process
- Assure Quality at the Source
- Improve Flow and Pull
- Think Systemically
- Create Constancy of Purpose
- Create Value for the Customer

These 10 principles represent an extension of Womack and Jones' 5 Lean Principles – Value, Value Steam, Flow, Pull, Perfection.

Of course, the Shingo Principles are about tools, systems and people. Although the focus of the book is on people, many tools and systems have a major influence on people at work. In this book, the appropriate tools and systems are mentioned but not described in detail. (Detailed explanation of tools and systems is given in many other texts including *The Lean Toolbox*.)

1.5 The Agile Manifesto

Two decades ago a group of software developers proposed a new approach to software development. This was the Agile Manifesto and the Four Values. Since that time the manifesto has not only been widely adopted amongst software developers but has spread and been adapted to many situations – work and play, private and public, service and manufacturing. We believe the concepts are highly relevant. Individual concepts appear in various discussions throughout the book.
- Satisfy the customer
- Welcome changing requirements
- Deliver working software frequently
- People and developers must work together

- Build projects around motivated individuals
- Face-to-face conversation is most effective
- Working software is the primary measure
- Agile processes promote sustainable development
- Continuous attention to technical excellence and good design enhances agility
- Simplicity is essential
- The best outcomes emerge from self-organising teams
- The team regularly reflects on how to become more effective.

There are also the 4 Values
- Individuals and interactions over processes and tools.
- Working software over comprehensive documentation.
- Customer collaboration over contract negotiation.
- Responding to change over following a plan.

As the influence of the Agile Manifesto grows, and as VUCA develops (see below), both Leadership and Organisations will need to adjust. Exciting changes in Leadership and Organisation herald a 'New Lean' that is emerging alongside traditional Lean.

1.6 Complexity

Particularly over the past two decades, the world of operations has moved relentlessly towards VUCA (volatility, uncertainty, complexity, and ambiguity). The acronym VUCA emerged in about 1987 but has since become widely accepted.

But many of the theories and concepts of what is now called Lean (and was previously known as the Taylor System, or Just-in-Time, and more lately 'Operational Excellence') relate to more stable, predictable environments. Dave Snowden named these as Clear (formerly called Simple) and Complicated environments as opposed to Complex. (See Section 8.9).

There is much to say, and to speculate, about Lean and Agile in the complex VUCA world.

"The greatest waste ... is the failure to use the abilities of people...to learn about their frustrations and about the contributions that they are eager to make." W. Edwards Deming

What Caulkin commented about Japanese car plants in Britain in 1993, now applies much more widely, and certainly to any aspiring Lean organisation. He said: *"Everyone now has two jobs. First to build the car, second to find ways of doing the job better."* (Caulkin, 1993). An excellent quote from Seddon and Caulkin follows:

"An organization organized around 'pull' and flow needs a very different kind of leadership from the traditional command-and-control where decision-making is distant from the work and based on abstracted measures, budgets and plans. Because of the emphasis on the system rather than individuals, however senior, descriptions of the TPS use the words 'leader' and 'leadership' sparingly. Here leadership consists in making it easier for others to achieve mastery and to work with the system to improve it rather than to make heroic changes..... (It places) the development of workers, individually and collectively, at its heart.
From Seddon and Caulkin, *Action Learning: Research and Practice* Vol. 4, No. 1, April 2007, pp. 9–24

...and from Johnson and Bröms.

"The proper role of management is to lead people to understand business as a system of work, a system that links each worker's capacity to serve with a specific customer's needs. The goal of a business is to nurture continually the creative talents of company members. By focusing on its members' activities, the manager will thereby improve the system's capability to serve the needs of customers. To help each employee and supplier realize his or her potential in the company, management's main job is to learn exactly what people do in their jobs and how what they do serves customers. Such learning is difficult, if not impossible, in companies that manage by results."

Further Readings.
Thomas Johnson and Anders Bröms, *Profit Beyond Measure*, Nicholas Brealey, 2000, page 2

1.7 Why 'Human' and Lean?

This book is a Toolbox for the Human aspects of Lean. It is deliberately eclectic – because it is our belief that there is no one best way for managing people. The human element is culturally and process dependent. Certainly there are indisputable best practices (such as managing by Gemba) but there is a range of approaches covered in the book all of which have had successes and failures in Lean environments. Toyota has been the Lean exemplar and whilst many human practices can be learned from Toyota, (especially that TPS is a Thinking People System) not all Toyota concepts will work everywhere and there are numerous successful people practices that have been demonstrated outside of Toyota in the wider Lean world.

We believe that intelligent people have the ability to see alternatives from different perspectives. Abraham Lincoln would sometimes argue with a friend from one perspective, and then they would switch and argue from the opposite perspective.

Almost everyone in 'Lean' and 'Continuous Improvement' recognises the vital role of Humans. Transformation is unthinkable without a full commitment to the people involved. Lean is ultimately a 'Human system'. Not just a Human system but a Human development system, and a nursery to grow 'thinking people'. Thinking people are grown by continually learning better ways to deliver value.

Of course, this is not news. So, why read this book? Because…

- First, the world of work is changing. Workforces are changing in age, diversity, education, and aspiration. Workers demand greater participation and better leadership, but also bring with them vast opportunity for betterment to their organisation, to society, and to the environment. Lean's 'eighth waste', recognises this and indeed it would be a waste to neglect the opportunity.
- Although much is known about good Human practice, there remains many a gap between actual and potential performance.
- The gap is widening. There has been a veritable explosion in knowledge in fields related to effective 'human' practices. These fields include leadership, psychology, organisation, anthropology, decision making and problem solving.
- Technology developments in areas such as Artificial Intelligence, robotic process automation, virtual reality, the 'digital twin', and the cloud, (to mention only a few) are not only accelerating but are also complimenting human development. Through Moore's Law, information is vastly more widespread and rapidly available. The implications for Humans are uncertain but will be profound.

In short, whether it is called 'Lean', 'Continuous Improvement', 'Operations Excellence', 'Process Excellence' or 'Lean Six Sigma' the emerging world of the more effective use of Humans at work - Head, Heart, Hands, Health, Habitat – is tremendously exciting. This book builds on many predecessors, discusses some common misconceptions, and lays foundations for a better mindset.

Many topics relevant to the future of Human Lean will be presented. But by no means will all topics be relevant to every Lean manager. A single model or framework will not be presented. We would not be so bold as to suggest (like Fred Taylor!) the 'one best way'. For a particular Lean manager some topics will always be relevant, others sometimes, yet others not at all. Several topics will be situational – they might work well in some situations but not in others. Hence, the topics are presented not as one joined-up concept. The choice is dependent on the mindset of the organisation, the location, the technology, and the person. But all topics share a common theme of performance improvement through humans.

Lean is an open-ended learning system so there will never be a static framework or a single formula. In fact, a new mindset could bring vast new opportunity.

Cautions

Although you may read this book…*"Understanding the Theory (Lean Production) in the head is not the problem. The problem is to remember it in the body."*   Taiichi Ohno

Scientific tools and human variability…

Much of science is based on the repeatable experiment. Cause and effect are linked by scientific laws. If you drop an apple, it will fall down at a predictable acceleration and speed. Calculate takt time, design an assembly line to match, and expect it to work. The rational decision maker, cold-blooded, impervious to emotions, has been assumed in much management theory, practice and writing (including in Lean) until quite recently when 'Behavioural Economics' began to have an impact. (For example, Levitt and Dubner, 2007; and Kahneman and Tversky, early 2000's)

The majority of concepts described in this book is not like that. Humans are much less predictable. They are emotional, and subject to many biases. Their behaviour depends on a large variety of factors any of which can change. Unfortunately, to judge by numerous publications and web blogs, the full rational model is still widespread in the Lean and Agile community. We try to keep in mind a balance between the rational and the emotional throughout this book.

The essence of pure Scientific Management is based around the repeatable experiment. This is fine for environments that are Simple (or 'Clear' to use Snowden's 2020 version) or Complicated (concepts that are discussed later in the book). Scott Page uses a landscape analogy to explain these types. In the analogy we try to reach the peaks. Simple has a single peak, like Mount Fuji. Complicated has numerous large and small peaks such as a mountain range. Both Simple and Complicated are stable environments where repeatable experimentation to find the peaks will yield good results. In Complex environments the landscape can shift due to earthquakes, tsunamis, floods and volcanoes. Here, experimentation, although highly desirable in order to learn, is much less dependable. Treat experimentation with caution. In a VUCA world (volatile, uncertain, complex, ambiguous) we need open-minded caution.

"To learn anything other than the stuff you find in books, you need to be able to experiment, to make mistakes, to accept feedback and to try again. It doesn't matter whether you are learning to

ride a bike or starting a new career, the cycle of experiment, feedback and new experiment is always there."

Charles Handy, of London Business School and author of numerous books on Organisation.

Psychological findings are frequently referred to in this book. But keep in mind that many of the findings in psychology are based on 'lab' situations often using university students, from a particular country, age group, intelligence level, and with particular motives. That is not to say that all psychology is invalid – far from it - there are certainly well founded and accepted concepts.

Much of Lean stems from Toyota and the 'Toyota Production System' (TPS). We have all benefitted from TPS, and will certainly continue to do so. TPS has incorporated thinking from Training Within Industry (TWI), from developments in psychology and engineering, and from other sources. TPS has adapted successfully to various national cultures. Today, TPS also influences thinking in service and administration.

And yet....

We feel that an exclusive focus on TPS is unwise. Remember that Toyota manufacturing is dominated by the assembly line – short cycle near repetition, low variation, high homogeneity. Such organisation has direct human implications. But obviously, many organisations are just not like that. One of the great findings of psychology is that behaviour is governed strongly by environment – so we have tried to attain a more general perspective.

Here are some tough words for those who still, after 30 years, think that Lean can be learned in a few weeks sitting in a classroom…

"Vulgar and inactive minds confound familiarity with knowledge and conceive themselves informed of the whole nature of things when they are shown their form or told their use; but the speculatist, who is not content with superficial views, harasses himself with fruitless curiosity, and still, as he inquires more, perceives only that he knows less."

Dr. Samuel Johnson, (poet, moralist, and founder of the English Dictionary), *The Idler*, 1758

People as a Concern

An old (1999) survey of 454 members of AME (Association for Manufacturing Excellence) of the impact of Lean showed…
- Over 80% had improved throughput time
- About 80% had improved Internal Quality Levels
- Over 70% had improved Productivity
- Over 65% had improved External Quality Levels
- BUT only about 50% had improved Employee Behaviour

We would hope that in the intervening years gains in understanding employee behaviour have been made, but the large volume of articles and books in the area suggest that human aspects remain the most challenging aspect of lean transformation. If only 50% had improved employee behaviour, was there a one-sided view of Lean implementation – and has Lean been sustained?

1.8 A House of Lean?

There are literally hundreds of versions of the house (or temple) of Lean, often company specific, with many based on some Toyota originals. One Toyota early-version is shown. A point about the house is that it is an attempt to integrate the various concepts of Lean into a unified whole or system rather than as a collection of separate techniques. It also suggests a sequence from the foundations upwards. This early version shows a strong preponderance of tools. This is not to say that without strong employee engagement all of the tools would be unlikely to succeed. For instance, Jidoka is people-centred semi-automation. It is just that no specific mention is made of people.

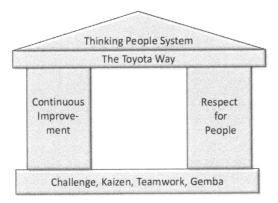

Later versions of the house almost reversed mention of tools and became very strongly people-oriented. An example is shown, similar to a version used in Jeffrey Liker's 'The Toyota Way'. Liker's 2021 book shows a TPS house not unlike the version above, but adding culture and 'flexible, capable, motivated members' in the centre.

This version of the house is crucial for an understanding of Lean as it is perceived today. The two columns – continuous improvement and respect – are balanced and both are needed. The house falls if only one of these is present. This is exactly in-line with the Socio-Tech concept that is discussed in Section 5.2. Specifically, do not run-away with CI or 'tech' without balancing it with Respect (so often the case with early Lean). And do not focus too much on People and Respect whilst downplaying CI. (A tendency today in some organisations claiming to be Lean?). The two columns, together, enable a 'Thinking People System'.

Lean Enterprise Institute (John Shook) has a related, excellent, version that covers the five areas of the house:
1. Roof: Situational: 'What problem are we trying to solve?'
2. Left wall: Process improvement – the way work is done
3. Right Wall: Capability development – of all people

4.   In the centre: Leadership
5.   Foundation: Thinking, mindset, assumptions.

Training Within Industry (TWI) has had long-term links with Toyota. Ohno made use of the WW2 US-originated TWI concepts, and the TWI legacy remains at Toyota today. TWI migrated around the world, including to Japan, following WW2. The UK government became a strong advocate. They developed an Arch or 'Gateway to Efficient Production' instead of a house or temple. This is adapted as shown below.

The original TWI thinking was (and still is) that Knowledge is specific to the organisation or area and much of it is acquired externally but developed internally. For example, chemical engineering or computer programming have their own specific bodies of knowledge relevant within an organisation. They form the foundation of what the enterprise does. But there are also skills or capabilities that are more widely applicable. Such capabilities are the focus of this book.

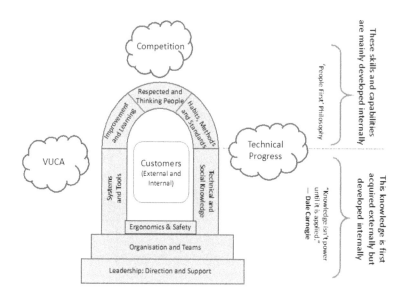

The Arch is explained as follows, and links many aspects in this book, just like the House of Lean:

- In engineering or architecture, the arch was considered an advance over the temple, allowing greater spans to be built. Think of span being analogous to opportunity.
- The arch protects customers, both external and internal.
- The foundation is Leadership. Without this, there is no purpose, no organisation.
- Organisation and Teams set the framework. Both organisation structure and layout are crucial enablers for a Human Lean enterprise.
- The walls are the Systems and Knowledge that allow purpose to be translated. The structure is built around customers.
- The **Keystone** is Respected and Thinking People. (An arch will collapse if there is no keystone.)
- Supporting the keystone is Improvement and Learning, and habits, methods and standards.
- Work safety is a vital part of the structure that prevents it from pulling apart.
- There are threatening clouds that surround the structure, and are capable of destroying it. They are: Competition, Technical Progress, and VUCA.

In the Organisation section of the book, the widely-used analogy of a sandcastle is used. Think of the Arch as made of sandstone – capable of being eroded by the tides of time.

All of these models are useful. (Or as George Box - surely a candidate for the title of Statistician of the 20th century – said "*All models are wrong, but some models are useful.*")

Further Readings.
Jeffrey Liker, *The Toyota Way*, Second edition, McGraw Hill, 2021
F.H. Perkins, Training Within Industry for Supervisors, *U.K. Ministry of Labour and National Service*, 1946, *pp. 24-25,* ProQuest, 2013

The Chapters and the Arch

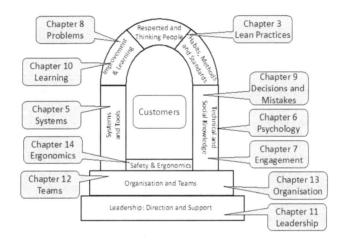

Chapter 2
Antecedents and Myths

While it may have taken until *The Machine that Changed the World* (Womack et al.) was first published in 1991 to bring the term lean and lean manufacturing into popular usage, examples of lean thinking can be traced back to 1780s – 1790s when the Royal Navy introduced standard operations and quick-change overs, or even earlier when the Venetian Arsenale in the 12th century pioneered the assembly line for ships. We should also not forget the contributions of Lilian Gilbreth and Mary Parker Follet – those two wonderful forward-thinking ladies from 100+ years ago – both of whom will be quoted often in this book. Less clear however is how these revolutionary manufacturing systems impacted on the way those in charge managed their subordinates. Before we investigate this however, it is worthwhile reminding ourselves of the most influential theories over the past 100 or so years that helped shape the way today's managers view their people.

2.1 Scientific Management

Scientific management, also often known as Taylorism, is a management theory first advocated by Frederick W. Taylor. It uses scientific methods to analyse the most efficient production process in order to increase productivity. Taylor developed his theories while working as an employee of the United States steel manufacturer, Bethlehem Steel. With a background in mechanical engineering, Taylor was obsessed with efficiency and began designing workplace experiments to determine optimal performance levels. His observations were that most workers deliberately took their time when working, and worked inefficiently. The solution he maintained was to identify, through scientific analysis "the one best way" to perform any task.

One of his most celebrated experiments was aimed at improving the rate at which gangs of workers moved "pig-iron" bars of steel. Armed with stop watches, Taylor's assistants came to the conclusion that a worker could, under proper supervision, load $47\frac{1}{2}$ tons a day. A remarkable figure which was almost four times greater than was currently being achieved. In another, he experimented with shovel design until he had a design that would allow workers to shovel for several hours continually. Looking at ways to improve the rate at which workers shovelled, his analysis showed the optimum shovel for moving any particular materials is one that should lift $21\frac{1}{2}$ pounds. Anything greater than that, and the worker would not be able to maintain the pace all day: anything less and the worker was working below optimal capacity.

In 1909, Taylor published "The Principles of Scientific Management" in which he proposed that by optimizing and simplifying jobs, productivity would increase. He also advanced the idea that workers and managers needed to co-operate with one another. Taylor's principles retain strong influence but certainly require modification.

Taylors Four Principles of Scientific Management:

1. **Replace** working by "rule of thumb" or individual preference. Use scientific methods to determine the most efficient way to perform specific tasks.
2. Instead of randomly assigning workers to any open job, **allocate workers to tasks based on their aptitudes**. Assess which ones are most capable of each specific job and train them to work at peak efficiency.
3. **Monitor** worker performance. Provide training, instructions and supervision to ensure workers are using the most efficient process.

4.   Properly **allocate the workload between managers and workers**. Managers should spend their time planning and training, allowing the workers to perform their tasks efficiently.

Cautions

- Taylor's research methods have long been disputed with many accusations of fabrication which places question marks over his subsequent findings.
- When searching for the most efficient one best way, don't forget that it is only the current best way. People performing the work should be encouraged and trained to find an even better way.
- Unlike in Taylor's era, today's employees are highly educated. Standard work that doesn't allow some flexibility may lead them to become bored, dis-engaged or apathetic.
- When all decision making is taken away from employees, they no longer feel accountable, and are unlikely to contribute discretionary effort.
- When relying solely on work study (based on external observation) to create the most efficient method, the danger is missing out on the valuable tacit knowledge which the person performing the task possesses.

2.2 The Hawthorne Studies

The Hawthorne Studies are one the oldest and most frequently cited studies of people's behaviour at work. The studies were carried out by Elton Mayo at the Hawthorne plant of the Western Electric Company in Chicago between 1927 and 1933 in co-operation with the Massachusetts Institute of Technology (MIT) and Harvard University.

The aim of the study was to identify any linkage between the workers working environment and their productivity. Among the many changes introduced were: relocating workstations, adjusting lighting, changing break times, positioning the supervisor closer to the workers, rotating out some team members and introducing payment incentives. The results of the study were published in 1939 by Mayo's assistants Roethlisberger and Dickson. They described a continuous increase in productivity observed during the test which suggested that the most important factor behind this continuous increase in output was the improved personal relations between workers and management - now commonly referred to as the Hawthorne Effect. This proposition was based on the informally expressed opinions of the workers participating in the experiment, as well as the general impressions of Mayo and his team of investigators. The proposition evolved into a "conclusion" and became the basis of the "Human Relations School" of management, which quickly took over the leading role from the "Scientific Management School" in American industry.

History however has cast doubts over Mayo's study with many researchers questioning the methods employed and the validity of his findings. By far the most disturbing fact unveiled was Mayo's failure to disclose that the workers involved in the study received close to double what they would normally have expected to earn for taking part in the research. It was also found that Mayo had displayed a tendency to discard particulars of the study which did not support his theory. Despite this criticism however, the Hawthorne myth lives on. This is mainly because while Mayo's research methodology was severally flawed and the findings fabricated, Mayo, accidently or otherwise, had identified something significant. When employers and managers engage with employees in a meaningful way, productivity increases.

The Hawthorne legacy is that

- Worker-manager relations play a large role in worker motivation and productivity.

- Financial incentives matter more to workers in low paid employment.
- The workplace is a social system.
- Work group norms affect productivity.

2.3 Samuel Smiles and Toyota

Where did Toyota's unique culture come from? Some organization theorists like Warren Bennis and David Snowden believe that the founder often has huge and sustaining influence. Apparently, Sakichi Toyoda (1867-1930) the founder of Toyota, was a great fan of Samuel Smiles' book *Self-Help*, originally published in 1859. This book is the only book on display at Sakichi Toyoda's birthplace, the shrine of Toyota. Sakichi Toyoda schooled his family, including Kiichiro Toyoda (1894-1952), founder of Toyota Motor.

Smiles' bestselling book is still in print, and was probably the first self-help book written. It tells of the great innovators of the Industrial revolution, such as Watt, Davy, Faraday, Stephenson, Brunel, and Wedgewood, artists such as Reynolds and Hogarth, writers such as Shakespeare, and soldiers such as Wellington and Napoleon. The majority of them beavered away through hard work, often with little technical education but great practical experience, often over considerable periods with patience and continual experimentation, to realise their goals. And their goals were firmly linked to the needs of customers. They were, in general, good businessmen although their primary motivation was not the accumulation of wealth. Some were Quakers who believed in a fair deal for their workers and a fair but not excessive profit over the longer term. 'Attention (to detail), application, method, perseverance, punctuality, despatch are the principal qualities required…', 'Accuracy in observation…' (Newton and Darwin were astute observers.) 'Method is like packing things in a box; a good packer will get in half as much again as a bad one….' and 'the shortest way to do many things is to do only one thing at once'. Most worked with 'constant modification and improvement, until eventually it was rendered practical and profitable to an eminent degree.' And 'the highest patriotism and philanthropy consist, not so much in altering laws and modifying institutions as in helping and stimulating men to elevate and improve themselves by their own free and independent individual action.'

Does that sound like the Toyota we often hear about today? (See, for example, Liker's *Toyota Way* principles numbers 1, 9, 10, 11, but especially 12, 13, 14.) Respect for people, Gemba, Kaizen, Observe deeply, Improvement Energy of your People, Some large and many small steps – it's all there – but not necessarily in those words. To reinforce these ideas Terence Kealey has written on how many great innovations in history have come about not through science driving technology, but technology driving advances in science through hands-on application at the workplace. 'Were the increases in productivity primarily a consequence of the great technical advances such as the spinning jenny or of the myriad small technical advances that innumerable workers and manufacturers made to their machines alongside the big advances? Romantically, we attribute the increases in industrial revolutionary productivity to the great individual innovations such as the jenny, but when the economists do their sums they show that the vast number of small technical improvements overwhelmed the impact of big innovations.' (p169)

Further Readings.
Terence Kealey, *Sex, Science and Profits*, Heinemann, 2008
Jeffrey Liker, *The Toyota Way*, McGraw Hill, 2021
Samuel Smiles, *Self-Help*, Oxford World's Classics, 2002 (originally published 1859)

2.4 Theory X and Theory Y

In his book "The Human Side of Enterprise" (1960) 'The American social psychologist Douglas McGregor, proposed his famous X-Y theory which suggested that there are two fundamental approaches to managing people.

Theory X managers believe that the average person:
- Dislikes work and will avoid it at every opportunity.
- Will only apply themselves to work when the threat of punishment is present.
- Is unambitious, doesn't want responsibility and prefers to be directed.

In short, Theory X is a 'carrot and stick' approach.

Theory Y managers however are of the opinion that the average person:
- Gets satisfaction from performing work.
- Will gladly use their initiative and imagination in pursuit of organisational goals and objectives.
- Has no problem accepting a reasonable level of responsibility.
- Possesses intellectual potential that is only being partly utilised.

While managers may have a natural tendency towards one or other, in practice most are likely to use a mixture of both Theory X and Theory Y. For example, a Theory X approach might be deemed appropriate for managing new hires (who may appreciate the guidance) or teams who are carrying out repetitive and boring work which is unlikely to stimulate them. On the other hand, when managing high performing individuals or teams, a Theory Y approach is more appropriate as these employees most likely would feel they are being micro-managed, or not trusted using a Theory X manager approach.

Theory X and Theory Y are still commonly referred to in the field of management and motivation. McGregor's ideas influenced todays understanding of the psychological contract, which is an unwritten set of expectations between the employee and the employer. The psychological contract is that employees balance what effort they put into their job with how they feel they are being treated by their employer. If they are putting more in than they feel they are getting back in return, the balance is skewed and the psychological contract is breached.

From a lean engagement perspective, Theory Y managers are much more likely to achieve sustainable improvements. However, many lean journeys begin with a "burning platform" situation, which requires urgent action with little time for gathering consensus - which may be best suited to a Theory X manager.

2.5 Herzberg's Motivation-Hygiene Theory

Fred Herzberg's motivation-hygiene theory (also known as the two-factor theory) proposes that there are certain factors in the workplace that cause job satisfaction while a separate set of factors cause dissatisfaction, all of which act independently of each other. The theory resulted from a study conducted by American psychologist, Frederick Herzberg to better understand employee's attitudes and motivations. After completing an extensive literature review of 2,000 job satisfaction studies, Herzberg and his fellow researchers developed a hypothesis which they later tested in an empirical study of 203 engineers and accountants. The research subjects were asked to recall events that made them especially happy or unhappy about their jobs. When Herzberg published the results of the study in his 1959 book "The Motivation to Work" it led to him becoming one of the most influential names in business management, revolutionised thinking about employee attitudes and, subsequently, management policy and practice.

The most significant factor from the research interviews, was that the themes which emerged from the stories about satisfaction were not the same as the themes of the stories about dissatisfaction. For example, the stories about dissatisfaction were linked to poor company policies, but the stories about satisfaction were not linked to good company policies. Similarly, the stories about satisfaction involved accomplishment, but the stories about dissatisfaction did not involve failure. Herzberg labelled the themes of the satisfying incidents "motivators" and the themes of the dissatisfying events "hygiene factors." The term hygiene was borrowed from epidemiology, the branch of medicine which deals with the control of diseases. This was simply because, as he observed, while good medical hygiene will not make people healthy, it can certainly help to prevent illness. Herzberg and his colleagues observed that, similar to medical hygiene, fair pay, good interpersonal relationships, just policies, and agreeable working conditions do not appear to provide much long-term satisfaction, they do prevent dis-satisfaction. As can be seen below the motivating factors are primary related to the job content, whereas the hygiene factors are mainly associated with the job context.

Dis-satisfiers	Satisfiers
Company policies	Achievement
Supervision	Recognition
Relationship with management	Meaningful work
Working conditions	Responsibility
Salary	Advancement
Relationship with peers	Growth

Herzberg's model exploded the myth that salary was the principal motivator. He understood that it was much more nuanced. While employees in very poor circumstances will be very grateful for any increase in earnings that will improve their circumstances, other employees in a better financial position will not be as motivated by a similar increase. Over sixty years later the Motivation-Hygiene Theory still has particular relevance for leaders looking at ways to engage their employees in lean activities.

Cautions
- Fixing the causes of dissatisfaction will not create satisfaction.
- A weakness in the theory is that it assumes a strong relationship between job satisfaction and productivity - something which is certainly not true in every case.
- There are two steps when adopting the theory to motivate employees: (a) Identify, eliminate or reduce the causes of dis-satisfaction and (b) Work with them to find satisfaction in their work.

2.6 Maslow's Hierarchy of Needs

In 1943, American psychologist Abraham Maslow published a paper for Psychological Review 'A Theory of Human Motivation' which first introduced his theory about how styles at work satisfy various personal needs in the context of their work. His theory contends that humans have a series of needs, some of which must be met before they can turn their attention toward others. From the bottom of the hierarchy upwards, the needs are: physiological, safety, love and belonging, esteem, and self-actualisation. These are commonly shown as a pyramid.

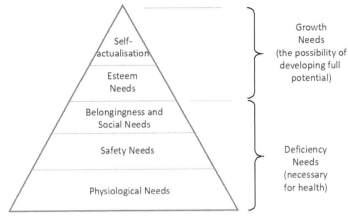

Maslow's Hierarchy of Needs

Maslow's theory remains one of the most influential theories on workplace motivation. Regarding the structure of his hierarchy, Maslow recognised that the order of needs may change, based on an individual's circumstances or personality. For example, some people may place more importance on recognition and status, than love and friendship. The hierarchy is open ended: Maslow suggested that as we reach higher levels even more potential becomes apparent. Later, he wrote of 'reversal', saying that not all individual's lower needs need to be met in some situations.

At the heart of Maslow's research was his interest in human potential, and how we fulfil that potential. He regarded motivation as the natural need for personal growth and discovery which lies within all of us. His positive approach to people and psychology is widely recognised as leading the way for later movements such as humanistic and positive psychology.

Maslow's hierarchy of needs continues to be popular and is relevant to leaders, across all industries and continents, who struggle to fully engage employees in their work and organisations. Safety needs should certainly be met in any organisation. Involvement in lean activities in their workplace can certainly help to fill most employees' psychological needs and potentially lead to self-actualisation.

2.7 Social Exchange Theory

To understand why some people are engaged in their work while others remain unengaged or indeed disengaged many researchers look to social exchange theory. Social exchange theory has evolved over time to explain the establishment, reinforcement and on-going maintenance of interpersonal relationships in organisations. Importantly in relation to employee engagement, social exchange theory provides a basis for understanding the relationship between employees and their organisations.

The genesis of social exchange theory goes back to 1958, when American sociologist George Homans published an article "Social Behaviour as Exchange." Social exchange theory is a concept based on the notion that a relationship between two people is created through a process of cost-benefit analysis. In other words people are only willing to put as much effort into a relationship as they are likely to get back in return. This is often depicted as a set of scales. If one side of the relationship feels that they are being short changed, they are most likely to withdraw benefits until the scales became balanced.

Social exchange theory is therefore based on the principle that exchange in a relationship must be of mutual benefit. Homans' hypothesis is based on three assumptions. Firstly that people behave in a rational way and make decisions accordingly; secondly that these rational decisions are based on the perceptions of likely net gain and, finally, that net gain is based on internally perceived gain minus perceived effort. (But note the comment on rational decisions and behavioural economics in Chapter 1).

In the context of social exchange theory, reciprocation is the process by which an individual who receives a benefit feels obliged to return the favour. Within a work context the relationship can be seen as a trade-off in effort on the part of the employees for benefits provided by the employer. Employers as a rule see a value in having their employees fully engaged as it demonstrates loyalty, commitment, and dedication which can deliver positively in terms of improved performance and discretionary effort. Employees in contrast see the rewards of being valued by the organisation, through improved pay and conditions, as well as through less tangible benefits such as access to information and respect. It is through the norms of reciprocity that employers and employees can reconcile opposing positions.

Some critics are of the view that Homans' theory is too simplistic. They argue that people and employees do not always make rational decisions. In fact sometimes, people influenced by their emotions, will make decisions which will have adverse repercussions for themselves. They also point that it fails to grasp how influential social structures are in shaping people's perception of the world around them.

Despite these reservations, social exchange theory and particularly the process of reciprocation provides valuable insights for leaders endeavouring to fully engage their people.

In summary

- Social Exchange Theory proposes that social behaviour is the result of an exchange process. This is sometimes also referred to as reciprocity and captured in folklore 'One good turn, deserves another.' or 'What goes around, comes around.'
- Social Exchange contracts are implied, rather than written.
- It takes time to build up a "Social Exchange" as both parties weigh each other up; it can very quickly end if one partner believes the other is not keeping up their side of the bargain.

2.8 Pay for Performance Incentive Programs

If we look at the number of organisations across the world that have incentive schemes as part of their overall compensation package, then the answer to the question 'Do incentive schemes work?' is a resounding yes. In fact 50% of American workers' annual salary is made up of incentives. As with most of life's big questions however, things are never as simple as they might first appear, but incentive led pay-for-performance can potentially be a highly effective form of compensation. This is because it can benefit both the employer (through increased productivity) and employee (though increased pay) simultaneously.

Lincoln Electric

Lincoln Electric, a welding manufacturer based in Cleveland, Ohio with operations across the globe, in 1934 introduced one of the most celebrated pay for performance systems in industry, which was widely copied by other U.S. manufacturers. Founded in 1895, Lincoln Electric is the leading producer of both arc welding machines and consumable products for those machines. Over the 70 years, Lincoln Electric have grown their business significantly, building a reputation for producing high value, high quality products, at competitive prices, with outstanding customer service. This resulted in a number of their main competitors, including household names such as General Electric and Westinghouse, and some Japanese, deciding to exit the arc welder market.

The pay for performance / productivity at Lincoln Electric has four main pillars.

- Piecework wages.
- A discretionary annual bonus based on individual and company performance and, as a result, compensation packages well above industry norms.
- Individual merit ratings used to determine the annual bonus element.
- A voluntary employee advisory board (works council) to ensure good lines of communication are maintained between workers and management.

The company recognises the need for trust and has in place complementary management practices which sees front line employees having the autonomy to set piece rates, record output etc. and operate with minimum supervision. Factory workers are graded twice yearly under four performance measures; the quality of their work, the quantity of their work, their dependability and their cooperation. The first two measures were to ensure the workers were motivated to perform to the best of their ability on an individual level, while the latter two were to encourage employees to work together and contribute ideas and improvement suggestions. The success of the program is evidenced with historically low absenteeism and employee turnover figures.
The Lincoln case can be seen as a challenge to Lean in as far as it is a strong pay-for-performance company. Is this so? Well, Lincoln has a highly focused product range, fairly modern technology, and a process that allows a high degree of individual work and incentive. In this environment, the Lincoln system works exceedingly well.

A word of caution however. When Lincoln Electric expanded their operations in the early 1990's they found that European culture could often be very hostile to the introduction of piece rate and bonus systems. This was particularly the case in countries where restrictive work practices were traditionally the norm. Lincoln is a special case: intermediate technology, a stable product line, and fairly balanced individual work enable a very high bonus to be paid. In many situations, however, a bonus system can and has destroyed teamwork.

Ford and Scanlon Plan

In 1914 Henry Ford shocked the US Automobile industry by doubling the minimum wage to $5 per day, as well as reducing the daily hours worked. Henry Ford claimed this was sharing the profits of a then highly profitable company amongst the workforce. In fact, this was probably done with an eye on reducing the exceptionally high employee turnover rate and absenteeism. Although greeted with dismay by competitors, the results were spectacular. More than 10,000 people applied for work the following day and subsequent employee turnover fell dramatically. Ford also introduced employee monitoring, something that would not be acceptable today. Employees were expected to be temperate, to keep their houses clean and tidy and not to run up loans.

The 'success' of the Ford plan laid the foundation for subsequent profit sharing amongst companies in the US and possibly the world.

A Scanlon Plan, versions of which are still used by several companies, is a form of profit-sharing, whereby employees are awarded a pre-determined portion of whatever profits they are responsible for bringing in. The main benefit of using this system is that it directly links employees' work with company results and employee compensation. It motivates employees to increase their personal earnings, while simultaneously contributing to company growth.

Joseph Scanlon worked as a cost accountant for Empire Steel in Mansfield, Ohio when it was incorporated in 1929 after a consolidation of six smaller steel companies, giving a total workforce of 5,000. However, the steel industry was a major casualty of the Great Depression and in 1931 Empire Steel went into receivership. Two years later the company returned as the Empire Sheet and Tin Plate Company with 1,900 employees. In 1937 Scanlon was elected President of Lodge 169 SWOC, the fulcrum for members to survive the devastating recession, as well as demonstrating the benefits of union membership to non-members. With demand for steel continuing to decline, by 1938 Empire's workforce had reduced to 900. It was against this background that the company President announced a 25% salary cut for all employees. Suspicious that this was a management plot to exploit them further, workers appealed to SWOC headquarters to investigate the company's financial situation. When SWOC confirmed that the company was heading for bankruptcy, union members voted a 25% salary cut. Aware that the salary cut provided only a temporary stay of execution on the company's future and that something radical was required, members of the management team met with union officials in June 1938 to formulate a strategy that would sustain the company for the long-term. The outcome was the establishment of a Joint Research Committee which would meet monthly to discuss workers' ideas of how to cut waste and improve productivity and profitability. This is where Scanlon in his role as Union President was able to use his accounting background to great effect. The union – management collaboration was a tremendous success. By 1941, output had doubled, pay had been restored and employment had risen to 1,200

In 1945 Scanlon, joined MIT where he expanded his ideas on how to establish a cost-saving program which would be divided among all employees, not just those involved in the manufacturing process. One of his first studies was with the Lapointe Machine Tool Company. The system proved very successful, resulting in significant productivity increases for the company, and corresponding bonuses for the workers. With Scanlon's ideas being widely adopted across the U.S. in 1947 MIT hosted a Scanlon Conference which ran annually until his health deteriorated in 1955. The idea, first mooted by Scanlon almost 100 years ago to boost profits by establishing a direct connection between work and reward, is even more relevant today. The employee of the 21st century is highly educated, fully aware of their entitlements and demand to be involved in changes which affect them. The main drawback businesses have with using the Scanlon Plan model have to do with sharing data. The plan requires full transparency including profits, projections, expenses and employee bonuses. All of this information is required to ensure that a Scanlon Plan is being fully implemented. For many businesses, this can be seen as a major disadvantage.

Cautions

- Because each company has different circumstances, there is no 'one size fits all' solution.
- Poorly developed incentive programs can reduce performance and morale, as well as stifling creativity, innovation and flexibility.
- Monetary rewards cannot substitute for a working environment where teamwork and trust is high and the work has meaning.
- Monetary rewards only work well in specific situations with specific job types.
- It can be very difficult to balance worker preference when setting incentive programs. Some workers may favour a lower percentage incentive which will shield them should performance drop. Others may prefer a high-performance percentage, believing it be a more accurate reflection of individual effort and productivity.

Further Readings.

John Bicheno and Matthias Holweg, *The Lean Toolbox: A handbook for lean transformation.* Buckingham: PICSIE books, 2016

D.F. Hastings, Lincoln Electric's harsh lessons from international expansion. *Harvard Business Review*, 77(3), 1999, pp. 163-164.

Frederick Herzberg, B. Mausner, and BB Snyderman, *The motivation to Work.* Aufl., 1959

G.C. Homans, 'Social behaviour as exchange', *American Journal of Sociology*, 63(6), pp. 597-606, 1958

Douglas McGregor and J. Cutcher-Gershenfeld, *The Human Side of Enterprise*, McGraw-Hill, 1960

Jeffrey Pfeffer, 'Six dangerous myths about pay', *Harvard Business Review*, 76(3), pp. 109-120.

F.J. Roethlisberger and WJ Dickson, *Management and the Worker*, Cambridge, 1939

D.A. Sachau, 'Resurrecting the motivation-hygiene theory: Herzberg and the positive psychology movement'. *Human resource development review*, 6 (4), 2007, pp. 377-393.

F.W. Taylor, *The Principles of Scientific Management.* New York, 1911

G. Wickström, and T. Bendix, 2000. 'The" Hawthorne effect" — what did the original Hawthorne studies actually show?', *Scandinavian journal of work, environment and health*, 2000, pp. 363-367.

James Womack, Daniel Jones, and Daniel Roos, *The Machine that Changed the World*, Rawson Associates, 1990

D. Wren, 'Joseph N. Scanlon: the man and the plan'. *Journal of Management History',* 2009

Chapter 3
Established Lean Practices to Managing People

The importance of people for Lean success has been recognised for at least as long as the word 'Lean' has been used in an operations context. It is also true that emphasis on topics such as 'culture', 'leadership', 'respect', and 'empowerment' have grown steadily. Early publications on JIT / Lean, such as Schonberger's 'Japanese Manufacturing Techniques' (1982), Robert Hall's 'Zero Inventories' (1983) and Womack, Jones and Roos' 'The Machine That Changed the World' (1990) made some reference – but probably insufficient - to people policies. Even earlier, Training Within Industry (TWI) (1940's) saw 'job relations' (JR) as one of the trilogy of job instruction, job methods, and job relations.

It's interesting to note that despite all the advances we've witnessed in technology and communications over the years, when it comes to managing people one key principle remains the same as ever; *"You cannot do things to people, but only with them."* said Kurt Lewin in 1954 and later elaborated with *"If you want any change to succeed, get the gatekeepers in on it early. Otherwise you will start over again with every stakeholder group."*

In this section we summarise established Lean 'people practices'.

First, we consider Respect and Humility – essential characteristics that apply to all sections below. Then, the next four sections (Gemba Walks, Questions, Leader Standard Work, and Gemba Meetings) are closely related and often used together.

The key leadership traits for all 'people' aspects of Lean are the twin concepts of Respect and Humility. (The foundation stones of the Shingo Prize Model are 'Respect Every Individual' and 'Lead with Humility.')

3.1 Respect

'Respect' is a word widely used in Lean. But what does it require?

John Seddon caused a stir at a Lean conference by saying *"Respect is horseshit"* (gasps and outrage from the audience!). What he meant was that 'lip service' and statements such as 'people are our most valuable asset' are too often a useless cover-up. True respect needs to be demonstrated, day-in day-out, not just mentioned in corporate literature, or spoken about whilst 'letting people go'. The true test of respect is what people experience, not what they hear about or read about in corporate missives. (Gasps unjustified?)

Attitudes to Respect have changed, we hope. Roman galleys had slaves with numbers, overseers with whips and a drummer beating out the rate ('takt time?'). (See the movie *Ben Hur*). Henry Ford set up a Sociological Department to monitor workers 'thrift, cleanliness, sobriety, family values and good morals.' Internal spies. Yet even today some organisations monitor key strokes, e mails, and conversation lengths in a call centre. Many have legions to track expenses and variances. Some 'Lean' organisations still highly monitor minute outputs from their 'human resources'. Is this different from *Ben Hur*? Is this Respect?

Let us begin with a quote from Isao Yoshino: *"If I am asked what made Toyota one of the top-ranking automakers in the world, I would say, we make people while we make cars. It's our people who make cars, not machines. That is respect."*

…and the African word 'ubuntu' – a person becomes a person through other persons.

To reinforce this…

In 2007, Jim Womack asked Toyota leaders how they show respect. What they said was a surprise: Managers begin by asking employees what the problem is with the way their work is currently being done. Next they challenge the employees' answer and enter into a dialogue about what the real problem is. (It's rarely the problem showing on the surface.)

Then they ask what is causing this problem and enter into another dialogue about its causes. (True dialogue requires the employees to gather evidence on the gemba – the place where value is being created -- for joint evaluation).

Then they ask what should be done about the problem and ask employees why they have proposed one solution instead of another. (This generally requires considering a range of solutions and collecting more evidence.)

Then they ask how they – manager and employees – will know when the problem has been solved, and engage one more time in dialogue on the best indicator.

Finally, after agreement is reached on the most appropriate measure of success, the employees set out to implement the solution.

Womack realized that *"This problem-solving process is actually the highest form of respect. The manager is saying to the employees that the manager can't solve the problem alone, because the manager isn't close enough to the problem to know the facts. He or she truly respects the employees' knowledge and their dedication to finding the best answer. But the employees can't solve the problem alone either because they are often too close to the problem to see its context and they may refrain from asking tough questions about their own work. Only by showing mutual respect – each for the other and for each other's role – is it possible to solve problems, make work more satisfying, and move organizational performance to an ever-higher level."* From Jim Womack Newsletter, 20 December, 2007

There are two dimensions to Respect: That which is visible in the actions of managers and can be observed, and that which is bias in the minds of managers and cannot be seen. We will call these (unsatisfactorily) as Visible and Invisible Respect.

Visible Respect

A good starting point to understanding Respect is the 'Foundations for Good Relations' used in TWI Job Relations (JR). A general statement from TWI JR is 'People must be treated as individuals'. Too often, people in organisations are treated as a collection of 'resources' (hence HRM) instead of as individuals. Building on TWI JR, there would seem to be five dimensions to the meaning and practice of Respect. All five are necessary.

1.   Trust

- Trust is arguably more important, more fundamental, than respect. Would you be rather be led, or lead, by someone you trust or someone you respect?
- Being honest and consistent with honesty. The first of Deming's 14 Points is 'Constancy of Purpose'. (The story of the well-kept goose until Christmas Eve is pertinent. Unlike geese, the story gets around.) 'Lip service' and hypocrisy will always undermine.

- Lifetime employment, as offered by some Japanese companies, is a strong indication of trust and consistency – but some of these also employ large numbers of 'temps' who might feel less respected. But Trust goes further: No modern organisation can control all of the actions of its employees. Flexibility in a VUCA world is a must. So people need to be trusted to respond appropriately to changing circumstances.
- Sharing relevant information and strategy. The TWI guideline is 'Tell people in advance about changes that will affect them'. 'Confidentiality' sends out warning signals, so treat with care. The growing Open Book Management approach (See Section 13.9) where financial and operational information is widely shared, is a powerful signal about trust.
- Catalysts. Amabile and Kramer in *The Progress Principle* say that respect is gained by both catalysts (for instance, allowing autonomy, providing resources and time, helping with work, learning and listening), and by….
- Nourishers (for instance giving encouragement and emotional support)
- The opposite of 'command and control'. Of course, full autonomy is often difficult but allowing maximum feasible autonomy sends out a message of trust and confidence.

2. Appreciation

- Acknowledgement of contribution. Individuals and not 'human resources'.
- A simple 'Thank you'. When was the last time you gave or received thanks? (Note: Not corporate or general thanks, but individual thanks based on a specific achievement.)
- Recognition. 'Give credit where due', says TWI JR. (Did that consultant steal your ideas?)
- 'Expressions of value'. Amabile and Kramer say that Respect refers to either explicit or implicit expressions of another person's value.
- Active listening, without interruption. 'Seek first to understand, then to be understood', said Steven Covey as one of this '7 Habits'.
- Genuine questioning.
- The good Gemba Walk (See Section 3.3 below.)
- Asking people what they think. 'We need and appreciate your views.' Front line workers have unique insights. (See Kurt Lewin's Force-Field Analysis in Section 4.5) George Koenigsaecker, as CEO of famous Lean company Jake Brake, insisted that C level execs participate in a number of kaizen events each year – or automatically lose their bonus. This was not for the wonderful ideas that C level execs would bring but rather for the execs to realise what good ideas front-line workers have.
- Sharing positive experiences. Not only an ego boost to the individual, but an improvement opportunity.
- The suggestion box containing ignored ideas. Disrespect!
- Of course, making improvements that result in the loss of jobs for a team shows ultimate disrespect by those responsible for the decision.
- Collective rewards, and beware of unearned, excessive, individual rewards. The steadily diverging 500+ multiple of senior management compensation over junior compensation is a clear problem for Respect. ('*I'm worth it!*', said Andy Harrison of EasyJet about his $4.5m package in 2009. Perhaps. Or, as Napoleon the pig said in Orwell's Animal Farm, '*We are all equal but some are more equal than others.*' (!))

3. Ability

- 'Make best use of each person's ability', goes the TWI JR statement.
- Awareness and, even better, use of non-work-related skills. Find out about these and you may be surprised.

- By contrast, not being aware of skills, ignoring skills, sending people to courses and conferences and then showing no interest, is de-motivating and disrespectful as well as being a huge waste. The 8th waste!
- Overload (Muri). Overload of work causes stress and, probably, quality problems. As shown by Kingman's equation, queues accumulate where utilization goes above about 90%. Then customers and schedules suffer.
- Is it respectful to give workers highly repetitive, boring jobs – even (as Henry Ford did) with much higher pay?

4. Psychological Safety

- Making people feel safe and secure – as in a family. Excluding a person from a group (deliberate or not) has been shown to have severe psychological consequences. Respect implies inclusivity.
- Fostering work as a learning, growing process. (See Section 9.9 on Psychological Safety in the Decisions and Mistakes Chapter)
- A willingness to admit mistakes. This works two ways: humility from top down, and confidence and security from bottom up. (Pulling the Andon cord with confidence. Thomas Watson (IBM founder) and his famous reaction to an employee who made a $1m mistake: 'Fire you? Of course not! I have just invested $1m in your education.') (Refer to section 9.7 on Mistakes.)
- Replacing blame with curiosity.
- Openness and accessibility. The boss on the shop floor; at the Gemba – but as a person who is there to help and learn, not to inspect and criticise. (See section 3.5 on Leader Standard Work.)
- The analogy of the 'Hot Stove Rule'. A family gathers around the hot stove. Support, help and encouragement (warmth) is given. If a transgression occurs (touching the stove) instant discipline is administered (burn) but the stove has no memory and continues to give warmth.

5. Civility

- Working environment (e.g. 5S) is a 'litmus test' for Respect. You would not like your family to live in a 'pigsty'. So allowing and ensuring a good, clean, healthy work environment is the most outward sign of Respect.
- Striving to understand people's viewpoints – not only about work but about personal concerns.
- Avoiding rudeness and sarcasm. Corporate intolerance of these is policy.
- Personal conduct, and ignoring the person. (In some cultures, not acknowledging a person's presence is an insult!)
- Of course, sensitivity towards age, sex, race, religion is fundamental.
- Appearance, parking, timekeeping, canteen and queuing priorities.
- Making eye contact.
- Care with reprimands.
- Toleration of expressed ideas – but agreement not necessary. Everyone should be treated with respect, but not everyone's opinions can be respected. Respect 'cannot be given, unless felt' says Stephen Fry, and 'a free mind is obliged to respect only the truth'. So, viewpoints should always be tolerated or listened to, even if they cannot be 'respected'. Woke culture?
- Being 'nice' is not respect if it is insincere.

Humility and respect are also the foundation of both Edgar Schein's book 'Humble Inquiry' and Gerald Egan's 'Skilled Helper' approach. Both rely on sympathetic, careful listening and probing, open questions.

A final word… In 2016 the Natural Environment Research Council (NERC) decided to launch a campaign to let the public decide what its polar research ship should be called. 'Boaty McBoatface' easily won the poll. However, NERC didn't like the answer, and the ship was named RSS Sir Richard Attenborough. The 'Boaty' name was instead given to an underwater research vehicle. How many leaders do the same when they ask for comment? Is this Respect?

Invisible Respect

Everyone has biases. There are two types that are of relevance to 'Respect'. First is the *Objectivity Illusion*. Everyone has opinions and viewpoints: about football or rugby, Democrat or Republican,, pull or push system, and so on. These colour your judgement to a greater or lesser degree. Everyone has the bias that their viewpoint is correct. Beware! As Abraham Lincoln said, *"I don't like the man. I must get to know him better."* Second is the *Fundamental Attribution Error* or (FAE). This is where your opinion of someone or something is coloured by situation or status. The person is blamed rather than the situation. You believe someone because he is a published author (!); you don't think much of a person because he drives a jalopy or is poorly dressed. As Amy Edmondson point out, if I am late, I blame the circumstances but if you are late I blame the person – perhaps for lack of commitment or motivation! Again, Beware!

As an example, there are many excellent consultants with relevant experience but there are others who simply trade on the basis that they once worked for a great company. Does that warrant automatic respect?

3.2 Humility

It is a leader's humility which makes him or her receptive to learning new skills and ways of managing people. Ego, on the other hand is a barrier to true learning. Arrogance is the opposite of humility. If a 'leader' believes that he already has all the desired skills, knowledge and experience, learning stops and 'them and us' grows. From an operational excellence perspective, leaders display humility by recognising that they can learn from all employees, regardless of their position on the organisation chart. There are always things to learn, simply because associates are closer to the action, so their opinions are sought and valued. Associates often have unseen skills from outside of the organisation (Sporting coach? Computer whizz? Volunteer? Artist?). Steven Johnson's thesis is that almost all innovation comes from the 'adjacent possible'.

In a similar vein, humble leaders are relentless in the pursuit of improvement. They actively benchmark both inside and outside of their industry.

Edgar Schein, in his essential book, 'Humble Inquiry', points out three types of humility: humility that we feel around elders and dignitaries; humility that we feel in the presence of those who awe us with their achievements, and 'here and now humility' that results from being dependent on someone else in order to accomplish a task. It is this third type, according to Schein, 'that is the key to Humble Inquiry and to the building of positive relationships'. There are three requirements, according to Schein: do less talking; do more asking, and do a better job of listening and acknowledging. It is particularly the second one (humble asking) that is often neglected.

There is a fine line between humility and over-confidence. Confidence has been shown to be trait for success. Over-confidence, on the other hand, is an undesirable but widespread bias.

- Confidence with humility is the gold. Be confident but listen, and be prepared to change.
- Confidence without humility can lead to disaster. (Who has seen the movie 'A Bridge too Far'?)
- Humility without confidence, might make you a nice person, but ineffectual.
- No humility and no confidence, could lead to a label of know-all, do nothing.

Lean Leaders should be aware of the Dunning-Kruger effect. This is the bias that people with low ability tend to over-estimate their ability. And, conversely, those that under-estimate their abilities are generally the most competent. In self-assessments studies carried out by the authors using, for instance, The Shingo Prize framework or the Goodson Lean audit, those who assessed themselves as good often had the worst plants – and vice versa. Ignorance is bliss?

There is an associated graph of confidence against competence.

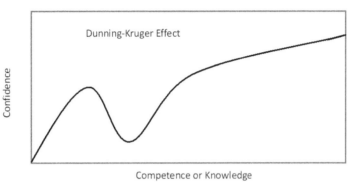

Kruger and Dunning found that 'participants scoring in the bottom quartile on tests of humour, grammar and logic grossly overestimated their test performance and ability.' So the least skilled were not only poor at their tasks, they were also poor at estimating their competence!

The effect is about the arrogance of ignorance, something we have found in a distressing number of cases (and we have certainly been guilty of this ourselves). Adam Grant, Stanford Professor, calls the first hump 'Mount Stupid', and of course this is a lack of humility. Grant describes two possible cycles:
- The rethinking cycle: Humility drives Doubt drives Curiosity drives Discovery drives Humility. This is a good learning cycle, but there is also…
- The overconfidence cycle: Pride drives Conviction drives Confirmation Bias drives Validation drives Pride.

Grant also describes two syndromes: the 'armchair quarterback' (who knows the rules better than the ref), and the 'imposter syndrome' where a usually competent person nevertheless realises the limitations of his or her thinking and feels reluctant to opine. To quote from Adam Grant's book *Think Again* (which every aspiring Lean manager should read): *"Great thinkers…..don't boast about how much they know; they marvel at how little they understand. They're aware that each answer raises new questions, and the quest for knowledge is never finished. A mark of lifelong learners is recognizing that they can learn something from everyone they meet."* (In short, Humility and Respect).

A prominent British consultant (and Deming fan) is often very critical of, and vocal about, of approaches other than his own. The result is that many managers are reluctant to ask or query for fear of being 'shot down'. Ironically, one of Deming's 14 points is 'Drive out fear'. Speakers need humility, honesty and to foster a *No Fears* culture when talking to others. This takes time. It can only be built by demonstration over an extended period, but can be destroyed in the very short term. Recall the story about the farmer who builds confidence amongst turkeys until the week before Christmas…

And to quote Edgar Schein: *"When I talk to senior managers, they always assure me that they are open, that they want to hear from their subordinates, and that they take the information seriously. However, when I talk to subordinates in those same organisations, they tell me that either they do not feel safe bringing bad news to their bosses, or that they have tried but never got any response or even acknowledgement, so they concluded that their input wasn't welcome and gave up."* (This is Psychological Safety, a topic that is discussed in Section 9.9.)

Arrogance and a lack of humility are major barriers to good decision making. See Section 9.4.

Finally, a quote from Pfeffer and Sutton…
"The implication is that leaders need to make a fundamental decision: Do they want to be told they are always right, or do they want to lead organizations that actually perform well?"

…and on Respect and Humility…

- Small spans of control for front line leaders, as practised by Toyota, enable them to listen, take ideas forward, probe, help solve problems and be aware of issues that might affect work.
- Outward signs of respect and humility include: No reserved parking, same rules for all, uniforms (?), a single canteen, who shows visitors around, the relative pay and bonus of the CEO, new managers begin with a period of working on the shop floor or at customer-interacting locations.
- Respect does not mean being nice, but rather a deep-seated appreciation of colleagues.
- Visitors to good Lean plants are invariably struck by the humility of their managers ('we still have lots to learn') and their willingness to learn from others, no matter who.
- Developing your people to achieve their full potential shows respect for them. (In this regard it is a 'Theory Y' attitude (see earlier) and a 'Growth Mindset' (see later).)
- A good test for Leaders: Ask yourself 'When was the last time a subordinate got me to change my mind?'

Further Readings.
Adam Grant, *Think Again*, WH Allen, 2021
J. Kruger, and D. Dunning, *Unskilled and unaware of it: how difficulties in recognizing one's own incompetence lead to inflated self-assessments.* Journal of personality and social psychology, *77*(6), p.1121. 1999
Jeffrey Pfeffer and Robert Sutton, *Hard Facts, Dangerous half-truths and total nonsense: Profiting from evidence-based management*, Harvard Business School Press, 2006
Edgar Schein, *Humble Inquiry*, Berrett-Koehler, 2013

3.3 Gemba and Gemba Walks

Note: Genba may be the more correct term, but here the usual 'Gemba' will be used.

Gemba is the 'real place' or actual place where value is created… It is where you go to see first-hand and get information by direct observation. 'The gemba' could be anywhere – the factory floor, a customer site, a supplier's process, a front office or a design centre. It is where value is added.

First, however, understand that Gemba is part of a trilogy. Gemba is the real place. Gembutsu is the real part or object. Gemjitsu is the real or actual facts. Go to the Gemba. Observe gembutsu. Collect gembutsu.

A Caution: Although Going to the Gemba is essential for first-hand observation, it is not that easy. Be aware that people's behaviour often changes when they are observed. Trust must be established first. A classic is changeover reduction in early stages of Lean: the standard time for the changeover often falls dramatically when observed even before any SMED (quick change-over) activity has taken place! Alternatively, it is the experience of many old-style Work Study officers that workers go into slow motion when the stopwatch comes out.

Let us remind ourselves that Gemba is not a 'Japanese thing'. They learned it from the Americans – specifically the famous Hawthorne experiments at General Electric that were discussed earlier in this book. What was happening was that workers were responding not to the lighting levels but to the interest being taken in them by esteemed researchers. This became known as the Hawthorn Effect. But the West promptly forgot this lesson. The Japanese took it on. So, don't sit in the office looking at an excel spreadsheet and imagine that you are improving productivity – that is management by looking in the rear-view mirror. Instead, as was said by Union soldiers to General Burnside in the American Civil War "*Move your hindquarters from the headquarters.*"

A now popular approach in companies who implement lean principles is called "Gemba Walks," which denote the action of leaders going to see the actual process, understand the work, ask probing questions, and learning from those who do the work. This should become a routine activity – a habit. By so doing, leaders not only learn the issues first hand but demonstrate humility and that people are the critical value adders. The objective is to understand the value stream and its problems, rather than review results or make superficial comments from their office or conference room.

Since about 2005, 'Gemba Walks' have catapulted in popularity. They are now considered an integral part of 'Leader Standard Work'. The Gemba Walk concept applies to several levels of management. Thus a director might walk once per month, plant managers once per fortnight, a division manager weekly, and a value steam leader daily. Gemba walks are a good way to create visible leadership. It is desirable to have a Gemba Walk schedule showing who is to walk when and maybe where (The area, not the route).

However, the purpose and methodology of a Gemba Walk is sometimes not understood, so potential is lost. A walk may do more harm than good. What it is NOT is:

1.   A casual walk-through or tour.
2.   Management merely showing their face or flag waving on the shop floor or office.
3.   An inspection – demanding action on anything out of place that is spotted, or to catch people out.
4.   A routine walk-through, following the same route.
5.   Giving answers. Telling.
6.   Giving direct orders on the spot, rather than coaching front line leaders.

So, what are the characteristics of a good Gemba Walk?

1.   Purpose: teaching others and learning yourself
2.   Focus: on the student, or mentee, not the work; like a teaching hospital round
3.   Time: allowing sufficient time for discussion and for follow up by the mentee.

4.   Assignments: agree on what to do.
5.   Follow up: next time
6.   Objective: learning to see, to question
7.   Servant Leadership: Identifying obstacles that need to be removed by management so that work can be improved.
8.   Communication and Trust: Building working relationships
9.   Emphasise the value stream, not vertical silos

Two types of walks:

1.   End to end walk – development of the value stream
2.   Area walk – development of the area

Note that a Gemba Walk is different from MBWA 'Management by walking around' – a phrase made popular by Peters and Waterman in their book 'In Search of Excellence'. MBWA is unfocused and random. Not necessarily a bad thing – anything that gets senior managers to the Gemba has virtue – but MBWA lacks the follow through and relationship building that are features of Gemba walks. MBWA sounds more like a President's or Queen's visit, a special event that happens only occasionally.

Gemba walks typically involve:

- Beginning with a review of a performance board, with charts and measures, to identify actions relating to new and current problems.
- A journey along a value stream for a first-hand, direct observation experience. (Perhaps start at the end, nearest the final customer, seeking upstream issues.)
- Showing true respect for front line associates.
- Clarification and seeking mutual understanding of issues. *"Can you show me…",*
- A way for leaders to observe, teach and learn. (But not to humiliate operators or over-rule direct line management.)
- A form of servant leadership that enables managers to identify opportunities for improvement and remove barriers to better work.
- Visits to the actual problem areas to discuss with the people directly involved.
- Discussion on actions taken or needed, for flow and improvement.
- Identification of barriers or obstacles that are preventing the problem being resolved.
- Follow up with line managers as to the agreed next steps.

A summary of Gemba Walks is the 7 G's:

1.   GO to the actual place.
2.   GET the facts from the actual situation by direct observation.
3.   GATHER ideas and suggestions. Ask and listen – very little tell, unless asked.
4.   GIVE credit where due.
5.   GRASP the current condition and clarify the problem.
6.   GUIDE the implementation through support, coaching, and feedback (Please see Feedback in Section 5.3).
7.   GENERATE and agree improvement proposals together with the people at the gemba. (Establish the next target situation. This will often mean breaking down the problem into manageable chunks.)

A good Gemba Walk means that team leaders and workers get an opportunity to be heard, and to demonstrate pride in their work and achievements. Leaders, at all levels, learn respect, have the opportunity to coach, and better to understand people and process. As a leader visits the gemba, there is the opportunity to question, but certainly not to command. The choice of words is very important. Keep humility in mind. Never accuse. Swop 'you' for 'we' (for instance, instead of 'Why do you not keep to the schedule?' try 'What can we do to make hitting the schedule easier?'). Never try to boost your own ego ('I fully appreciate how difficult your job is.')

…and don't be afraid to say 'I don't know…', or 'That's new to me', or 'What a valuable insight that is.'

Of course, familiarity with the work, machine, or process leads to better questions. 'Are the stoppages on that dynamo still a problem?' and maybe as a follow up, 'Excellent! Tell me what was done to solve the problem?'

Gemba Experiences: A True Gemba?

- Anthropologists are the true Gemba experts. They study the culture of societies and groups by typically spending weeks or months with the group. They don't begin with 'a problem' but with an open-minded quest to learn how the group behaves or thinks. Today, major tech companies such as Apple, Alphabet, and Intel employ anthropologists to study how different societies regard and use, for instance, their products. If you are an engineer in California can you possibly understand how an iphone could be regarded and used by a farmer in central Africa? (See more about Anthropology in Section 11.10)
- In the early 1970's, one of the authors (Bicheno) was a student of Peter Checkland – he of 'soft systems' fame. (See Chapter 5). Checkland's methodology has similarities with anthropology in as far as it requires a 'rich picture' of the situation to be developed. This leads onto several 'root definitions' each reflecting the viewpoint of a different stakeholder. For instance, the view of a particular prison by the governor, the religious minister, the guards, the prisoners, the victims, the psychologists, and more. None of this can happen without Gemba experience.
- In the 1980's, one of the authors (Bicheno) was lucky enough to be associated with legendary Operations Research professor 'Gene' Woolsey. Woolsey insisted on a Gemba approach amongst his Masters students – although the term was then unknown. In one typical case the operations in a 24/7 warehouse were studied by a student who brought his camp bed to the warehouse and did not emerge for a week. Just drawing a value stream map would be totally inadequate!
- Steve Spear's Harvard Business School case study 'Jack Smith' tells of a senior management recruit to Toyota who spends 8 weeks working on the line in both USA and Japan.

Cautions

- Gemba walks require humble leaders with the self-awareness to know that they may not have all the answers.
- A leader's role is to provide support and direction, not to fix every problem.
- The focus should be on strengthening systems, developing personnel and identifying improvement opportunities.
- Leader's failure to attend prearranged Gemba Walks will send out a clear *'We are not important"* message to those employees concerned.
- A title leader doesn't automatically make you a coach or mentor.

Further Readings.

David Mann 'Making the Connection to the HVSF Real' in *Accelerate the Journey*, Vol 01, Issue 09, June 2014 (horizontal value stream flow).
Edgar Schein, *Humble Inquiry*, Berrett-Koehler, 2013
Jim Womack, *Gemba Walks – Expanded Second Edition*, LEI, 2013

3.4 Questions and Listening

Sincere questioning, showing interest and follow through, is a positive feedback process. If associates learn that responses are taken seriously, they will be encouraged to offer more ideas and suggestions. Responses that illicit a punishment response will inevitably close down further dialog. And vice versa - when associates learn that measures are there to expose problems and opportunities rather than to appropriate blame, the information itself is likely to be more genuine. Psychologists refer to this circular process as 'the norm of reciprocity'.

A question such as 'How is it going?' could get the response, 'OK', but a better reflective question would be 'What opportunities are there for improvement? – And then, of course, it is vital to follow up answers with further probes.

More detailed guidance on Questioning is given in Section 9.10.

In this respect, Gemba walks have similarities with the Socratic method (See Section 3.14). Questions cannot be effectively asked or answered by managers sitting at their desks. A true questioning culture is only possible if you are at Gemba. Apart from Gemba walks, the Gemba attitude breaks away from the 'it's not my problem' attitude and 'I only work here', moving towards 'servant leadership' and the 'inverted organization triangle'.

Spending time at the front line, call centre, or service counter listening to actual customer words is a great way to raise manager curiosity and motivation - far better than market survey, monitoring KPI's, or 'mystery shopping'. Ohno was famous for his 'chalk circle' approach - drawing a circle in chalk on the factory floor and requiring a manager to spend several hours inside it whilst observing operations, noticing variation, and taking note of wastes. The West too has its devotees. John Sainsbury who ran the supermarket chain could pass a shelf and see at a glance if prices were wrong. An open plan office, with senior management sitting amongst 'the troops' is Gemba. Gemba is, or should be, part of implementation. How often is the Western way based on 'change agents', on simulation, on computers or information systems, on classroom-based education? These have a place, of course, but Gemba emphasises implementation by everyone, at the workplace, face-to-face, based on in-depth knowledge with humility and respect. And low cost, no cost solutions rather than big-scale expensive information or technology solutions.

Finally, as was said in Pilgrims Progress, 'To *know* is a thing which pleases talkers and boasters; but to *do* is that which pleases God'.

3.5 Standard Work and Leader Standard Work

Leader Standard Work (LSW) follows on from the Gemba principles. But, first, a word.

Standards. Lilian Gilbreth, perhaps the 'mother of scientific management' points out three things: A standard is 'a unit of reference', 'a basis of comparison', and 'a model'. A standard derives 'not from theories, but from scientific study of actual practice.' And 'a standard is progressive' – it 'remains fixed only until a more perfect standard displaces it.'

Some confusing phrases: *Standard Work* is the practice of setting, documenting, following and improving standards. *Standardised Work* is the aim, and the objective of kaizen activities.

Standard Work is the documented and current best way to do a particular task, procedure or process. Employees are involved in developing the standard for their work, and following it until an improvement process results in a new standard. Standard work ensures that results are consistent and forms the foundation upon which all improvements are made. Leader standard work applies this same concept to the task of driving Lean thinking and behaviour throughout the organization. Leader Standard Work is a set of behaviours and recurring activities that advances a Continuous Improvement culture. The practice also incorporates coaching and mentoring opportunities, surfaces immediate opportunities to improve processes and, through LSW, leaders get to understand what is working well, what isn't, and where change is necessary.

Here are some famous quotes from Henry Ford and Taiichi Ohno.

From Henry Ford:

"To standardise a method is to choose out of many methods the best one, and use it. What is the best way to do a thing? It is the sum of all the good ways we have discovered up to the present. It, therefore becomes the standard."

"Today's standardisation is the necessary foundation on which tomorrow's improvement will be based. If you think of 'standardisation as the best we know today, but which is to be improved tomorrow' - you get somewhere. But if you think of standards as confining, then progress stops."
Henry Ford, Today and Tomorrow, 1926

From Taiichi Ohno:

"But in the beginning, you must perform the Standard Work, and as you do, you should find things you don't like, and you will think of one kaizen idea after another. Then you should implement these ideas right away, and make this the new standard. Years ago, I made them hang the standard work documents on the shop floor. After a year I said to a team leader, 'The colour of the paper has changed, which means you have been doing it the same way, so you have been a salary thief for the last year.' I said 'What do you come to work to do each day? If you are observing every day you ought to be finding things you don't like, and rewriting the standard immediately. Even if the document hanging there is from last month, this is wrong.' At Toyota in the beginning we had the team leaders write down the dates on the standard work sheets when they hung them. This gave me a good reason to scold the team leaders, saying 'Have you been goofing off all month?"

L.M. Gilbreth, *The Psychology of Management*, New York, 1921
Taiichi Ohno, *Workplace Management*, originally published in 1982, from translation by Jon Miller, Gemba Press, 2007.

Standardisation

Standardisation, as opposed to Standard Work, is a trade-off decision. There is a need to be flexible for innovation and for customer service (for instance to avoid failure demand) against requirements to follow procedures for instance in health and spare parts. A great selling point can be consistency through standardisation. What would happen if McDonalds allowed every franchise the freedom to make changes? Do customers, and the organisation, want cost and consistency, or flexibility? Pressures for standardisation increase with the size of the organisation. Flexibility is fine, even desirable, for 'Mom and Pop' concerns but, increasingly, as an organisation grows, it becomes a challenge – consistency against adaptability.

Key Points and Standard Work

In TWI Job Instruction (JI) there are three stages to documenting a job: Main steps, Key Points, and Reasons for the Key Points. In may be argued that EVERY job, manufacturing or service, has a number of Key Points. In many customer-facing jobs, and in design and many office tasks, considerable flexibility can and should be allowed. Nevertheless, there will remain some Key Points that should always be followed, together with clear explanation or understanding of why the Key Point is necessary. Key Points could constitute a very small proportion of some jobs (See the Kaizen Flag in Section 3.11) but they remain Key.

Job Instruction is now beginning to be taught using Augmented Reality (AR). The jury is out on the effectiveness of using AR for TWI JI. (AR certainly has a great future in much of wider Lean teaching and experience building.)

Beware

Once rework, or rework processes or even departments, become a part of standard work, we promote it from waste to 'value-adding'. The abnormal becomes normal and appears to have belonged there all along.

Window Analysis and standards

Work standards will only 'work' if operators are prepared to follow them! Certainly, this is partly dependent on 'culture' – both company culture and national culture.

Window analysis is a framework used to confirm that standards are being followed, and to identify potential problems. It is particularly appropriate for assembly operations where following standard work is critical to quality. The method helps to establish the reason for the failure of a standard – whether caused by establishing the standard, communicating the standard or adhering to the standard. The method is used by, for example, Sony. The method seeks to understand whether the issue identified is confined to one person or group, or is more widespread. In the figure Party X may be a manager, Party Y an operator.

The categories are: 'Known' or 'Unknown' – whether the correct methods are established and known – and 'Practised' or 'Unpractised' – whether the correct methods are practised 100% of the time.

There are then four conditions – refer to the figure below:

A – only if methods are known and practised by both parties 100% of the time.
B – an adherence problem, when a method is established and understood, but not practised by all parties.
C – a communication problem, when the method is established, but some individuals are not informed about it.
D – a standardisation problem, where the right method is not established.

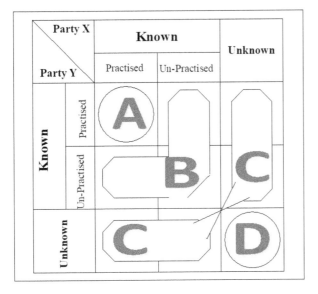

Standards taken too far?

Standard work is not the same as close monitoring. The UK Sunday Times Business Section of 7 Feb 2021 reported that Amazon workers, "after swiping in, collect a hand-held scanner that records their every move for the next 10 hours, feeding productivity data to team leaders and managers. When pickers scan an item, a countdown begins on their scanner showing how much time they have before they need to scan the next one. …If warehouse workers aren't hitting their targets, an alarm sounds on their scanner telling them to report to their agency's desk where they are made to sign a form acknowledging they are falling short of expectations." Repeated failures lead to dismissal. Amazon claims that performance is measured over a long period (workers are given private medical insurance and nurses are on site). This may sound harsh. But the questions are, is this used for improvement or for close control of behaviour? Trust or big-brother watching? Excessive top-down or a learning system?

Leader Standard Work

LSW is a system to support leaders in:

- Focusing on the critical tasks / activities.
- Defining and exhibiting ideal behaviours, and mentoring and coaching of their people.
- Recognising employees for their commitment and performance.
- Engaging with their employees to understand the issues that affect them in performing their daily work and displaying a "Lead by Humility" approach.
- Demonstrating their commitment to employee engagement.
- Structuring and prioritising their tasks and activities.
- Managing their time efficiently.

In his excellent book, *Creating a Lean Culture*, David Mann says that there are four principal elements of Lean Management. These are Leader standard work, Visual controls, Daily accountability process, and Leadership discipline. Of these, LSW has the 'highest leverage' and helps consolidate the other three. LSW work involves drawing up a timetable of activities that each leader in the organization, from team leader to Vice President needs to follow. Maasaki Imai's famous diagram on how people spend their time in a Kaizen organisation (a version is given in the later section on Kaizen) shows the proportion of time spent on Kaizen activity decreasing with management level. Just so with LSW. A senior manager may spend only a little time regularly on LSW – but note, not zero!

While every LSW document is specific, the example presented below is typical of those used by front line team leaders. It specifies the key tasks which have to be performed on the first hour of shift e.g. check manning, ensure efficient start up, gather data for the daily Gemba meeting. Hourly tasks might include walking the lines to monitor output and engage with the operators. Off-line tasks which while critical, can be done at any stage throughout the shift are also included. Note also, how it incorporates the team leader auditing the layer below, while the manager above also reviews and signs off on the team leader standard work daily. The authors would recommend using a hard copy LSW for a number of reasons. Its physical presence is in itself a reminder, leaders can carry it about with them as they go about their work and most importantly it becomes a living document which leaders are constantly updating.

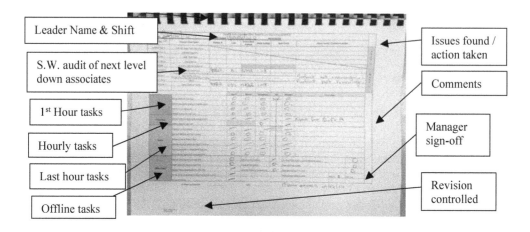

LSW Rules; (a) Every layer supports and audits the layer and process below it, (b) It should form part of regular 1-1's, (c) Process is the main focus, not only the result, (d) Should be concentrated on improving the process and supporting the people.

Cautions

- While LSW helps to establish and sustain a particular leadership style across the organisation, it does reduce leaders' discretion. Some leaders may not like this.
- LSW requires considerable discipline.
- LSW should be reviewed and updated on a regular basis.

A variation on LSW is to use 'leaders' to audit a selection of standard work procedures. This is done at the Gemba, and is standard practice at Toyota plants. Perhaps a senior manager would do so once a month, a department leader once a fortnight, and a section leader once per week. What they would look for is an associate's ability not only to follow the standard steps, but also their knowledge of key points and the reasons for key points. A 'Job Breakdown Sheet' may be used by the leader for the task. This task not only clearly demonstrates the importance of Standard Work but also builds an understanding by leaders of the process steps.

Standard Work System

The figure below explains how TWI, LSW and problem solving knit together as one overall system to drive and sustain a continuous improvement culture. This system evolved from a lean transformation led by one of the authors, Noel. Interestingly the TWI, LSW and problem-solving systems were introduced separately and only joined together once they were deeply embedded in the organisation.

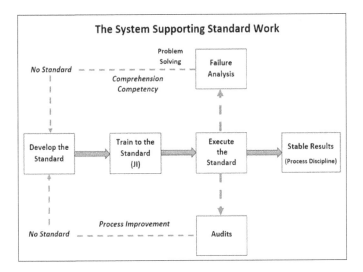

Key Points and Reasons are discussed in a following section (3.8) on TWI

Further Readings.
John Bicheno and Philip Catherwood, *Six Sigma and the Quality Toolbox*, PICSIE, 2005
Robert W Hall, 'Standard Work: Holding the Gains', *Target,* Fourth Quarter, 1998, pp 13- 19
Taiichi Ohno, *Toyota Production System*, Productivity Press, Portland, OR, 1988
Mike Rother, *Toyota Kata*, McGraw Hill, 2010
Spear and Bowen, 'Decoding the DNA of the Toyota Production System', *Harvard Business Review*, Sept/Oct 1999
Timothy Martin and Jeffrey Bell, *New Horizons in Standardized Work*, CRC Press, 201

3.6 Daily Gemba Meetings

Daily Gemba meetings are the key component of a lean company's management system. It allows them to know on a daily basis if they are on track to meet line, department and ultimately site goals. Gemba meetings are a way of involving employees at all levels of the organisation to meet briefly to identify and resolve issues which are preventing them from achieving their goals. General agendas are fixed with safety usually the first item on the agenda, but other items can be raised. These are normally stand-up meetings, are of fixed duration – typically 10 to 15 minutes, and should always start and end on-time.

A word of caution: Professor Wu of Harvard Business School found that stand-up meetings are "great for implementation but actually undermine idea generation". A stand-up explicitly "refocuses the energy of members on targets but doesn't leave members feeling open to searching for other avenues." We would add, Stand-up meetings should not be used for important decisions.

Gemba meetings are centred on an area performance board or screen, where daily performance achieved and issues of concern are shown. Non-production visuals, like training matrices, recognition and site communications may be displayed. The best examples include a visual display of KPI status (Red, Amber, and Green), trended graphs, and agreed actions and target dates with the appropriate owners identified. Many companies adopt the 1-3-10 second rule of visual management. Can we see in one second if we are on target? In three seconds, what is the trend and in ten seconds what actions have we taken to resolve the problem and get us back on target.

By the way, it is good psychology to start with a look at some of the Green status points, and particularly any that have recently changed from Red or Amber. Complimenting people first on achievement helps to build confidence rather than giving the impression that the Gemba Meeting is a 'policing activity' and (worst of all) that any Red status should be hidden.

An essential component of the Gemba meetings process is the tier management system. The meetings ensure the close monitoring of key performance measures, as well as enabling a two-way transfer of knowledge – coaching, mentoring, explaining and communicating in one direction and listening and facilitating in the other direction. Issues are raised for upwards communication. Escalation is incorporated – each level decides what to bring to the next level.

In summary, Gemba meetings are a highly effective, and very visual means of communication. As well as providing clear alignment and direction, they also help to create a positive culture of engagement, teamwork and efficiency.

Cautions

- KPI data and associated comments must be written up before the meeting.
- Gemba meetings should be focused on ensuring that daily and weekly targets are met.
- Every action raised must have an owner and target completion date.
- It is essential that the appropriate decision makers attend the meetings.
- Discussions on any item that exceed two minutes should be taken offline

Reference.
D. Dukach and A. Wu, 'Stand-up Meetings Inhibit Innovation', *Harvard Business Review*. Jan – Feb. 2021

3.7 Quality Circles

Having originated in Japan, Quality Circles are an integral part of the Toyota Production System. At Toyota, QC presentations to senior management occur almost every day. Quality Circles, at least of the Toyota variety, seem to be less popular in the West but the broad concept remains valid and powerful.

A quality circle is a participatory management technique that enlists the help of employees in solving problems related to their own jobs. Circles are formed of employees working together in an operation which meet at intervals to discuss quality problems and develop solutions for improvements. Quality circles are usually small, (7 or less?) and are led by a supervisor or a senior worker. Employees who participate in quality circles receive training in recognised problem-solving tools such as brain-storming, Pareto analysis, and cause-and-effect diagrams. Having applied these tools to locate the root cause of the problem, the QC team will present their findings and improvement plan to management for approval to proceed with implementation.

The format varies widely. Some circles are voluntary (the best ones seem to be), some take place in company time, others take place immediately before or after a work shift. Some have their own specific areas set aside, others use shared meeting spaces. Many use facilitators, other more experienced circles manage themselves. Some have limited authority and funds to proceed directly with small changes, most require approval from a higher level. Some have regular presentation time spots with managers and members from other circles in attendance.

QC's are a form of self-managed team. As such they may be seen as first stage leader-building or devolved management.

Edward Lawler (a famous authority on teams) has described a 'cycle of failure' for many Western QCs. The following sequence is typical. In early days the first circles make a big impact as pent-up ideas are released and management listens. Then the scheme is extended, usually too rapidly, to other areas. Management cannot cope with attending all these events, and is in any case often becomes less interested. In the initial phases, the concerns of first line supervisors, who often see QCs as a threat to their authority, are not sufficiently taken care of in the rush to expand. Some supervisors may actively sabotage the scheme; others simply do not support it. Then, as time goes on, with less support from management and supervision, ideas begin to run out. The scheme fades. (This is also the Cycle of Failure' found in many Suggestion Box schemes.)

Cautions

- A common mis-perception is that QCs are a Japanese idea which do not work in a Western culture.
- QC team skillset may not be adequate to resolve all problems.
- Constructive feedback is essential. (See Feedback, Section 5.3)
- Management support may reduce over time as skills develop, but not out of disinterest.

3.8 Training Within Industry - Job Relations

Training Within Industry (TWI) is arguably the most effective and influential industrial training programme ever developed. TWI methods had massive impact on Japanese industry, including Toyota. The thought was, and is, that it is the front-line supervisor who has the greatest impact on day to day productivity and process stability by instructing on how to do a job, by improving the work, and by dealing effectively with any operator problem or motivation issue. Today, many Toyota team leaders still carry quick reminder cards based on TWI. TWI methods cover what was considered to be the three essential areas for a supervisor – job instruction (JI), job methods (JM), and job relations (JR). Each has a four-step standardised procedure, summarised below. Those three skills are, still today, considered the essential tasks for any team leader at Toyota. The package of skills is what makes team working effective – all three are necessary. The original TWI name 'Job Relations' ceased to be used at Toyota in 2000 – but the essential steps form the backbone of the 'people' expectations of team leaders and supervisors.

Note: In the UK, TWI may be confused with the long-established 'The Welding Institute'. No connection, except that Training Within Industry certainly applies in welding.

TWI job relations addresses one of the most challenging parts of a supervisor's job – establishing and maintaining good supervisor–employee relations and dealing with problems when they arise. Job Relations is aimed at giving supervisors basic skills in behaviour in organizations, motivation, and communication. The Four 'Foundations of Good Job Relations' are 'solid gold' for every person in a management position. They are:

- Let each worker know how he/she is getting along.
- Give credit when due.
- Tell people in advance about changes that will affect them.
- Make best use of each person's ability.

And the TWI four steps on how to handle a people problem are:

1. Get the facts. ('Be sure you have the whole story.' Find out what rules and customs apply. Talk with the individuals concerned. Get opinions and feelings.)
2. Weigh up and decide. ('Don't jump to conclusions.' Fit the facts together. Check practices and policies. What possible actions are there? – note plural 'actions' not 'action'. Consider the effect of possible actions on the individual, the group, and on production. Sometimes a period of reflection is helpful.
3. Take action. ('Don't pass the buck.' Consider if you are going to handle the problem yourself, whether you need help, and whether the actions should be referred to others. Consider the timing of the action.
4. Check the results. (Did your action help?) How soon and how often should you check? Watch for changes in output, attitudes, and relationships.

It will be noticed that these four steps align with PDCA, although, wisely, it is PDAC – perhaps a better version of the original!

Cautions

In hierarchical organisations, line managers, more than any other group in the organisation, are challenged by the need to communicate upwards to senior managers, downwards to their sub-ordinates and frequently across departments. This requires skill and tact. It would be unusual for such skills to develop without training. Likewise, front-line managers must have the support of, and confidence in, their respective managers.

Further Readings.
Patrick Graupp and Bob Wrona, *The TWI Workbook*, CRC Press, (This remains the best guide and overview of TWI)

3.9 Lean Coaching

One of the most critical tasks leaders at all levels in organisations face today is in assisting their subordinates to achieve their full potential. A key component in making this happen is the leader's ability to develop coaching skills that can release their employee's capability in a structured, safe environment. In fact, according to Mike Rother (*Toyota Kata*, 2018) coaching has become so critical in developing both individuals and organisations, that it is likely to become a significant factor in career progression and consequently a subject at business schools.

While coaching encompasses many activities and techniques borrowed from other disciplines such as counselling, psychology, education, and consulting it is best defined by Whitmore (1992) who suggests that: *"Coaching is unlocking people's potential to maximise their own performance."*

Lean coaching is a fundamental requirement in creating an environment where sustainable continuous improvement can take hold and thrive. In a Lean coaching relationship, the coach will ask questions that stimulate critical thinking skills and reinforce systematic approaches for improving how leaders lead, and how work is done.

An important point is that coaching allows empowerment, participation, and delegation. Why? Because coaching your team, allows them to take on more responsibility. This is exactly in line with the Lean concept of 'creating thinking people' (TPS = Thinking People System). So, coaching should be done by every Lean manager, not by the HR function.

Lean coaches are often referred to as a sensei. A lean sensei is a master teacher of lean tools, systems and principles. While similar in experience to a Black Belt or Master Black Belt in the Six Sigma methodology, the sensei is more focused on facilitating and teaching lean than on the actual practice of it. A lean sensei typically stands outside of an organization, allowing him or her objectively to see what needs to be done and to develop a true continuous improvement culture without having to worry about internal politics or strong personalities.

In Michael Bungay Stanier's excellent book *The Coaching Habit* (a book that every aspiring Lean Manager should have) he gives 'seven essential questions'. (There are certainly similarities with the Socratic Method – see Section 3.14) You should read the book on the questions, but briefly they are a series of open questions beginning with 'What's on your mind?', followed by 'and what else?'. The questions are not a strict series but often involve cycling back to probe further. Resist giving your 'solution' but instead ask about the challenge. Another question is particularly interesting for fans of the '5 Whys': Stanier suggests asking What instead of Why, particularly why followed by 'did you…' (Of course, the 5Whys does have its place. See later in this chapter). Later comes 'How can I help? And, throughout, never underestimate silence and listening. (The Quakers have a tactic that has been used to good effect for 350 years - if there is a disagreement, then 'let's just have 2 minutes silence'.)

Note: See more on Questions in Section 9.10.

Further Readings.
Michael Bungay Stanier, *The Coaching Habit*, Box of Crayons Press, 2016. Note: Access the web site www.boxofcrayons.com for several resources.
John Whitmore, *Coaching for Performance*, Nicholas Bearley, 2017

3.10 Quick Response

Quality Circles and Kata (see below) are proven to be effective. However…

A variation found at Nissan, J&J and others is a Quick Response system whereby problems are addressed immediately. At J&J, where there are high levels of automation, if process control detects an unsatisfactory condition, a klaxon sounds, the process steps, and a multidiscipline team immediately assembles at the problem point (the gemba). A whiteboard, configured with A3-type steps, is wheeled to the point. Countermeasures are put in place and longer-term solutions discussed. Prioritisation is not considered 'We simply can't wait'. And, of course, in a medical situation, patient safety overrides trade-off decisions.

Some organisations have a response procedure which uses Pareto analysis and PDCA. The 80/20 Pareto system collects up all defects and non-conformities during a period and prioritises the top problems. (Sometimes an impact-cost matrix is used for prioritisation.) From an organisation perspective this is slower-response because the solution team (whether QC, kaizen group, or whatever) is assembled periodically and the solution may be subject to management approval. By contrast, a Quick Response system aims to address EVERY problem immediately without an up-

and-down approval process. PDCA could be followed, but there would be hierarchy of PDCA loops, as discussed by Shingo with reference to poka-yoke. The little and fast PDCA is the immediate countermeasure; the bigger and slower PDCA aims for the root – if it has not been solved during the little PDCA loop.

A variation at Toyota is the classic Andon cord. When pulled by an operator, the team leader will go to the problem immediately. Usually a quick solution is found within the takt time, but if not, the section of the line will stop. A recurring problem will result in escalation. (A Short story: On a group visit to Toyota Kentucky, a group member asked 'How many stops are there per day?' The answer: 'Over 1,000!' Group member, 'You must have lots of problems!' The response, 'We stop for our mistakes; others ship their mistakes!')

Further Readings.
Michel Baudin's Blog discussed Nissan's QRQC system on 15 December 2020.

3.11 Kaizen

Kaizen – Kaizen is a Japanese term which means "good change", "change for the better", or "improvement". As a philosophy, kaizen promotes a way of thinking wherein small incremental changes create a massive impact over time. It is based on the idea that improvement is a continuous process, not achieved by a first big step but over many small steps.

The essence of kaizen is (with quotes from Masaaki Imai, author of the original book on Kaizen):
- Continual improvement (*'Every day improvement'*)
- Involving all (*'Everyone improvement'*)
- Small changes (*'Everywhere improvement'*)

This implies a continual process of discovery – as Dan Jones has said *'peeling the onion'* to reveal more opportunity. And, by everyone - top to bottom – every day. Each small change necessarily uncovers another opportunity. For instance, reducing machine downtime leads to reducing buffer sizes leading to line rebalancing leading to exposing quality issues…and so on and on. Changeover reduction should lead to smaller batches which should lead to less buffer which should lead to improved layout which should lead to improved visibility which should lead to improved quality…. There is almost an infinity of such paths (as discussed by Bicheno in *Fishbone Flow.*) One improvement necessarily leads to another.

Kaizen is about growing a questioning culture. Curiosity is closely aligned to kaizen. As Bertrand Russell, noted mathematician and philosopher said, 'It is a healthy thing now and then to hang a question mark on things you have long taken for granted'. As an example, Sir William Armstrong founder of BAE Systems, that became one of the largest engineering groups in the UK, had a questioning, enquiring mind. For instance, walking past a water wheel, he asked himself what was the most effective way for it to operate: water input at top, clockwise or anticlockwise; water at bottom, clockwise or anticlockwise? And how to collect the water? Asking such questions led, little by little, onto great engineering innovations – hydraulic cranes, shipbuilding, and Tower Bridge in London.

But also realise that Kaizen achievements by employees is a great opportunity to show recognition and appreciation, and to reinforce a Lean mindset. This is an opportunity not to be missed! It strengthens the motivation feedback loop as discussed under Expectancy Theory (Section 4.1)

Daily Kaizen is just what the name says – daily and continuous. It is the practice of seeking opportunities for improvement across the entire organization every day. These improvements are usually small and incremental and often the result of repeated PDCA cycles. Daily Kaizen is about guiding and encouraging employees to be aware of waste, to question why processes are producing as they are, and how processes can be improved. Daily Kaizen offers several advantages including:

- It allows all employee to become involved in the continuous improvement process
- Small, reoccurring problems can be addressed quickly, by the people they affect
- Daily Kaizen can take place without interfering with the normal daily work
- No need to follow normal project management rules 'Just do it'
- It increases employee engagement and creates a momentum for improvement.

The Kaizen Flag™

The Kaizen Flag is a famous diagram developed by Maasaki Imai and widely copied and adapted. The flag portrays the three types of activity that everyone in a Kaizen organization should be involved with. These three are 'Innovation, 'Kaizen', and 'Standardization' against the level in the organization. (An adapted version is discussed below). In the original, senior management spends more time on 'innovation' (to do with tomorrow's products and processes), a definite proportion on 'kaizen' (to do with improving today's products and processes), but also a small proportion of time on 'standardisation' (that is, following the established best way of doing tasks such as, in top management's case, policy deployment and budgeting). A standard method is the current best and safest known way to do a task, until a better way is found through kaizen.

Middle managers spend less time than top managers on innovation, about the same time on kaizen and more time on standardisation. Operators spend a small, but definite, proportion of time on innovation, more time on kaizen, and the majority of time on standardisation.

Kate Mackle, former head of the British Kaizen Institute and now Principal in the consultancy Thinkflow, explains that innovation is concerned with preventing waste from entering tomorrow's processes, kaizen is concerned with getting waste out of today's processes, and standardisation is concerned with keeping waste out.

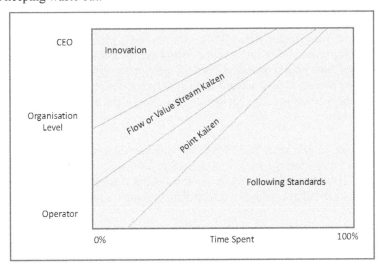

The version of the flag shown in the figure above has been developed based on Imai's original. (In Imai's original, the standards line goes from the bottom left corner to the top right hand corner. Only one category of Kaizen is shown in Imai's original.)

Another way of looking at the flag is that standardisation involves keeping out waste, kaizen is about getting waste out, and innovation is about preventing waste from entering.

Imai's point is that all levels in an organisation must split their time between the three activities. To not do so would mean that the organisation would not be a kaizen organisation

Further Readings.
Maasaki Imai, *Kaizen: The Key to Japan's Competitive Success*, McGraw Hill, New York, 1986
Maasaki Imai, *Gemba Kaizen*, McGraw Hill, New York, 1996

3.12 Kata

Kata (or Toyota Kata) has begun to have a major influence in Lean since Mike Rother published *Toyota Kata* in 2010. It may even be the most important development in Lean for a decade. Rother defines a kata as a well-rehearsed routine that eventually becomes second nature or habit. The word stems from Karate where basic sequences are rehearsed even by high-Dan black belts such that the actions establish and reinforce pathways in the brain and become automatic or a habit. (Many will have seen the famous sequence with Mr. Miyagi: 'wipe on, wipe off'!)

Kata is now a proven methodology in manufacturing, service, healthcare, and government.

The following is an important point at the outset: Kata is not only an improvement approach but is an approach to develop people into orderly, scientific thinkers. To this end Kata, as briefly described below, is not explicitly used by Toyota although the development of scientific thinking certainly is.

By the way: *"For any theory to be scientific, it must be stated in a way that it can be shown to be false as well as true."* says Tavris and Aronson in *Mistakes were Made.*

The Kata experience has much in common with TWI. (In recent years there have been several joint Kata-TWI conferences.) Kata overlaps with the Gemba and Leader Standard Work approaches, and can fit in well with Hoshin Kanri (Policy Deployment) planning. Hence this section on Kata is placed after Gemba and LSW sections and before the Hoshin Kanri section. Kata also has close links with several other important concepts and theories, amongst them: (a) Small Wins, (b) Habits, (c) System 1 and System 2 (Kahneman) and (d) Mindset (Dwek). (e) Coaching. All of these are discussed in separate sections. In that sense, Kata is a 'meta methodology', combining several forms of best practice.

Establishing Kata aligns with the PDSA incremental experimental method. Rother defines management as *"the systematic pursuit of desired conditions by utilizing human capabilities in a concerted way"*. But Rother has been at pains to point out that Kata is not a tool but one of several ways to ingrain Lean behaviour. It is a teaching or learning routine.

In both Kata and TWI, skills are built up by repetition. Very often learners get it wrong for the first few times and need coaching. But confidence is built through feedback 'at the gemba'. Hence there are unique improvement and leadership routines referred to by Rother as Improvement Kata and Coaching Kata.

There is the realistic assertion that one must have a target condition to know where one is going. With a target condition the direction and first few steps can be attempted. Unlike the assumptions of much of project planning, one is not quite sure or confident about the overall path leading to achieving the target condition. So one proceeds in small steps as with the experimental method. What is the first step? Try it. Does it move you closer? Reflect. Adjust. Avoid blame. What is now preventing us from moving ahead? What is the next specific small step to take? – not some big, vague step like 'reduce inventory', but perhaps 'let us try running the workstation with a container of 8 parts rather than 10'. Small wins build confidence and motivation. Practice builds mindset. The habit is established with each 'que' of going to check.

The **Improvement Kata** is a routine for moving from the current situation to a new situation in a creative, directed and meaningful way. It has four elements:

- Understand the direction
- Grasp the current condition
- Establish the next target condition. A measurable target.
- PDSA toward the target condition

Then repeat, and repeat again. This last step would often require several iterations, or PDSA cycles. Have patience.

One small step at a time, and learning from each step. Don't try to take big steps, containing several smaller simultaneous steps. Why? Because some small steps will work but others may not – but you may not be able to distinguish the successful from the unsuccessful if several initiatives are attempted at the same time. This is really the essence of scientific method – set a hypothesis, test it, reject if necessary. (Of course, a full scientific approach would today (especially in healthcare) require a randomised trial. Although very seldom possible in operations rather than research, do think about the possibility – for instance, with two cells, making a change in one cell but not in the other and observing the difference.

The **Coaching Kata** is a pattern for teaching the Improvement Kata. It is a set of coaching routines to practise in order to develop effective coaching habits. It gives managers and supervisors a standardised approach to facilitate Improvement kata skill development in daily work. The Coaching Kata uses a standard set of five questions that are primarily focused on the leader or coach in an improvement area. The five are:

1. What is the target condition? What is it we are trying to achieve?
2. What is the actual condition now?
3. What obstacles do you think are preventing you from reaching the target condition? Which one are you addressing now?
4. What is your next step? What do you expect to happen? (This is the start of the next PDSA cycle)
5. When can we go and see what we have learned from taking that step?

Feedback and review are integral to both Kata and Hoshin. Remember, Kata is a PDCA / PDSA improvement cycle. Rother suggests that there are four 'Reflection Steps' for each small step carried out in an experimental cycle. The writers of this book believe that the Reflection Steps, if conscientiously carried out, are a principal benefit of Kata. They are...

1. What did you plan as the last step?
2. What did you expect?
3. What actually happened?
4. What did you learn?

Sometimes there is a second coach, whose role is to make sure that the five steps and the four steps are followed, and to give guidance when they are not followed. Rother suggests these steps should form a daily 20-minute coaching cycle!

Kata and Hoshin

Rother has pointed out that there are two phases to Kata – Planning and Execution. Planning establishes the longer-term vision or strategy. (Hoshin, discussed in the next section, is the Lean approach to deploying the vision and associated KPI's.) A Hoshin cycle applies to an organisation, department, and the associated value streams. Under Hoshin, within each value stream, there will be several processes each of which will have challenges to address in order to meet the higher level Hoshin targets. This then sets up a framework for a whole series of Katas, each working towards their own desirable future states or target conditions. Hoshin is appropriately also called Policy Deployment and this deployment, level by level, establishes the full integrated plan.

Now, having established the target condition for the value stream, and often for a particular process, the Kata Execution phase can begin.

It is good practice to display the hierarchy of Katas on a visual management progress storyboard. Of course, a Kata approach does not necessarily have to be integrated with Hoshin. It can fit in with other integrated transformation frameworks, with Shingo Prize aims (see Section 3.17), or with a local initiative aimed at, for instance, defect reduction or lead-time reduction.

Wider Areas of Application

It is interesting to note that Kata has been, and is, used in teaching pupils. This is Kata in the Classroom (KiC). In one intervention with which one of the authors (John) was involved, Kata was used successfully to improve reading with dyslexic children. The teaching assistants found that with the Kata approach they and the pupils both learned at an accelerated rate as opposed to traditional methods. The KiC website is inspirational. The potential is huge!

Cautions

- The Kata method is straightforward. That is a great attraction. But the practice is not so simple. Skill is required in each of the steps. Learning to ask the right 'small step' questions needs to be developed, again and again through deliberate practice.
- Powell and Heathcote warn that there are two types of manager. The teacher-manager can steer the inquiry by posing thoughtful questions to the learner, which often unearths shared unknowns. Controlling managers, on the other hand, coax learners towards their own thinking, sometimes using Toyota Kata as the vehicle. Control-managers get what they want, and the learner believes it was their creation, but, in reality, thought-potential and creativity were unwittingly muzzled. The ultimate learning experience is suppressed.
- Despite what was said about the many related concepts, Rother suggests that we should not 'implement or add on some new techniques, practices, or even principles', but rather seek 'to develop consistent behaviour patterns across the organisation.'
- The Improvement Kata is an incremental process in small steps. Rushing, trying several steps simultaneously, risks failure
- Taking time to think through the long-term vision is most worthwhile, *'If you don't know where you are going, any path will get you there!'*

Further Readings.
Rose Heathcote and Daryl Powell, Improve Continuously by Mastering the Lean Kata, *The Lean Post*,
December 9, 2020
Mike Rother, *Toyota Kata*, McGraw Hill, 2010
Mike Rother, *The Toyota Kata Practice Guide*, McGraw Hill, 2017
Mike Rother and Gerd Aulinger, *Toyota Kata Culture*, McGraw Hill, 2017
Numerous Kata videos, many of them featuring Mike Rother, are available on the web. See
http://www-personal.umich.edu/~mrother/Homepage.html
The following two single-page information sheets provide a quick summary that explains TK and
its role well:
• What is scientific thinking?
http://www-personal.umich.edu/~mrother/KATA_Files/Scientific_Thinking.pdf
• What is Toyota Kata?
http://www-personal.umich.edu/~mrother/KATA_Files/TK_Definition.pdf

3.13 Hoshin (Hoshin Kanri, or Policy Deployment.) and OKRs

First, Hoshin is not about developing high-level strategy. It is about the effective deployment of
a given strategy throughout an organisation and ensuring that the whole organisation is aligned to
support the strategy. In other words, it is about the 'how' of strategy deployment, not the 'what' of
the strategy. Russell Ackoff talked about doing the right thing, doing things right, and the danger
of doing the wrong thing right. (See Ackoff in Section 5.5). Thus there should be clear separation
between corporate strategy and Hoshin. The development of strategy is a huge field in itself,
certainly not limited to Lean organisations. (There are many publications on strategy development.
We recommend 'Good Strategy, Bad Strategy' as an excellent lead into the what, followed by
Hoshin or OKR for the how.) In Lean the strategy is sometimes referred to as 'True North'.

A critical, and distinguishing, feature of Hoshin is engagement and participation in the
development of plans – projects, tactics, and improvements – that are necessary to achieve the
overall strategy. This involves identifying what is necessary to be done, no less and no more. The
combination of Strategy, Hoshin, and Kaizen is summarised by the figure below adapted from
Cowley and Domb. At each stage of deployment PDCA is required. It is often said that Hoshin
requires a much longer time to develop, through participation, but a much shorter time to execute
than old-style MBO but is much more effective.

Planning and Hoshin

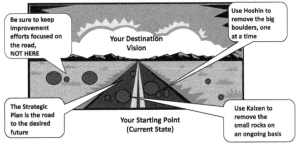

Adapted from Cowley and Domb 'Beyond Strategic Vision'

Hoshin Kanri (or simply Hoshin) is the Japanese term for Policy or Strategy Deployment. The term derives from the helmsman of a ship. Thus, the captain may determine where the ship is headed and set an arrival time target, but all functions need to be subservient to the goals. Navigation must determine the route (and adjust for weather). The engine room needs to ensure appropriate propulsion capability. And so on. At lower levels there will be necessary supporting activities such as catering and deck cleaning. The Hoshin process seeks to translate the top-level goals into appropriate aligned measures for the entire organisation. Policies (or strategies) are deployed to achieve an aim. The strategies are brought about by tactics (or projects). Tactics are, in turn, brought about by various processes or deliverables. These in turn produce results.

A quote from Churchill during WWII helps clarify:

"You ask, what is our policy? I can say: It is to wage war, by sea, land and air, with all our might and with all the strength that God can give us..... You ask, what is our aim? I can answer in one word: It is victory, victory at all costs, victory in spite of all terror, victory, however long and hard the road may be; for without victory there is no survival...."

Following this, tactics could then be specified by theatre: first The Battle of Britain, then North Africa, Italy, Burma, Europe, and finally Japan. Processes (or Deliverables) would be all the (high level at this stage) activities necessary to achieve these - involving the USA, supporting Russia, securing supply lines, finance, ramping up war production, building and training resources. Results could be specified in terms of achieving the tactics against time horizons and costs.

There would be much discussion and participation on the tactics and processes, although not about the top-level strategy. Then the Processes would be deployed to a second level. Here, each main process becomes a sub-strategy. The sub-strategy of 'Supporting Russia' could involve tactics (or projects) of organising convoys, allocating navy resources, securing armaments and vehicles, and so on. The processes would be the activities involved in, for example, convoys.

Thereafter implantation of the convoy sub-strategy is thoroughly discussed. Participation and ideas from those with convoy expertise is vital, before deployment of the plan. Now there would be greater detail and plans for specific ships, sailings, crew, navy support vessels. The broad concept is shown in the figure below.

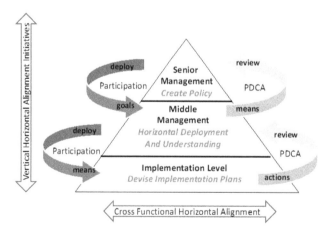

Referring to the figure, the 'catchball' analogy from netball is frequently used. In netball, the ball is passed between players on the same side to gain the best positional advantage before being sent over the net to the other side. The analogy is about firming up the goals and alternatives before passing them on. Sub-strategies are broken down into shorter term challenges. At the same time, unconventional approaches to attaining the goal are discussed. Detail is worked out in a participatory methodology using the X matrix – or sometimes a series of A3's – or both. In addition, a series of X matrices are sometimes displayed in an 'Obeya' room. (Both A3 and Obeya are discussed briefly in a section below and in the chapter on Problem Solving). Of course, plans require review and change. PDCA is necessary.

The deployment process is sometimes referred to as 'The Big W'. Imagine beginning with the desired strategy at the top left of the W. The strategy is thrown down to the level below for implementation development. The resulting proposals are then returned to the top level for comment, adjustment and approval. Some changes are made, and then returned to the level below. The adjusted proposals are then returned to the top level. Once again comment and adjustment take place and returned to the level below. Fine tuning takes place before returning the proposed actions to the top level for final approval. (This is also known as 'Nemawashi'.)

At the implementation level there should be emphasis on developing people through (according to Isao Yoshino) assigning people to teams, allowing flexibility in instructions, encouraging people to think creatively, listening and discussing, checking progress and giving advice or help when necessary. Further, in line with psychological safety, tolerating failure is a means to learn valuable lessons. Participation encourages development as well as 'buy-in'. As Jack Stack of Open Book Management states, 'People support what they help create', and Frank Devine (see Engagement Section) says 'If people help to plan the battle they won't battle the plan.'

The Hoshin Kanri process identifies goals, initiatives, and owners at each level. Benefits of using the process include; it can be used to refine the sub-strategies through participation, and it helps break down objectives into manageable parts that people can start to work on immediately. The measurement section (of an X matrix or A3) gives employees a way to see how incremental improvements can address both short and long-term needs. It fosters cross – collaboration by giving everyone the same view of success. It is an effective communication tool to monitor progress and quickly flag if roadblocks start to appear.

Speaking at the 2018 European Lean Educator conference, Isao Yoshino, former Toyota executive in charge of Hoshin, gave the key characteristics of Hoshin-Kanri as follows:

- Employee engagement. Both top-down and bottom-up.
- Focus on the current 'big issue' and prioritise.
- Setting a clear target and expectation. A numerical target or concrete milestone
- The process must match the result. (A good result with a poor process is mere luck.)
- Fact-based rather than assumption-based. (Including Gemba, 5 why)
- Regular review (PDCA process)
- People development
- Not hesitating to bring bad news

Once the goals have been set for the year, various teams across the organisation apply problem solving techniques such as A3, Kaizen, and PDSA to move towards the goals. A fundamental requirement of Hoshin Kanri is the requirement to have a monthly review process where each project or initiative is tracked against set milestones. This ensures that potential roadblocks are identified early. Good Hoshin involves three levels: 1. Tracing and correcting; 2. Researching why things did not work out; and 3. Learning how to improve the system itself. (As per Argyris in 5.5)

Visuality is important. Clear X matrices (which show goals, processes, and measures) or Planning A3's should be shown and updated at every group meeting place. These show the clear link between the group's targets and initiatives and the overall corporate strategy.

At the end of each year a comprehensive assessment of the organisations progress is carried out. This may result in some of the key goals and time-lines changing for the coming year.

A critique: Hoshin is most suitable in businesses that have stable operations. In a fast-changing business such as IT project work, or in a VUCA environment, Hoshin may be less suitable. There is an analogy with the rejection of the 'waterfall' method in many IT projects and the adoption of agile approaches (Sprint? Scrum?). This leads onto the growing adoption of OKR, as outlined in the next section.

OKRs

The Objectives and Key Results (OKRs) framework has become a popular, and simplified – but not necessarily simple – alternative to Hoshin. Introduced by Andy Grove at Intel and subsequently introduced to Google in 1999 by John Doerr (who worked with Larry Page, Alphabet co-founder) whose book is *Measure What Matters.* Amazon, Google and Oracle remain enthusiastic.

Start with one Objective, or goal. For a team, this could be derived from corporate objectives, and could be broad. The point is, it is simply stated and easy to remember by all. Note that an objective should not be confused with a slogan. (See Section 13.13 on Bullshit).

Then, a small number – two or three, absolute maximum of five, specific key results (KRs) are set that directly relate to the objective. For a team, quarterly is usual. These are SMART (specific, measurable, actionable, reachable, time limited). Clear, Yes or No results. If all key results are achieved, this would indicate that they have been incorrectly set.

Objectives are the *what* statement, and key results are the metrics that relate to the *hows*. There should be clear transparency between objectives and results – probably in line with Andy Grove's outlook as an engineer.

OKRs work with a CFR (Conversations, Feedback, Recognition) methodology. This is a key feature, bringing some of the tasks of traditional Human Resources to line managers - not dissimilar to Blanchard's One-minute manager concepts. In his book, John Doerr points out the similarity with Amabile and Kramer's concepts in *The Progress Principle* of Catalysts (OKRs) and Nourishers (CFRs). (Refer to section 4.2 on Amabile in Small Wins). Recognition, of course, shows Respect.

As with Hoshin, there is a cascade. Begin with the broad and long-lasting Mission statement and Company values. These are cascaded down by level, perhaps company, department, team, individual – from longer-term to short-term. The cascade is not introduced as a 'big-bang' but gradually, say from two levels to eventually reaching the team and individual.

Where we have observed Hoshin and OKR, it would seem to us that Hoshin is more participative but slower and more detailed. (Bureaucratic?). OKR is more top-down and shorter. CFR, however, makes OKR more human. We see no conflict with Lean or Agile.

Cautions
- Hoshin and OKR require a long-term commitment, patience, ongoing support and energy from senior management.
- A rigorous implementation is necessary.
- Breakthrough objectives should remain stable during a three to five-year period.

Further Readings.
Michael Cowley and Ellen Domb, *Beyond Strategic Vision: Effective Corporate Action with Hoshin Planning*, BH, 1997 (A book that gives an excellent overview of strategy with Hoshin.)
John Doerr, *Measure What Matters*, Portfolio Penguin, 2017
Thomas Jackson, *Hoshin Kanri for the Lean Enterprise*, Productivity Press, 2006
Richard Rumelt, *Good Strategy, Bad Strategy*, Profile Books, 2011

3.14 The Socratic Method

"Never tell, explore together"

Although it would horrify philosophers and does no justice to Socrates, these four words are a 'quick and dirty' indication of the Socratic Method, and could also be a powerful way into a Lean transformation.

Eli Goldratt once said, *"Anytime you tell someone something you take away the opportunity for the person to discover it themselves"* (this was the approach used by Jonah in Goldratt's book 'The Goal'). David Meier, (co-author of 'Toyota Talent') at a seminar arranged by one of the authors of this book (John), always answered a question with a question and never gave a direct answer. That is classic Toyota. The reaction of attendees was evenly split between 'Brilliant' and 'Very poor'. Clearly, Goldratt and Meier wanted people to think for themselves, but many people are conditioned to expect 'answers' (The irony is that this book is largely about telling!).

The Socratic method of learning is named after Greek philosopher Socrates who taught students by repeatedly asking question after question.

The idea is that by getting the learner to agree with a set of statements, the 'truth is drawn out'. By taking this approach Socrates aimed to expose contradictions or doubt in the students' thoughts and ideas which would guide them to solid, tenable conclusions. The technique involves the students self-discovering holes in their own theories and then working out a better solution for themselves. Socrates believed that the first step to knowledge was recognition of one's ignorance. But this works two ways: both learner and teacher can discover different viewpoints. Ideally, learners must learn to think critically and talk persuasively. Teachers get to learn viewpoints that may not have been apparent. Both sides require good listening. All these are skills that need to be developed and encouraged. Be humble with claims about knowledge – be aware that there is often no one right answer for all circumstances.

However, most people in the Lean world, including the authors, are not philosophers (or lawyers) and find the Socratic Method difficult. There are, however, similarities with Humility, with 'The Five Whys' and with Coaching (See separate Sections 3.5 and 3.16). On Humility, philosophers talk about 'intellectual modesty'. Socrates said the only way in which he was wiser than other men was that he was conscious of his own ignorance, while they were not. So, this is 'bottom up' humility not 'top down' arrogance. The classic 5 Why method is often excellent for homing in on the root cause, but there is a risk of lack of respect, and of insufficient time to explore wider issues. The 5 Whys is suitable for some types of problem solving (See Chapter 8 on Problem Solving), but the Socratic method is suitable perhaps always, except where a quick decision is vital.

Why is the Socratic Approach difficult but effective? Because admitting you are wrong is difficult. It affects status, and hence builds in resistance to change. On the other hand, it helps build an open-minded, humility-based, culture.

If you really must do a 'telling' lecture, at least begin by posing a few questions. This is not just Greek philosophy but well-founded learning theory. As the questioning conversation continues, the leader needs to re-state opinions, clarify statements, and use 'and' instead of 'but'.

An Example: Reduce Batch Size – a conversation between associate (or learner (L)), and manager (or teacher (T):

L: We ought to make larger batches while the machine is already set up. This would save wasting time on numerous change overs. Productivity would increase!
T: Good point! Let us explore. What do you think are the goals of a concern like ours?
L: Make more money!
T: Do you mean money or profit?
L: Well, OK, profit!
T: What drives profit?
L: There seems to be much attention given to Quality, Cost, and Delivery.
T: Yes, certainly. Would you say that these three are independent?
L: They are probably inter-related.
T: How so?
L: Well, quality affects cost. Being more careful takes longer and costs more but leads to better quality.
T: Ah! So, do you mean that being able to detect problems faster leads to better quality?
L: Yes, I suppose so.
T: When is the best time to detect problems?
L: As soon as possible.
T: Fine. We agree on that. And when do you sample for quality?
L: Twice per batch. One the first and last pieces.
T: How long does that take
L: About 10 minutes per piece.
T: So, about 20 minutes per batch.?
L: Yes.
T: And what is the usual batch size, and time per unit?
L: 60 pieces takes about 2 hours.
T: Does it sometimes happen that the first piece is OK, but not the last piece?
L: Yes. But only occasionally.
T: Then what would happen?
L: The whole batch needs to go to audit.
T: Presumably, with a larger batch more audit time would be required in the case of a defect?
L: Well, yes, but that would happen only occasionally.
T: OK, we need to think about that. Also, we probably need to look into the inspection procedures. Batch size and inspection time could be related. Will you do that?
L: OK, I will look into both.
T: Great. Thanks. Please let me know when we meet next Monday.

What can be noticed from this conversation?

- It takes time
- Asking not telling. Self-discovery.
- It shows respect. Focus on agreement, not faults.
- The learner is not told that he is wrong. Keep asking questions, but…
- Never argue. 'As soon as you tell a person that he is wrong you have already lost'.
- Both sides have learned. Issues are exposed.
- Many issues remain. One thing leads to another.

Sometimes we have to choose one lean principle over another. For example, on a production line we might want to introduce one-piece-flow to reduce throughput time and inventory. This may however result in increasing an associate's time on non-value adding activities to physically move the parts. So the 'never tell, explore together' Socratic approach could help. For instance, begin by asking, 'We need to reduce throughput time to stay competitive. How could we do this?'

There are similarities with Action Learning – a topic that is discussed in Section 10.21

3.15 People Development Concepts from Deming, Ohno and Spear

The work of W. Edwards Deming, Taiichi Ohno, and Steve Spear is usually thought of in terms of quality, waste reduction, and flow. But all three recognised that these aims could only be achieved through people. Here we select a sample of their most important people-related ideas. (It must be said that reading the original works is highly beneficial to any aspiring manager!).

Deming.

- 94/6 rule. Deming said that 94% of problems are due to the system, and only 6% are due to the people. Where did Deming get those figures? It doesn't matter, the point remains – don't start problem solving or improvement by blaming people. People do things because of the system – and the system can only be fixed by management. The 'system' (the source of the problem) would include lack of clarity of purpose, of standards, of feedback, of training as well as a climate of fear.
- Red Blue and variation. Deming was often critical of senior management, saying that they often did not understand variation, particularly the difference between common cause and special cause variation. Deming illustrated this with his famous Red-Blue skit which amusingly but worryingly shows good 'workers' being blamed or fired, and poor workers getting undeserved praise. (Was that reward truly earned, or was it just a piece of good luck?)
- 14 principles. Deming's 14 Principles include
  - The necessity for a consistent message.
  - Change from chasing to support.
  - 'Drive out fear'. Challenging - but can only be done by demonstration over the long term. But, of course, fear works two ways – fear by the boss of delegation (top down) and fear of being thought stupid (bottom up).
  - Remove organisational barriers and improve visibility, particularly customer feedback. Flow of information may be more important than flow of physical goods.
  - Eliminate slogans.
  - Eliminate standards and numerical quotas. (Controversial, but Deming was referring to those that are fixed and prevent improvement.)
  - Train and educate.
- Profound Knowledge. The four aspects can also be used as a checklist for why things go wrong. They are:
  - A failure to understand 'system'. Local suboptimization working against value stream improvement.
  - A failure to understand variation.
  - Misunderstanding of scientific method. See PDCA below.
  - Reliance on extrinsic rather than intrinsic rewards.

Ohno

- Go to the Gemba and see with your 'own eyes'.
- There are always further opportunities for improvement and unseen wastes that must be challenged. Never be content.
- Tough but supportive. Respect for workers is not the same as being nice.
- Knowledge and wisdom. Knowledge can be taught but wisdom can only be gained by practice.
- Chalk Circle and detail. As mentioned, Ohno drew a circle on the floor and insisted that a new worker stand in the circle and identify wastes in detail. "Look again!" and again!

Spear

- In a famous 1999 *Harvard Business Review* article, Steve Spear wrote of 'The Four Rules of the Toyota DNA'. The four rules are unstated at Toyota but the contention is that they drive much behaviour:
  - 'All work shall be highly specified as to content, sequence, timing, and outcome.' Standard work for all tasks, but standard work is not fixed forever in stone, but is the platform for further improvement.
  - 'Every customer-supplier connection must be direct, and there must be an unambiguous yes-or-no way to send requests and receive responses.' Communication channels should clear, known, studied, mapped.
  - 'The pathway for every product and service must be simple and direct.' Layout must evolve towards clear value streams.
  - 'Any improvement must be made in accordance with the scientific method, under the guidance of a teacher, at the lowest possible level in the organization.' That is PDCA. See below.

Further Readings.
Joyce Orsini (ed), *The Essential Deming*, McGraw Hill, 2013
Taiichi Ohno's Workplace Management: Special 100th birthday edition, McGraw Hill, 2013
Spear and Bowen, 'Decoding the DNA of the Toyota Production System', *Harvard Business Review*, Sept-Oct 1999, pp. 97-106

3.16 People Development through PDCA, A3, 5 Whys, Kaizen Blitz and Andon

All the concepts mentioned in the section headline are classic tools for waste reduction. They are widely used for this purpose. But they should also be regarded as people development tools. Here, we will consider the second aspect – which should be weighted at least equally with the waste reduction tool aspect. Our view is that statements such as 'Lean is not about tools', or 'tool heads', misses the point in that many tools can be powerful ways to 'create thinking people' as George Davidson, manufacturing manager of Toyota South Africa was fond of saying.

PDCA and Scientific Method

Plan Do Check Act (PDCA) or another version Plan Do Study Act (PDSA) is the classic Deming or Shewhart Cycle for the scientific method. It is probably also amongst the least understood.

Too often it is Plan (briefly), Do, and no check or act.

In 1964 Richard Feynman (Nobel laureate, polymath, and Challenger shuttle investigator) gave a now-famous lecture....

"Now I am going to discuss how we would look for a new law. In general we look for a new law by the following process. First we guess it. Then we compute the consequences of the guess to see what would be implied if this law that we guessed is right. Then we compare the result of the computation to nature, with experiment or experience, compare it directly with observation, to see if it works. If it disagrees with experiment it is wrong. In that simple statement is the key to science. It does not make any difference how beautiful your guess is. It does not make any difference how smart you are, who made the guess, or what his name is - if it disagrees with experiment it is wrong. That is all there is to it"

and later...

"Another thing I must point out is that you cannot prove a vague theory wrong. If the guess that you make is poorly expressed and rather vague, and the method that you use for figuring out the consequences is a little vague - you are not sure, and you say, 'I think everything's right because it's all due to moogles, ...do this and that more or less, and I can sort of explain how this works ..' then you see that this theory is good, because it cannot be proved wrong!"

One of the authors of this book (John) had an experience that made him realise that he did not understand the essence of PDCA. An industrial engineering student project in the early 1980's, with the author as supervisor, was concerned with setup reduction at a Toyota supplier. The students did a good job, using classic Shingo SMED that reduced the time to less than half the original. At the presentation, management and supervisor (author) were very pleased. The presentation was attended by the Jishuken facilitator from Toyota who also congratulated the students. The Toyota facilitator then asked the supervisor about how the project met expectations. The supervisor said that the expectation was that time would be reduced. But what was the specific aim and what had the students learned asked the facilitator. After several embarrassing rounds of discussion, it became apparent that proper PDCA had not been followed. It is not good enough just to do a setup reduction project. What should have happened was to set a specific aim (or hypothesis) (Plan), carry out the project (Do) and to then to judge the outcome against this (Check). If achieved – good and confirmation – but if either the time was worse OR BETTER – then what was it that had been learned? (Act). The Toyota facilitator was more interested in what the students had learned than the actual time reduction! This is 'win-win' and proper PDCA.

Steve Spear had a similar light-bulb moment, explaining 'High-velocity organizations insist that "the scientific method" be used in a disciplined fashion.... Fixing the problem isn't good enough; they want to fix it while gaining a deeper knowledge of how their own processes work (Spear, 2009, p.25).

A3 Problem Solving

The A3 methodology is discussed in the chapter on Problem Solving.

As a tool, A3 Problem Solving and Reporting - made popular by Toyota - is a way to concisely guide users through the critical problem-solving steps. This involves understanding and clarifying a problem and its root causes, and then identifying countermeasures and experiments to close the gap between the target and the current situation.

John Shook describes A3 in his book *Managing to Learn* as not just a problem-solving process, but a critical part of a management system. The book is an extended case study of interchanges between mentor and mentee that result in homing in on the core problem that was not apparent in the earliest stage. The mentee is continually challenged, not aggressively but with respect, to review his assumptions and data.

John Shook writes that

(A3 is) *"...a visual manifestation of a problem-solving thought process involving continual dialogue between the owner of an issue and others in an organization. It is a foundational management process that enables and encourages learning through the scientific method."*

and

"It takes two to A3." A3 should not be done alone but as a conversation between manager and subordinate (but better to think in terms of mentor and mentee). The interchanges foster and build wider perspectives and critical thinking. Going through an A3 can be gut-wrenching the first few times and a continuing check on thinking that is too narrow"

Common questions that will be asked in the dialogue include:

- 'Have you been to the Gemba to see it first hand?'
- 'What do you see as the gap that should be addressed?'
- 'How do you know that?'
- 'That data seems important. Did you check it?'
- 'Would that data be better shown on a graph?'
- 'Tell me how this problem arose'
- 'Did you ask the customer?'
- 'How will you know if your proposed solution works?
- 'What do the associates say?'

The mentee learns that making mistakes is part of the development process and will not be seen as a reflection on skill or status. We can all learn. Note: See the earlier Questions Section 3.4 The mentee will often proceed from a jump-in-to-the-obvious problem to a more considered, fact-based solution. The mentee's scope will often be widened as the problem is viewed from different perspectives. The mentee may develop more of an in-depth appreciation of classic Lean tools, and ways of analysing and presenting data.

In particular, an appreciation of 'real' PDCA will be developed. Of course, the mentor must have knowledge and experience of Lean, as well as patience, and a way with words that supports rather than give offence. What a challenge!

Three Essential Points!

A3 is often thought of, or presented, as a problem-solving tool. But, reading the above it will be realised that the A3 steps should be carried out in parallel with developing the person who is trying to tackle the problem. Learning the associated tools is one thing, but developing a critical, scientific way of thinking is quite another. Too often training and literature on A3 (and Six Sigma DMAIC, and Ford 8D) merely treat these as mechanical or statistical problem-solving steps, but say nothing about developing people's ways of thinking along with addressing the problem – including an attitude of reflection, or Hansei (see Section 3.19).

Numerous experiences with the problem solving A3 reveal that the majority of users (at all levels, junior to top) jump to a conclusion as to what the real problem is, and hence the solution. Or, they think they know what the problem is and go through the motions of the left hand side of the A3 to confirm their belief. Confirmation bias! In fact, most real-world problems have several possible 'solutions', some of them wide ranging such as 'training', or 'education'. A 'conclusion' like this is too wide – useless? But a major aim of the left-hand-side of the A3 is to home in on the 'big-one', to select the most beneficial aspect to tackle first. This means keeping an open mind, and not pre-deciding the aspect to tackle.

A main aim of the left-hand side of an A3 is to home-in on the specific problem. This is highly desirable and guards against widening-out the problem so that, almost inevitably, the result is that the problem becomes unmanageable with conclusions such as 'it's a training problem', 'it's a strategy issue', or 'the problem is lack of direction'. The mentor is supposed to keep the mentee focused and prevent widening out. But beware! A mentor can direct the focus towards a particular pre-meditated conclusion. It may be that the mentee, or the A3 problem-solving team, may have an insight into a wider issue that the mentor is unaware of. A problem solving mentor should always be generous enough to allow the possibility of an unforeseen 'Gee-whiz' or 'Ah-ha' moment for the mentor.

Further Readings.
John Shook, *Managing to Learn*, Lean Enterprise Institute, 2008
Durward Sobek and Art Smalley, *Understanding A3 Thinking*, CRC Press, 2012

5 Whys

5 Whys is a well-established tactic, aimed at finding the root cause of a problem. Ask why several times – perhaps 3 to 6 times – successively. Poor customer service? Why? Deliveries are often late. Why late? Inventory is often out of stock. Why out of stock? Often other products have to be made first. There is a queue. Why a queue? Because batches are large and it takes time to process them. Why large? Because changeover time is long. Why is it long? Don't know. It has never been studied. Voila!

Great if this works. Certainly try it. Certainly don't accept the first reason without further probing. Unfortunately in practice there is not often one answer to each why. But aim at homing in on the crucial main cause by a succession of Pareto analyses. By contrast an expanding tree will lead to either an unworkable number of avenues to pursue or to the vague 'the problem is the people' or 'the problem is management'.

Hence, a few rules for more effective 'people' use of 5 Why:

- 'People' reasons for the problem are not acceptable. Remember Deming's 94/6 rule. Most problems lie with the system or the process, not the people. It is just too easy to blame 'people'. What is causing 'the people' to behave in that way?
- Do not allow Whys to become personal or accusing.
- At each Why stage, prioritise. A rule of thumb: don't allow more than two reasons for every why.
- Home in, not home out. For example: We have unreliable machines. Why so? Allow 'Because we don't have regular maintenance'. Do not allow 'Because we have no TPM'. Then further 'Why no regular maintenance?' Allow 'Because maintenance priorities are not clear' but do not allow 'Because no one has worked out a schedule'. In each case, the first answer allows one to be more specific, the second answer runs a risk of widening out the reasons.

- Stop when you get to a reason that is beyond your control of frame of reference. Finlow-Bates suggests that there are no ultimate root causes. It just goes on and on. (A delivery failure is due to a van running out of petrol, caused by a leaking tank, caused by a weld failure, caused by quality of weld, caused by poor material, caused by cost cutting, caused by financial pressures, caused by…)

These cautions, if not taken up, will result in the vague, ultimately unhelpful conclusions such as 'the problem is our people', 'management doesn't get it', 'training is required', or 'we can't fix it because it is outside our scope'.

The 5 Whys is also discussed in the chapter on Problem Solving. See Section 8.6

Kaizen Events

Kaizen Events (or Kaizen Blitz) are focused events typically held over 4 or 5 days in an area or value stream. Perhaps a dozen participants from the area with a few from outside the area take part, led by a facilitator. There are often several aims but waste reduction is the general case. But, like other methods discussed in this section, Kaizen Events are as much a people awakening and development approach as a waste reduction approach. Both manufacturing and office areas have been targeted.

Blitz events have declined in popularity from their heyday in the late 1990's probably due to the problem of sustainability of results. In the short-term, results are often dramatic – say a 30% reduction in lead-time together with enhanced productivity – all within a few days – are not uncommon. Sustainability depends upon several people factors but also upon the nature of the area. Layout changes and elimination of pent-up frustrations are usually sustained, but method changes less so.

For participants, the experience of an event is often liberating. In fact, it is the impact on managers, and particularly on associates that is probably the main benefit rather than the impact on productivity.

Why? Because during an event…

- Hierarchy is downplayed. Everyone's opinion is sought and considered. The benefits of participation and active listening become apparent.
- Managers learn that associates have many good, previously untapped, ideas. Respect grows.
- Permission to make changes is minimal except for changes that involve large expenditure or affect other departments. A realisation grows of the opportunity afforded by reducing permissions and bureaucracy.
- Pent up frustrations are removed. Associates are encouraged when they see their ideas, some previously ignored, are acted on almost immediately.
- The realisation grows, amongst both managers and associates, of the extent of waste even in areas previously thought to be good. Moreover, a repeat event later in the same area often reveals further opportunities.

There are caveats, however, that partly explain the decline in popularity…

- Kaizen events can be a threat to managers. 'Why was that opportunity not seen by you before?' can lead to defensive behaviour. Reasons can always be found. An insecure manager can seek reasons why a change is not as good as it appears. Allowing such excuses is a management failure rather than a failure of the event.

- Expectations are not made clear. Events can have dramatic results but should not be over-sold beforehand.
- Team composition must include appropriate managers, not just operators and a facilitator. A classic program in the TV series (and book), 'Sid's Heroes' shows management defensiveness when presented with operator achievements with no manager participation. Expectations were also unrealistic.
- Failure to follow through. Some changes cannot be made during the event, so rely on follow through that may not take place due to a host of reasons – made worse by reluctant managers. Of course, discouragement and scepticism follow.
- Rewards and recognition must be considered. Monetary rewards for achievements may not be appropriate, but some form of recognition must be given – and not just as an afterthought.
- 'OK, that was fun, now back to work!'

Further reading
John Bicheno and Matthias Holweg, *The Lean Toolbox*, 5th edn, PICSIE, 2016
Sid Joynson, *Sid's Heroes*, Taozen, 2001
Anthony Laraia, Patricia Moody, Robert Hall, *The Kaizen Blitz*, Wiley, 1999

Andon

Andon or Line Stop is the famous Toyota method whereby an associate typically on an assembly line, can pull an overhead chord if a problem is experienced. Pulling the cord results in a light flashing on an overhead board and possibly a warning sound. The team leader responds immediately and if the problem is not resolved within a takt time cycle, the line or a section of the line, will stop moving ahead.

The point is that this is not only a method to highlight and resolve quality problems quickly at the point of use but, crucially, is a demonstration of empowerment of the worker. If things are not correct the worker, and the worker's team leader, can stop the line without seeking higher permission. Stories are legend about the Toyota Andon experience – how reluctant and unbelievable it is for a new worker to pull the cord, and how he or she is then thanked for so doing. This is now called Psychological Safety (See Section 9.9 on Mistakes). Of course, if there is little Psychological Safety an Andon system will fail, as indeed it often has.

3.17 The Shingo Model™ and Supporting Principles

In 1988 the Jon M Huntsman School of Business at Utah State University introduced the Shingo Prize, to promote excellence in manufacturing companies in the USA. Since then it has become a global standard for Enterprise Excellence across multiple sectors. The Shingo Model™ is both a vehicle for Organisational Transformation and a Global Recognition Program. It was named in honour of Shigeo Shingo (1909:1990), a Japanese industrial engineer who was involved in the development and promotion of the Toyota Production System (TPS), and specifically tools such as SMED, Poka-Yoke and Zero Quality Control (ZQC).

The model has three insights of Organisational Excellence. The beliefs are:

1. **Ideal Results Require Ideal Behaviours.** The results of an organization depend strongly on the way its people behave. To achieve ideal results, leaders must do the hard work of creating a culture where ideal behaviours are expected and evident in every team member.

2. **Purpose and Systems Drive Behaviour.** It has long been understood that beliefs have a profound effect on behaviour. What is often overlooked, though, is the equally profound effect that systems have on behaviour. Most of the systems that guide the way people work are designed to create a specific business result without regard for the behaviour that the system consequentially drives. Managers have an enormous task to realign management, improvement, and work systems to drive the ideal behaviour required by all people to achieve good business results. (Note: see JCM Model: Section 4.3)

3. **Principles Inform Ideal Behaviour.** Principles are foundational rules that govern consequences. The more deeply one understands principles, the more clearly people will understand the ideal behaviour. And the more clearly one understands ideal behaviour, the better he or she can design systems to drive that behaviour to achieve ideal results.

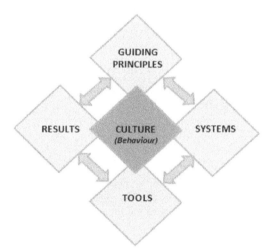

Leaders must drive principles and culture while managers must design and align systems to drive ideal, principle-based behaviour. Involvement of the entire organization—every team member—is essential for genuine, sustainable improvement. Systems, tools and culture, should be influenced by the principles. Culture arises from all behaviours in an organization, so if systems are aligned to principles, they will drive behaviour ever closer to the ideal. Finally, systems determine the necessary tools to enable the system to achieve results. The level of results achieved determines if the tools need to be refined within the system.

Shingo Guiding Principles

The Shingo Guiding Principles are the basis for building a sustainable culture of enterprise excellence. The ten principles are: respect every individual, lead with humility, seek perfection, embrace scientific thinking, focus on process, assure quality at the source, improve flow and pull, think systemically, create constancy of purpose, and create value for the customer. Because Shigeo Shingo encouraged us to think categorically, the principles are divided into three dimensions: Cultural Enablers, Continuous Improvement, and Enterprise Alignment.

Respect Every Individual – this includes employees, customers, suppliers, the community and society in general. When people feel respected, they give more than their hands: they give both minds and hearts.

Lead with Humility – Humility is an enabling principle that precedes learning and improvement. A leader's willingness to seek input, listen carefully, and continuously learn creates an environment where team members feel respected and energised and will give freely of their creative abilities.

Seek Perfection – Perfection is an aspiration not likely to be achieved, but the pursuit of perfection creates a mindset and culture of continuous improvement.

Embrace Scientific Thinking – Innovation and improvement are the consequences of repeated cycles of experimentation, direct observation and learning. A relentless and systematic exploration of new ideas, including failures, enables us to constantly refine our understanding of reality.

Focus on Process – All outcomes are the consequence of a process. It is nearly impossible for even good people to consistently produce ideal results with poor processes. Experience has informed us that an issue is usually rooted in an imperfect process, not in the people involved.

Assure Quality at the Source – Perfect quality can only be achieved when every element of work is done right the first time. If a defect occurs in a product or service, it must be detected and corrected at the time it is created.

Improve Flow and Pull – Value for customers is highest when it is created in response to real demand and at a continuous and uninterrupted flow. Waste is anything that disrupts the continuous flow of value.

Think Systemically – By understanding the relationships and interconnectedness of a system, people will make better decisions and improvements that will more naturally align with the desired outcome of an organisation.

Create Constancy of Purpose – An unwavering understanding of why the organisation exists, where it is going, and how it will get there enables people to align their actions, as well as to innovate, adapt, and take risks with greater confidence.

Create Value for the Customer – Ultimately, value must be defined through the lens of what a customer wants and is willing to pay for. Organisations that fail to deliver both effectively and efficiently on this most fundamental outcome cannot be sustained long term.

Values are cultural, personal, interpretable and variable. Our personal values influence how we see the world and ultimately our choices on how to behave. Principles govern the outcomes of our choices. In other words, the values of an unprincipled person will very likely lead to behaviours that have negative consequences. For example if a leader does not respect his workers they are likely to become dis-engaged from their work. Principles determine the consequences of human relationships and, ultimately, principles influence the successful outcome of every business venture. Similarly, the values of a corporation, not grounded in enduring principles, are largely unsuccessful in influencing the creation of a consistent and lasting organisational culture.

Shingo Recognition Process

The decision to award Shingo recognition is based on a complete assessment of an organisation's culture and how well it drives world-class results. Shingo examiners focus on the degree to which the Guiding Principles in the Shingo Model™ are evident in the behaviour of every employee. The examiners observe behaviour and determine the frequency, duration, intensity and scope of the desired principle based behaviour. They also observe the degree to which leaders focus on principles and culture, and managers focus on aligning systems to drive ideal behaviours at all levels.

The first step for organisations that feel they are ready to challenge (The term used for the official recognition process), or simply just want to learn more about the Shingo Model™ is to send some of their Senior Leadership Team members on a 2 Day Shingo Discover Excellence Workshop. These interactive workshops, organised by Shingo affiliates, provide a thorough understanding of the Shingo Model™ and are usually held at plants already on the Shingo Challenge journey. Affiliates also run Shingo Workshops on Systems Design, Cultural Enablers, C.I., Enterprise Alignment and Build Excellence.

Organisations are encouraged to have a minimum of three years of sustained improvement before submitting their intention to challenge. A company profile sheet must accompany the application. Based on the application, the Shingo Office will decide whether or not the plant is ready to proceed to the next stage. This requires the plant to carry out a Shingo Insight Survey among their employees and submit with it a report detailing at least three years of sustained improvement under the following headings;

- Safety / Environment / Morale
- Financial / Cost / Productivity
- Delivery
- Quality
- Customer Satisfaction

If the Shingo Office are satisfied the results, the organisation will proceed with writing their Achievement Report. The Achievement Report is a 40 to 50 page document which details how the organisation has transformed its culture based on the principles of organisational excellence represented in the Shingo Model™. The Achievement Report is reviewed by a team of Shingo examiners who will determine if the organisation merits a site visit from the Shingo examiner team.

At their annual International Conference, held in the US, the Shingo office celebrates organisations that have successfully challenged over the previous 12 months. Recognition is awarded at 3 levels; The Shingo Prize, Silver Medallion and Bronze Medallion.

The rigour of the Shingo Model™ is reflected in the fact that on average less than 10 organisations, worldwide receive Shingo awards each year. It should however be noted that the "Real Prize" for organisation who adopt the Shingo Model™ is building a sustainable continuous improvement culture which delivers improved business results for all stakeholders.

Cautions.

- It is not about chasing the "Prize". The reason organisations adopt the Shingo philosophy is to create a sustainable continuous improvement culture that provides increased value to their customers and ensures the long-term success of their businesses.
- Many people have acquired leadership positions using traditional command and control behaviours. These people will struggle with the "lead by humility" approach which is a fundamental requirement of the Shingo Model™.
- Possibly the best reason for using the Shingo Prize model is that it allows a fairly unbiased, external view of an organization's strengths and weaknesses with respect to Lean.

- Remember that although the Shingo Prize criteria have been developed over many years it remains their viewpoint, but not necessarily the most appropriate viewpoint for a particular organisation.
- Of course winning a Shingo Prize is no guarantee of business success. In fact there is the danger that an organization could become lulled into believing that no further improvement is necessary. This may well be one reason why Toyota does not participate in the Shingo Prize

Reference.
Shingo Model Booklet 14.6 Accessed Feb 2021
For more information go to the official Shingo website https://shingo.org

3.18 Sensei, Sempai, and Consultants

Sensei and Sempai are Japanese words frequently used in martial arts but which have become widely used in a Lean context.

A Sensei is a teacher, master, or instructor. According to Wikipedia, a Sensei is an 'honorific term …. translated as "person born before another" or "one who comes before". In general usage, it is used, with proper form, after a person's name and means "teacher"; the word is also used as a title to refer to or address other professionals or persons of authority…or to show respect to someone who has achieved a certain level of mastery…'

A true Sensei, then, brings another way of looking at the world, and works to bring such insight to others. 'Understanding' seems to be a key word – but fostering understanding indirectly – by challenging, changing thinking, and not by telling.

A Sempai is a teacher, mentor or senior. In martial arts and war a Sempai is the most senior warrior, responsible to the commander for the development of lower warriors.

In the world of Judo and Karate there are many Sensei, both Japanese and other. They are invariably high-dan black belts, and an older Sensei may not even fight but just talk and guide.

In the world of Lean, a Sensei is usually a high-status external consultant (although initially at Toyota internal) whilst a Sempai is internal. Both terms cannot be self-appointed, but must be earned.

The original Lean Sensei were people who worked directly under Taiichi Ohno or with early Toyota suppliers with guidance from Ohno. Many became consultants to major companies in the West and often had a major impact. Several seem to have followed Ohno's reputation as a no-nonsense, impatient, taskmaster. For instance, in one intervention, by bringing parts directly to the line, a warehouse was closed down almost overnight. In another, a flow cell comprising machines from several functions including a heijunka scheduling board and kanban, was set up in weeks.

Why were the original Sensei so effective? Some reasons were reputation – bringing the wise words, experience, and insights from Ohno himself (or perhaps a direct associate) – together with, often, very high fees. Reputation and fees grabbed the attention of top management – hanging on every word that was said. In one example, the Sensei, arriving at a plant and discovering that his thinking had not been followed, simply left to play golf whilst charging his fee, and informing the CEO that he would return after the company had thought through his words.

A Sensei will have 'True North' in mind and try to influence thinking towards that state. Encouraging a questioning culture rather than direct telling what to do. Often, a good Sensei will begin by asking about purpose. (Certainly 'make money' would not meet with approval!) Moving to the operation, a Sensei will usually be very reluctant to give suggestions but will ask the student to *'Look again'* without further comment, and then *'Look again'*, and yet again until finally the student gets the message. Only then will some brief comment be made. Of course, this 'discover for yourself' and 'learn to see' is good psychology – self learning will have much greater impact.

To become a Sensei, therefore, one must learn from a Master. One cannot follow a relatively short course or do a project – please take note Lean Sigma Black Belts and other forms of 'certification'. However, to progress in the Toyota TPS organisation, a person must learn a range of skills on the job and then be deemed 'ready' to move to the next stage. Normally moving to the next stage requires an increasingly demanding project. Building up to a senior (Sensei?) level would take years, and most would not get there.

Three of our favourite books that give a real sense of a true Sensei are given in the further readings below. These contain a myriad of sayings, quotations, lessons, and advice. Note that, apparently, Ohno was for years reluctant to write down or 'codify' the Toyota Production System because he feared misinterpretation would stultify further development.

Today there are very few Sensei who were directly influenced by Ohno. Exceptions are Isao Yoshino (especially on Hoshin), Takehiko Harada, and Isao Kato (especially on TWI).

Was Shigeo Shingo a Sensei? Shingo spent many years as a trainer at Toyota, mainly with Industrial Engineering topics. Some credit Shingo with developing TPS, but this is disputed within Toyota. No doubt Shingo had a significant influence within Toyota with Lean tools, particularly SMED, poka-yoke, and 'Job Methods'. Never a Toyota employee, he also worked as a trainer with many Japanese companies. As author of several books translated from Japanese, Shingo is almost certainly better known in the USA than in Japan. It is interesting that in Japan there is the Deming Prize, and in USA there is the Shingo Prize. (Something about a prophet in his own land?). Shingo's sayings are widely quoted. So, would Shingo be regarded as a Sensei today? Almost certainly yes, but not in the usual sense of someone working with people on the shop floor and managing by asking questions and requiring direct observation.

Is a new generation of Sensei emerging? We hope so. With skills in service and hospitals, electric cars, robots of all types, artificial intelligence, and analytics and big data. The wisdom of the old Sensei is likely to continue but to be joined by the emerging world.

Some controversial speculation: Could it be that the fading of original Toyota Sensei has corresponded with the decline in Toyota inventory turn performance? Richard Schonberger (one of the original Western authors of JIT/Lean - a decade before *The Machine that Changed the World*) believes that inventory turn performance is a good surrogate for Lean performance, and has tracked inventory turn performance of hundreds of companies for decades. Toyota's turns peaked in the late 1990's and have worsened fairly steadily ever since.

A Lean Sensei and a Lean Consultant.

To stimulate readers' thinking and discussion about Consultants - a quote from Chris Smyth, Health Editor of *The Times*, London, 21 February 2018, reporting on a study by Andrew Sturdy, professor in management at Bristol University, who said *"Consultancy firms make hospitals worse"* and *"Our research has clearly shown that management consultants are not only failing to improve efficiency in the NHS but, in most cases, making the situation worse . . . this is money which, many argue, could be better spent on medical services or internal management expertise"*

A Lean Consultant is usually a very different person from a Lean Sensei. Of course, consultants come in many flavours – from highly competent to ultimately destructive. No doubt there has been a band-wagon effect. Phil Rosenzweig's delusions as pointed out in *The Halo Effect* also apply to consultants. These include the delusion of correlation (perhaps success would have happened anyway), the delusion of lasting success (almost all have both successes and failures) and the delusion of organizational physics (there are no immutable laws that will predict success). The table below probably presents an extreme view of a notional Lean consultant.

	A Lean Sensei	A Lean Consultant
Title	Earned by respect	Appointed (by self?)
Experience	Vast	Varies hugely
'The Answers'?	Not given	Given
Approach	Asks questions	Gives solutions
Where?	Gemba	Office?
Relationship	Long term?	One-off?
Methods	Direct observation	Begins with mapping
Orientation	Make them think	Solve their problems
The Vision	'True North'	Cost Quality Delivery
Focus	Wide (whole co.)	Narrow (technique)
Developing..	The people	The systems
Communication	Challenging	Recommending

And what of old (pre-Toyota) Sensei and non-Toyota Sensei…

William (Bill) Knudsen – the greatest vehicle engineer in history (he of Ford Model T, Chevrolet, WW2 Jeep, army trucks, tanks and even aircraft) certainly deserves the accolade. Quotes: *"be sure the flow of material coincides with the sequence of operations'*, and *'I learned that when you shout at someone, you make him afraid, and when he is afraid, he won't tell you his troubles.'*

And Robert (Doc) Hall – a JIT pioneer since the early 1980's and still making a case for 'Compression' – was always and still is, decades ahead! And, what of Carlos Ghosen and Elon Musk? Although not Sensei in the classic sense, their impact is undeniable!

Further Readings.
Takehiko Harada, *Management Lessons from Taiichi Ohno: What every leader can learn from the man who invented the Toyota Production System*, McGraw Hill, 2015
Taiichi Ohno's Workplace Management, (Special 100th Birthday Edition), McGraw Hill, 2013
Phil Rosenzweig, *The Halo Effect*, Free Press, 2007

3.19 Hansei

Hansei is reflection. Pause for thought, sometimes deep reflection.

But why a Japanese word? Probably because Hansei is an integral part of Japanese national culture. (Note: Japanese culture, not only Toyota). 'Han' is change; 'Sei' is look back.

Because Hansei is strongly linked to the quest for perfection, this means that hansei, kaizen, humility, and learning are part of the same package. Hansei could also be regarded as part of the Deming Cycle – combining the Check and Act stages of PDCA: Plan, Do, Hansei? In fact, the PDCA / PDSA cycle (suitable for science experiments) could well be improved for management by specifically incorporating reflection.

Donald Schon made a useful distinction between two types of reflection. Reflection-in-action takes place through ongoing experiments like Kata. It requires active participation. It is messy but important and relevant. This guides us to the path to be taken. Reflection-on-Action is look-back and takes place after the event, such as with an After-action review (AAR). This is only effective if it leads to changes next time around. Much academic research into Lean has been of the latter type. Rigorous but only a partial picture. But it is the relative absence of rigour and practice in Reflection-in-Action that is the weakness and opportunity. See: https://youtu.be/Ld9QJcMiNMo

Then there is also individual reflection and group reflection. There should be time for both.

It is important to note that Hansei is not criticism or disgrace, but rather is seen as an opportunity to do better or differently. Although sometimes associated with mistakes, the wider view can be taken that there is always an *opportunity* to do better, so in that respect there is always a 'mistake'. Culturally this can be difficult for Westerners who love to celebrate success, even marginal success, with 'high fives' but then fail to think about an even better way.

Too often Hansei has become associated exclusively with failure. Equivalent to 'Go and sit on the naughty step and think about what you have done.' That would be to miss the point. Hansei should be associated with both failure and success. Far better would be 'Let us think about this overnight. Sleep on it. Discuss in the morning.' Let your brain do much of the unconscious sorting out and reflecting. It also helps to take some of the emotion or elation out of the situation.

This section on Hansei could well have been included in the Psychology chapter because it is what some psychologists ('shrinks') encourage their patients to do: think about themselves, reflect – but overcome their concerns rather than try to do better.

Building-in reflection as part of any improvement cycle is most desirable. In AAR's (After Action Reviews – see Section 10.20) participants consider:

- This is what we set out to do.
- This is what happened – facts not opinions. Also no personal accusations.
- What went well?
- What did not go well?
- What should we do better next time?

This automatic sequence, through the last three steps, builds in reflection as part of the package.

Further Readings.
Donald Schon, *The Reflective Practitioner*, Routledge, 1991

3.20 Short Interval Tracking

SIT allows companies greater agility to plan work, people and equipment in order to maximise the use of resources, aid decision making and respond to issues effectively. SIT is a process for driving improvements on the production floor during each shift. The shift is split into short intervals of time e.g. four hours, within which the production employees and support staff use data to identify and implement improvement actions. These actions may be countermeasures to address a gap between actual and target performance, or actions to improve current performance. SIC is in essence a form of Kaizen as it encourages teams to work together to achieve regular, incremental improvements to the manufacturing process.

SIC works in tandem with the daily Gemba meeting. It engages and supports the production team to address problems which are likely to cause them to miss their shift targets. Crucially SIT enables the team to react at an early stage, to minimise damage and implement containment measures while the root cause is being identified. At the meetings the team should focus first on the performance since the last interval. Where targets are not being met, they should prioritise and implement corrective actions; if this is not possible, they should escalate the problem for assistance and direction. Lastly, they should look ahead to the next interval for any potential problems.

Cautions

- Often, there are two SIC meetings per shift
- Meetings should be focused around a cell board
- Meetings should be less than 10 minutes.

3.21 Pull Systems: Kanban and Information

This is not a book of Lean tools, so we will not go into details on the workings of kanban and CONWIP. These are pull systems, as are more esoteric types such as Drum Buffer Rope and POLCA.

A central aim of pull systems is to control the flow and timing of materials along the value steam – perhaps along the full value stream from customer to raw material. A pull system is driven by the needs of the next downstream process, whereas a push system moves work from the immediate upstream process in anticipation of needs by the next process. As such a pull system places an upper limit on work-in-process (WIP) inventory.

However, from a human perspective, pull systems are also effective visual information systems. A set of kanban cards (or electronic equivalents), for instance, conveys information on quantities as well as production instructions in a loop between pairs of workstations. Kanban automatically signals when production should start and stop. If any stoppage occurs the movement of pull cards stops. This takes place rapidly and often independent of a computer system. When the pull system signals a stoppage or problem, human action should respond. A pull system is therefore an excellent way to surface problems and an excellent work scheduling system.

The problem-surfacing feature alone favours the introduction of kanban or CONWIP, as opposed to MRP where most of the information is in a computer 'black box', and is forecast driven – and a forecast is often wrong. MRP is not as people-friendly as kanban.In a software development environment, kanban (or pull) also serves to limit the amount of WIP and to display and highlight problem areas – again making best use of human resources.

Further Readings.
Christoph Roser, *All About Pull Production*, All About Lean, 2021 (The most comprehensive guide on kanban, by far!).

3.22 Visual Management and 'Visuality'

It almost goes without saying that visual management is an important enabling methodology for Lean. Gwendolyn Galsworth, perhaps the 'doyenne' of visual management, prefers to call it 'visuality'.

What makes good visuality effective is that it operates at the speed of light, far faster than any computer system. Can a manager walk into a production area and determine the status within minutes, just by standing and looking? Speed is one thing – 'shouting' for action to be taken is another. Good visuality highlights a problem and indicates a solution.

So visuality is more than painting lines on the floor and putting up boards. There is passive and active visuality. Good visuality means that an operator should not have to ask or guess what to do or where to place an item. It also means active, natural, expected follow through. Examples are shown in the table.

Topic	Passive Examples	Active Examples
5S	Clean and tidy; Shadow boards	No place for loose items; Ergonomic workplaces
Standard Work	Long lists of instructions	Only key points. Auto checks. Active Computer visuals. AR.
Schedule	On a computer screen	Day-by-the-hour board with active reasons for under or over
TPM	Start-up checklist. Recording OEE	Active red card; Stoppage response shown by lights. Auto kamishibai
Inventory	2 bin system	2 bin with auto notification
Quality	SPC chart	SPC with auto call
Ideas	Placed on a board	Progress stages shown
Material handling	Clearly marked locations	Lights; poka-yoke

In each of these, whenever a 'deviation' occurs, a good visual system should evolve to avoid the issue happening again. For instance, if inventory is found in the wrong location, that would indicate that the visual system is deficient. If a schedule is missed, why was the cause not made clearer earlier – visually. Here, a useful hierarchy is suggested by Galsworth: (Can you move to the next level?)

1.   Visual indicator (a warning sign at a railroad level crossing)
2.   Visual signal (lights flash when train approaches)
3.   Visual control (a barrier comes down)
4.   Visual guarantee (physical separation of train and car)

Visuality is therefore an inherent part of, amongst others:

- Leader standard work. (What does the leader need to focus attention on? Not just red lights.)
- Continuous improvement. (Where is the current most pressing problem?)
- Scheduling. (At a glance: Are we ahead or behind? What is the next job? Shortages?)
- Hoshin Kanri. (The visual connection between strategy and operations, and how well are we doing? If behind, how can management help?)
- TPM. (At a glance: What is the current status?)
- Kata. (The 5 Questions : Easy to see? – for both types of Kata.)
- Gemba walks. (Is progress from the last walk visible?)

Gwendolyn Galsworth suggests that good visuality is an empowerment concept by getting operators, supervisors, designers, engineers to ask 'what (information) do I need to know?', and then later 'what (information) do I need to share?' These must be easily and visually communicated. Note that it is the 'I' question, not the 'we' question. The 'why' is known by the person, better than anyone. Then, ask the person to design his or her own visual display. Try to avoid the top-down, 'you will use this / fill this in / report on this'. That temps 'cooking the books'.

Some Visual Tools

The following visual tools are some of many that have been found useful:

- 'Bodystorming' (instead of brainstorming) is a concept used by IDEO that asks participants to act out their ideas with suitable full-scale props.
- Kamishibai. A board with slots for two-sided cards each of which requires an action to be carried out. The card is then turned around. Common with TPM. Comments and stickers can be added.
- Day by the hour / Heijunka / short interval control. Visually showing the levelled schedule across the day, and requiring action if output in any period is not achieved.
- Yamazumi. A board used for line balancing. Workstation activities are accumulated and adjusted until planned cycle time is reached.
- Single Point Lessons. Temporary boards that emphasize a correct procedure. Pictures rather than words.
- 'Pick to Light' Systems. This is a company that markets an extensive range of visual picking systems that highlight the appropriate parts needed for assembly. See their web site.
- Follow the colour routes. For example in a hospital, directing people to the right department.
- Roadmaps. A graphic display showing the past and planned Lean journey with cartoons.
- *Back of the Napkin*. A great little book showing how simple drawings can aid planning and problem solving. Use with an A3! Simple diagrams have a great history for clarification – for example, in Physics, from Michael Faraday to Einstein.

Finally, visual displays are an art in themselves. See, for example, Edward Tufte or Howard Wainer. Both contain wonderful examples and severe warnings. Of course, intuitive usage has been one of the hallmarks of Apple computer.

A final story
New neighbours moved in next door. After a day or two the new neighbour hung washing on the line. The wife of the original household said to her husband, 'That washing is dirty. I think the new neighbour does not know how to do a proper wash!' This sequence was repeated several times. After a few weeks the wife said, 'Wow, suddenly their washing is clean! What has happened? 'Well', replied her husband, 'I have just cleaned our windows…'

Further Readings.
Gwendolyn Galsworth, *Work that Makes Sense: Operator Lead Visuality*, Visual Lean Enterprise Press, 2011. This book contains hundreds of colour photos. Everyone will find several ideas!
Edward R Tufte, *Visual Explanations*, Graphics Press, 1977
Howard Wainer*, Graphic Discovery: A Trout in the milk and other visual adventures*, Princeton University Press, 2005
Dan Roam, *The Back of the Napkin: Solving problems and selling ideas with pictures*, Penguin, 2008

3.23 Habits

Lean relies on good habits. Lean is not an occasional or sporadic activity but needs to become a set of habits, just like brushing your teeth or wearing a seat belt. A habit is very often a small action, but small actions repeated regularly often accumulate into big benefit.

In 1959 Volvo became the first car company to install three-point seat belts as standard. It was considered an unnecessary waste by many, and even opposed by some saying, for instance, that in an accident it would be safer to be thrown clear. But today, seat belts have simply become an activity that has become automatic and is given little thought. One estimate is that belts have saved more than a million lives. The habit sequence of Que, Action, Reward is in place. The Que or trigger is sitting down in the car. The Action is putting on the belt. The 'Reward' is a by now unconscious feeling of safety. If the sequence is not carried out, a car driver or passenger feels awkward or that something is missing. The reward is very seldom extrinsic, but more often just an alleviation of a concern, or a satisfaction. On occasion a reward may be, for instance, a chocolate bar received after a morning run.

The point is that a habit can easily be learned and widely adopted if it conforms to good and easy practice. Regularity is a key. Be reminded (light? iPhone? diary?) every time until it becomes standard. The sequence of Que, Routine, Reward (after Duhigg; B J Fogg calls the sequence Anchor Moment, Tiny Behaviour, Instant Celebration.) needs to be established. If a seat belt was uncomfortable or hard to find it would not become a habit. (Think if a seatbelt had first to be taken out of the trunk.) The sequence, together with feedback is a motivation loop not unlike Expectancy Theory discussed in Section 4.1.

(It now appears that with the growing popularity of 4x4 vehicles, seat belt use has declined in the UK. Apparently, people find 4x4 seat belts more awkward or perhaps feel more secure. So a habit can be broken – unintentionally – and a new habit is called for.)

Always remember that a habit is a subconscious decision triggered by an environment or situation. (Watch a movie? Buy popcorn! Don't even think about it. It's your reward.) Advertisers spend huge sums linking environments with products. Watch rugby on TV = Have a beer – your reward! So with Lean, think about what situations should eventually trigger what subconscious action or decision. (Log on to your computer in the morning = Check daily stats, respond and be rewarded with up to the minute team information. ??)

Maurer has pointed out that the human brain finds it easier to accept small changes than big changes. Little changes add up. It's kaizen. In Lean and CI, the goal of a habit is not to solve a problem, but to become a problem solver. The goal is not to improve relations with a particular team member but to become an excellent team facilitator. At home, the goal is not to cook a good meal but to become a good cook. There is much in common with Carol Dwek's mindset and her plea for a 'yet' outlook. (Section 7.4) and the Kahneman's 'System 1 and System 2' (Section 8.14)

Accumulation, like interest in a savings account, compounds. A positive feedback loop. But note that a positive feedback loop can compound good, like friendship or respect, or bad like dissatisfaction or ignoring contribution. Both become confirmation bias, where reinforcing evidence is sought. In management (and sport) situations both good and not-so-good outcomes will happen. But regularity and accumulation will determine whether the good or not-so-good mean will tend to predominate. As with the Learning Curve, repetition usually makes the routine easier. These are good reasons for management to nurture habits by their own regular actions and by allowing time for accumulation. Have patience.

Good habits are facilitated by making them easier to do. (Pulling the Andon chord at line side). Bad habits are decreased by making them harder to do. (Avoiding defects by poka-yoke. Removing the large batch ordering default in an MRP system. Put that chocolate bar on the top shelf.) This is not unlike Thaler and Sunstein's 'Nudge' concept.

The bottom Line on Habits for Human Lean:

- Set up an easy-to-do Queues or Triggers: We always have a morning meeting at Gemba. We always do an After-Action Review (AAR). We always use PDCA.
- Then follow through with an Action procedure: Who will be present? How will it be done? Make it easy to do. (Close by; easy to see; convenient.)
- Reward: Make the action satisfying: Show progress, Share information, Share discussion at tea break, Comment on achievement.)

Further Readings.

Charles Duhigg, *The Power of Habit*, Heinemann, 2012
James Clear, *Atomic Habits*, RH Books, 2018
Robert Maurer, *One Small Step Can Change Your Life: The Kaizen Way*, Workman, 2004
B J Fogg, *Tiny Habits*, Virgin Books, 2020
See also Russell Poldrack, *Hard to Break*, Princeton Univ Press, 2021 for an academic study

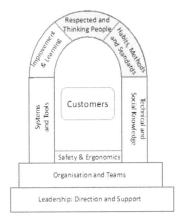

Chapter 4
Eight Models of People at Work

In this chapter, eight of what are considered the most useful models relating to human performance in a Lean and Agile context are presented.

The table below gives an overview of areas of applicability.

Name	Focus	Scope	Main Sources
Expectancy	Motivation	Individual, team?	Vroom, Porter and Lawler
Trilogy	Improvement	Individual, group	Bicheno, based on many
Job Characteristics	Task Design	Individual, team	Hackman and Oldham
Performance	Performance	Individual	Mager and Pipe
Force Field	Change	Group	Lewin
Change curves	Acceptance	Indiv and Group	Ross; Katzenbach+; Scholtes
Diffusion	Buy-in	Group	Rogers; Kotter; Bicheno; Devine
Queues (Waiting Lines)	Muda Muri Mura	Group	Kingman model

4.1 Expectancy Theory

Expectancy Theory has been a consistently popular theory of motivation since introduced by Victor Vroom in 1966. An important modification and extension was developed by Porter and Lawler into a more comprehensive theory of motivation. Several others have suggested further modifications. Here we present our version, with comments relevant to Lean.

Although the model is focused on the individual, many concepts are also applicable to a team.

Like virtually every theory of motivation it has significant critics but the basic framework remains very useful to practitioners. Over the years it has been discussed and added to by many.
The underlying concept is:

Motivation = Valency x Expectancy x Instrumentality

In short, an individual is motivated towards that activity which she is most capable of undertaking and which she believes has the highest probability of leading to her most desirable outcome. People are motivated when they believe that behaviour will lead to rewards (intrinsic and extrinsic), that such rewards are valuable to them, and that their behaviour will result in a certain probability of success.

There are two types of 'Expectancy': Effort – performance, and Performance – Outcome. 'Instrumentality' links performance to outcome. 'Valency' is the strength of a person's feeling about specific outcomes and links outcome and satisfaction with the perceived value of the outcomes.

The factors are all modified by resources, skills, values, trust, perceptions and probabilities. Unlike Maslow and Herzberg who focused on needs, Porter and Lawler's theory is a dynamic feedback model that separates effort, performance and outcomes. As such, Expectancy Theory can be regarded as a meta theory linking various other theories. It is learning theory – people learn from their experiences and behave accordingly.

Importantly, the theory breaks with the formerly accepted view that there was a simple and direct relationship between job satisfaction and performance – still widely held, but much too simple! Motivation is not a simple cause and effect relationship (By the way, beware of reading Vroom's original papers – unless you can cope with mathematical gobbledygook).

Here, we present our adaptation of the Vroom (and Porter and Lawler) model, and attempt to examine the linkages. The numbers refer to the figure.

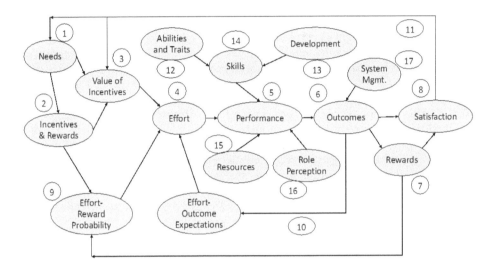

1. Needs. This may include Maslow's Hierarchy. But 'Needs' may also be those of the wider peer group (at work and at home). For instance, the Socio-Tech needs of coal miners in the classic Emery and Trist case. (See Section 5.2). Herzberg's Need Hierarchy is relevant – higher needs cannot be met unless lower needs, such as safety and survival, are already met. But there are always exceptions – the starving artist? (As Berthold Brecht wrote in The Threepenny Opera, 'First comes a full stomach, then comes ethics'.)

2. Incentives (or Rewards) may be Extrinsic (such as money or bonus) or Intrinsic (the work itself, or recognition). Deming and many others have been critical of extrinsic incentives, claiming that such incentives have only short-term effect. Alfie Kohn's book *Punished by Rewards* is a devastating critique of incentive plans. But, beware, some extrinsic rewards may be very powerful depending on Need.

3. Do the incentives match the needs? Don't assume you know! People vary. A TWI Job Relations mantra is 'People must be treated as individuals'. And one of Stephen Covey's '7 Habits of Highly Effective People' is 'Seek first to Understand, then to be Understood'.

4. Effort is dependent upon the value of incentives and the perceived likelihood that the incentives or rewards will be achieved, and upon the persons belief that effort will lead to outcome.

5. Performance is influenced by Effort, but modified by the person's Skills and by the availability of appropriate resources.

6. Outcomes are determined by Performance but the Management System (17) – including attention to Flow and to the '7 Wastes' also has influence. 'A bad system will beat a good person every time', said Deming.

7. Rewards are generated by both the outcomes and satisfaction. Rewards (or lack thereof) may be intrinsic or extrinsic or both. An important factor is whether the Rewards are perceived as equitable or fair by the person. Managers may disagree with the perception. Therefore managers need an understanding of the person's circumstances and of the wider environment. (One reason why Toyota teams have a small span of control.)

8. Outcomes result in Satisfaction to both the worker and to the organisation. Satisfaction follows from intrinsic and extrinsic rewards.

9. The receipt of equitable rewards will feed back to Effort-Reward probability. To what extent were the rewards compatible with the outcome? Were expectations met? People will learn about the relationship and future behaviour will be influenced. The Mager model (See Section 4.4) asks the tough question: Will performance make a difference? Mager also asks, 'Will an outcome be punished?' ('You do such good work; here is more for you to do!). Will a non-outcome be rewarded? (A person does pretty poor work, but gets the pay increase anyway. A poor worker is not fired because of union intervention.) Note that, at work, most behaviour is voluntary. The person may choose to work hard or not work hard, depending largely on expectations, and on experiences from the past.

10. Likewise, did the outcomes meet expectations? A person may find that she can do the work easily, or alternatively however hard she tries it will not result in a desired outcome. On both feedback loops, management can learn about the expectations by interview. A team leader has an important role here. Were ideas listened to or just a waste of time? TWI Job Relations' 4 foundations are excellent. Possibly the Yerkes-Dodson hypothesis is relevant here. (See Sections 3.8 and 13.6)

11. How does Satisfaction relate back to Needs and to the Value of the Incentives? Note that Job Satisfaction does not directly influence performance.

12. An influence on Skill is the person's Ability. This may be natural ability such as physical strength, or intelligence (IQ?). Selection has a role to play. Skills also develop through Habit and Deliberate Practice. (See Section 4.2)

13. Development also affects Skill. Training, mentoring, and education. TWI Job Instruction and Job Methods certainly has a role. Carol Dwek has proposed 'Mindset' – a fixed or growth mindset. A growth mindset can be developed. Angela Duckworth proposes 'Grit' (See Section 7.4).

14. Skills are a composite of ability and Development. $S = f$ (Ability, Development). Nature, nurture, and noise. ('Noise', a concept used in forecasting, is the unpredictable element. Identical twins, brought up in identical circumstances still behave differently.)

15. Appropriate resources must be provided. Appropriate resources include sufficient time. (note 'Muri' overload, perhaps 90% of takt time if takt is used). It also includes hard tools (computers? pull-down drills? etc.), ergonomic workplaces, and soft tools (basic training, computer software).

16. Role perception is how the person sees her role. There is the story of the washroom cleaner who saw his job at NASA as helping to land a man on the moon.

17. System management would include Lean facilitation and system design. How much genuine effort by the employee is wasted by poor system design? The classic 7 wastes are relevant. System management opens up a full range of Lean practices, including visual management, andon-type signals, maintenance (TPM?), morning meetings, and idea management.

Implications for Managers.

The Expectancy model developed by Vroom, Porter and Lawler has significance for Lean managers:

- Employee needs must be understood, not assumed.
- Incentives and rewards must be appropriate to the individual. Find out from employees what rewards and incentives would be meaningful. Don't assume.
- Feedback is experienced by employees and affects future performance. It is the actual experience, not what the manager thinks it should be.
- Clear expectations on performance must be given.
- Task design is important. The work must be such that there is room for feedback related performance improvement.
- Self-feedback must be possible. Is there a way that a worker can obtain self-feedback against expectations?
- Performance depends on effort but also skills, resources, and role perception.
- Attention must be given to rewards, both intrinsic and extrinsic. The TWI Job Relations foundations are always relevant:
  o Let each worker know how he/she is doing. (Note: not only the group, but the individual.)
  o Give credit where due. Notice unusual performance.
  o Tell people in advance about changes that will affect them – and manager expectations!
  o Make best use of each person's ability.
- Beware of simply matching rewards with outcomes.

Practice does not make perfect, but it may take you to the next level. There is no perfect. Rather, practice could make temporary best – until the next breakthrough in technology or method takes place. An example: Olympic High jumping transitioning from the Western Roll to the Fosbury Flop https://www.youtube.com/watch?v=CZsH46Ek2ao

Note: The feedback loops in the Expectancy Theory Diagram have a parallel with the motivation feedback loops discussed in the feedback section of the Systems Chapter. (Section 5.3)

By the way (for Engineers): Expectancy Theory can be thought of as a control system that continually adjusts, like a thermostat. A desired temperature is set (the outcomes), the system is monitored (feedback) and heat is applied (management action) when the temperature (employee satisfaction) falls below that desired. There is a lag between detection and meeting the desired outcome. There is also Entropy: any system will run down to its lowest level (chaos) if energy is not put into the system.

Further reading
- Victor H. Vroom, *Work and Motivation,* Wiley, 1964
- Lyman Porter and Edward Lawler, *Managerial Attitudes and Performance*, Irwin,1968

Deming's Red Bead Game

Deming's famous Read Bead Game can be linked to Expectancy Theory. In his sessions 'Four Days with Dr. Deming', Deming had a group of 8 volunteers (6 workers, one scribe, one inspector) play the game. In addition, the instructor plays the role of a manager. Workers were given a wooden paddle with holes for 50 beads. Many red and while beads were held in a bucket and all workers were asked to dip their paddle into the bucket to retrieve 50 mixed (red and white) beads. Red beads are 'defects' and are counted by the inspector. Of course, each of the 6 players get different numbers of defects. Deming (or the manager) praised those workers with fewer beads and admonished those with more defects. ("Of course it is possible to get fewer defects! Look at the results of others!") The unsatisfactory workers were given a warning to improve or be fired. The workers were then told to do another dip of 50 beads each. What usually happened? The 'good' workers got worse results; the bad workers got better results. Why? Look at the figure below showing the distribution of red bead samples.

Of course, if a high number of read beads (poor) is obtained with the first dip, what is the probability of getting a lower number next time? Very likely! And the other way around if a worker got a low number on the first dip.

Distribution of Red Beads (Defects)

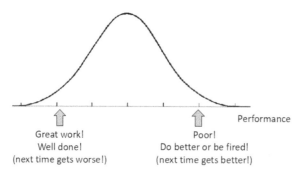

Performance

Great work!	Poor!
Well done!	Do better or be fired!
(next time gets worse!)	(next time gets better!)

Conclusion: Rewards don't work; Punishments do work!

Deming's (sarcastic) conclusions:

- Warnings for low achievement get results!
- Do not praise good performance – the workers will take advantage!

Of course, these are rubbish! Deming's proper conclusions were:

- Workers often can't do much to improve their performance. So don't blame them!
- Only changing the system will improve performance, and only managers can do this.
- Deming's 94/6 rule: 94% of problems are due to the system; only 6% due to people.
- Many managers just don't understand variation. They hand out rewards and punishments without knowing anything about statistical variation. Rewards are often given when they are not deserved; Punishments likewise.
- To judge if performance is really good or poor, one needs to know the distribution. Use a statistical process control chart (SPC) to see if performance falls outside the control limits. (In the game all readings fall within the control limits, and therefore are common cause variation. No action should be taken!)

Discussion of the game is often best done with reference to Expectancy Theory and the Mager and Pipe flowchart – both discussed in this chapter.

Notes on playing the game: We have played the game numerous times with various groups. Our experience:

- Play the game with people from the same organisational level. Mixing levels can lead to un-needed controversy.
- After playing, ask for a short period of silent reflection before discussion.
- The game can be a revelation to some. But some argue that it is unrealistic. Performance cannot easily be measured. True, but it is the principles that matter.
- A few, more statistical savvy, will raise Type 1 and Type 2 error possibilities. Type 1 is where worker is accused but should not have been. (This is what the game is about. A Type1 has more serious consequences than a Type 2.) Type 2 is where a worker is not blamed but should have been.

    Video: https://youtu.be/geiC4UgpDyw

An update on motivation…

Nitin Nohria, Boris Groysberg and Linda-Eling Lee outlined how new research in fields like neuroscience, biology and evolutionary psychology suggests that people are directed by four basic emotional needs or drives:

1. The drive to acquire – we all aware of just how happy it makes us when we get something we have longed for. Not only physical goods but experiences like holidays, a job promotion or moving to a more upmarket neighbourhood.
2. The drive to bond – at its most basic this is about love and caring. A homeless person with addiction issues may nevertheless have a dog to care for. At another level humans want to be part of something greater than themselves such as organisations and associations: a football team, a religion, a pop group, an 'eco' grouping - but also a work group.
3. The drive to comprehend. Everyone has basic curiosity but this may fade with age. When small children "play" with their food they do so through sight, touch, smell and taste. This desire to make sense of the world around us never leaves us.
4. The drive to defend – like all animals we instinctively protect our family, friends and possessions. When we fill this drive we feel confident and secure. Nohria believes that this also extends to a desire for a fairer and more just society.

The authors' suggestion that organisations should design their work systems to tap into these four drives. This will have positive outcomes for both the organisation and its employees. Refer to the example below.

Primary Drive	Work System	Possible Human Lean actions
Acquire	Reward and Recognition	Personal recognition and feedback Investment in employee training Provide development opportunities
Bond	Culture and Engagement	Build community spirit (Social, Sports Clubs) Engagement initiatives Foster teamwork; Downplay status
Comprehend	Job Design	Whole jobs (See JCM) Involvement in problem solving Use visual management systems
Defend	Performance Management	Clear and transparent policies Group loyalty. Trust. Shared communication.

Further Reading.
Nohria, N., Groysberg, B. and Lee, L., 2008. Employee Motivation: A powerful new model. *Harvard business review*, *86*(7/8), p.78.

4.2 The Lean People Trilogy

There would seem to be three inter-related emerging 'people' concepts of particular relevance to managing a person with Lean aspirations. They are the concepts of Practice (closely linked to Kata and TWI), Small wins motivation (closely linked to Kaizen), and Belief and Bias (closely linked to Respect and Humility). These three mutually reinforce each other. They form a set, the combined power of which is significant for Lean transformation. All three are necessary. This Trilogy model brings together several concepts discussed at greater length in this book.

We know now that effective learning and training for Lean requires practice and repetition. One off instruction – and particularly classroom instruction without practice simply does not work in a Lean context. It is soon forgotten, if indeed it was learned in the first place. As Benjamin Franklin said almost 300 years ago, *"Tell me and I forget, teach me and I may remember, involve me and I learn"*.

'Small Wins' is the essence of Kaizen and Continuous Improvement. (Kaizen is continuous change for the better). Many small wins add up to a big win. Of course, there may be occasional 'Kaikaku' or breakthroughs but many such innovations rest on combining several previous smaller gains. Steven Johnson calls this 'the adjacent possible'. Thus, the iphone combined developments in the web, micro-processors, glass, music, memory chips and more. The implementation of small wins is a powerful feedback motivator.

Belief in people's potential is the essential third component, creating the climate for Practice and Small Wins to flourish.

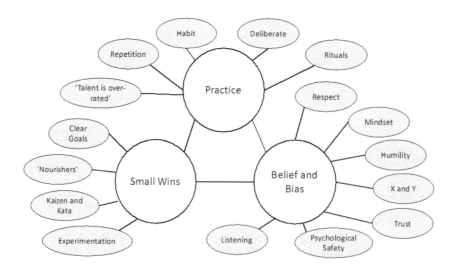

Practice

Two stories about practice: Gary Player, one of only 5 golfers (and the only non-American) to win The Career Grand Slam (Masters, PGA, US Open, British Open) said, *"Yes, I am lucky. And, you know what, the more I practice the luckier I get"*. Then there is the tale of the lost tourist in New York City who enquires how to get to Carnegie Hall, *'Practice, man, Practice!'* is the response. Malcolm Gladwell in his popular book *Outliers* discusses the '10,000 hour rule for Mastery'. Quoting a string of famous people including The Beatles, Mozart, Bill Gates, and many sportspeople, Gladwell proposes that it is hours of practice that is a large determinant of success. *"We do owe something to parentage and patronage.... But they are invariably the beneficiaries of hidden advantages and extraordinary opportunities and cultural legacies that allow them to learn and work hard...in ways others cannot"*. Although it might not necessarily take 10,000 hours to become a Lean master, certainly a Lean Six Sigma Black Belt with a 40-hour course and a project under his belt would not come close.

Deliberate Practice

It is not just practice that is needed but deliberate practice. Deliberate practice, as described by Anders Ericsson involves observation, constructive feedback and correction. Mozart did not just practice but was coached by his father – a talented teacher. Practice is necessary but not sufficient and the extent of practice depends on the field of endeavour. So, a coach or tutor is required.

Repetition

We all know that repetition is necessary for improvement. This is not something new. For centuries the church has relied on weekly or daily repetition to reinforce religion. Repetition is the premise of TWI. TWI's effectiveness is embedded in the repetition and practice over the 10 hour (two hours per day for 5 days) class. ('Continue until you know that they know'). These are discussed in a separate section on TWI in this book. In Steve Spear's Shingo award winning book 'The High Velocity Edge' he gives examples of repetition combined with scientific method – for example Admiral Rickover's continual insistence on questioning and uncovering things that are unknown.

Habit

Aristotle is reputed to have said, *"We are what we repeatedly do. Excellence, then, is not an act, but a habit."* The effectiveness of habit is something that is becoming established in Lean – Leader Standard Work, Yamazumi, 5S, A3's, Lean scheduling – all emphasize regularity. Most effective habits are not only regular but also small actions. See below. Establishing good habits is very important in Lean. (Habit is discussed several times in this book. See particularly Section 3.23 but also Sections 3.9, 3.12 and 7.6.)

Rituals

Schwartz, in a HBR article refers to 'rituals' at Sony, where daily walks, meetings, and periods when e mails are prohibited, are compulsory. The US Army now regularly uses After Action Reviews (AAR's – See also Section 10.20). As the name suggests an AAR is conducted as soon as possible after every action or exercise. It is conducted by a trained facilitator almost invariably in the field. Status or rank is downplayed, but personal criticism is not allowed. The phases are: What did we set out to do? What went right? What went wrong? What can we learn and how can we do better next time? The effectiveness of AAR's is discussed by David Garvin of Harvard in his book *Learning in Action*. Garvin warns that AARs fail where facilitation skills are inadequate. AAR's have lots of similarity with A3 mentoring described by John Shook. Focus on the problem, not the person. Direct observation is required. Fact based, not opinion based.

Small Wins

Recent years have revealed the power of small and 'varied wins' motivation. In a seminal 1984 article, Karl Weick said; *"By itself, one small win may seem unimportant. A series of small wins at small but significant tasks, however, reveals a pattern that may attract allies, deter opponents, and lower resistance to subsequent proposals. Small wins are controllable opportunities that produce visible results. Once a small win has been accomplished, forces are set in motion that favour another small win. When a solution is put in place, the next solvable problem often becomes more visible. This occurs because new allies bring new solutions with them and old opponents change their habits."* (A crucial quote for Lean transformation!)

More recently, Teresa Amabile and Steven Kramer's momentous work at Harvard Business School has elaborated on the power of small wins on 'positive inner work life'. Small wins are shown to be the most powerful motivating factor, but need to be supported with 'catalysts' (for instance clear goals, providing resources and time) and 'nourishers' (for instance, respect, encouragement). Moreover 'setbacks' (like small losses and negative leader behaviour) can overwhelm small wins. An enthusiastic medical doctor, Robert Maurer, explains the power of small wins and kaizen with reference to the human brain. Humans find small changes far less threatening. Large changes provoke fear that automatically restricts access to the cortex (for safety and survival). But failure often results. Small changes bypass the amygdala giving access to the cortex. Success is more likely. Hence ask small questions, take small actions, solve small problems, and bestow small rewards. (This seems similar to Kahneman's System 1 and System 2 brain concepts.)

All these give justification for Rother's Toyota Kata concept. Small wins, with PDSA and learning. Kata is discussed at length in Section 3.12.

Small wins is also the essence of 'The Lean Startup' methodology. Here, instead of spending huge amounts of time on lengthy project definition and specification, an experimental approach is used which tests out 'minimal viable products'. Where the small test product succeeds it is gone ahead with; where it fails it is abandoned. A low risk and learning methodology. Fail fast and learn. The small wins idea is absolutely integral to learning with Experiments as used by Google, Amazon, Microsoft and now many others. These organizations conduct literally hundreds of experiments each month (See Section 4.2)

As an aside, why was Eisenhower chosen as supreme allied commander for D-Day? He had very little battle experience against the huge experience of Patton, Montgomery, Bradley. Well, some say he was chosen because of his excellent consensus building skills. Also, humility and respect. He made progress through splitting the vast requirements into 'small wins' packages that everyone could agree on.

Belief and Bias

What VS Mahesh calls 'Pygmalion' and Kahneman and many others calls 'Confirmation Bias' has long been known. We selectively seek out information that confirms our beliefs, and tend to ignore information that contradicts our beliefs. Margaret Heffernan calls this 'wilful blindness'. We all have 'filters' and build on flimsy evidence. This is a type of cognitive bias that everyone has. So, for example, Israeli drill sergeants are told that one group comprises specially selected achievers and other group comprises the less able. The groups, however, unbeknown to the sergeants, were randomly selected. Nevertheless the 'superior' group performs much better. So do randomly selected maths students. A self-fulfilling prophesy.

The distinguished psychologist Carol Dwek classifies people according to a 'fixed mindset' or 'a growth mindset'. (Actually a continuum.) People with a fixed mindset think their intelligence is static, a fixed trait. They avoid challenges, deflect criticism, and feel there is no point in effort. By contrast, those with a growth mindset embrace challenges, work hard to improve, and learn from criticism and feedback. Intelligence is not fixed, but can grow. Countless 'under-achievers' (Churchill, Branson, many sportspeople) have demonstrated this through determination. As Henry Ford said, *"Whether you think you can or whether you think you can't, you're absolutely right."* The growth mindset is captured in Dwek's word 'Yet'. The attitude is that a person can't do it yet, but will be able to with effort and support. The point is a growth mindset can be learned! And taught. A good teacher motivates by giving constructive feedback, linking effort to achievement. Praise effort rather than success.

Of course, to give genuine constructive and specific feedback one must believe in the potential of the mentee. One must be aware of confirmation bias. George Davidson, former Manufacturing Director at Toyota South Africa, when asked about the aim of TPS simply said 'To create thinking people'. In other words, change their mindset.

Listening and Respect go hand in hand. Genuine listening implies respect and vice versa. It begins with the recognition that the person doing the job is the real expert about that job.

Humility is required. The sub-title of Edgar Schein's excellent book is instructive: 'The gentle art of asking instead of telling'. Very hard for most people, including the authors of this book. But remember, you never learn from telling. Schein makes an early point about how annoying it is to be told something you already know by someone who assumes you are ignorant. He tells of examples from the Deepwater gulf spill and from the Columbia and Challenger shuttles where information that could have prevented the disasters was known but not listened to. A climate of both feeling safe to tell, and the ability to be listened to, is required. Not easy with a powerful boss.

This is best summarised by the important concept of *Psychological Safety*. This is the lack of fear that bringing bad news to the boss will be treated positively not negatively. As Amy Edmondson of HBS explains the concept as 'People are not hindered by *interpersonal* fear' and where 'they fear holding back their full participation *more* than they fear sharing a potentially sensitive, threatening or wrong idea'. So people realise that their job may be lost due to economic or company competitiveness, but not through highlighting defects and mistakes. It is vital for leaders and managers to cultivate the characteristics of trust, respect, humility, listening, and psychological safety in any Lean-aspiring organisation. *'Approach problems as a joint collaborator' and 'replace blame with curiosity'*, says Laura Delizonna. (See also Section 9.9 on Mistakes)

Margaret Heffernan tells of how threatening and how common is 'wilful blindness' amongst senior people from all walks of life. An ostrich mentality is far from unusual. So is Groupthink (See Section 9.4). Heffernan praises the former CEO of British Airways who appointed an official 'corporate fool' who had a licence to speak up and challenge. Apparently, the Catholic Church, for several hundred years, had a person whose task was to challenge any proposal for sainthood.

Bringing the People Trilogy Together

The three factors of the trilogy are mutually reinforcing. When brought together they form a powerful system for the softer side of Lean Transformation. A common theme is that training and doing should not be separated. This theme is echoed by TWI, by Mike Rother, and by many in the field of Learning. (See Chapter 10)

Between Repetition and Small Wins. Repetition and practice need to be deliberate and coached with a goal in mind. But small wins along the way are vital to retain momentum. The linkage might explain the disenchantment with week-long Kaizen Events that has set in. Whilst changes can be dramatic, they are often not sustained. Why not make the small, non-threatening changes as opportunities arise, coupled with experimentation as suggested by Rother's Kata methodology? Rother explains that whilst the 'target condition' might be known, the route to get there is uncertain. Many small steps, some of which will fail but from which we will learn, is the way to go. According to Rother *"Because the improvement kata is a set of behavioural guidelines, it is something that we learn through repeated practice. It takes conditioning to make behavioural routines become second nature, and consequently a lot of Toyota's managerial activities involve having people practise the improvement kata with their guidance. For team leaders and group leaders, this teaching occupies more than 50 percent of their time, and for higher-level managers it can also occupy up to 50 percent."*

David Mann's thesis on 'Creating a Lean Culture' is through Daily Accountability, Leader Standard Work, Visual Controls, and Discipline. Daily means repetition. Leader standard work, visual controls and discipline together imply directed small wins becoming the norm. Specifically, the rapid problem solving and feedback that these four result in, stimulate culture change.

B.F. Skinner. Some may wonder if Skinner's classic work on behaviour modification is appropriate here – linking repetition with small wins. Alfie Kohn, in *Punished by Rewards* page 6, wrote (somewhat unfairly?) that Skinner *'...could be described as a man who conducted most of his experiments on rodents and pigeons and wrote most of his books about people'*. More recently a phrase, and several books, discuss *Lab Rats* as becoming a form of work that is beginning to appear, but such work is definitely Non-Lean!

In line with expectancy, Skinner talked about positive reinforcement (such as praise) and negative reinforcement (such as punishment or withdrawal). Both types increase the probability of behaviour modification. Behaviour is modified by future goals. He discussed, amongst many other theories, Continuous Reinforcement whereby every time a specific action takes place the person receives a reinforcement. This method is effective because it quickly establishes a link between the behaviour and the reinforcement.

Skinner held that people (and rats!) don't just respond to stimuli, they respond to patterns of stimuli. It is the pattern of stimuli rather than the stimulus itself that is important. This is profound - a one off incentive (or reinforcement) will not be effective. Initially, to establish a desired behaviour, reinforcement should be 'fixed' (at a regular time, or following a given achievement), but then, once established, reinforcement should be variable (with time or achievement) in order to sustain the change. However, there must be 'contiguity' – in other words as short an interval as possible between the behaviour and the reinforcement. (An annual Christmas bonus will do nothing to affect behaviour in mid-year!).

Between Repetition and Belief. Gladwell wrote of the 10,000 hour rule for mastery. But two comments: The 10k rule really only applies to world-leading performance, and practice without belief – for however long - will fail.

Mike Rother, discussing Kata as an improvement approach, emphasized the duo of an 'improvement kata' and a 'coaching kata'. Both are necessary.

Carol Dwek's examples of people moving towards a growth mindset show a determination to get there, a belief that it is possible, as well as sustained practice.

Geoff Colvin says about deliberate practice: *"It is an activity specifically designed to improve performance, often with a teacher's help; it can be repeated a lot; feedback on results is continuously available; it's highly demanding mentally, whether the activity is purely intellectual, such as chess or business-related activities, or heavily physical, such as sports; and it isn't much fun"*. For people who have been guided through a successful A3 problem solving exercise, including the frustration of having to repeat the analysis in order to get to 'root cause', that sounds just about right!

Between Small Wins and Belief. These are mutually necessary. Mindset can be learned. It has been said that Toyota achieves excellent results with average people, but many others achieve mediocre results with excellent people. Although we feel that this is rather insulting to Toyota people, the sentiment is clear. Take an excellent person and put her in an organisation that does not believe in using or growing her talents, and her results will disappoint. But talent CAN be developed….

Mike Rother claims that *"We have misunderstood why Toyota is more successful than other organisations in achieving the challenges (target conditions) it sets for itself. It is not primarily because Toyota people have greater discipline to stick with a plan or experience fewer problems, as is often thought. Rather, they spot problems at the process level much earlier, when the problems are still small and you can understand them and do something about them."*

This however is no easily accomplished task. Steve Spear describes how Dallis, a successful auto-manufacturing manager, upon joining Toyota is developed as a Toyota manager through a painful process of being mentored. Dallis learns to see, understand and solve many small problems at several Toyota locations before being released into the position he was hired for. 'Dallis spent 12 weeks learning about the importance of observation as the basis for improvement and of using the scientific method of being clear about expectations before making changes and following up to observe the results of those changes.'

Further Readings.
Teresa Amabile and Steven Kramer, *The Progress Principle: Using Small Wins to Ignite Joy, Engagement, and Creativity at Work*, Harvard, 2011
Geoff Colvin, *Talent is Overrated*, Nicholas Brealey, 2008
Daniel Coyle, *The Talent Code: Greatness Insn't Born, It's Grown*, Arrow, 2010
Laura Delizonna, 'High Performing Teams need Psychological Safety', *Harvard Business Review*, 24 August 2017
Carol Dwek, *Mindset: The new psychology of Success*, Random House, 2006
Amy Edmondson, *The Fearless Organisation*, Harvard Business School Press, 2019
David Garvin, *Learning in Action*, Harvard, 2000
Malcolm Gladwell, *Outliers: The Story of Success*, Penguin, 2009
Margaret Heffernan, *Wilful Blindness*, Simon and Schuster, 2011
Daniel Kahneman, *Thinking, Fast and Slow*, Allen Lane, 2011
David Mann, *Creating a Lean Culture*, Second edition, CRC Press, 2011
Robert Maurer, *One Small Step Can Change Your Life: The Kaizen Way*, Workman, 2004
Robert Maurer, *The Spirit of Kaizen: Creating Lasting Excellence One Small Step at a Time*, McGraw Hill, 2013
Eric Reis, *The Lean Startup*, Portfolio, 2011
Michael Roberto, *The Art of Critical Decision Making*, The Great Courses, 2009
Edgar Schein, *Humble Inquiry: The Gentle Art of Asking Instead of Telling*, Berrett-Koehler, 2013
Steven Spear, *Chasing the Rabbit*, McGraw Hill, 2009, and the later edition, *The High Velocity Edge, 2010*
Karl Weick "Small Wins: Redefining the Scale of Social Problems," *American Psychologist*, January 1984.

4.3 The Job Characteristics Model

Hackman and Oldham's Job Characteristics model (JCM), developed in 1975 and expanded in 1980, continues to have great relevance for the design of effective jobs. An adapted version is shown in the figure. JCM applies equally to manufacturing and service.

The model can be linked to Expectancy Theory in as far as the underlying belief is that enriched jobs lead to job satisfaction, increased intrinsic motivation, and to improved work performance. Feedback is another link with Expectancy Theory. It is also linked to Herzberg's model, and can be seen with the Lean 'Drivers' model in Chapter 1. Moreover, JCM is clearly in line with Organisation Development theory which proposes that to change a culture requires defining the desired actions and behaviours and then designing the work that reinforces such behaviours.

As shown in the figure there are three stages: Good Job Characteristics lead to improved Psychological States that in turn lead to good work outcomes. In 1980, 'moderators' were added. We have slightly modified and extended Hackman and Oldham's model following ideas from de Treville (2006) and Emiliani (2007).

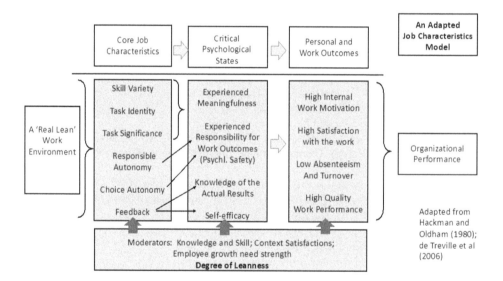

A 'Real Lean' Work Environment

Bob Emiliani made a useful distinction between what he called 'Fake Lean' and 'Real Lean'. Real Lean 'is the simultaneous deployment of both Continuous Improvement and Respect for People'. Respect is not the same as friendliness but does involve appreciation. Fake Lean is the employment of just one of these, typically 'the tools' of CI. Lack of respect for people, says Emiliani, is widespread and involves a focus, for instance, on 'earned hours, purchase price variance …batch and queue thinking, fire fighting, and the blame game'.

Importantly all of the following core job characteristics can be influenced by management, particularly in a Lean environment.

Core Job Characteristics

- Skill variety. A good job requires having a variety of different activities and challenges, and would involve the use of several different skills. This can be achieved by job rotation, involvement in team meetings, 'quality at source', and participation in improvement.
- Task Identity. As far as possible a job should involve a complete job, start to finish. It is not necessary for a person to actually carry out all the tasks to make a product, but participation as a team member in a recognisable aspect or distinct stage is desirable. Manufacture of a subassembly, field maintenance, a class teacher, and customer support are examples. Unlike Charlie Chaplin in 'Modern Times', not a small, repetitive task with little link to the wider product or service.
- Task Significance. The job is seen as having substantial impact on success. Recall the story of the NASA toilet cleaner seeing his job as helping to get a man to the moon. The famous CEO of Scandinavian Airlines, Jan Carlsson, emphasised 'moments of truth' that involved every employee playing an important role in the customer journey. Carlsson emphasized that a single negative moment of truth could lose or win customer loyalty.
- Autonomy (here subdivided into Responsible Autonomy and Choice Autonomy) involves substantial own responsibility, for instance, for quality and meeting the schedule and timing – without close supervision. Standard work should not be limiting, but be seen as a platform for further improvement. For responsible autonomy there would need to be some flexibility with respect to buffer inventories, and recognition of inevitable variation. Utilization as a percentage of takt time (where used) should be less than (say) 90%, so as to avoid instability. (See Section 4.8 referring to Queues and utilization.) Choice autonomy would recognise a worker's variety of skills and allow sensible adjustment to changing circumstances, again without close supervision. Lateral task assistance, including the sort of mutually supportive team activities observed by Emery and Trist in their 'socio tech' studies, would be allowed. The role of the supervisor or manager would be to facilitate flow and improvement, rather than act as 'controller'.
- Feedback on work carried out needs to be given to the worker from a variety of sources – the job itself, from supervisors, and from co-workers probably from further downstream. Such feedback needs to be constructive. Classic stories tell of Toyota managers thanking workers for stopping the line when a problem becomes apparent.

Critical Psychological States

- Experienced meaningfulness of the task stems equally from Skill Variety, Task Identity, and Task Significance. The three are equally weighted.
- Experienced responsibility for work outcomes stems from Responsible autonomy and Choice autonomy. We could add, following the Trilogy model above, a climate of Psychological Safety as a Critical Psychological State.
- Knowledge of the actual results stems from feedback
- Self-efficacy is a worker's belief in the effectiveness or impact on him- or her-self of the work itself.

Personal and Work Outcomes

All the critical psychological states, when positive, together influence High internal work motivation, High satisfaction with the work, Low absenteeism and turnover and High quality work performance.

Moderators

Hackman and Oldham later introduced Moderators as a recognition that there were other factors involved. Not all workers want the same levels of work outcomes. Perhaps there is a lack of resources or skill capability (knowledge and skill). Note here the Mager and Pipe framework later in the chapter. Many stories tell of people whose real satisfaction lies outside of work, say with the kids' football team. Others perhaps are dissatisfied with salary, supervision, or working conditions. Note here Herzberg's 'Hygiene' factors. Stress and frustration? (Context satisfaction). Yet others have varying degrees of need and of interest and opportunities to learn (Employee growth need and strength). Note here links with Maslow's hierarchy.

De Treville and Antonakis used the six job characteristics to derive what they called the Degree of Leanness. Thus, when all 6 are low the job is 'too Lean'; when the characteristics are a mix between high and low the job is 'somewhat right'; and when all characteristics are high the job is 'just right'.

The mix of Personal and Work Outcomes leads on to Organizational Performance. Lawler and Worley's concepts are relevant. They maintain that there are three primary organizational processes which contribute to organizational effectiveness. The sequence is important. First, Strategizing (a process which establishes 'strategic intent'). Second is Creating Value through competencies and capabilities. Third, Designing the structures and jobs that enable the organization to achieve effectiveness.

A note on Job Characteristic types

Job rotation is the process by which employee roles are rotated laterally in order to promote flexibility in the working environment.

Job enlargement is the process of allowing employees to determine their own work pace (within limits), to self-inspect the product, and be responsible for their own machine maintenance, their own workplace, including 5S, and the maintenance and improvement of standard work, all within certain limits.

Job enrichment allows a degree of autonomy in the planning and execution of work. This may include tasks formerly undertaken by people from higher levels. There is greater responsibility for the complete job outcomes. Participation in scheduling or TPM may be examples.

Criticisms of JCM

The criticisms of Hackman and Oldham's Job Characteristics model include ignoring organization structure, ignoring extrinsic rewards such as pay, as well as ignoring some intrinsic elements such as participation. Nevertheless, JCR remains probably the most significant and widely used model for job design.

Extending the JCM

More recently, in the light of changes in work organisation such as autonomy over work hours, service working, and emotional and social pressures, Parker reported that Morgeson and Humphrey added an additional 15 job characteristics covering knowledge motivation (e.g., problem-solving demands), social characteristics (e.g., social support), and contextual characteristics (e.g., work conditions). These additional factors explained 34%, 17%, and 4% respectively of the variance in job satisfaction. Other studies, reported by Parker showed that for a large sample of UK workers, individual autonomy was more strongly correlated with well-being and satisfaction than participation in a semiautonomous work group. But participation in a semiautonomous work group was better for learning.

There are other studies which reported that teams with high task interdependence perform better with high levels of team autonomy, whereas low-interdependence teams perform better with high levels of individual autonomy. Further, Parker reported that at Toyota NUMMI 'motivation arguably does not come from job autonomy; rather, employees are motivated by participative leadership, extensive training, employment security, engagement in continuous improvement, and other such positive features of the work context. The enabling context, combined with a clear understanding of the organization's mission, allows employees to experience identified motivation, that is, the internalization of values.' Further, de Treville and Antonakis similarly argued that 'a lack of autonomy over work timing and methods can be compensated for by other positive aspects of work design, including high levels of accountability (because employees can influence decisions), high skill variety and task identity (because employees are involved in repair and improvement), high levels of feedback (because employees have access to information), and high work facilitation (because lean production emphasizes the removal of obstacles to help performance).'

Further Readings on the JCM.
Bob Emiliani, *Real Lean*, Centre for Lean Business Management, 2007
Richard Hackman and Greg Oldham, *Work Redesign*, Addison Wesley, 1980
Sharon Parker, Beyond Motivation: Job and Work Design for Development, Health, Ambidexterity, and More, *Annual Review of Psychology*, 65:661-91, 2014
Suzanne de Treville and John Antonakis, 'Could Lean Production job design be intrinsically motivating? Contextual, configurational and levels-of-analysis issues', *Jnl of Operations Management*, 24, pp 99-124, 2006

4.4 Mager and Pipe on Performance Problems

This superb flowchart should be the starting point for any manager experiencing a shortfall in performance from any individual worker.

The Mager and Pipe flowchart, taken from their excellent book and reproduced with permission, has been a mainstay of one of the authors this book for over 30 years, and has been used in a variety of settings – manufacturing, service, health and academic. The latest version of the flow diagram is reproduced in the figure, but Mager and Pipe's whole book is a highly recommended, in-depth look at the questions raised.

The main questions are given in the flowchart, but these are subdivided into broad issues on the left and right of the flowchart, as follows, (A flavour is given on the sub-questions).

What is the performance discrepancy?
- The starting point is to describe the shortfall in performance. Not the solution (such as 'we have a safety training problem') but the performance (such as 'we are experiencing an increase in accidents on the shop floor'.)

Is the problem worth pursuing?

- Mager and Pipe suggest the shortfall be quantified in terms of time delay, damage, quality, extra supervision needed, loss of customers, etc. Perhaps draw a trend graph. Note that sunk costs and potential future costs should not be included.

Are the expectations clear?

- A fundamentally important question!

Are resources adequate?

- 'Resources' include time, information, expertise, as well as physical resources such as hardware and software.

Is the problem visible?

- A hidden problem will not be recognised, never mind solved. How to make a problem visible?

Can we apply fast fixes?

- Sometimes a fast fix is possible. This is similar to …
- This could include, is the task clearly specified?, (standard work?), are there adequate resources (such as equipment, and time)?, is the problem known to the employee?

Are the consequences 'right side up'?

- Is performance punishing? ('Joe always does such good work, we need to get him to work on the overload this weekend.')
- Is non-performance rewarding? ('Don't ask Sue to do that work. She is always late.')
- Does it make a difference, or are there consequences?

Do they already know how?

- Did the person once know how?
- If yes, has the task been done recently? (if no, provide practice or feedback)

Are there other clues?

- For instance, task simplification or obstacles. The 7 Lean 7 wastes, plus 5S, would be good aspects to consider.
- Only now should moving or replacing the person be considered! (The long list of prior checks above should prevent hasty blame taking place!)

Which solutions are best?

- Finally, we get into selecting the best option.
- And after, check the results.

Clearly there are overlaps with TWI Job Relations, but Mager and Pipe's flowchart includes aspects not directly covered by TWI JR. Why not use both together?

Note: These Questions refer to the Mager and Pipe flowchart. A general section on Questions is given in Section 9.10

Performance Analysis Flow Diagram*

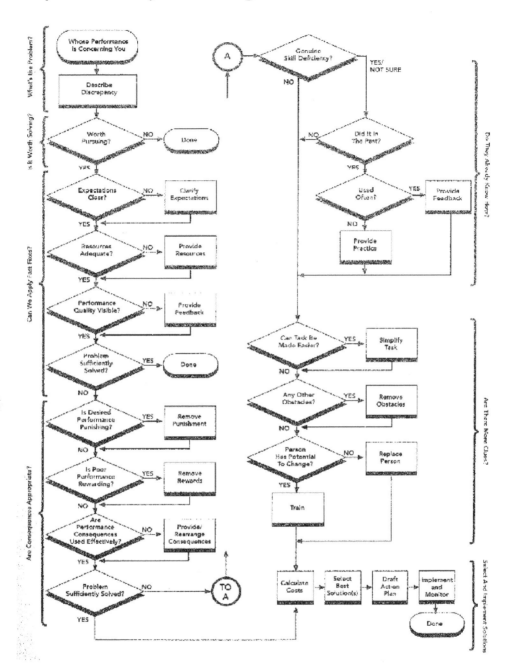

4.5 Kurt Lewin and Force Field Analysis

Kurt Lewin (d. 1947) was one of the most influential management psychologists; his legacy lives on. His work overlaps and reinforces Socio-Tech as discussed in the Systems chapter (Section 5.2). Lewin is widely recognised as being one of the fathers of Organization Development, or O.D.

OD was much in favour in change management from approximately the 1960's to the mid 2000's. From around the 1980's OD tended to fall out of favour with criticism that it was too focused on the individual rather than the organization, that it ignored organizational politics and power, and had unclear goals and values. Pettigrew said that OD was too rational, too linear, too prescriptive. Others criticised Lewin's three step model as applying only to groups, not to an organization. In OD, a 'culture of excellence' as put forward by Peters and Waterman (*In Search of Excellence*) It became and still remains popular despite several of the excellent companies they described falling into hard times. A CEO 'Halo Effect' developed but in turn was massively criticised by Phil Rosenzweig.

Of late, however, there seems to be have been a renaissance – in particular of the theories of Kurt Lewin. Lewin believed that planned change comprised four inter-related elements:

- Field theory (as discussed below).
- Group dynamics (a group's behaviour changes with conditions within and ouside. For a leader to be effective, she must first learn about her own behaviour, and be prepared to change that behaviour before attempting to change the behaviour of the group.)
- Action research. Education and change without hands-on experience is futile. A joint collaboration between 'experts' and workers, studying the jobs, the tools, the situation, and the people is required. Every organization is unique and the change process must be designed appropriately. (Surely a plea for 'Respect'.)(See also the section on Action Learning 10.21)
- The three-step model of change (unfreezing, change, refreezing).

Lewin viewed motivation as an interaction between the person and the specific situation. Written as $(B = f(p,e))$. That is behaviour is a function of person and environment.

Force Field analysis is a most useful and powerful tool suggested by Lewin that exemplifies the equation. In any change situation there will be forces for and against change – 'driving forces' and 'restraining forces'. Behaviour can only be understood in relation to all the forces acting at that moment on the situation. The forces emanating from the person or team and from the environment result in an equilibrium or 'status quo'. This can be shown in the simple but powerful Force Field Diagram. It allows the individual, organisational, and environmental factors to be included. Such a diagram should be set out for discussion in any change situation. It facilitates participation and discussion. Forces for and against the change are added to the diagram with the length of arrows roughly indicating the intensity of the force. Perhaps begin by a manager adding the forces for change and then eliciting forces against the change. Participants can add forces both for and against. The idea is to reduce the restraining forces, and to amplify the driving forces, by discussion. So a change is not just announced, it is discussed. Such participation increases the likelihood of acceptance. Experience in using Force Field is that several restraints are surfaced, without which would have limited or cancelled the success of the change. Bringing issues to the surface is an important aim. It is not the aim to make a decision, but a way to understand the system and to improve the chances of successful acceptance.

Force Field is a learning process both for those proposing and opposing the change. See the figure, as an example.

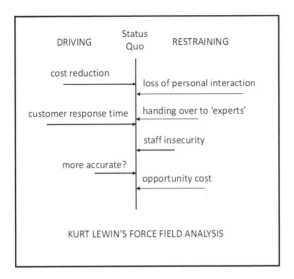

KURT LEWIN'S FORCE FIELD ANALYSIS

Of course, participation and respect are integral. Everyone participating should have a chance to contribute. It is also essential that follow up is required. It is fatal to do a Force Field exercise where the results are just taken away with no feedback or action.

Use a flip chart, even if this analysis is being done through Zoom or MS Teams. This could be done in stages: First, draw a vertical line to indicate the 'status quo'. Second, (management) should explain the driving forces for the change. Write them down on the chart. Third, solicit the restraining forces or reasons that will work against the proposed change. If done in a group setting, participants should first write down their own points privately on paper and then add them to the chart. The relative strengths of the forces can be determined by voting: each person has (say) two votes. Fourth, draw in the arrows with lengths corresponding to the number of votes. Fifth, discuss. Ensure all have a say, and limit length of talking by each participant.

Force Field analysis is a powerful tool for engagement in any transformation. For instance, if using Kotter's 8 step Transformation concept, (see below) use Force Field at every stage.

4.6 Change Models and Curves

Kotter's 8 Steps (or Errors)

John Kotter of Harvard Business School, undoubtedly one the greatest authorities on change, developed a by-now widely adopted Change model – a general model and not specifically for Lean. The 8 stages are shown in the table, based on Kotter's huge experience, and with our own comments added. In the original HBR article, Kotter listed 8 errors rather than 8 stages, and emphasized the significant challenge of each. These are certainly worth reading and re-reading. In the table below each Stage could be considered as a reason for failure if not adequately explored.

The original Kotter model is now more than 25 years old. The stages have become well accepted – so much so that some Lean managers we know are taking the steps (but not necessarily in sequence) without realising that they originate from Kotter. The 'gold' in Kotter's model are the 8 error areas that derive from the stages. A powerful checklist!

Stage	Content	More detail and comment
1	Create a sense of urgency	A burning platform is always there. If you doubt, look again! A SWOT-type analysis?
2	Recruit a guiding coalition	Multi-discipline. A line manager to lead. Remember the accountants and unions. A Champion? Not necessarily the top managers.
3	Form a vision for change	ONE specific, concise 'True North'. Requires many revisions.
4	Communicate the vision	Don't assume. Level-by-level buy-in. Two way. Force field? Credible! Reinforced. Walk the talk. Later, Kotter talked about 'enlisting a volunteer army'.
5	Remove obstacles	Some may have to go. Empower the rest. Do measures support the change? 'Drive out fear' said Deming. (But note: fear works two ways – boss fearing delegation, and subordinates fearing being thought stupid or cheeky.)
6	Generate Short-term wins	Demonstrate. Several short-term aims. Select 'difficult' area? Reward?
7	Consolidate (Don't declare victory too soon)	Spread the knowledge. Build on the momentum.
8	Anchor. 'Institute Change'	Learn specifically. Show. Next generation managers.

From a Lean perspective, there are cautions:

- The sequence of 8 Stages is a long process. Kotter's model is often presented as either 8 steps – and then seen as complete, or in a loop with Anchor feeding back into Creating urgency. Neither of these are satisfactory. Lean transformation is not a one-off project. Feeding back after 8 steps is just too long. Much change usually happens during the 8-step period, and revision and re-start is often necessary.
- Kotter's model is essentially top-down, in contrast to Hoshin-type planning where there is more emphasis on participation and level-by-level discussion, specific feedback, and buy-in.
- Kotter's HBR article uses 8 errors rather than 8 stages. This is far more satisfactory. The errors are worthy of serious consideration in any Lean transformation.
- Many PDCA / PDSA loops should occur at each stage of the sequence. The PDCA learning sequence is not sufficiently emphasised.
- The original model is 25+ years old. During that time, much instability has crept into operations – both manufacturing and service. Therefore the stages model is probably more applicable in Clear and in Complicated situations rather than in Complex environments. (See the CYNEFIN model in Section 8.9.)
- Many of the concepts mentioned in this book – for instance Problems, Motivation, Positive Psychology, Leadership – can be used alongside Kotter's Model. Kotter's model is therefore a 'meta model' providing a framework for many other concepts and tools.

Note: Later, Kotter followed the original book and articles by valuable books on Change such as *A Sense of Urgency* (2008), *Our Iceberg is Melting* (2020) and *That's not how we do it here.* (2016)

Change Curves

There are at least three change models that use a curve to show the stages that a group may expect during a change process. The three chosen here are the Kübler-Ross curve that can be applied to an individual or group, especially when an unexpected shock occurs or is anticipated (Covid?); the Katzenbach and Smith curve for project teams; and Peter Schotes' learning experience curve.

The Stages in the table refer to the Figure.

Concept or Model	Stage	Activity	Comment
Kübler-Ross	A	Shock	Surprise
	B	Denial	Disbelief
	C	Frustration	Anger or blame. Early recognition.
	D	Depression	A low point in energy and mood
	E	Experiment	Beginning to engage the reality
	F	Decision	Learning the new ways
	G	Integration	Becomes embedded
Katzenbach And Smith	B	Working Group	A group is not a team
	D	Pseudo Team	Need to work together recognised
	E	Potential Team	Loose dependencies developing
	F	Real Team	Goal and interdependencies clear
	G	High Performance Team	Successful working together
Scholtes	A	Illusion	The illusion of learning. Know the words. 'Knowing enough to be dangerous'(!)
	B	Realisation	Oh gee, we didn't really understand.
	D	Real Learning begins	Humility. The path ahead will be long and continuous.

Covid has meant that most organizations have been through a transition period and have had to adjust and to learn new ways. All three concepts have probably been relevant.

Kübler-Ross

Kübler-Ross was developed by Elisabeth Kübler-Ross to understand the stages of grief following the loss of a loved one, in her book *On Death and Dying*. (The five original stages are described as DABDA: Denial, Anger, Bargaining, Depression, Acceptance. Each stage is distinct.) The more general applicability to organisational change – 7 stages - was recognised later, and is given above. To judge by the large proportion of Lean transformation failures, perhaps a model based on death and dying is appropriate!

An interesting, and worrying, story about Kübler-Ross is told by Michel Baudin in his excellent Lean Blog. Michel tells of France Telecom that used the Kübler-Ross concept to downsize their workforce 'to shed 23,000 of its 130,000 employees. It also wanted to change the jobs of many of the remaining workers. Consultants trained the managers to expect their subordinates to follow the theory. Based on the "five stages of grief," they were going to move along the following orbit in energy versus satisfaction. It did not work. Tens of employees committed suicide and three top managers eventually went to prison for moral harassment.'

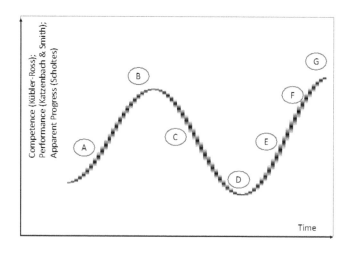

Change Models
and Curve

Adapted from
Kübler-Ross (1969)
Katzenbach and Smith
(1993)
Scholtes (1998)

Note:
The shape of the
curve is a composite
Sine Wave that differs
From the originals,
but attempts to
capture the essence

Peter Scholtes (d. 2009) worked closely with Deming for many years. His books are classics on Leadership and on Teams. The Scholtes curve has certainly been experienced by many in the Lean area – except that it recurs several times – just when you think you know it, another iteration opens up! Dan Jones calls this 'peeling the onion'.

4.7 Diffusion and Adoption Curves

Various authors have presented conceptual curves to show the distribution of people's attitude towards a change initiative. In the figure that follows, the curve is shown as a bell shaped, normal distribution. This is speculation, but is nevertheless conceptually useful. The area under the curve represents the total population of concern.

The Diffusion Curve

"The part of the diffusion curve from about 10% to 20% is the heart of the diffusion process. After that point, it is often impossible to stop the further diffusion of a new idea, even if one wished to do so."

- Innovators   2.5%
- Early adopters   13.5%
- Early majority   34%
- Late majority   34%
- Laggards   16%

"Early adopters are a more integrated part of the local social system than are innovators.... They serve as a role model for many other members of a social system.... The early adopter decreases uncertainty about a new idea by adopting it, & then conveying a subjective valuation of the innovation to near-peers through interpersonal networks."

From E.M. Rogers, *Diffusion of Innovations*
4th ed., The Free Press, 1995

Everett Rogers produced an early version in 1962 relating to innovation that was probably based on the adoption of farming techniques, such as the use of fertilizer, in the 1920's. (Rogers has refined his theory several times since.) Rogers thought that the factors driving the spread of a new idea were the innovation itself, communication channels, and the social system – all spreading gradually through time. Innovation (for example the use of a smart phone) starts with a small minority (called the innovators) and spreads through the population.

In a later version, Rogers included a 'chasm' (of understanding, suspicion, trust) that had to be breached before the early majority could be won over. So here the distribution is not continuous but is in two pieces – before and after the chasm. Rogers identified 4 stages and 5 influencing factors that determine the adoption of an innovation. These are important for Lean Transformation:

The Stages:

- *Awareness of need.* It is the wide experience in Lean that when an organisation in a sector adopts good Lean practice, others are forced to follow due to the advantages gained by the Lean innovator. Of course the classic case is cars, but other cases are computers (HP then Dell), supermarkets (Tesco), and aircraft (Boeing – at least initially!).
- *Decision to Adopt.* In Lean, often cost and quality. Sometimes lead-time.
- *Initial Use.* Perhaps a pilot, but a critical stage. Can the financials be shown? Also, who does it - Sensei led? Resourced? Distracted by other initiatives (Six Sigma? Automation? Redundancy?)
- *Continued Use.* Does management lose interest. Seen as a project?

The Factors:

- *Relative Advantage*
- *Compatibility* – with people and existing systems
- *Complexity.*
- *Trialability.* Can the innovations be tried out at little risk or cost? Roger identified this as a major factor. This is now common in software – distributing a free trial version, or even the full version valid for a limited period. In fact, the basis of much of Agile software development is moving from 'Waterfall' to Agile and Sprints. Can a low cost pilot be done using Lean? Several Lean Sensei's recommend this path.
- *Observability.* A classic conflict sometimes arises between the clear physical advantages (lead-time, quality) and the less-clear financials (obscured by overheads). A good reason to get management to the Gemba, and to encourage inter-plant visits. 'Seeing is believing.'

The Figure on the next page is a composite of several approaches.

Bicheno uses the analogy of a farmer. A Lean Champion is a farmer not a hunter. *Farmers* take the long view, and win in the long term. *Hunters* take the short view, get early gains but ultimately die out. Farmers are shepherds. Early adopters are found on the right-hand side of the figure. These people are 'gung ho' for change. They require very little convincing. But experience shows that there are two sub-groups here. *Dogs* are faithful, but are also intelligent. This valuable group will be the core of the change initiative. By contrast, *Lemmings* are easily up for change, any change, and, in a sense, are not the people you want. ('If he thinks it is a good thing, then it must be a bad idea.') They leap in just too quickly, without thought. *Horses* are the key group. They need guidance from a Lean champion. They require training to be broken in. Horses are also intelligent. Most horses work well in teams. The strategy to be adopted with horses depends on the situation. In normal circumstances the rider is in control, and the horse will take instruction except in emergencies. When there are fences and jumping is required, horse and rider act synergistically – the trick is to find the right balance between guidance by the rider and initiative and judgement by the horse. On a mountain hike, however, the best strategy for the rider is to let the horse take most of the control, relying on it to pick out the safest path. *Sheep* can be led by riders with horses and dogs. Generally they cannot be relied upon to get there without considerable guidance. Shepherding is required. Sheep are multi-functional providing wool and mutton. They are adapt to a wide range of climates. Sheep can also be led to an extent by *Goats*, either into the abattoir or into a lush field. (Note: Sheep is not a derogatory term – they are the backbone of much farming.) *Goats* are much more cautious. They have good reason to doubt, and some of those doubts are valuable insights. They climb trees and look around. But they can be made into valuable assistants. Finally *Jackals* cannot be trained. They eat goats and sheep, and may scare horses. They are the true anchor draggers. Note that in this analogy, groups traditionally regarded as anchor draggers and early adopters each have sub groups. These sub groups need to be distinguished. Beware of lemmings. Listen to the goats – they may have good, thoughtful reasons for any reluctance.

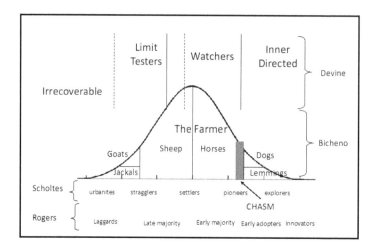

As an aside on what are here called Goats, Kegan and Lahey contend that a major reason why some people (and groups) are reluctant to change is 'competing commitments'. For example a manager is offered promotion but is committed to spending time with an ageing relative. His superior then makes a 'big assumption' that the commitments are mutually exclusive. This is destructive. To uncover this, Kegan and Lahey suggest that managers ask a series of questions. For instance, what would you like to see changed? Then, what commitments does your reservation imply? And, what are you doing that is keeping your commitment from being realised?, leading to working out a way to reconcile this big assumption with the change. Use Force Field analysis?

Peter Scholtes, who worked with Deming, uses different labels, as shown in the Figure.

Frank Devine, a UK based consultant, has a very useful related concept. The 'Inner Directed' are self-motivated and go along easily with changes. At the other extreme are 'Irrecoverables' that are negative and highly resistant. Ultimately, these may have to go. Towards the negative end are 'Limit Testers' who 'try their luck' and test the boundaries. Perhaps some frequently come late to work, others don't participate in problem solving, some always complain, yet others cut corners on standard work. 'The Watchers' are a central group that observe management reactions to the Limit Testers: are they allowed to get away with it, does their behaviour lead to any consequences? Depending on the managers' reaction the proportions of Watchers will shift to left or right. (Note an overlap with Mager and Pipe.) Of course, this implies that a management that adopts a passive role will fail. Ongoing understanding and communication are required.

Andrea Shapiro has a similar version. She built on the ideas of Gladwell (see below) to form a change management theory that has been used in several major Lean transformations in the UK. She uses the categories of 'apathetics', 'incubators', 'advocates' and 'resistors'. Thus advocates influence the apathetics, some of whom become incubators. Some incubators turn into advocates, others become resistors. Managing these flows is critical to achieving change.

The Adoption Curve and Key People

Malcolm Gladwell talks about *Mavens* – people who accumulate knowledge and get into the detail. But not only do they know, they want to tell – not in a know-all kind of way but in honest assessment; they like to help. They are 'students and teachers'. So mavens spread the good or bad news. If Lean is working or not working they will know, and will say so. People listen. Then there are *Connectors*, who have lots of contacts and put people in touch. And then there are *Salespeople*, who often unconsciously sell ideas. Generally these people are known, and they carry huge influence. Change will be easier if these people are made use of. Mavens, connectors and salespeople constitute a very small but highly significant number of people. The Tipping Point is reached quite suddenly when a critical mass is persuaded. Hence the importance of the adoption curve. Gladwell also talks about how change spreads – like a virus. There are three factors: content, carriers and context. *Content* is the value of the message itself. The ability to get things done. The value of the change will influence the support it receives. The message has to be powerful and relevant. *Carriers* are infected and move the message. They comprise the three types described earlier. *Context* is the environment – is it hostile or conducive to the virus. There are external and internal factors. Externally it is about the current climate in which the organization finds itself, and internally the support that the message receives from senior management is decisive.

Time to Adopt?

Delay can be a self-fulfilling prophesy. As Johann Goethe so elegantly wrote:

"Until one is committed there is always hesitancy, the chance to draw back, always ineffectiveness. Concerning all acts of initiative (and creation) there is one elementary truth, the ignorance of which kills countless ideas and splendid plans: that the moment one definitely commits oneself, then providence moves too. All sorts of things occur to help one that would not otherwise have occurred. A whole stream of events issue from the decision, raising in one's favour all manner of unforseen incidents and meetings and material assistance which no man could have dreamt would come his way."

(Thanks to Lee Flinders for bringing this excellent quote to our attention.)

It is unfortunately the case that in every organisation there are, undoubtedly, 'anchor draggers'- or apparent anchor draggers. But before dismissal, we would urge:

- Using the Mager and Pipe flowchart from the earlier section. Yes, there are performance problems' but why?
- Think about Ken Blanchard's statement: *"God does not make junk."* The person may well be 'junk' but what has led to that?

Take-up of Lean and Complex Systems

Adoption curves are interesting models. We should consider whether there is a 'tipping point' where, relatively suddenly, almost everyone becomes a Lean enthusiast? And, a related point, why is it that many organisations have taken on Lean despite some organisations being currently unsuitable either because of the people or the operating environment? Here, we can turn to Thomas Schelling (1921-2016) (Nobel Prize winner in economics and systems theory) and his theory on feedback loops and diversity. (Diversity here is cognitive- or opinion-based, not necessarily of origin, class or race.) What follows is speculation on our part, but has relevance for the spread of Lean both within and between organisations. This tipping point concept is also referred to as 'diffusion' or 'contagion'. (Virus?)

First, people are known to be strongly influenced by other people with whom they routinely come into contact with. Everyone in an organisation has a different tipping point with respect to enthusiasm for Lean. A tipping point for an organisation or site occurs when the proportion of people in the organisation who believe that Lean is a good idea reaches a critical level. This is equivalent to Rogers' 'late majority' or Bicheno's 'sheep'. Thereafter, take-up is easy – the doubters are won over by the majority. This is like the old saying: 'Getting ketchup from a bottle; some will come and then the lottle'.

By the way, systems people distinguish a 'tipping point', that happens suddenly, from 'path dependence' where large change grows more gradually. An example of a tipping point would be the supply chain chaos following the Suez Canal blockage in mid 2021. Path dependence would be the consequential impact as COVID-19 developed.

Path dependent change has been studied by systems people. Each individual has their own tipping point. For an individual, below the tipping they remain unconvinced but once the tipping point is reached the person changes her mind. For some, the tipping point may be very low, for others it may be high. Imagine that some intervention happens that convinces the very low tipping point people to become Lean enthusiasts. Now the proportion of Lean enthusiasts has increased. This in turn means that others now reach their tipping points. And so it grows, until all but the die-hards or extreme anchor-draggers are won over. There is a positive feedback loop. Growth of the number of Lean enthusiasts may initially be very slow but the rate of adoption grows rapidly – sometimes unexpectedly so. So 'small wins' demonstrations are a good idea. It can also happen between organisations when success at one organisation convinces others that Lean is a good idea. Lean may be a good idea at some but not at others. This may explain a number of Lean failures.

This tipping point sequence can happen in reverse. Imagine many people are keen on Lean but some negative event turns people off. The proportion of sceptics grows, and the negative influence grows. This convinces others to become sceptical, and so it grows.

Note that if there is no diversity of opinion, Lean will not take off unless there is a huge change effort. For example, if everyone has the same tipping point at (say) 60% then all 60% will first have to be convinced before everyone is won over. Also, if Lean begins demonstrably to fail, growth can go into reverse as a small but growing minority of sceptics gradually convince others that Lean is not working….

In the next section, we consider queues. Queues are also subject to rapid exponential growth.

4.8 Queues: Muda, Muri, Mura and Kingman

Queues (or Waiting Lines) are the most widely occurring phenomenon in Operations Management, including Lean. They occur in manufacturing, service, government, and health. When Ohno said about TPS *"All we are trying to do is to reduce the time from order to cash"*, he was really talking about the sequence of queues. Understanding the human implications for queue reduction is the intention here. Queues take up space, cost money (if the queue is of inventory), annoy customers, and importantly directly affect quality because of the time delay to pick up problems.

Refer to the Figure. It shows relative queue lengths against utilization, for various values of the coefficient of variation, CV. (A CV of zero would mean no variation; values of between 0.8 and 1.5 are common in service and manufacturing.) This figure would apply almost everywhere – from call centre to highway traffic to car assembly.

Notice…

- The exponential shape. Queues are very small at low utilization levels, but rise steeply above 80% or 85%. Beware!
- Variation (the CV value) makes little difference to queue length at low utilization levels but makes a significant difference at high utilization levels.
- If variation can be reduced, this would make a big difference at high utilization but little difference at low utilization levels.

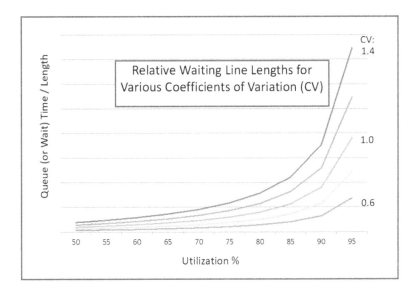

The curves shown can all be calculated from Kingman's equation. (The actual equation is given after the readings.) There are three factors that influence queue length: the arrival variation, the process variation, and the utilization. For example, the arrival variation could capture the pattern of customer or order arrivals, and process variation could capture the customer service times or assembly times. Utilization is load divided by capacity, or the time taken to do the work divided by the total time available.

Readers will be familiar with 'Muda' or waste. Mura is variation. Muri is utilization (or more accurately 'overload' – or high utilization). The cause of much Muda (or queues in this case) is Mura and Muri. So Kingman's equation includes mura, muri and the muda of queues or delays.

And: utilization = load/capacity = (Value demand + unnecessary demand) / (base capacity – waste)

Where:

Value demand is first time actual demand that 'customers are prepared to pay for'.
Unnecessary demand, or failure demand, results when rework or re-visits occur.

(Note: See also Seddon's "Check" model in Chapter 5 on Systems.)
Base capacity is the capacity of the production facility if everything works perfectly.
Wastes detract from capacity and include the 7 classic Lean wastes.

A Caution: Shifting Bottlenecks

Kingman's equation and the extensions is one of the most powerful and illuminating concepts in Lean. It is most suitable in situations of stability, where demand varies only a little, where there is process stability and where the product or customer mix is fairly stable. Examples would be a call centre, car assembly, fast food, process industry and repetitive medical situations. However, if the highest utilization resource shifts due to product mix changes, breakdowns, or quality issues, there may not be sufficient time to establish the queue characteristics.

Utilization and Efficiency

During the COVID pandemic the effects of utilization were dramatically illustrated in Italy. Lombardy and Veneto are closely situated geographically and share similar demographics and wealth. They also have similar health care systems. During the pandemic the two regions had vastly different mortality rates. As expected, mortality rates in both regions increased as utilization of intensive care units (ICUs) increased becoming noticeable at about 40% utilization. But then, in Lombardy, the increase became dramatic when utilization exceeded about 50% reaching nearly 5.5 deaths per 100,000. In Veneto, meanwhile, ICU utilization remained below 50% and mortality rates remained nearly flat at fewer than 1.3 deaths per 100,000. (Reported by Matthias Holweg, in an HBR newsletter, June 2020). Likewise, we all have experienced dramatic increases in queues on a highway when 3 lanes are reduced to 2 by roadworks.

Implications for people at work

- Don't plan for 100% utilization! Excessive queues will result! Beware of utilization above about 85% (Even Toyota has 55 seconds work content in a 60 second takt time. Line stop, or Andon could not work if there was 100% utilization.)
- Lower utilization not only reduces queues but allows for flexibility, recovery, and innovation.
- There are two types of variation – arrival and process. They are equally weighted in Kingman's equation. Many Lean programs give much attention to reducing process variation (often related to people) but ignore arrival variation! Customer arrival variation can often be reduced by providing information, incentives, and priorities. Some arrival variation is self-imposed by, for example batching, quantity discounts, or 'end-of-moth hockey stick' reporting. Such changes are often hugely cost-effective.
- Ignoring arrival variation, but focusing all attention on process variation reduction, would be like a marriage of one person. Ridiculous!
- 'Variation is the enemy' at higher utilization levels. Standard work and 5S will pay off.
- If utilization is low, improvement programs that aim at reducing variation (such as Six Sigma) will probably yield meagre results.
- Demand is of two types – value and unnecessary. Many (particularly service organisations) don't even know how much failure demand they are experiencing. Reducing failure demand can yield very impressive results particularly at higher utilization levels. Such reduction is strongly dependent on people's engagement and motivation.
- Ignoring failure demand risks the level of total demand becoming regarded as normal value-added work! The waste comes to be ignored - but the opportunity is huge!
- Reducing unnecessary demand > reduces load > reduces utilization > reduces queues EXPONENTIALLY

- Reducing waste > increases capacity > reduces utilization > reduces queues EXPONENTIALLY
- Hence from these last two, there results an exponential 'people payoff'!

Further Reading on Change Curves and Queues.

John Bicheno and Matthias Holweg, *The Lean Toolbox*, 5th edition, PICSIE Books, 2016 – especially chapters on 'The Science of Lean' and Innovation.
Suzanne de Treville and John Antonakis, 'Could Lean Production job design be intrinsically motivating? Contextual, configurational and levels-of-analysis issues', *Jnl of Operations Management*, 24, pp. 99-124, 2006
Bob Emiliani, *Real Lean*, Centre for Lean Business Management, 2007
Malcolm Gladwell, *The Tipping Point*, (Chapter 'The Law of the Few'), Abacus, 2000,
Richard Hackman and Greg Oldham, *Work Redesign*, Addison Wesley, 1980
Robert Kegan and Lisa Lahey, 'The Real Reason People Won't change', *Harvard Business Review*, November 2001, pp. 84-92.
John Kotter, *Leading Change*, Harvard Business School Press, 1995; and "Leading Change: Why Transformation Efforts Fail', *Harvard Business Review,* May/June 1995
www.kotterinc.com
Edward Lawler and Christopher Worley, *Built to Change*, Jossey Bass Wiley, 2007
Kurt Lewin, *Field Theory in Social Science*, Harper and Row, 1951
Robert Mager and Peter Pipe, *Analysing Performance Problems*, Revised 3rd edition, Center for Effective Performance, 1997. (Obtain directly from www.magerconsortium.com/publications)
Scott Page, *The Model Thinker*, Hachette / Basic Books, 2018
Everett Rogers, *Diffusion of innovations* (5th ed.). Free Press, 2003 (An excellent, and long, discussion on Rogers' and others' ideas on innovation is to be found on Wikipedia.)
Peter Scholtes, *The Leader's Handbook*, McGraw Hill, 1998
Andrea Shapiro, *Creating Contagious Commitment*, Strategy Perspective, 2003
B.F. Skinner, *Beyond Freedom and Dignity*, Alfred Knopf, 1971

Note: Kingman's Equation: Average queue time = $T \times (CVa^2 + CVp^2) / (U / (1 - U))$

Where;

   CVa is coefficient of arrival variation; CVp is coefficient of process variation
   U is utilization expressed as a decimal; T is average process time.

Chapter 5
Systems, Systems Thinking, Socio-Technical Systems, and Complexity

"Without conscious attention to systems, we will focus on people. That is what we have been trained to do. Rather than understanding and improving our systems, we seek better results by exhorting and seeking to motivate our people. When we don't understand systems we equate improving our people with improving our system."... Peter Scholtes, (long-standing Deming associate), 1998

Why This Chapter?

'Systems thinking' has become synonymous with Lean. This is most welcome provided, of course, that the term is understood and not mis-used. Sometimes 'systems thinking' is too narrowly interpreted or understood, perhaps limited to Value Stream Mapping or thoughts from Deming.

In the last two decades or so there has been much attention to problem solving and in particular to A3 problem solving. There is much to be said for this. A3 has often been limited to what systems people would call 'hard systems' – this does not mean 'difficult' but rather to situations where people issues are not the focus. But there is a continuum of problem types from hard to soft, and as soft or people issues become more important, or wider issues become prominent, so the importance of wider systems thinking becomes necessary.

But...
We live in a VUCA world (Volatility, Uncertainty, Complexity, Ambiguity). Several recent events have illustrated this – COVID, the Tsunami hitting Japan, 9/11, Brexit, the relatively sudden importance of global warming. And the effect of the internet on retail. All of these have had an impact on the world of Lean. We can't control the emergence complex events, but we can seek to understand and then adjust so that negative effects are reduced.

So, yes, we certainly need an appreciation of Systems Thinking but today we also need an appreciation of Complexity. Complexity is also discussed in Section 8.9 on Cynefin.

This chapter gives an overview of and an introduction to aspects of systems thinking and complexity that are more applicable for people aspects of Lean. It should be said upfront that both 'Systems' and 'Complexity' are large and developing areas of study.

5.1 Systems: Background

Systems theory pre-dates Lean and some of it has little to do with Lean. The literature is huge – for an overview, see Jackson. In the sections that follow only 'human activity' or 'purposeful' systems are considered. There are other types – natural and mechanical systems are examples – that are not considered. A little history is useful.

Fred Taylor broke jobs down into small elements and studied the elements in detail. It was called 'scientific management', which was appropriate since science has mightily progressed, and still progresses, by reduction combined with experimentation. Taylor's assumption was that the elements could then be successfully combined. By contrast, says Peter Checkland, Emeritus Professor of Systems at Lancaster University, 'The systems approach seeks not to be reductionist.' ('seeks' because it is challenging.) As has been said, if you study a dog by taking it apart and studying the elements, the first thing you get is a non-working dog!

'The Blind Men and the Elephant'. A thousand-year-old (?) classic story from India describes how a group of blind men set out to describe a strange beast – an elephant, it turns out. One describes the trunk, another the tusks, a third the ears, and so on. They come to blows because each thinks his view is correct. They then collaborate to learn the true picture and each learns he was only partially correct.

Another example: If the aim is to reduce lead time by (say) 20%, it does not mean reducing EVERY STAGE in the chain by 20%. In fact, some stages may have to INCREASE in the time taken in order for overall lead time to reduce.

Ohno said, "*All we are trying to do is to reduce the time from order to cash*". Note the systemic nature of this statement. Lean is not about manufacturing or service but about the system that brings both of these together. Toyota is a 'systems' company rather than a manufacturing company. Toyota learned their systems craft from, amongst others, Deming. Ohno saw economies of flow rather than economies of scale.

The 'Systems' movement goes back long before the word Lean came into being. For instance, Jan Smuts in 1926 proposed 'Holism' ('the whole is greater than the sum of the parts'). Creativity on levels from cell to society comes from the 'intermingling of fields'. (Similarly, the science writer Stephen Johnson says that much innovation has come from 'the adjacent possible'). And von Bertalanffy talked about open systems in biology as early as 1950.

It is perhaps a pity that the word 'system' has been used instead of 'holism'. 'System' is so widely used a word that often it has no relationship to the 'systems thinking' as described here.

During WW2, the British and later the Americans developed 'Operations Research' (O.R.). The original teams were highly eclectic and multidisciplinary and were hugely successful in developing solutions to complex problems. It was certainly systems thinking. After the war and still continuing today, O.R. and OR/MS (for management science) became highly mathematical and statistical, much of it focused on 'optimisation'. (Russell Ackoff, systems 'guru', wrote a famous critique in 1979 'The Future of Operational Research is Past', an article that many 'experts' in Lean and Six Sigma should read!). This is not to suggest that O.R. techniques such as linear and dynamic programming, game theory, Markov chains, Bayes theorem, and more recently the widespread and growing use of algorithms are not useful to a Lean manager. They certainly often are essential. But the human element, and multidisciplinary insights, have too often been downplayed.

Non-Systems Thinking

In Jeffrey Pfeffer's book *What Were They Thinking?* numerous examples are given of top management from major corporations adopting practices that could be termed non-systems thinking. (Pfeffer does not use the term systems thinking.) Examples are top-down announcements of unilateral cutting of staff or wages when a company gets into financial trouble, believing in driving staff with threats and rewards, or introducing IT systems based on 'golf-club' conversations. These practices ignore the impact on the system in favour of short-term 'solutions', and with minimal discussion except at board level. They prove ineffective, even disastrous, for the organization - sometimes immediately and almost invariably in the medium term – although, unfortunately, not always disastrous for the executive himself. "*Systems bite back*" says John Gall.

5.2 Socio-Tech

An early challenge to Taylorism was the 'Socio-Tech' investigations by Emery and Trist who studied the introduction of longwall mining in Yorkshire coal mines in the 1950's. Longwall machines involving continuous mining that took out whole coal seams using far less labour were seen as the way forward. The results were disappointing. The investigation revealed that the social system had been broken – miners could no longer mutually support for safety, support, and productivity. It was the total system, not just the new machines that was important. Group tasks were replaced by individual tasks. Hence was born 'socio-tech'.

'Socio' factors include psychological and social needs, formal and informal communication including reporting, skills, and the work itself. 'Tech' factors include machines and equipment, processes, maintenance, materials and also, from a Lean perspective, layout, flow and ergonomics. All need to 'gel' together.

Eric Trist (1978) compared the two paradigms (Taylorism and 'Socio-Tech'), including:
- Technology first vs. Social and technical together
- People as machine extensions vs. people complement machines
- Narrow tasks and simple skills vs. multiple, broad skills
- Many levels and autocratic vs. flatter and participative
- The sole purpose is the organisation vs. the organisation and the people.

This awakening led Emery and Trist to the 'open system' viewpoint. It is the inter-connections, and the feedback – both internal and external – that is important. A learning system. Of course, this is just what the Wright brothers did in developing the airplane, not as individual parts but all parts working together, including the pilot.

Weisbord says there are two 'profound' lessons from the Socio-Tech studies. (These have big implications for Lean managers and consultants!)
1. '...given some minimal guidance, most work groups produce (work) designs (that are) 85 to 90 percent congruent with what the best outside pros can do – with vastly more commitment to implement.' (Our comment: Wow! The exact opposite of Taylor!)
2. A work design should not be thought of as a 'big bang', all-at-once activity. Managers should learn to give only 'minimal critical specifications' and then leave design and development to the group. Weisbord says that the best engineers have failed to figure out every contingency, so 'you and I' should not try. Doing so reduces the possibility for 'learning, self-control, and ownership. Paradoxically ...slow is fast, less is more.' (Our comment: This gels with Peter Senge (see later). 'Well-designed by experts' examples include Three Mile Island, Chernobyl, Boeing's problems with the 787, Skylab astronauts switching off the radio from Houston to limit the number of instructions, and Captain Sullenberger's successful landing of his aircraft in the Hudson River. See also the 'Serious Systems Fun' section later in this chapter.

In contrast to Taylor, Emery's list of factors for satisfying work (1964) are:
- Variety and challenge
- Contributions to decision making
- Feedback and learning
- Mutual support and respect
- Wholeness and meaning
- Room to grow.

Surely, this is a list for every Lean aspiring organisation! This theme is further taken up in the Organisation Chapter.

As a follow up, the Tavistock Institute in 1995 produced a guide to teamwork in manufacturing that proposed that for a successful change initiative 7 aspects needed to be considered simultaneously. 'Change Everything at Once!'. These are:

- Strategy and organisation structure. (Clear purpose, the starting point.)
- Job design (see Job Characteristics Model, Section 4.3)
- Employee and industrial relations (see Section 7.2 on Engagement).
- Manufacturing and engineering systems (for instance, cell layout, problem solving, waste reduction and including 'muda, muri, mura'; level scheduling).
- Quality systems (for instance, quality at source, andon, poka-yoke, standard work, PDCA)
- IT ('Lean IT' to support flow, quality, problem identification, inventory, etc.)
- Financial and accounting systems ('Lean accounting' and measures)

Certainly a tall order, but a list that may help explain why so many Lean transformations have failed to meet expectation. A reminder of what 'systems thinking' really implies!

Some concepts from Systems Theory that are of particular relevance to Human Lean include:

5.3 Feedback

Feedback has been mentioned several times in this book. It is an essential feature of coaching and mentoring, of Kata, and of A3 problem solving. (By the way, 'coaching' is narrower, relating to improving work or performance; 'mentoring is wider, taking in life aspirations over a longer term.)

Systems have feedback loops. Many feedback loops have delays. So it takes time for success or failure to develop. Small things can set off chain reactions in connected loops, which may amplify. For instance, the actions of a manager who ignores waste, whilst walking past the waste, sends out a message about the importance of waste. Loops may have several stages, as in a hierarchical production control system. Drawing out some of these causal loop diagrams can be thought provoking. Understanding that there are many loops at work at any time, and that they take time to work through is important for Lean transformation.

"A real irony is that respect for people requires that people feel the pain of critical feedback.... ..the job of a leader is not to put them in positions to fail, but to put them in positions where they must work hard to succeed and still see how they could have been even better."   Akio Toyoda. CEO of Toyota

Seddon and Caulkin make the point that 'the power and originality of the TPS lies in the fact that the feedback or learning loop connects downstream to the external or internal customer, whereas in conventionally managed organizations feedback connects upstream, to the manager.' These are learning cycles which enable frontline employees to be part of the processes of decision making and improvement.

Feedback is a skill. Here are a few pointers.

- Feedback must always be constructive, never destructive.

- Effective feedback must be specific. General feedback, such as 'You have done well' can come to be regarded as meaningless. Specific feedback requires close observation and familiarity, both of which add to the credibility and value of the feedback. This is directly in line with 'evidence-based' thinking.

- Deming's 94/6 rule is a golden nugget. That is 94% of problems ultimately lie with the system, and only 6% with the person. It makes sense, therefore, if there are issues, to begin with the system. What are the barriers that are limiting the person from achieving his or her goals?

- Following Deming, Adam Grant discusses two types of conflict: Task and Relationship. Although Grant was dealing with conflicting opinions it is very useful for feedback. The idea is to separate tasks from relationships. High performing groups spend lots of time on task conflict, but keep personality out of the equation. Task disagreement is very healthy – a great source of innovation. Some of the most innovative groups argue extensively over tasks – new products, web design, improvement. Low performing groups are the reverse – tackling personalities rather than tasks.

- The Mager and Pipe performance flowchart (given in the Eight Models chapter) is an excellent checklist to go through before giving feedback.

- If you have not already done so, take a look at the Expectancy Model and The People Trilogy in the Eight Models chapter.

- Push and Pull Feedback: According to an excellent section first published on 2 February 2021 on Knowledge@Wharton, performance, after receiving personal feedback, actually gets worse one-third of the time. If feedback is positive, there is no need to change but if negative there is often scepticism, discouragement, or it is seen as unfair. So, Wharton academics suggest "pulling" is a better idea than "pushing." (Sound like Lean?) "Pulling entails teaching, coaching, and developing employees rather than pushing—or correcting—them. Pulling says, "Here's how to get ahead in this company… Pushing says, 'You're not doing very well.' In employees' eyes, it's likely to be the difference between challenge or inspiration and criticism."

- Reassurance should be given to new employees that most will find it difficult to attain good performance early on. Hence coaching feedback should be expected by new employees aimed at narrowing any performance gap.

- Similarly, Gilovich and Ross recommend that honest feedback always be given, but explaining any shortfall by saying that such shortfall is being judged against best-of-the best, or world class. So it is not criticism, it is positive aspiration.

- It is good psychology to begin feedback with the positive. At a Gemba meeting, begin with the Green items – particularly those Green items that were previously Red. Show recognition and appreciation of achievement. But beware – undeserved or excessive praise is counterproductive. (Don't get a reputation for always chasing, never praising!)

- Bland feedback is a temptation for the mentor or coach. A Mentor may find it less awkward to avoid giving criticism. They may think that is the route to popularity. But by so doing the mentee is deprived of an opportunity to learn.

- Deliberate practice is recommended by Anders Ericsson. Practice does not make perfect unless accompanied by feedback. Simply trying harder will not work by itself. Deliberate feedback, according to Ericsson, involves immediacy – or as soon as possible, pushing people to get outside their comfort zone, striving for things that are not easy, identifying best in class performance as a benchmark, and clearly identifying the particular skills that are lacking – specific not general.

- Mindset. Carol Dwek's concept of a Growth Mindset and a Fixed Mindset were discussed in the Eight Models chapter. Dwek's research shows clearly that encouraging a Growth Mindset can have a very positive outcome. Encourage the YET mindset ('You may not be able to do it YET'). Dwek recommends praising effort rather than achievement.

- TWI and key points. TWI Job Instruction for a task includes main steps, key points, and reasons for the key points. Unless the reasons for following the key points are clearly understood, motivation and growth will be lacking.
- Instead of feedback sessions, would an Apprentice Model be more appropriate? In other words, have the mentee 'study at the feet of the master' for prolonged periods. Of course, apprenticeships have been used for centuries. The apprentice learns much from osmosis and direct observation rather than instruction.
- The One Minute Manager. Blanchard and Johnson's famous million-copy bestseller emphasises frequent (daily) feedback with one minute on goal setting, one minute on praising, and one minute on 'reprimands'. Reprimands take place immediately and involve telling the person what they did wrong, but then boosting their confidence about their capability. Also, in line with Deming and Grant above, it is about the task, not the person.
- Finally, have feedback on your feedback. 360 degree feedback or anonymous feedback on the feedback.

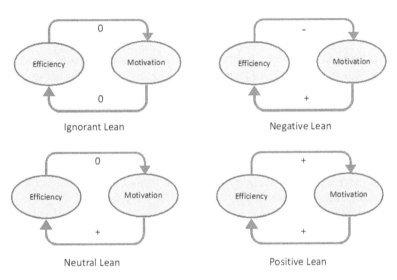

Adapted with permission from Wallace Hopp
'Positive Lean: merging the science of efficiency with the psychology of work'
International Journal of Production Research, 2018, Vol. 56, Nos. 1–2, 398–413

Wallace Hopp, in his excellent article on Positive Lean shows four feedback loops linking motivation with efficiency. In the 'Ignorant Lean' scenario, efficiency does not drive motivation, nor does motivation drive efficiency. The links are not established in workers' minds. This is a management failure. There is no improvement. In 'Negative Lean', workers are motivated to make improvements, but this backfires because, as a result, workers are dismissed or given more work. Negative Lean represents the classic case of Taylorism gone bad – a system in which improvements in efficiency come at the expense of worker satisfaction. Performance eventually declines to zero. In 'Neutral Lean' workers are motivated to make improvements but recognition is withheld. Slow improvement results. In 'Positive Lean' workers are motivated to make improvements and are given recognition (intrinsic or extrinsic) that encourages further motivation. Improvement is accelerated. 'Only the Positive Lean scenario in is self-sustaining. Improvements in all other scenarios must be driven from the outside, either by forcing efficiency improvements or by exogenously enhancing motivation.'

On feedback, one of the authors of this book (Noel) is reminded of meeting a Toyota Production Manager many years ago in Kentucky. In the course of conversation, the manager outlined how his annual performance review was based on three elements of equal significance; (a) How he applied the Toyota Production System, (b) How he developed his people and (c) Did he achieve his production targets.

Further Readings.
Wallace J. Hopp (2018) Positive lean: merging the science of efficiency with the psychology of work, *International Journal of Production Research*, 56:1-2, 398-413, DOI: 10.1080/00207543.2017.1387301

5.4 System Boundary

An important concept, and vitally important in Lean, is that of the boundary of the system under consideration. West Churchman, in 1968, made the point that a system boundary was not necessarily physical but a 'mental construct' about who and what to include. Too narrow a boundary risks suboptimization. Too wide becomes unmanageable. There will always be systems within systems.

In 2020, Dan Heath in his book *Upstream* gave the example of the travel company Expedia where it was discovered that 58% of calls to their all centre made a second call for further explanations or details. This was a huge surprise, amounting to roughly 20 million calls or $100 million. But how to reduce this? Move the system boundary upstream so as to get to the cause of duplicate calls. In Lean parlance, the value stream does not start when a call is received and thereafter mapping the next steps downstream, but instead should begin with an analysis of types of demand, including the reasons for duplicate calls. After a detailed analysis of demand types, a 'war room group' was set up with the specific aim of eliminating duplicate calls or the reasons why customers sought additional support. In other words, get it right the first time. It took time to do, but eventually duplicate calls were reduced to near zero.

Dan Heath explains that a cause of the duplicate calls was that the company organisation – with marketing to attract customers, the product team to complete reservations, and IT to keep the system running included no group to ensure no duplicate calls. A system boundary issue! A major system boundary problem is 'It's not my problem' explains Heath. The statement may be stated out load, but far more common is the unstated attitude, whether deliberate or simply unconsidered.

Dan Heath labels this approach 'Upstream'. John Seddon, in his 2003 book *Freedom from Command and Control*, proposed eliminating 'failure demand' – 'a demand caused by a failure to do something or to do something right for the customer'. (More detail is given below under Seddon's Check Model.) Study demand at the point that it arises, says Seddon. In other words, be sensitive to the appropriate boundary of the problem. It is the well-established maxim: prevention is better than cure, - a standard approach in Lean towards defects and maintenance. (Failure demand, is also discussed in the Eight Models Chapter under Queues: Muda, Muri, Mura and Kingman.)

Further Readings.
Dan Heath, *Upstream,* Bantam Press, 2020

5.5 System Concepts and Major Contributors

Kurt Lewin. In the 1920's, Kurt Lewin, whose work is discussed in the Chapter on Eight Models, proposed his 'Field Theory' of change. A change must consider all relevant personal and environmental factors and understanding these factors grows with the change process. Increasing the involvement of participants in a system increases the likelihood of changing their behaviour. An appropriate approach should be developed internally with participation by those who will be affected by the change. Hence Lewin's famous statement, *"you cannot understand a system until you try to change it."*

Hard and Soft Systems.

'Hard systems engineering' would include systems such as an engine, car, computer network, or a suspension bridge. The human aspect tends to be downplayed. Today, many former university departments of Industrial Engineering have re-branded as 'Industrial and Systems Engineering'. Much of this change follows traditional OR/MS. See below under Ackoff.

'Soft Systems', started by Peter Checkland at Lancaster university in the 1970's, emphasized not optimisation but 'moving from a mess to an improved mess'. Checkland's methodology uses the excellent CATWOE considerations:

- Clients: customers, yes, but for some a 'customer' may not be appropriate – a prison, a hospital.
- Actors: all the categories of the 'players' – managers, workers, unions, suppliers, distribution workers, contractors, 'temps', and others. Some may become 'victims' of the system, other may be 'beneficiaries'
- Transformation: Inputs, Process, Outputs. Not a value stream map, but a list of characteristics. (Six Sigma would call this SIPOC). Constraints could also be considered here.
- Weltanschauung or 'world view' or beliefs. Culture. Every system has its own, mainly unstated, beliefs and biases. Hard to determine the set, but be assured these world views will have a major influence.
- Owners: Perhaps the shareholders, investors, the government, the debtors. Who are the real owners who 'call the shots' (the managers?)?
- Environment. Increasingly relevant! (social, technical, economic, political, natural)

Note that each category would contain several possible elements so as to help 'appreciate' the system's structure and process. (The 'what is'.) 'Root definitions' (RD's) are proposed (usually more than one – reflecting several viewpoints).

For instance, a RD might be 'A system to design a Yaris that will appeal to motorsport enthusiasts' (impossible, one might say, but it has been done with the GR-Yaris!). Another might be 'A parallel system to allow traditional Toyota Yaris design thinking to merge with the aspirations of young drivers seeking performance at reasonable price.' (These alternate RD's are made up, of course.)

From the RDs, and bearing in mind CATWOE, conceptual models are drawn. Start with a blank sheet of paper with only the RD at the top. These 'what might be' models (called 'rich pictures') are developed to answer the question 'What are the minimum necessary activities to achieve the RD? The best conceptual models are developed by inter-disciplinary teams – from a diverse group of the actors. Activities begin with verbs – e.g. 'analyse xxxx' and not nouns – e.g. 'Supplier'. The activities show what needs to be done to achieve the RD.

This is a radical departure from the idea of starting with a value stream map drawn from the existing system. It allows a total re-think.

Thereafter the conceptual model(s) is compared with the existing system – if there is one. Then, a list of 'feasible desirable changes' is developed in discussions with the relevant parties – owners, managers, engineers, workers. Finally, the implementation plan is developed – but continually reviewed.

Ackoff

Russell Ackoff (1919 – 2009) was a distinguished, profound and witty professor of systems. His books and videos remain classics, which every Lean-aspiring manager should access.

First, Ackoff distinguished 'Purposeful Systems' (such as are discussed here) from natural systems (such as eco-systems) and physical systems (such as an engine).
According to Ackoff, two of the most important properties of a system are;
- Every system has properties that it loses when separated from the system.
- Every system has properties that none of its parts do.

'Machine Age' thinking involves (1) decomposition of that which is to be explained; (2) explanation of the properties of the parts taken separately; (3) aggregating these explanations into an explanation of the whole.' This would be typical of many Scientific management and improvement projects!

Systems thinking reverses the order: '(1) Identifying the whole of which the thing to be explained is a part; (2) Explaining the properties of the containing whole; (3) Explain the behaviour or properties of the thing to be explained in terms of its roles or functions within its containing whole." *Ackoff's Best*, p16/17).

Another Ackoff gem: Effectiveness is efficiency multiplied by value. "Intelligence is the ability to increase efficiency; wisdom is the ability to increase effectiveness." Of particular interest in today's AI world is Ackoff's thought that, in principle, efficiency can be programmed by computer but effectiveness requires judgment and is never independent of the judge. (*Ackoff's Best*, p 170/171)

An important idea from Ackoff: *"Successful problem solving requires finding the right solution to the right problem. We fail more often because we solve the wrong problem than because we get the wrong solution to the right problem."* And *"Getting the right problem wrong is better than getting the wrong problem right."* (Hear Ackoff say this in various U Tube videos.)

Ackoff's Fables are witty, amusing, and often of great relevance for Human Lean. Samples, from *The Art of Problem Solving....*
- "One can enjoy a game played by others, but one can only have fun by playing it oneself." (Gemba, participation, consultants?)
- "The end of one problem may be the beginning of another." (Improvement never ends. 'Peeling the onion' says Dan Jones.)
- "Irrationality is usually in the mind of the beholder, not in the mind of the beheld." (Change not working? Blame yourself, not others!)

Ackoff's witty but serious 'f-Laws' are a series of sharp observations: Samples, from *Management f-Laws...*
- 'The lower the rank of managers, the more they know about fewer things. The higher the rank of managers, the less they know about many things.' (No 13) (We are reminded here of the parable: 'The scientist knows more and more about

less and less until he knows practically everything about almost nothing. The manager knows less and less about more and more until he knows practically nothing about almost everything.' (!))

- 'Managers who don't know how to measure what they want settle for wanting what they can measure.' (No 51) (A widespread problem in the Lean world. Measure schedule attainment as defined by the organisation but not the customer.)
- 'A corporation's external boundaries are generally much more penetrable than its internal ones.' (No 60). (Silos between departments? Include detailed info flows in a value stream map!)

Deming.

In line with the open systems concept, Deming in 1950 produced his now famous diagram linking suppliers, production, testing, distribution, consumers, consumer research and design in a feedback loop, showing their inter-dependency. The goal of management is to support and create positive interactions. The entire system needs to be 'optimised' together rather than the individual parts. In fact, improving individual parts without reference to the whole can make things worse. (In Lean, speeding up an individual machine may lead to overproduction.)

Stafford Beer

Stafford Beer (1926 – 2002) developed the Viable System Model or VSM (note this is not Value Stream Mapping) over several decades as a practising manager and academic. VSM has a large following in the IT and public sectors. The model is based on the human body which is 'viable' in as far as it responds to changes, both internal and external. The three basic elements are the Operation (organs and muscles that carry out the work; the 'metasystem' – brain and nervous system that plan and coordinate; and the environment.) VSM works on five levels (S1 to S5) with decisions and controls being carried out at the lowest appropriate level, often subconsciously but transferred to higher levels dependent on circumstance. For instance, reacting to changes in temperature in the human body is carried out first at lower subconscious levels – by sweat or shivering – then with heart and lungs – and may only reach top level consciousness if warranted – perhaps by putting on a sweater.

In an emergency, S1 can link directly to S5.
- o   S1: primary activities (organs and muscles)
- o   S2: stability (nervous system)
- o   S3: optimization of internal system (base brain)
- o   S4: planning and intelligence (mid brain linking with the senses)
- o   S5: policy and identity, and arbitration between S3 and S4 (higher brain)

The model is recursive in as far as there can be models within a model.

The model is related to the 'Law of Requisite Variety' (the variety of the regulator must equal or exceed the variety of that being regulated, or 'Robustness requires that for every disturbance there must exist a response.') Note that, for Lean, standard work or scripts in a call centre that do not allow for sufficient adaption to variety of circumstance will fail! In fact, the possible 'disturbances' are almost infinite so any standardised scripts will not be robust.

VSM is used for organisational diagnosis, including manager responsibilities, information flows, and system failures - for example, the failure of emergency services in the Manchester terrorist bombing. If the system were organised as a human body, would it have responded in the same way? A case study of VSM used in a Lean/Six Sigma context is given in Lawrence Miller's book *Getting to Lean*.

One problem with Beer's concepts is the strange language: How about purposive, homeostasis, autopoiesis, variety attenuation? (It is bad enough having to learn Japanese words!)

A final thought from Stafford Beer (it is written on his gravestone): 'The purpose of a system is what it does.' Provocative! Never mind the CEO's lofty-sounding words, start with what the organisation does. 'People are our greatest asset.' (Maybe, but what does the organisation do?) Is the purpose of a company to reward its executives as much as possible? Will a tax incentive encourage tax avoidance? 'Our customers are our first priority'. Is the purpose of a hospital to provide a place to die? (Because that is what it does...)

Oshry
Perhaps an easier system concept than the VSM is Barry Oshry's 'Seeing Systems'. Oshry sees 3 groups in any organisation – 'tops', 'middles', and 'bottoms' – each with their own culture, beliefs, assumptions, and attitudes to other groups. Tops may suffer from turf wars. Middles may suffer from alienation, say between disciplines. Bottoms may suffer from lack of individual recognition. Useful language for discussion!

System Dynamics, started at MIT, uses feedback loop models to understand systems. Jay Forrester's work on supply chains and the bullwhip effect were early examples. A system dynamics model could be a conceptual 'causal loop diagram' or a computer model using software. A famous example of the latter was the 'Limits to Growth' study of the interactions between population, pollution, non-renewable resources, food production, and industrialization. Some scenarios of this late 60's model predicted catastrophe in the early 2000s. (We are pleased to report that we are still here.)

Feedback loops can be positive (showing growth or decline) or negative (seeking stabilization). Elements are connected by arrows. Elements that move in the same direction are shown with a +; in opposite directions with a –. The infamous 'R' infection factor in Covid-19 is an example. An R greater than 1 leads to exponential growth (like interest from a bank); less than 1 results in decline towards zero.

An example, based on Repenning and Sterman (2001): There may be two responses to a gap in desired output from a system: the 'work harder' loop, and the 'work smarter' loop. (For a diagram see 8.3).

> Harder: Performance Gap →+Pressure to work→+Time spent working →+Actual performance →-Performance Gap
> Smarter: Performance Gap →+Pressure to improve→+Time spent on improvement→(delay) + →Capability→+Actual performance→-Performance Gap
>
> But there is a third interaction.....
> Time spent working→-Time spent on improvement
> The result is that the work harder loop has short term gains but long-term decline; the work smarter loop has short term decline but long-term gain.
> Such diagrams can be very useful to a Lean analyst. See *The Lean Toolbox*. The effect of feedback loops is simply not captured in a Value Stream Map.

This leads onto the late **Chris Argyris** – single and double loop learning. Single loop learning improves the system or solves the problem. Double loop learning asks why the problem arose in the first place. A famous example comes from the surgeon Atul Gawande: Single loop involved improving the surgical procedures for eye injuries that arose with soldiers in Iraq. Double loop asked why they arose and what could be done. It turned out that soldiers were not using the protective 'shades' because they were not 'sexy' enough. The solution? Issue redesigned glasses. The result: A dramatic fall in eye injuries. This involves going 'Upstream' as Chip and Dan Heath refer to it. In fact the eye story may represent what some refer to as 'Triple Loop Learning' – a joint problem-solving approach which improves the learning method itself, and thus accelerates improvement.

Single loop includes scanning the environment (conventional 'SWOT'), setting objectives and KPI's, and monitoring performance. Double loop occurs when reflection ('Hansei') takes place allowing a possible change in direction – now known as 'pivoting'. The analogy of the thermostat – setting the temperature and controlling it as against reflecting and deciding to change the setting when the season changes. Argyris' ideas are central to 'intervention theory' – getting leaders to think through their assumptions for themselves.

By the way, Argyris was also sceptical of 'Culture' – believing that the underlying beliefs of managers are similar irrespective of culture. This is discussed in the Organisation chapter.

Following on from Argyris, MIT System Dynamics, **Peter Senge**, an influential systems thinker from MIT, has proposed 10 systems 'laws' that not only help us to understand systems better, but which are also an excellent aid to avoiding implementation pitfalls. The laws are set out below, with some additional comment on the relevance for Human Lean:

- 'Today's problems come from yesterday's 'solutions''. This could be a re-statement of the 'push down, pop up' principle. Attack one problem, stemming from past actions, and another pops up. This is the fundamental problem of reductionist rather than holistic thinking. In administration, using a new target to solve the problem often leads to unexpected behaviour.
- 'The harder you push, the harder the system pushes back'. Most systems are in a state of natural balance. When one factor is altered others compensate. Hence the rapid growth of wildlife when predators are removed, but then stabilising due to food shortage. This happens in organisations also. People react to change in direct proportion to the amount of change. Senge calls this 'compensating feedback'. (Newton's Third Law?)
- 'Behaviour grows better before it grows worse'. The wildlife story in the last point is an illustration. Management is often deluded (and rewarded!) by short-term results. Why? Because the whole system is not appreciated.
- 'The easy way out usually leads back in'. There are many quick and easy solutions to problems in organisations – and they are all wrong! Juhani's law states that 'the compromise will always be more expensive than either of the suggestions it is compromising'.
- 'The cure can be worse than the disease'. Help may induce dependency – ask Africa!
- 'Faster is slower'. Perhaps the supreme implementation law! Take time to achieve buy-in. The essence of what strategy deployment should be about.
- 'Cause and effect are not closely related in time and space'. If there is a problem in the office, the solution lies in the office.... Very likely not so!
- 'Small changes can produce big results – but the areas of highest leverage are often the least obvious'. Malcolm Gladwell in *The Tipping Point* talks of 'mavens' in an organisation that have great influence despite their apparent lowly status. Find them!
- 'You can have your cake and eat it too – but not at once'. The essential aim of Lean is to seek short lead-time, high quality and low cost – but it takes time to achieve.
- 'Dividing an elephant in half does not produce two small elephants. Again, a warning on reductionism. Focusing on improving the point, but ignoring the whole, may make things worse. Improving throughput in a hospital theatre may clog the subsequent beds.

- 'There is no blame'. Senge's point here is similar to Deming's 94/6 rule – 94% of problems lie with the (management) system; only 6% with the people.

Further Readings.

Russell Ackoff, 'The Future of Operational Research is Past', *Jnl. Opl. Res. Soc.,* Vol 30, No 2, pp 93-103, 1979

Russell Ackoff, *Ackoff's Best*, Wiley, 1999

Russell Ackoff, *The Art of Problem Solving*, Wiley, 1978

Russell Ackoff and Herbert Addison, *Management f-Laws*, Triarchy Press, 2007

Chris Argyris, *Organisational Traps*, Oxford, 2010

Stafford Beer, *Diagnosing the System for Organisations*, Wiley, 1985

Stafford Beer's Falcondale lecture set of videos (1994): https://opendata.ljmu.ac.uk/id/eprint/6/

Nicholas Brealey, 2002 (Note: for System Dynamics)

Peter Checkland, *Systems Thinking, Systems Practice*, Wiley, 1981

Robert Flood, *Rethinking the Fifth Discipline*, Routledge, 1999

Barry Oshry, *Seeing Systems*, BK, 1996

Repenning and Sterman, 'Nobody ever gets credit for fixing problems that never happened', *California Management Review*, pp 64-88, Summer 2001

Peter Senge, *The Fifth Discipline*, (Revised and Updated), Random House, 2006

Denis Sherwood, *Seeing the Forest for the Trees: A manager's Guide to applying Systems Thinking,*

5.6 SIPOC, Value Stream Mapping, and Theory of Constraints (TOC)

In this section we briefly discuss the relationship between systems thinking and some frequently used approaches. This is not intended to be an explanation of the approaches themselves.

- A SIPOC diagram is often used in a Six Sigma project. The Suppliers, Inputs, Process, Outputs, and Customers are listed. SIPOC can be regarded as an extension of Deming's system diagram. It encourages thinking about the various different elements in each. The central stage of SIPOC is process. Note also the Inputs, Process, and Outputs all show variation. This variation should be studied – common cause and special cause. So SIPOC may be regarded as a 'quick and dirty' systems approach – although far better than nothing at all!

- Value Stream Mapping (VSM, as opposed to Viable System Model) does show the main steps in an end-to-end process, plus a supplier at one end, a customer at the other end, some production control information flows, and basic data. As such, it is far better than looking at an individual process. But VSM ignores feedback, rework, variation, and the people element. Shared resources are generally also ignored. To add all these would add massively to complexity. That is the point! It is an overview tool for participation. VSM is also a snapshot in time, crucially dependent on when the snapshot was taken.

- Theory of Constraints (TOC) may be regarded as a partial systems approach in a far as it seeks to identify the single constraint, or bottleneck, in a system. A constraint is something that limits the system and prohibits it from achieving its goal. The constraint may be finance, marketing, operations, human, or even wider such as political and environmental. A bottleneck is a stage that limits flow within a system. "*An hour lost at a bottleneck is an hour lost for the whole system*" said Eli Goldratt, founder of TOC. The bottleneck is identified, then exploited, other resources are subordinated, the bottleneck is elevated (broken), and the sequence repeats with the new bottleneck. All good systems thinking, but limited in much the same ways as VSM. Too often, we feel, the true bottleneck is human, but ignored because of uncertainty of how to measure.

- So
    - Why not use VSM, SIPOC, and TOC together?
    - Why not also use other systems concepts, such as those described, to add insight, and improve the likelihood of success?

Beware: A bottleneck may shift if the product mix changes. It may also shift due to resource changes such as absenteeism or breakdown. Variation upstream of a bottleneck can de-stabilise the system. Conclusion: TOC's Drum Buffer Rope Concept is more suitable to a stable system.

5.7 Seddon's 'Check' Model

John Seddon's Check (or Vanguard) model has become a popular approach to service systems, particularly in the UK. Although the model has at its foundations the work of Deming and of Toyota, the model is uniquely service oriented. Seddon believes that much of Lean Thinking is not suitable in a service environment. See Jackson's Classification below.

However, several aspects of the Check (Vanguard) model give very useful insights into Human Lean – in as far as no manufacturing organisation is purely manufacturing and necessarily has service aspects.

'Check' derives from the Deming Cycle – Plan Do Check Act – but begins with Check. The stages are called Check, Plan, Do. Seddon may or may not agree with our following comments!

The Six Stages of 'Check' are:

1. Purpose: *What is the purpose – from the viewpoint of the Customer or Client?*
Purpose is the reason why you are doing the task. It is not 'Vision': Vision is where you want to be. It is often worth writing down both Purpose and Vision. Purpose should be an 'outside in' view, not an 'inside out' view.

'What does the customer want from the system?' is an outside-in question. *"How can I get these bastards to do more work?"* (Seddon's words) is, he says, a (wrongheaded) inside-out question. This requires taking a 'helicopter' view. Of course there may be several customer categories. If you get a list of things you are probably not high enough in your helicopter. So first seek the overall purpose – then you can get into the lists. You may then decide to home in on the most relevant item on the list – being the system or sub-system of immediate concern.

Why do this? It is simply an opportunity to stand back and consider why the organisation exists, without getting into organisational functions or departments, an attempt to avoid sub-optimisation, to remain holistic. The purpose statement should lead to the critical measures that enable a judgement to be made on whether the purpose is being achieved.

Note that 'Purpose' is never profit. Profit is one measure of success in achieving the purpose.

Sometimes, the 'customer' is an object like an aircraft or building or pipeline. It can be valuable to put yourself 'in the shoes' of such 'customers' – asking what they would want if they could talk. This is a powerful insight!

2. Demand: *What is the nature of the demand?* Having defined the purpose of the system, now you can consider the demands that are placed on the system by customers. Seddon uses the very powerful concept of Value Demand and Failure Demand. Value Demand is demand that is in-line with the purpose. It is what the system is there to do, what it exists to serve – 'it represents the demands customers make for things they want'. Failure demand, by contrast, is "demand caused by a failure to do something or do something right for the customer" (Seddon). But, says Seddon, failure demand is not caused by people doing wrong things – it is caused by the system.

Beware! Do not do mapping before you understand demand. You will not know what questions to ask. You may miss failure loops. You may conclude that the process is good, when it is actually generating failure. Your capacity calculations are likely to be wrong. This situation is much less of an issue in manufacturing because there is usually relatively little external rework imposed on a factory.

Why do this? To understand how much work is being loaded unnecessarily on the system, and hence possibly overloading the system, with severe consequences on response times and generating even more failure. There is little point is studying the flow of work when only a small percentage of demand is should actually be present. Importantly, failure demand also destroys the morale of workers who may see themselves as 'fire fighters'. When workers begin to see their work not as repetitive drudgery but as actually improving the system for customers and themselves, morale can improve more dramatically than by sending them on motivational courses or by imposing KPI's and hoping for the best. The latter is the classic 'beatings will continue until morale improves'.

This is not simply 'muda' or 'necessary non value added' work. Activities such as 'waste walks' simply will not pick up the extent of failure demand.

To understand demand, listen to the actual voice of the customer. Do not rely on market surveys or questionnaires. Write down what they actually say or write in emails. Classify and record the frequency.

Once you have this very valuable information, you should do two things:
>   (a) Re-design the system to make sure the value work flows more efficiently, and
>   (b) Set up ways, including the root causes, of eliminating the failure demand.

There is Preventable Value Demand and Predictable Value Demand. This is another valuable insight. As examples:
- Preventable Value Demand may arise in healthcare when there are earlier stages that could have occurred but did not – vaccination? A failure to visit the doctor when a heart murmur occurs. As is invariably the case, problems are much more cost-effectively addressed at source. Of course, this is a system boundary issue – but could the boundary be moved? Maintenance demand is also relevant – design for maintenance (as in 'power by the hour' aircraft engines.)
- Predictable Value Demand. Of course, today there are many very sophisticated forecasting models, such as Box-Jenkins. But again, looking at the wider system can give good indications. For example, supermarket groups target nappy (diaper) purchasers with follow-up offers of baby food. Huge amounts of data are routinely collected via the web. And more simply, knowing that trees growing under power lines keep growing, and traffic volumes wear out roads, give predictable demand.

3. Capability: *What is the system predictably achieving?*
This sets out to answer whether the system is able to meet the load put on it in a stable, predictable way. Of prime concern is the end-to-end service time and its variation. The word 'predictable'

refers to the stability of the system – is it 'in control' or 'out of control'? You will probably need a run diagram or Statistical Process Control (SPC) chart to answer the question. There is a fundamental difference between a system with a response time that on average is OK but that has unstable variation, and one with similar average response but highly stable performance. To know whether the system is capable it is necessary to know the purpose, and the critical measure or measures.

4. Flow: *How does the Work Work?*
Now that there is an overall appreciation from the customer's viewpoint, begin to look at how value is delivered to the customer. Only now is it appropriate to map the process.
Is there flow? Is customer flow smooth, swift, simple, steady, and slim? Note that we are concerned here with flow that meets the purpose – not just flow for the sake of flow. Don't attempt to flow activities that should not be there in the first place – failure demand. And we are concerned with the customer. If there are stages that don't contribute to the purpose they should not be on the 'main line' of flow. Stalk and Hout's Golden Rule: "*Never delay a customer value adding step by a non-value-adding step.*" Support activities should be done off-line, in parallel where delays don't bother the customer.

Why do this? Because flow is primary to customers – but you cannot understand flow unless you know purpose and capability.

5. System Conditions: *Why does the system behave this way?*
The system conditions are what cause the system to behave as it does. It is structure, the processes, the measures, the managers and maybe the people.
There will very likely be 'dirty data' flowing around the system, and several inappropriate measures. These will cause distortions. Measurement: "Tell me how you'll measure me and I'll tell you how I will behave", said Goldratt.

6. Management Thinking: This is the true 'culture' of the system, because the beliefs of the managers flow down into the employees. A Toyota saying is that 'the shop floor is a reflection of the management'. In some (many?) organisations the managers are primarily focused on satisfying their own managers' (or 'corporate') purpose rather than the customer's purpose. That is what has happened in many hospitals, banks, and universities, which are often so focused on meeting targets that the customer is forgotten.

In manager-focused organisations, frontline employees react to managers, not customers. Many measures and standards prevent these systems from absorbing variety. Hence costs are high and service is poor.

These 6 stages would complete the 'Check' stage. Thereafter would follow the Plan and Do stages.

Plan involves:
- What needs to change to improve performance against purpose?
- What action could be taken and what would be the consequences of taking the action?
- What measures are appropriate that will signal that action needs to be taken, and which will lead to learning?

Do involves
- Implementing the planned action.

This then would complete Check, Plan, Do cycle, and lead on to the next cycle.

Study. This final step is not given in the Seddon Check methodology, but the current writers feel that it should be made more explicit. Whereas the 'Check' stage includes studying the situation before the intervention, 'Study' includes recording what worked and what did not work, after or during the intervention. This allows learning and not having to repeat mistakes. Perhaps some critical, repeatable activities could have 'standard work' developed for them – for instance a doctor washing hands, or recording critical information so that the cause of failures can be diagnosed without having to rely on memory, but beware of standards that reduce responsiveness.

Potholes: a mini case.

Why Potholes? Potholes have become a big story in the public sector. It is estimated that there are at least 4 million holes in English and Welsh roads, and £60+ million was spent on damage claims resulting from potholes, to say nothing of the administrative costs and legal costs involved! In common with other services such as health, delaying pothole repair leads to non-linear cost escalation. Possible causes are almost endless, from trapped water turning into ice to uneven wear, with remedies ranging from 'cold mix to hot mix' (with endless formulations), temporary through to permanent.

Wiltshire County Council reported the case of the application of systems thinking to potholes. Previously it took 45 days on average from call to repair. Now it takes 12 days. Productivity (measured by the amount of road surfacing material applied) has increased five-fold, and pothole teams now actually repair roads for '7, 8 or 9 hours' per day as opposed to '2 or 3 hours' previously. This 'systems thinking' approach involves, apparently:
- The use of 'parish stewards', with local knowledge to feed jobs into the system.
- 'Trying to fix all the things' when the gang is there.
- Different methods used to fix different types of potholes.

It is worth quoting from a Vanguard newsletter (2009), written by John Seddon:

"Imagine the typical design: if you were a pothole, how many people turn up to see you, what do they do, who does the 'value work' (fills you in)? When you study potholes as a system, much of the crazy behaviour you discover is driven by measuring, recording and sorting potholes into their relevant target category, and management's perceived need to control the people who do the work. Systems thinkers design the pothole service against predictable demand, organising workers into geographies, capturing data on potholes when the work is done (thus once only and accurately) and ensuring that the workers use their own data on potholes to manage their own work. The result is as much as a five-fold increase in productivity and, most importantly, massive reductions in failure demand."

Clearly, this approach is effective. Also, as West Churchman said, 'The systems approach begins when you first see the world through the eyes of another'. So, this is not only through the eyes of another person, but also the 'eyes' of the object! Useful!

But first, what is a 'pothole'? There is no clear definition. The perception of a pothole from the public can range from a small shallow depression (from a notorious 'Mrs. Bucket' figure of BBC TV fame) to a major series of holes in a rural road that has remained unreported for several weeks. The area over which potholes appear is also relevant – from a single depression to a road looking as though it had been the target of a cluster bomb exercise. And...
- How about prevention? Better prediction? (Big data?)
- A quick fix, a longer fix, or a really substantial fix?
- The cause (or 'root cause') of the pothole, not just repairing it.
- Purpose: fixing potholes or ensuring safe flow?

It may be possible, with considerable time spent, to achieve a minimum cost solution for a section of road. But, following Scott Page, what happens if the 'landscape' changes while the optimal minimum cost solution is being developed? Perhaps new legislation allowing heavier trucks has been introduced. Perhaps a new housing estate down the road has been agreed. Perhaps COVID will affect traffic flows. There is no once-and-for-all optimum, especially in a VUCA environment.

A good start would be to give some thought to the system boundary, to 'upstream', to 'failure demand', to predictable demand rather than to reaction – and to experiment, monitor <u>and learn</u>. 'Better' will emerge, but 'best' is not possible. It is an emergent system.

As Mark Twain is reported to have said, *"For every problem there is a solution that is simple, neat – and wrong."*

Further Readings.
John Seddon, *Freedom from Command and Control*, Vanguard, 2003, and
the Vanguard web site www.beyondcommandandcontrol.com

5.8 A System Classification?

Jackson has suggested a classification, dependant on the problem. A 'horses for courses' approach. Jackson's classification is given, in part, for different system problem types as follows:

- For 'Technical complexity': Operations Research and 'Hard Systems'
- For 'Process complexity': Vanguard and the 'Check' model.
- For 'Structural complexity': System Dynamics
- For 'Organisational complexity': Socio-Technical Systems and the Viable System Model
- For 'People complexity': 'Soft Systems', and others
- For 'Coercive complexity': Legal and psychological types (not discussed here).

5.9 Systems and Serious Fun

For Serious Systems Fun….We thoroughly recommend John Gall's book 'The Systems Bible'. This is humorous, subversive, but highly thought provoking. Some favourite examples...

- 'The System always kicks back' (Think rainforest clearing, or 'letting people go'.)
- 'The old system is now the new problem'. (MRP? Office and home working?)
- 'The crucial variables are discovered by accident'. (Do you recognise that influential person?)
- 'Destiny is largely a set of unquestioned assumptions. (Body count will win the war. (aka Vietnam). Brexit?)
- 'If a system can be exploited it will be.' and 'Any system can be exploited.' (Every incentive scheme. Government aid.)
- 'Almost anything is easier to get into than get out of.' (MRP? Telephone contracts?)
- 'Do it without a new system if you can.' Why? Because a new system will bring its own overhead like HR, IT, accounting, and strategy – even Lean experts! Soon these attract consultants themselves or develop their own big problems. Think the scandalous NHS IT project.
- 'Great advances do not come out of systems designed for great advances.' – nor from the current major players. Take cars as an example. Cars were supposed to add to transport flexibility. They do – partly - but many end up in traffic jams.

- A hierarchy of systems (also in Lean organisations): 'Big fleas have little fleas on their backs to bite 'em, and little fleas have lesser fleas and so ad infinitum'.

Gall's many principles are a reminder, if one were needed, that any 'model', 'conceptual diagram' or 'map' of a human activity system will always only be a partial representation. How could you model the possibility of people's reaction to an organisation change, or the possibility of politics or corruption? So, beware!

Finally...

Beware of 'experts' who complain that others 'Don't get it'. This statement should be the other way around. It is the 'experts' who don't get it! It is not good systems thinking. Systems thinking and Lean thinking should involve humility and a willingness to learn from other viewpoints.

Further Readings.

Stafford Beer, *Diagnosing the System for Organisations*, Wiley, 1985
Nicholas Brealey, 2002 (Note: for System Dynamics)
Peter Checkland, *Systems Thinking, Systems Practice*, Wiley, 1981
Robert Flood, *Rethinking the Fifth Discipline*, Routledge, 1999
John Gall, *The Systems Bible*, General Systemantics Press, 2006
Dan Heath, *Upstream,* Bantam Press, 2020
Michael Jackson, *Critical Systems Thinking and the Management of Complexity*, Wiley, 2019
Barry Oshry, *Seeing Systems*, BK, 1996
Repenning and Sterman, 'Nobody ever gets credit for fixing problems that never happened', *California Management Review*, pp 64-88, Summer 2001.
Peter Senge, *The Fifth Discipline*, (Revised and Updated), Random House, 2006
Denis Sherwood, *Seeing the Forest for the Trees: A manager's Guide to applying Systems Thinking,*
Marvin Weisbord, *Productive Workplaces Revisited*, Jossey Bass, 2004

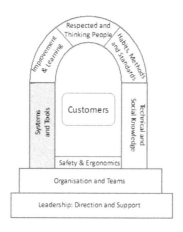

Chapter 6
Psychological Aspects

First, consider the guidelines that Benjamin Franklin, one of the founding fathers of the United States, developed for himself. He wrote down, and continually evaluated himself against, the following 'virtues': temperance, silence, order, resolution, frugality, industry, sincerity, justice, moderation, cleanliness, tranquillity, chastity, and humility. We are not sure about chastity and perhaps temperance, but possessing all the others would make for an ideal Lean practitioner!

The writers of this book are not professional psychologists, but have a deep interest in personality, roles, and traits that contribute to success or failure. Lean is a multidisciplinary endeavour and it behoves both Lean practitioners and psychologists to work together. This chapter gives a basic introduction.

The contention, or hypothesis, is that an understanding of personal characteristics is a first step towards improvement.

6.1 Testing, Personality, Behaviour and Helping

There are words and phrases that have come to be strongly associated with successful Lean. These include

Respect
Humility
Participation
Team work
Mutual trust
Reflection (Hansei)
Following Standard Work
Problem solving skill
Improvement
Ideas

These characteristics might be desirable in a Lean Leader, but are by no means characteristic of all leaders that are well considered by some, but certainly not by all! (For instance, the words are not strongly associated with Trump, Putin, or Kim Jong-un.)

The words are strongly correlated with personal traits, personality and roles. The relative ease of Lean transformation with groups having different psychological characteristics would be challenging to study. Randomised trials would be necessary – something that is difficult in most work environments. Whilst it is not impossible to change someone (or a group) not having the appropriate personal traits, it seems highly likely that a Lean transformation would be much slower and more problematical with a workforce that has a preponderance of unsuitable traits. (A classic study was the GM/ Toyota NUMMI experience in California where a problematical workforce was transformed into a highly productive workforce. This involved a strong contingent of GM workers spending time at Toyota in Japan, and a large commitment of Toyota coaches at the California plant.) We used to think of changing thinking to change behaviour. Now we think of changing behaviour to change thinking – changing the 'cultural artefacts'.

For decades psychological researchers have struggled with identifying which factors might best be needed to define personality. Why be concerned with personality at work? Because personality influences both counterproductive workplace behaviours and organisational citizenship. The former includes 'goofing off', working deliberately slowly, failing to do tasks, and may extend to sabotage and theft. The latter includes high commitment, helpfulness, motivation, and 'going the extra mile' – all desirable, if not essential, for Lean.

Of course, these are behaviours of relevance to every manager and organisation, not just Lean managers. However, Lean is particularly strongly associated with people's contribution without which Lean cannot hope to be successful.

Throughout this chapter keep in mind that the characteristics and roles to be discussed are each on a continuum – perhaps normally distributed. Extremes are rare. For instance, it is rare that a person is either highly introverted or extroverted - it is the case that a person may tend to some degree towards introversion or extroversion. Moreover, characteristics are situational – for instance, a person may be more of an extrovert at home but more of an introvert at work.

It is apparent that, in recruitment and selection, testing of IQ has declined in popularity in favour of testing for OCEAN characteristics and Emotional Intelligence, concepts that are briefly explained below.

Importantly, both Carol Dwek (in her book *Mindset*) and Angela Duckworth (in her book *Grit*) make the point that IQ tests and many psychological assessments mentioned below have their strengths, but are not great indicators of follow-though achievement and perseverance. For this, a Growth Mindset (Dwek) and task determination (Duckworth) are better indicators. (See Section 7.4)

6.2 Myers Briggs

The Myers-Briggs Type Indicator (MBTI) is a well-known and widely-used personality categorisation. MTBI is a theory that proposes that there are four principal psychological preferences that we use to interact with the world. Each preference is a continuum but is expressed in one of two states. Hence there are 16 personality types. The basic four (very briefly summarised) are:

- Extraversion (E) – Introversion (I). This is the Energy continuum. E types receive their energy from interacting with people. I types prefer their own world of ideas and experiences. Energy comes from reflecting on their own thoughts, memories, feelings.
- Sensing (S) – Intuition (N). This is the way of getting information. S types like real, tangible information. They observe the detail. N types prefer intuition and grasp patterns, relationships and connections.
- Thinking (T) – Feeling (F). This is the style of decision making. Logical, objective, and energised by the evaluation process (T), whereas F types prefer feelings, identify with the people concerned, to create harmony.
- Judging (J) – Perceiving (P). This influences the way in which the person relates to the wider world. J people live in a planned, orderly way, seek to get things done and stick to the plan. P people are flexible, spontaneous seeking to understand rather than to control.

Combining gives the 16 types. Typical or classic occupations for the different types are suggested.

ISTJ Inspector	ISFJ Protector	INFJ Counsellor	INTJ Mastermind
ISTP Crafter	ISFP Composer	INFP Healer	INTP Architect
ESTP Promoter	ESFP Performer	ENFP Champion	ENTP Inventor
ESTJ Supervisor	ESFJ Provider	ENFJ Teacher	ENTJ Admiral

The Myers-Briggs web site suggests that the MBTI 'reveals how we see and interact with the world, giving insight into our motivation and the motivation of others. This provides a strong foundation for personal growth and development, underpinning enhanced personal effectiveness.' Where MBTI used, team members can relate to one another by appreciating their particular inclinations.

However, MBTI has been criticised by a variety of academics as being a fad, simplistic and unscientific. There is a significant amount of published material on MBTI but debate continues.

As with several of the theories in this chapter a free assessment is available on-line, but the official MBTI can only be administered by practitioners trained by the Myers-Briggs organisation.

One Lean consultant uses the MBTI with early-stage Lean groups. All members take the test and the consultant gathers participants into groups. One group for the E's and another for the I's before explaining typical characteristics of each group. The point is made that there are no good and bad characteristics, just different strengths and ways of looking at the world. Then the whole group is re-grouped into the S's and the N's. Again explained. Then again for T's and F's, and yet again for J's and P's. The idea is that awareness of different strengths is fostered, leading to closer co-operation and 'respect'.

6.3 The Big Five

Lean managers have to manage both physical and human resources. That means understanding different personality types including their own.

A dominant personality theory and associated test is The Big Five, or Five Factor Model, that has developed gradually since it was first proposed in 1990. Today, the model is widely accepted and validated. The word OCEAN is a way to remember the five personality traits of Openness, Conscientiousness, Extroversion, Agreeableness, and Neuroticism.

Each of the five is further sub-divided into sub-traits. The OCEAN words are fairly self-explanatory. Here we will use the sub traits to expand on each together with a few comments from research. Remember that each is a continuum from very low to very high with frequency perhaps normally distributed. Everyone is a mix of all five OCEAN traits.

Openness: Ideas, Values, Fantasy, Actions, Aesthetics, Artistic, Liberal, Feelings, (High tend to be open to change, but there may be internal and external openness in opposite directions.) Openness is usually an expected indicator of success, but the opposite may be the case. Low: 'Simple', Practical, Shallow.

Conscientiousness: Competence, Order, Dutifulness, Self-discipline, Concentration on achievement, Meticulous, Deliberation. (High tend not to be spontaneous. Thought of as boring?) Also a trait sought in potential Lean employees. Low: Careless, Lazy

Extroversion: Warmth, Friendliness, Positive, Excitement seeking, Assertive, Gregarious. (High end extroverts tend to be risk-takers and make snap-decisions. Tend to be promoted but then may lack the skill.) Extroversion can be a two-edged sword. They are sociable, optimistic and energetic, and tend to 'think out loud'. But it is Introverts who are often more thoughtful and creative. Introverts have several virtues – for instance, better at reflection- but tend to be overlooked – one of several points made by Susan Cain in her book *Quiet: The Power of Introverts*. Ms. Cain, in her follow-up book *Quiet Journal*, suggests ways in which introverts can 'harness their hidden strengths'. There are also 'ambiverts' – people who become more extroverted or introverted depending on the situation. Karl Moore, of McGill University, estimates that 40% of the population are extroverts, 40% introverts, and 20% ambiverts. Findings suggest that extroverts tend to perform well (intelligence, creativity, learning, vigilance) under conditions of high stimulation, with introverts performing well under low stimulation conditions. Apparently, tasks in which extroverts show superior performance include dual-tasks, memory, and demanding tasks, but extroverts are normally poorer than introverts on difficult problem solving. (A huge number of studies have been carried out comparing extroverts with introverts.) Although more extroverts have been found to be in high-earning jobs than those who were less outgoing, another study found that introverts were more likely than extroverts to surpass the expectations of boards and investors. Karl Moore thinks that, in order to succeed, introverts must try to show more enthusiasm or make a stirring speech, while extroverts need to shut up and listen to their teams, not least because when the boss speaks first, subordinates will be reluctant to disagree.

Agreeableness: Modesty, Tenderness, Trust, Altruism, Compliance, Straight-forwardness. (High end are Eager to help and expect return behaviour, not always reciprocated.) People who test high in Agreeableness are often particularly sought after because they demonstrate high levels of trust, straightforwardness, compliance, and modesty. Low: Cold, unpleasant

Neuroticism: Self-consciousness, Anxiety, Angry-hostile, Depression, Impulsive, Vulnerable. (High neurotics are often worried about the future, and crave reassurance.) Neuroticism is associated with high levels of negative effect – they tend to become anxious and upset. Low: Calm, relaxed.

The OCEAN traits are now widely used in recruitment and selection. Once again, free assessment for OCEAN traits is available on-line. Take care, however: tests are not definitive but may be a useful indicator. Also, psychologists warn that self-tests of behaviour are sometimes invalid.

There are a few classic matches between traits and job categories. For instance, introverts make good train drivers because they pay more attention to signals and to safety. Extroverts make the best hotel receptionists. But generalisations like this should never be applied to a particular individual.

Being an extrovert or introvert is not necessarily an indication of managerial ability. According to Francesca Gino, in *Harvard Business Review, "Team leaders who are extroverted can be highly effective leaders when the members of their team are dutiful followers looking for guidance from above.... (but) when team members are proactive — and take the initiative to introduce changes, champion new visions, and promote better strategies — it is introverted leaders who have the advantage."*

Lean and Continuous Improvement begins with the individual. You. Self-assessment is a non-threatening way for an individual to get unbiased feedback – private, if necessary. So why not access one of the many free assessment tools?

We will now consider characteristics that tend to lead to counterproductive behaviours.

6.4 The Dark Triad

To begin, we should make the point that here we are not considering emotionally unstable, clinical or criminal traits – that is a specialist topic. The so-called Dark Triad are three sub-clinical characteristics that may lead to detrimental effects on individuals and organisations. Let us be clear – some organisations at some stages can benefit from people with Dark Triad characteristics, but the Dark Triad tends to leave a trail of destruction behind that may last for years. The Dark Triad traits are:

- Narcissism: 'I am the greatest', a grandiose self-view, egotistic, a sense of entitlement.
- Psychopathy: selfishness, remorselessness, superficial charm (In popular literature a psychopath is often a soulless killer – that would be an extreme, possibly clinical, case!)
- Machiavellianism: manipulative and exploitive of others. A focus on self-interest and deception to achieve personal goals or power. (By the way, Machiavelli's *The Prince* remains, after almost 500 years, the classic work on gaining power by ulterior motives. Don't be naïve enough to think that someone opposed to Lean initiatives will not use the methods!)

Studies have shown, for each of these characteristics, a fair correlation between increasing presence of the characteristic and counter-workplace behaviour. Managers with Dark Triad Characteristics tend to have less social responsibility and less support for employees. Respect (except for others with even more power) and Humility don't get a look in! It turns out that some Dark Triad characteristics make for success with junior managers, but limit their progression to more senior management.

Further reading on Tests and Personality Types.
Ben Ambridge, *Psy-Q*, Profile, 2015 (This contains several self-tests.)
Susan Cain, *Quiet: The Power of Introverts in a World that Can't Stop Talking*, Penguin, 2013
Francesca Gino, 'Introverts, Extroverts, and the Complexities of Team Dynamics', *Harvard Business Review*, 15 March 2015

6.5 Belbin and Team Roles

In the UK, Belbin's Team Roles model has been popular. According to the theory, a team with members having similar team roles will be out-performed by a team with a range of different team roles. (A 'role' describes a particular type of competency that a person displays at work or in social settings.) So a team selected on the basis of high IQ's is likely to be less effective than a team having a good mix of team role profiles. If all team members are, for instance, all good 'idea' people there is a fair chance that their ideas will not be successful. It is the combination of individuals rather than the merits of particular people that account for success. The 'Aha' moment is the realisation that recruiting the best people is not necessarily the route to success. (From a Lean perspective, Jim Womack controversially said that Toyota achieves excellent results with average people, but many others achieve mediocre results with excellent people. This would seem to support Belbin's view.)

Today one can take a free team-roles test on-line. Detail on Belbin's tests and the BTRSPI (Belbin Team Role Self-Perception Inventory) can be found on the website: www.belbin.com

Dr Meredith Belbin's team roles model is one of several and proposes 9 roles, subdivided into 3 main types. A similar team roles model (given in the same order as Belbin's 9 roles below, are Explorer, Driver, Completer, Chairperson, Team player, Executive, Innovator, Analyst, Expert.)

Action roles:
- Shapers, Often extroverts who stimulate, challenge and question. May be abrasive and offend.
- Implementers, The 'get things done', people. Usually self-disciplined, well-organised, efficient. May be inflexible
- Completer-Finishers. The detail people. Ensure timely completion. Perfectionists and conscientious. Not enough delegation?

People Oriented:
- Coordinators, The chairperson role. The value -appreciators. Too much delegation?

- Team Workers, The supporters and negotiators. Diplomatic and flexible, but possibly indecisive.
- Resource Investigator, Often extroverted, they seek to acquire necessary resources and work with external stakeholders. Sometimes too optimistic.

Thought Oriented:
- Plants, The idea people, but possibly impractical
- Monitor-Evaluators, The critical thinkers possibly detached.
- Specialists. The topic experts, the technical professionals, possibly too concerned with detail

These roles include weaknesses. The weaknesses could be worked on to reduce negative impact.

Please note that an effective team does not have to have 9 people, each with a different role type. It is quite possible that one person could have several role skills, so an effective team could have only a few members with different role skills. For effective team working and communication, a good team size would be about 7 – lower with complex tasks, higher with less complex tasks.

The next section is on Emotional Intelligence with Daniel Goleman being a leading figure. Goleman has suggested six distinct leadership styles. Perhaps then, various Belbin's roles can be adapted depending on the situation.

This also relates to 'Dominance Complementarity'. This is the tendency for people to respond oppositely to others along the control dimension of interpersonal behaviour. Factors such as expertise and enthusiasm for the task are likely to elicit submissive responses from fellow group members when the group is trying to generate creative ideas. The suggestion is that positive behaviours evoke positive behaviours, negative evoke negative, and dominant behaviours evoke submissive behaviours, and vice versa.

Further Readings.
R. Meredith Belbin, *Team Roles at Work*, Second edition, Routledge, 2010
There are numerous materials on the web, including U Tube and free tests.

6.6 Emotional Intelligence

Emotional Intelligence (EI) and Lean have travelled on parallel paths for decades. Since they share some common thinking it is surprising that they have not become more inter-linked. Both started in the early 20th Century. Both gained prominence with the launch of a book – *The Machine that Changed the Word* in 1990 (for Lean) and *Emotional Intelligence* in 1995. Both have grown strongly with large followings, multiple publications and conferences. Both share the concept of improving performance through developing people, reflection (Hansei), and critical thinking. Both share an interest in Leadership.

A definition of EI is:
"The ability to perceive accurately, appraise, and express emotion; the ability to access and/or generate feelings when they facilitate thought; the ability to understand emotion and emotional knowledge; and the ability to regulate emotions to promote emotional and intellectual growth."
(Sternberg and Kaufman, 1998)

In short, *"The ability to recognise, understand and manage emotions in ourselves and others"* (according to the Global Leadership Foundation).

For decades, and still continuing, the potential of people for work and leadership has often been assessed by IQ and technical skills. In the 1920's 'social intelligence' was mooted as a possible alternative. In the 80's and 90's researchers such as Jennifer George and notably Mayer and Salovey proposed that emotional capability has a major influence on people's ability to perform at work. Then in 1995 Daniel Goleman published the huge best-seller (5m+ copies sold) *Emotional Intelligence*. EI requires finding the balance between the emotional feeling-brain and the rational thinking-brain. (Slightly reminiscent of Kahneman's System 1 and System 2 that is discussed in Section 8.14). Goleman's book is really a self-help book. Emotional Intelligence (EI) has grown to be a major theory, with an entire box set of readings from Harvard Business Review, and adopted by many major companies including Johnson and Johnson. (J&J are also enthusiastic adopters of Lean.) It is claimed that EI is a strong predictor of success in life and work, with some claiming that traditional intelligence contributes only 20% to general life success, with 80% attributable to EI.

Today there is an explosion of material on EI, with many publications (not all of them good) and many consultants 'jumping on the band wagon'. (Again, similar to Lean). We may note that EI remains controversial amongst psychologist researchers, (As perhaps so does Lean, with Lean failure rates of 70% not uncommon) with some arguing that EI adds little, as a predictor of success, beyond the OCEAN characteristics discussed earlier and others disputing that EI can ever be reliably measured.

The claim is that persons with high EI are
- More articulate
- More perceptive at identifying the needs of followers
- Better at teamwork
- Better at building a supportive culture

(Wow!) (But see Mindfulness below.) Clearly, EI is more relevant to jobs requiring high people contact, and less to more physical work.

As Goleman says: *"CEOs are hired for their intellect and business expertise—and fired for a lack of emotional intelligence."*

Goleman's model contains 4 interacting Fundamental Capabilities that are further broken down into 12 Competencies. This forms a route map towards leadership, but is also relevant outside of the workplace.

- *Self-awareness*. This is the ability to be self-critical and self-reflective. It builds self-confidence. Self-awareness is the foundation leading onto Self-management and Social awareness. Competencies: Self-awareness: Emotional self-awareness, Accurate self-assessment, Self-confidence.
- *Self-management*. Competencies: Self-control, Adaptability, Achievement orientation, Initiative, Trustworthiness, Conscientiousness.
- *Social awareness*. Competencies: Empathy, Organisational awareness, and Service orientation.
- *Social Skill* stems from both self-management and social awareness. It includes a whole set of desirable leadership Competencies: Influence, Teamwork and collaboration, Building bonds, Influence, Change catalyst, Communication, Developing others, Conflict management, teamwork.

Simply reviewing the 12 competencies in your mind can give you a sense of where you might need some development. Note: Leadership is discussed in a separate chapter

Goleman, in a much-quoted *Harvard Business Review* article relating Leadership to Emotional Intelligence discussed six distinct leadership styles, each springing from different components of emotional intelligence. Importantly, the research indicated 'that leaders with the best results do not rely on only one leadership style; they use most of them in a given week—seamlessly and in different measure—depending on the business situation.' Goleman likens this to selecting the appropriate club from a golf bag, depending on the situation. The six styles are discussed in the Chapter on Leadership.

An important claim made is that EI can be developed by a person, and is not genetic as is usually assumed with IQ. Leadership flexibility can be learned according to Goleman. To grow personal EI is a long path, requiring <u>critical</u> self-reflection, not just self-reflection. One of the paths towards critical self-reflection uses a technique that is similar to a classic Lean tool: the 'Why' sequence. Critical Self-reflection is not unique to EI, but is widely used in teaching and psychology. For instance, the Open University has a free course 'Succeeding in Post Graduate Study' that has modules on reflection and critical thinking.

An example of the Why sequence could be that a manager has been asked to participate in a Gemba Walk and has refused. He should ask:

- Why did I refuse? (Because I don't feel comfortable in doing such a walk.)
- Why do I feel uncomfortable? (Because I might appear foolish to the operators.)
- Why would I appear foolish? (Because I am not familiar with the processes.)
- Why am I not familiar? (Because having an engineering degree people will expect me to know.)
- Why do I not know? (Because I have been too proud to ask. I realise that despite my background I cannot know everything, and should be prepared to ask and to learn.)

And Goleman and Nevarez suggest three questions to boost EI:

- What are the differences between how you see yourself and how others see you? (Clearly, this is self-reflection – Lean Hansei.) Begin with one of the several self-tests that are available free of charge. But then combine these insights with feedback from peers – including 360 degree feedback. (See also the section on Feedback)
- What matters to you? (Which are the most important gaps?)
- What changes will you make to achieve these goals?

This is broadly similar to Kata (See separate section, except that Kata would include an additional Check step.) Clearly, then, EI overlaps into the key Lean areas of coaching, problem solving, culture and motivation.

As with other sections, there are several free on-line assessments of EI that are available. Not all are reliable! But a well-established measure is MSCEIT which measures four EQ (Emotional Quotient) factors – perceiving emotions, using emotions, understanding emotions, and managing emotions.

Further reading on Emotional Intelligence.

Daniel Goleman, *Leadership that Gets Results*, Harvard Business Press, 2017
Daniel Goleman, *Emotional Intelligence: Why it can Matter More than IQ*, New edition, Bloomsbury, 1996

Daniel Goleman, "Leadership That Gets Results', *Harvard Business Review*, March-April 2000
Daniel Goleman and Richard Boyatzis, 'Emotional Intelligence Has 12 Elements. Which Do You Need to Work On?' *Harvard Business Review*, 6 February 2017
Daniel Goleman and Michele Nevarez, Boost Your Emotional Intelligence with These 3 Questions, *Harvard Business Review,* 16 August 2018
'Quiz yourself: Do you lead with emotional intelligence', *HBR.org*, June 5, 2020
Harvard Business Review Guide to Emotional Intelligence. Online.

6.7 Egan's Skilled Helper Approach

Gerard Egan, a distinguished professor (aged 91 in 2021) developed his approach in the 1970's to solve problems and develop opportunities in a counselling process. In the client relationship it uses a practical, three-stage model. One of Egan's books *The Skilled Helper* (in its 11th edition in 2020) is probably the most widely read book in the world on counselling.

Egan's model is designed for 1:1 counselling by helpers (such as psychologists, social workers, ministers of religion) in a problem situation. But other professionals, including consultants and managers in Lean settings, including performance management, could also benefit. So although the model is not an organisational change management model per sé there are many aspects that are of value – as indeed has been demonstrated in situations of which the authors of this book are aware. A 'problem' in Egan's terminology is not something that can be 'solved' but the aim is to help a person to manage the situation more effectively or to improve their effectiveness. So, for example, the Skilled Helper model can be used to improve training and also supervision. As with Appreciative Inquiry briefly described below, it may not begin with what is going wrong but with what could go better. (Therefore, closely aligned with Continuous Improvement).

The Three Stages of the Skilled Helper are:

- 1. Current State: What is going on? Help the person to tell their stories.
- 2. Preferred State: What do I need or want? Help the person set viable goals.
- 3. The Way Forward: How do I get what I need or want? Help develop strategies.

The stages could take place in three separate occasions. Traversing all three stages is a focus on 'How do I make it happen?' so action is required after every stage. The stages are not necessarily linear but may backtrack. Lean practitioners will immediately notice the similarity with the three stages of Value Stream Mapping: Current state, Future state, Action plan. Egan's model has nine boxes, three per stage, that delve into each of the stages. Very useful for Value Stream Mapping!

Egan's model can be shown as a 3x3 matrix with the columns being the three stages above, and the three rows respectively concerned with exploration, with challenging and selecting, and with commitment. What follows is a very brief overview of the 3 stage, 9 box model. The reader should certainly consult one of Egan's books for much more detail. There is no substitute for practice here. Try the stages with colleagues and friends first before using for real. Get feedback.

St1.1 Story. Where we have come from is told or related. Not an interview. Not reporting on themselves but reflecting on the events. Reframing and paraphrasing would be used.
St1.2 Blind spots. Empathy in moving the story towards new perspectives. How do you know that? Don't try to catch out or criticize, but try to see from different viewpoints.
St1.3 Leverage. Help identify those issues that will make a difference. Prioritise.

St2.1 Possibilities. Use creativity, brainstorming, imagination to develop ways to move forward.

St2.2 Change Agenda. Turn the promising possibilities into realistic goals.
St2.3 Commitment. Find the incentives that will lead to commitment. What habits will be necessary?

St3.1 Possible strategies. Review the possible strategies. Pros and cons.
S3.2 Best fit. Help in choosing the best fit strategy.
S3.3 Plan. Convert the chosen strategy into a (simple?) plan.

Gerard Egan tells a story that will fit well with Lean practitioners. A person walking along a river spots a lady struggling in the water. The person jumps in, drags her out, and begins artificial respiration. Just then another lady is seen struggling in the river. Again she is dragged out and respiration is started. A crowd gathers. Then yet another lady comes floating by and struggling. This time the person gives up and begins to run upstream. 'Why are you abandoning those half-drowned ladies', cries the crowd. 'You take care of them. I am going upstream to find out why ladies are ending up in the river, and will try to prevent more from falling or being pushed in!' (Similar to Dan Heath's *Upstream*, discussed in the Systems Chapter: Chapter 5.)

So, just as with quality at source and going to the Gemba, don't just try to fix the recurring problems, but get to the root. That is what a Skilled Helper should seek to do.

As with several aspects of Lean (for instance, Kata and Leader Standard Work) good questioning technique is important. (Refer to Section 9.10 on Questioning)

Although The Skilled Helper is focused around 1:1 interventions, the writers are aware of the use of the model in group settings. We believe that Egan's model would be very useful alongside a Lean Value Stream Mapping transformation, in A3 problem solving and in Kata. Indeed, Egan suggests using his model as a 'browser' to evaluate and expand on concepts and techniques.

A vital part of the work of the skilled helper is to do with conversations (as indeed is the case with Lean). Thus one interesting aspect is Egan's SOLER model, the aim being to improve communication with a client. Briefly, S is sit square facing the person; O is open posture – don't stand or sit with arms or legs crossed; L is leaning forwards giving attention; E is making good eye contact; R is be relaxed in talking. These can be linked to Carl Rogers' (a famous humanistic psychologist) '3 core conditions' for therapeutic change: empathy, congruence (i.e. genuineness) and unconditional positive regard.

Further Readings.
Gerard Egan, *The Skilled Helper*, (latest edition), Brooks Cole, 2008 / 2020
Val Wosket, *Egan's Skilled Helper Model*, Routledge, 2008
A large amount of material on the concept of the Skilled Helper is available on the web.

6.8 Persuasion and Influence

For anyone responsible for introducing change the ability to persuade and influence others is a critical factor in ensuring a successful outcome. All persuasion situations revolve around moving a group of people from point A to point B. However at point A the team may be resistant or uninterested in moving from A to B. To bring about a change in attitude the leader or change agent must be able to articulate their ideas or proposals so that their audience fully understand the proposals and, most importantly, believe the message.

Persuasive speakers are aware of the three distinct elements required in their communications sessions if they are to achieve maximum effectiveness. Firstly for the message to be believable, the person delivering it must have credibility. Secondly the speech must be constructed so that it appeals to the audience at an emotional level. Finally the choice of words and the use of facts, stories and quotations are critical. Assuming that trust is present, there are two paths towards persuasion i.e. the conscious and subconscious mind. People tending towards the conscious mind use logic to assess the facts of the situation before arriving at a rational decision. Others with a subconscious mind will process the information based on their intuition. Studies have shown that while most decisions are based on instinct and gut feelings (the subconscious element), logic is still important because it allows us to validate our decisions. (This is similar to Kahneman's System 1 and System 2 Thinking. See Section 8.14)

Behavioural research scientists have identified two qualities which have proved to be effective in moving people's mind-set towards a new perspective. These are empathy and sincerity. Empathy enables us to put ourselves in the shoes of others and to identify and understand their perspectives. Empathy also motivates us to look for solutions which can leave both sides satisfied. When people display sincerity about someone else's problems or concerns, their relationship moves onto a higher level.

However…
- Always be aware of your body language. Facial expressions, body movements and gestures can betray a person's true feelings.
- The golden rule for getting your message across is to first tell them what you will be speaking about. Then you actually tell them. Finally, recap on what you've actually said (Say what you're going to say, say it, say what you said).
- Remembering names is a powerful relationship builder.

When attempting to persuade, influence or even just have better interactions with our working colleagues what can be of enormous help is being able to identify and understand how they approach things differently. Dorothy Grover Bolton and Robert Bolton believe this can be achieved simply by observing their behaviour and listening to their language. They have developed the useful People Styles Model to explain this approach. The model is based on four different styles, none of which is better than the other. Refer to the figure. It is important to note that each style has strengths and weaknesses, and while each of us has a dominant style, that behaviour can stress others.

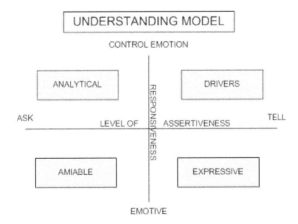

Analytical: These people sit back and consider all the facts before making decisions. They are cautious, precise, deliberate, formal and questioning. However, they can be seen as, stuffy, indecisive, suspicious, reserved and cold. This person may only make one decision in the day but it will most likely be the right one.

Driver: Typically competitive, demanding and determined, these people want results. They like to see progress happening, and they like directing things. But they can be seen as overbearing and aggressive. He or she will make six decisions in the day and be very satisfied if only four of them are very successful.

Expressive: These people are dynamic, enthusiastic, visionary, persuasive and sociable. They are dreamers who generate excitement about generalized ideas without having the specifics. May be seen as excitable, frantic and hasty.

Amiable: These are good, friendly and caring people who just want to help. They like to share and are more than willing to do as they're told. However, they can come across as being stubborn.

Tips on how to get the best from the different styles are given in the table below.

People Style	Do	Don't
Analytic	Be well prepared Put things in writing Allow them time to consider all the details	Be flippant Get too close and personal Change their routine.
Driver	Be direct Focus on results Be brief, be bright, be gone	Bore them with details
Expressive	Be friendly Be open and flexible Be entertaining	Bore with detail Tie down with routine Ask them to work alone
Amiable	Be patient and supportive Slow down to their pace Ask their opinion (they might not give it)	Take advantage of their good nature Push for quick decisions Spring last minute surprises

Note: All of the subjects introduced in this chapter have particular relevance for those who are, or who are aspiring to become better people managers, particularly in Lean environments. We will return to the most significant of these subjects in Chapter 11, Leadership, to explore them in greater detail.

Further Readings.

Dan Ariely, *Irrationally Yours*, Harper, 2015
Safi Bahcall, *Loonshots*, St. Martin's Press, 2019
Robert and Dorothy Bolton, *People Styles at Work*, AmaCom, 2018
David Robert Grimes, *The Irrational Ape*, Simon and Schuster, 2019
David Robson, *The Intelligence Trap*, Hodder and Stoughton, 2019
Phil Rosenzweig, *Left Brain Right Stuff*, Profile, 2014
James Surowiecki, *The Wisdom of Crowds*, Abacus, 2004
There are several free self-tests available for the work styles: See,https://mssic.org/wp-content/uploads/2020/04/IHI-QI-Team-Member-Work-Styles.pdf

6.9 Nudge

Thaler and Sunstein created huge interest with their book *Nudge* in 2008. This is about 'behavioural economics' and ways in which people can be positively, but gently, influenced to adopt behaviours that benefit themselves and society. Subsequently, a Nudge unit was established within the UK government with notable successes, for example increasing tax return punctuality.

Sunstein points out several advantages of using Nudges, including retaining freedom of choice and reducing the costs of one-size-fits-all approaches. But he also points out that Nudges don't always work (for example, printing the number of calories on a chocolate bar) and that trials or experiments should be held.

But Nudge applies to Lean implementation also. As Thaler and Sunstein point out, many good or bad practices in life result from habit or default rather than from deliberate choice. Thus 'culture' results from the 'ways things are done around here' that in turn often derive from habit or default rather than deliberate choice. Thaler and Sunstein make the point that the assumption that we are all 'economic man', always making rational decisions on the basis of weighing the evidence and considering alternatives, is highly flawed. In fact, most of us, including those with quantitative backgrounds, very often take the most convenient short cut. There is often no time, never mind the skill, to seek out and weigh all the alternatives. (Herbert Simon said the same thing years ago when he said most people are 'satisfiers' (good enough), not 'optimisers'.) This could be an important reason why, for example, MRP does not work too well - because the defaults are chosen and the computer rather than the scheduler runs the company. In Lean, there are many counterintuitive aspects, and many do the 'obvious', but wrong, thing. For example, larger batches and more inventory is good. In Theory of Constraints and to a lesser extent in Lean scheduling there are a lot of fairly complex calculations that need to be made and re-done when conditions change. So people will go through them and make the best decision. Right? Wrong! They will frequently make the easiest reasonable decision. So, try to 'nudge' them to make the easiest better decision. (This aspect is also discussed in Section 8.14 to do with Kahneman's System 1 and System 2 Thinking, and in the Appendix to Chapter 9 listing default decision making.)

Ways to Nudge include the following:

- The boss is regularly seen on the shop floor, always picks up any rubbish without comment.
- Any out of place tools are always placed in the manager's office. No comment is made when they are collected.
- No reserved parking. Common refreshment areas.
- Restricted line side storage space, and warehouse space. Limited space available.
- Schedulers and designers have to walk through the plant to get to their offices.
- Setting up default values in computer scheduling systems that encourage small batches.
- Designers are given the default option to select from standard components or fasteners.
- Small batch deliveries have wider delivery windows than large batch deliveries.
- Sales are given the default to select from discounts for multiple regular orders rather than quantity discounts. Orders over a certain size (a month's production?) cannot be entered into the system.
- Flow lengths are displayed on the shop floor.
- Production that is not for delivery today or tomorrow is stored in an area labelled 'Racks of Shame'. No comment is made.

- Operator jobs are routinely rotated.
- Building the expectation of regularity in, for example, material handling or tugger routes, repeater product schedules, morning reviews, operators showing visitors around.
- Forklift trucks are not used. No big containers are available.
- Multipurpose machines are vetoed.

Further Readings.

Richard Thaler and Cass Sunstein, *Nudge*, Penguin, 2009
Cass Sunstein, *How Change Happens*, MIT Press, 2019

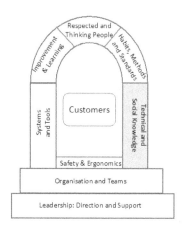

Chapter 7
Engagement and Applications

7.1 Overview

The focus in Lean was originally predominantly on tools and techniques. Education and training on these was paramount. Then the focus began to shift towards leadership and people – respect and humility between people. Good, and of course what this book is about. But now we realise that a further step has emerged – a focus on positive psychology. Today, numerous studies (by Gallup and by academics) have shown that employees who have a greater positive outlook and wellbeing at work are more productive, more engaged, more creative, and healthier. Too good to miss!

There are famous examples: Richard Branson of Virgin put employees first, believing that customer satisfaction would follow. Bill Hewlett and Dave Packard established the 'HP Way' focused on the people that made up the company rather than on the products. Alas, after 50 years, the ideal has faded. Vineet Nayar in his book *Employees First, Customers Second* showed how this philosophy led to the huge success of his IT company.

Glassdoor.com allows employees from companies to post comments about their experiences. As such Glassdoor is a mirror for wellbeing. There is a ranking of companies by employee satisfaction. (By the way, Toyota is some way down the list. Check this out yourself.)

Historically, psychology was strongly focused on what was wrong - mental illness, depression, and pessimism – the negative. Although the positive aspects have long been studied (for instance by Maslow – see Section 2.6) Positive Psychology as a field emerged strongly in the 1990's with work by, for example, Martin Seligman who is regarded as a pioneer of Positive Psychology.

Seligman's widely-used Positive Psychology framework is known as PERMA for Positive emotions, Engagement, Relationships, Meaning, and Accomplishment. PERMA is also a framework for understanding wellbeing – in work and outside of work – and mindfulness.

Engagement is a major theme in this Chapter. Positive emotions are discussed in the Psychological Aspects Chapter under Emotional Intelligence and also in this chapter on the closely linked concept of Flow. (The originator of 'Flow' is Mihaly Csikszentmihalyi, (or MC), who was mentioned in Womack and Jones' *Lean Thinking*. MC is discussed below in Section 7.3.) The other aspects of Seligman's framework relate to Appreciative Inquiry, Mindset, Mindfulness, and wellbeing – all of which are highly relevant to human aspects of Lean and are discussed in this Chapter.

7.2 Engagement

A practical definition of employee engagement is given by MacLeod and Clark (2009) in their report to the U.K. government:

> *"Engagement is about creating opportunities for employees to connect with their colleagues, managers and wider organisation. It is also about creating an environment where employees are motivated to connect with their work and really care about doing a good job ... It is a concept that places flexibility, change and continuous improvement at the heart of what it means to be an employee in the twenty-first century workplace."*

High levels of engagement are characterised with increased contribution, higher levels of discretionary effort, and increased job satisfaction and wellbeing. Increased engagement can provide positive outcomes for both organisations and employees. When employees become engaged they bring increased vigour, interest and dedication to their work and are also less inclined to leave, all of which increases organisations' competitiveness and profitability. At the same time employees also benefit as a result of developing new skills, knowledge and influence which makes their work more enjoyable, interesting and fulfilling.

However, in practice, employee engagement levels have over the past decade remained disappointingly low in organisations worldwide. Gallup's 2017 report 'State of the Global Workforce' stated that '85% of employees worldwide are not engaged or are actively disengaged in their job', but 'in the best managed companies' as many as 70% of employees are engaged. Moreover, Gallup found that 'Business or work units that score in the top quartile of their organization in employee engagement have nearly double the odds of success (based on a composite of financial, customer, retention, safety, quality, shrinkage and absenteeism metrics) when compared with those in the bottom quartile'. In a more recent article from 'The Insider' (HBR, 17 May 2019), Buckingham and Goodall report, following a huge US survey, that 'engagement averages a paltry 16%', but doubles when 'what really engages is their experience on a team' and further improves when the team is in a trusting environment.

Here we briefly mention just three of several routes to engagement. The Shingo Prize (2018) includes 10 principles of which two ('respect every individual' and 'lead with humility') are strongly aligned with engagement and three ('embrace scientific thinking', 'think systemically', 'create constancy of purpose') are indirectly aligned. In the *Toyota Way Fieldbook* (Liker and Meier, 2006, pp. 226-231) the responsibilities of team members, team leaders, and group leaders are detailed. This makes clear that engagement is not simply an edict from the top, nor a stand-alone bottom-up activity but requires active and ongoing involvement through all levels. TWI (Training Within Industry) is a set of concepts – Job Instruction, Job Methods, Job Relations – known as the 'three-legged stool', that had a major influence on early development of the Toyota Production System and is still used today, in modified form, for 'developing competent and able people' (Liker and Hoseus, 2008). Note the similarity of TWI Job Relations to engagement – 'the foundation for good relations' particularly 'people must be treated as individuals'.

Rapid Mass Engagement and the Cathedral Model

Frank Devine of Accelerated Improvement has had considerable success with his Rapid Mass Engagement (RME) and the related Cathedral Model for Lean culture development. The model has been used by several Shingo Prize winners (Gold, Silver, and Bronze.) in Europe.

Today the need for engagement is well established, perhaps even over-emphasized. However, in such conventional Lean transformations, even though employees 'have a say' or are involved or consulted, the power to make the final decisions remains with management alone. RME takes a different route, with the fundamental belief that true engagement must begin with employees themselves, reflecting their own beliefs and removing obstacles that prevent full participation. To do otherwise is merely 'pseudo engagement'.

Throughout the RME process employees are involved in adult-to-adult conversations and *make* decisions not merely *react* to management decisions. Employees never 'ask management' or 'make representations'; they make many operational decisions themselves and actively prioritise. As a result, employees are not the passive recipients of 'engagement' - rather they act on their system of work in such a way that they become actively engaged. In this sense, management doesn't engage employees; management *creates a process whereby employees become engaged* and then work to sustain the new system thus created. RME is therefore a radical alternative to the traditional top-down approach to engagement and enablement. In this approach:

- *All* the employees on a local site who constitute an interdependent system make decisions and are not merely 'involved' or 'consulted'.
- Employees create their Behavioural Standards in the language chosen by them, not in managerial or academic language.
- Employees agree, by consensus, not negotiation or compromise, with the local senior management team, a jointly-owned and prioritized change plan to overcome obstacles to achieving the site's Higher Purpose
- RME aims to undermine any legacies of negative and limiting assumptions and aims to create rapid momentum and sustainability from the bottom up.

By involving all employees the process ensures the *width* of ownership necessary for a new culture to withstand the kind of early challenges that can undermine it before it grows strong enough to sustain itself. *Depth* of ownership is achieved by the more intense experience of *collective, joint decision making* (known as Consensus Day). Both width and depth are sustained and leveraged by continuous improvement outputs and from joint decision-making. As Frank Devine says, *"If people help to plan the battle, they are less likely to battle the plan"*.

The overall process of RME has six phases as follows:

1. The process starts with *employees* rapidly creating a new and competitive culture. A Joint Decision-Making event called Consensus Day agrees, by consensus not negotiation, with the senior management, a change plan to enable (by removing obstacles to the organisations' Higher Purpose) and engages employees via the creation of a new, employee-owned continuous improvement culture.

   The approach is called the Cathedral or Higher Purpose Model. A core driver is that work is not just about earning wages but also can be harnessed to create jobs and sustain communities. When employees see the *genuine* focus on changing their experience at work, skepticism reduces and engagement deepens and widens. The engagement is deepened by the intensive nature of the process - e.g. 'Consensus Day' at Boston Scientific and Seagate involved 60-90 employees making joint decisions with their Senior Team about key business issues by consensus over 24 hours of contact time. The mass nature of the process widens engagement as <u>all employees</u> create their own culture.

2. To enable and sustain an initially fragile new culture, standards of leadership *outputs* have to be consistent and high. This makes it difficult for opponents of the new culture to point to examples of individual managers who are not both operating at a high-performance level and *modeling and referencing* the new culture in their day-to-day activities.

3. The new fragile culture needs to be sustained by process change as well as behavioural change and the elements of this combination are designed to be mutually reinforcing in nature. The leadership approach thus leverages improvement.

4. To sustain the new culture, multiple sustaining mechanisms are designed and implemented to avoid natural degradation over time and to *make the new culture independent from the energy and commitment of the original leadership group.* As an example the specific role of the internal facilitator group includes acting as a permanent 'conscience' of the new culture and helps ensure all new policies and procedures are measured against it.

5. Creating an environment where the new culture is reinforced every day. As an example, Boston Scientific have a standard internal workshop called 'Creating the Environment'

whereby the front-line leader and the team are taken through a process of agreeing how to make the new culture a reality and not just words on the wall. This includes ensuring that leaders can be challenged without consequence.

6. Once the new culture is created it will expose systems that are inconsistent with it thus creating the tension and pull to improve and align these systems.

Throughout the process, including the leadership development and continuous improvement aspects, existing systems and procedures are examined to identify potential conflicts and barriers - both social and technical. This is a specific design feature and aligns with 'Socio-Technical' design and 'Quality of Work Life'. The 'socio' aspects include issues such as the effect of changes on employees' social standing and self-image and which are sometimes missed even when employees are involved in substantial technical changes. (See 'Socio-Tech' Section 5.2)

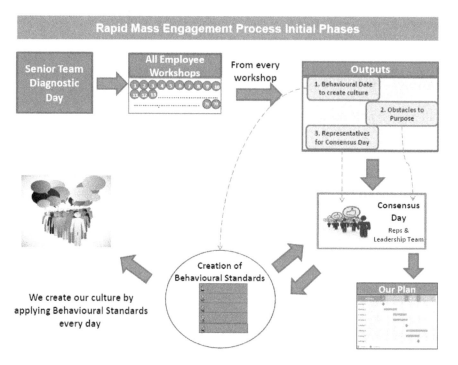

In this process, all employees diagnose the key obstacles to achieving the organisation's Higher Purpose and agree the nature of the new culture needed to overcome such obstacles. The early stages of RME are shown in the figure below.

The Cathedral Model is shown below. As the name suggests the model is a sort-of House of Lean, but specifically about people. The model shows a set of practices that must be carried through. It is called the Cathedral Model after a bricklayer who is building a cathedral – not just building a wall that could be anywhere.

The model is generic and Devine adapts each implementation to the specific circumstances by involving large numbers of staff in a participative dialogue. At its base are values and 'behavioural standards'. Values come from the organisation itself – for example Johnson and Johnson's Credo that is a one page statement beginning with 'our first responsibility is to the doctors, nurses and patients, to mothers and fathers and to all others who use our products and services'. The credo goes on to mention company responsibilities covering employees, communities and stockholders. Behavioural standards are then developed by employees at each site. They are concise statements that have to be bought-into by all. They are specifically 'bottom-up' not top-down, developed together with employees and unions, so are not 'lip-service' and become the daily expected behaviours. For example a standard such as 'Listen to people, involve them, and appreciate what they have done' is a statement developed through mass participation, not by consultation or negotiation, and certainly not by top-down edict.

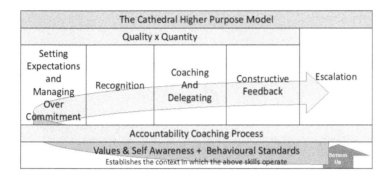

Upon this foundation is built the Cathedral's central pillars of Recognition, Coaching, and Constructive Feedback. In short, this puts specific meaning to the often-used word 'Respect'. The outer walls are Expectations and Escalation.

Expectations are set, bottom-up, through behavioural standards and values, and top-down though managerial goals – perhaps through policy deployment. Leader standard work plays a role here. The employees themselves manage recognition, coaching, and feedback. Time needs to be set aside for each of these. Recognition involves primarily intrinsic rather than extrinsic motivation, as discussed by Pink in this Chapter. Time should also be allowed for experimentation and initiative, or else improvement will not happen. All of these are managed visually where possible. Visual management is the mechanism that drives continuous improvement. The other wall is Escalation, where an agreed procedure is in place when things go wrong. Note here the Deming 94/6 rule about problems most of which lie with the system rather than the person. But, occasionally, escalation may involve a person.

Engagement and Continuous Improvement

In a Doctoral research study carried out in Lake Region Medical between 2014 and 2018 by one of the authors (Noel), the findings identified a significant link between involvement in continuous improvement activity and employee engagement through a process of social exchange. Social exchange is typically demonstrated in both parties displaying a sense of loyalty, feelings of trust and a desire to reciprocate for real or perceived favours. (See Section 2.7)

Within the CI process there are four key enablers which can become a catalyst for increased engagement. See the figure below.

The first and most significant of these is the role played by the leader in supporting the individual through the CI process which generates feelings of trust, loyalty, and a sense of obligation. The second relates to how the CI process can result in improvements to the employee's daily work, with social exchange developing as decisions and responsibilities are delegated to the employee. The third revolves around the recognition that employees receive from their involvement in CI. This begins when the manager selects the individual from among their peers. Then, and as the project progresses, more recognition comes in the form of presenting updates at cell meetings or presenting the completed project to members of management and other visitors. The final enabler is the opportunity for personal development that involvement in CI provides. This has special resonance for employees whose work is standardised. Consider for example a front-line assembly employee carrying out highly standardised work. That employee may have tremendous potential and great ambition, but no opportunity to display it.

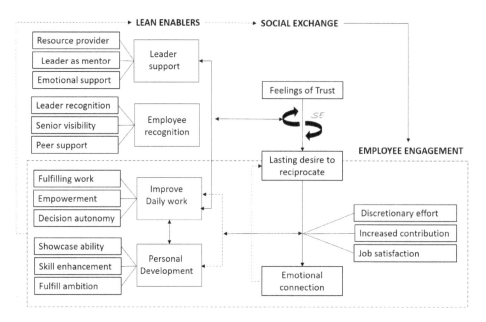

When employees are involved in CI their job satisfaction levels increase significantly. This arises from the pride and achievement they get in their own personal development and the pride of completing the projects or initiatives. The organisation also benefits through the wider implementation of improvement and cost saving ideas. Another major benefit is the shift in mind-set where engaged employees are now actively looking for opportunities to remove waste in the knowledge that their opinions are valued and will be listened too.

Cautions

- Managers must be willing to delegate some level of authority and responsibility to their subordinates.
- When managers begin to involve their people in CI, they open a door which is very difficult to close. Employees will expect on-going involvement in improving their work. If this doesn't happen, they are likely to become disgruntled.
- People have a special loyalty to managers who have helped launch their careers.

Toyota Engagement

In their seminal book *The Toyota Engagement Equation*, Tracey and Ernie Richardson hypothesise that Toyota's culture is built on two pillars; (a) Discipline to follow a path of continuous problem-solving improvement and self-development. (b) Accountability to exacting work standards, personal and company goals. Readers will notice the similarity with the House of Lean discussed in Chapter 1

The book is really an extended case study of the experiences of Tracy Richardson in joining Toyota and progressing through the ranks. As such it is a valuable insight into developing people and engagement. (All HR and other managers should read.) It also provides insight into how models such as Expectancy Theory and the Trilogy are effectively applied, although without mentioning these models specifically. (Refer to Chapter 4.)

The Richardsons' equation has three components. The first component comprises the six problem solving steps that are found in the Toyota A3 analysis. (Refer to Sections 8.9 and 8.13). The six steps, neatly encapsulated into 6 S's are:

1. Go to See.
2. Grasp the Situation.
3. Get to the Solution
4. Standardisation.
5. Sustain and systemise
6. Stretch: follow through by regular 'raising the bar'

The second component relates to people: Everybody, Every day, Engaged). These two components add up to the third which is their version of the Toyota DNA (for Discipline 'n Accountability). Clever!

While many organisations trot out the familiar cliché "Our employees are our biggest asset" Toyota practise people development on a whole different level. For example, regardless of what level you join the company at, the expectation is that you will be developed to advance by at least two levels. Responsibility for this development is split between the worker and his or her immediate leader.

Unlike many western organisation Toyota don't adopt the "biggest bang for my buck" approach when it comes to idea generation. In fact it is quite the opposite with a preference for the small incremental improvements. These of course will in time add up to significant change. Employees who come up with an improvement idea have to present it to their co-workers who will provide constructive feedback and encouragement. What's really significant is the coaching opportunity presented by the small ideas. The leader, using the Socratic Method, can get to understand the workers' thinking and logic, and where necessary point out any potential flaws. This helps to create an environment of trust where personal development and teamwork will flourish.

Another great example of how Toyota develop their employees, featured in the book but also in a video by Isao Yoshino, concerned getting the assembly lines in Kentucky ready for start-up. After the American workers returned from their training in Japan, the production equipment started to arrive. Workers then had to use their newly developed skills to set up and test new processes. While, as might be expected, mistakes were made, this was where the real learning occurred. In Toyota speak this is the difference between learning the "know-how" and the "know-why" which is fundamental to problem solving and continuous improvement.

When Toyota made the decision to start manufacturing in the US one of the big challenges they faced was transitioning American leaders who were conditioned to operate in a Command and Control environment towards a Servant Leadership style. Key to this was appointing individual Japanese trainers who were quietly observing and assessing in the background. Interventions were always in the form of questions e.g. *"What was the rationale behind that decision? Who did you develop today? What did you learn today? Given the opportunity what would you do differently?"* Trainers would often let the leader fail on purpose in order to learn a valuable lesson. The Japanese trainers also emphasised the need for leaders to view their subordinates as individuals rather than workers. Making this personal connection is essential to building mutual trust and respect.
In many organisations tribal knowledge (pertaining to a particular group) is a big problem. Many employees see this knowledge as power and guard it closely as something which may advance

their career in the future. Contrast this with Toyota where to advance your career, you must work as a team, share your ideas and develop your subordinates.

7.3 Mihály Csíkszentmihályi's (MC's) FLOW Concept.

This is not 'Flow' as Lean practitioners usually use the term – the aim being to make material 'flow' in an interrupted sense through the stages of a Value Stream. Here, Mihaly Csikszentmihalyi (or MC) described the experience of 'Flow' as when we lose our sense of self in carrying out a task, forgetting about worries and concerns, and becoming completely absorbed in the work. Flow occurs when, according to MC, *"a person's body or mind is stretched to its limits in a voluntary effort to accomplish something difficult and worthwhile"*. Our sense of time becomes distorted or lost, the experience is intrinsically rewarding, and our performance soars. Most people have probably experienced this at some stage.

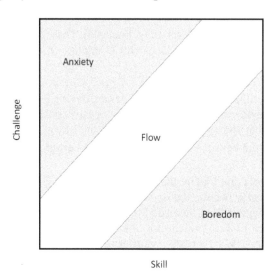

Flow', according to MC, requires a balance between skill and challenge. Too much challenge with insufficient skill leads to anxiety. Too little challenge with a surplus of skill leads to boredom. Both of these conditions have been, and to an extent still are, experienced in the world of work, play – and politics! Many will know of 'The Peter Principle' – people in an organisation rise to their level of incompetence. (!), and of skilled people working in jobs where their skills and talents – physical and mental – are under-used – and as a result are bored. Perhaps they do so for the money, for companionship, or because their talent is unrecognised.

'Flow' suggests matching skill with challenge, as shown in the Figure. To achieve a sense of Flow, MC suggests the following
- A clear goal
- A balance between challenge and skill
- Feedback
- No disturbance (switch off that mobile phone and e mail notification!)
- Personal control of the task
- Lack of awareness of physical needs
- The task itself is intrinsically rewarding. Not seeking extrinsic reward.
- Fun, play, and group working seem to make a difference.

That is the challenge! To design work having these characteristics that allows Flow to be achieved.

MC's work can be aligned with the Yerkes-Dodson Law, and with the so-called Goldilocks Effect (Please refer to Section 13.6). Yerkes-Dodson and the Goldilocks effect propose that there is an optimal zone of stress and utilization – not too much or too little, but just-right – where productivity is maximised.

In today's VUCA world, more and more tasks are challenging and complex, so an awareness of the Yerkes-Dodson curve is increasingly relevant. No longer the old linear idea that more work and longer hours lead to greater performance.

And certainly no longer the old Royal Navy adage, 'Flogging will continue until morale improves'!

7.4 Carol Dwek's Mindset

Do you believe that you are poor at (say) mathematics and so just avoid the topic, or are you prepared to spend some time to improve your competence?

Carol Dwek, professor at Stanford and author of the million-copy book *Mindset* would say that the former belief would indicate a Fixed Mindset, and the latter a Growth Mindset.
We believe that the development of a Growth Mindset in yourself and in others is closely allied with continuous improvement and should be regarded as an essential capability for every Lean manager. Every time a Lean manager provides feedback on an A3, on a kata cycle, on a kaizen event, or on any other CI initiative, he or she will be communicating a Growth Mindset or a Fixed Mindset. Be aware that this will feed through to, and influence, the future behaviours and motivation of people receiving the feedback. It seems likely that many Lean improvement initiatives have suffered this fate....

Now here is the great news: a Growth Mindset can be developed! Ability can be developed.

The following is a hypothetical situation inspired by Carol Dwek's book:

You are facilitator of a team that has just made its pitch in the annual 'Best Kaizen Improvement' event. A senior management group selects the best initiative of the year and the winning team gets sponsored to go with their partners to the corporate event held overseas. Unfortunately your team did not win. What is your reaction, in discussing the result with the team: Tell them...

- that you thought they should have won.
- that with their ability they are likely to win next year.
- that although they worked hard, the winning team made a superb presentation and set the benchmark for the team to exceed.

The first two encourage a Fixed Mindset. Your team is already good enough and does not need to work harder. The judges were at fault, not the team. The third option tells the harsh truth and encourages the team to try harder. What you say, and how you say it, really matters!

Dwek uses a word that has huge potential: YET. So, your, or your teams, Kaizen, or Kata, or Coaching (and on and on) may not be up to scratch YET. Dwek talks about the power of Yet versus the 'tyranny of now'. 'Now' is the attitude or belief that you are born with certain limitations that cannot be developed. Some are 'gifted' and don't have to make much effort to perform (at whatever) very well. Of course, DNA does play a role but, according to Dwek, every super sportsman, inspirational leader, or super achiever in any field, has worked hard, usually over an extended period, to achieve their supremacy. YET is a word that is incorporated in the Lean People Trilogy Model. See the Eight Models in Chapter 4.

People with a Fixed Mindset think that their talents and skills are 'all that they will ever have'. Their goal is to look smart or talented and, if shown not to be the case, look for someone or something to blame or for someone who is worse. There is no need to work hard or to collaborate. In the 1970s, says Dwek, the self-esteem movement 'took over the world'; tell everyone how good or 'gifted' they are. But this is now seen to have backfired.

People with a Growth Mindset see challenges and opportunities to develop. 'I am not there yet, but I can get there'. (Think the WW2 slogan used with TWI: 'We can do it'.). My goal is learning. I want to collaborate. DNA and inherent talent are but starting points from where I will grow.

Brain research (See section 8.14) shows that every time a challenge is taken on, the connections (synapses) in the brain grow stronger. The brain can, and does, develop – or fades away.

In fact, says Dwek, mindset is a spectrum from Fixed to Growth. People tend towards one or other. Moreover, mindset is situational – a person may tend towards a growth mindset in some circumstances and a fixed mindset in other situations. You never have permanently arrived at a growth mindset; it always requires work.

What to do and what not to do?

Continuing to praise and reward effort rather than achievement, and to emphasize YET, has been shown to shift the mindset. This has now been widely demonstrated amongst schoolchildren and amongst managers and teams – around the world. Others, such as VS Mahesh have used the 'Pygmalion' effect to turn 'hopeless cases' into high achievers (as witnessed by one of the authors, John, of this book) discussed in Mahesh's book with the subtitle 'The Corporation as a Nursery for Human Growth'.

Dwek says managers (or parents) should praise wisely. Beware of praising intelligence and of saying 'you are the best'. The problem is that such statements build undue confidence. No further effort is required. But sooner or later they discover someone who is more intelligent or is more skilled. So, instead, praise effort. Achievement can be acknowledged but put in the context of hard work or effort. Beware of using triggers such as 'You are smart' or 'You are clever'.

Praise the *process* of learning, praise their focus, determination, persistence, perseverance, ongoing effort, strategy, progress. But beware of praising getting the answer right, right now. Achievement, then, is a by-product of attitude. (The parallel being profit is a by-product of Lean.) From a Lean perspective this has parallels with a good Sensei. 'Look again', then 'Look again', and eventually 'You are making progress. Now what should you do next?'.

Companies - not just people - suggests Dwek, also have mindsets. Of course, this links in with 'Culture'. Moreover, talking to people in a company can give strong clues towards the mindset at a location or wider company. Thus, indicators are how did people get to their positions in the company ('talented' or hard work, and is credit shared?), how are mistakes dealt with (opportunity or blame), attitudes towards learning, and attitude towards developing people. Does the company expect people to improve towards the goal or to 'get it right first time'? If there is a challenge – take it, or make an excuse? If there is a reversal – what can be learned from this, or blame others? Everything worthwhile requires huge effort over an extended period or instant success?

Here, it will quickly be realised, that better Lean companies fit in very well with Growth Mindsets.

If Lean practitioners truly would like to build people, they need to take Dwek's research and guidance seriously.

Further Readings.
Angela Duckworth, *Grit: The Power of Passion and Perseverance*, Vermillion, 2016
Carol Dwek, *Mindset* (Updated edition), Robinson, 2017
(There are numerous videos on UTube about Mindset)
V S Mahesh, *Thresholds of Motivation: The Corporation as a Nursery for Human Growth*, Tata McGraw Hill, 1993

7.5 Appreciative Inquiry

Have you, dear reader, ever been in a meeting where the 'leader' goes straight into 'the problems', mistakes, complaints, costs….and blame. 'We must do better – and you need to help!' In essence, this is a focus on making more money by reducing costs, on problems, and blame. The alternative is how to grow the business by capitalising on strengths and opportunities. Enter Appreciative Inquiry!

Note: AI is frequently used as an abbreviation for Appreciative Inquiry but today is more frequently associated with Artificial Intelligence, so beware not to talk at cross purposes!

From its early beginnings around 1985, Appreciative Inquiry has grown into a significant methodology used by hundreds of companies and organisations, including many in the Fortune 500.

Appreciative Inquiry is a descriptive title because it encapsulates the critical phases of appreciation (positive psychology building on strengths, not criticism or weakness) and inquiry (asking a question is a first step towards change; it is conversational and seeks to reveal the hidden strengths and resources that are already there). 'Inquiry' should begin with appreciation, should generate knowledge, should be provocative and collaborative.

Appreciative Inquiry is in essence a change management philosophy, with the belief that every organisation contains elements that work well. These strengths are built upon to create a 'positive revolution'. The phrase 'unconditional positive question' gives a sense of how AI seeks out the achievements, strengths, potentials, and wisdom of participants.

There are clear overlaps with Lean Thinking is as far as Appreciative Inquiry involves listening with Respect, Humility, Participation, Team work, Mutual trust, and Ideas. In short, the majority of words in the opening section of this chapter. Both Lean and AI claim to use a systems approach. However, one important difference with classic Lean tools such as A3 is that these begin with a gap, or what has gone wrong, whereas AI begins with what we are good it. The argument is that a 'Deficit Approach' is ultimately de-motivating. People like to talk about their successes not their failures. When was the last time you attended a conference on failures?

In the British public service the phrase 'lessons have been learned' is often heard. Good if taken in a positive light. Not so good if blame is attached – which seems to be the usual case.

Consider these scenarios:

Situation A: 'We have too many clerical errors and complaints, and people need to be monitored more closely to reduce the errors.' (What is the team's reaction?)

Situation B: 'Bill, I have noticed that your customer satisfaction ratings are good and improving. Can we learn from your methods, so all in the team can develop better methods?' (What is the reaction this time?)

Situation C: 'Well, team, we need to consolidate then grow. Everyone needs to participate. You all have ideas about how to do this, but perhaps have not revealed them. So let us now have a session where your good ideas are brought out.' (The reaction this time?)

A: How does the manager know that the team is not doing their best? Could it be that they are working with an inadequate system? Blame! A focus on the negative.
B is much better, provided that the compliment paid to Bill is genuine. If not, it will quickly be recognised as ingenuous.
C, of course, needs to be followed through and acted upon. A positive focus.

B and C are what Stavros and Torres call 'Conversations worth having'. Based on much research, they recommend 'Positive Framing' that focuses on the positive, but also on 'where we want to go or on what we want more of'. They also recommend 'Flipping' – focusing on the 'positive opposite' – instead of the problems of being late, what are the opportunities of being early?

Be careful! Carol Dwek (see the earlier section) warns against giving high praise for achievement ('You are the best') rather than for effort. The former encourages a Fixed Mindset; the latter a Growth Mindset.

A positive approach should not be strange for a Lean practitioner. Consider...

- Deming: To repeat, Deming's '94/6' rule said that 94% of problems lie with the system, and only 6% with the people. Begin by examining the system instead of blaming the people. One of Deming's 14 points is 'Drive out Fear'. Blame creates fear. A quote: *"Interactions...may be positive or negative. As negative interactions they subtract from the benefit of the individual people. Why is a company not as good as the sum of all the people in it? With positive interactions it ought to be more than the sum of all the individual efforts."* (From *The Essential Deming*, p 155)
- A Sensei will never criticise directly but will often say 'Look again!' When the student finally sees the light, a limited compliment may follow but so too will encouragement to look ever deeper.
- And others...
- Peter Drucker said *"All of us have strengths on which we could capitalise....Weaknesses in all individuals are inevitable; however, so are strengths. In building an organisation, managers need to staff so as to capitalise on individual strengths, and to make weaknesses irrelevant."* (From William Cohen, *A Class with Drucker*, p 235)
- Carol Dwek, and her 'Growth mindset' (See the earlier section)
- McGregor's 'Theory Y' (See Section 2.4)

On a Gemba Walk, does the leader go to the performance board and home in immediately on the red areas, or does she go to the board and first ask about the green success stories? (Particularly those now Green areas that have turned from Red.) Will the former encourage hiding problems, open discussion and honesty?

On another level, AI is more fundamentally different from Lean in as far as, philosophically, it breaks with the ideas of the 'One Best Way'. Instead of homing in on a problem solution, AI widens out the range of possibilities or opportunities, building on strengths that are already there. Instead of PDCA, AI is, according to Lewis, Passmore and Cantore, a break from a 'modernist' towards a 'postmodernist' perspective. So knowledge is created through conversations rather than rational research, and different ways of doing things is to be welcomed rather than reducing variation in the interests of efficiency. Thus, for Lean, a real challenge but also a real opportunity. In this respect, AI has much in common with Anthropology, discussed in the Organisation chapter.

There are 4 classic stages to Appreciative Inquiry – known as the 4Ds (Note: Not the Ford 8D problem solving steps!). It is a process of engagement. The largely bottom-up process grows commitment. For an organisation that has been top-down, command and control, Appreciative Inquiry can be a significant shock, a credibility gap for many. However, in some Appreciative Inquiry concepts there is a first stage: Define. This would make it a 5D sequence.

Define (Focus)
- Concerned with defining the area of interest.
- The focus of the inquiry. (Note: Not a problem, but a positive aspiration.)
- It is important that Defining should be open-ended, positive and outward looking. (For example, not 'the sales shortfall', but perhaps 'creating positive customer reactions'.)

Discover (Appreciating)
- What do we do well, and have done well, in the area?
- Open Ended Questions.
- Capturing 'the life blood of the organization' (to quote Cooperrider, 'father' of AI)
- What are the positive events and experiences that have led to the organization's survival, reputation, and growth?
- Group and 1:1 interviews.
- Key stories relating to past successes are captured and mapped
- Main themes are identified, not pre-decided.
- Lean and Quality tools that are used are an Affinity diagram and a Relations Diagram. Possible main root causes of success are accumulated using Affinity. Then each root cause is compared with each other. An arrow is drawn from the influencing to the influenced card. Cards with the highest number of arrow tails are the drivers or forces behind the successes.

Dream (or Disrupt?) (Envisaging, Innovating)
- This is not 'blue sky' thinking, but grounded in the history and achievements as identified in the discover stage. It projects forward the positive thoughts, so the outcomes from the Discover stage should be known.
- It fosters inspiration. Of course, listening with respect is necessary.
- What might we do? / What would you do?
- What would be the ideal?
- Groups that share Dream ideas work together to refine the ideas.
- A poster showing a road with past events and moving into the future could be drawn. Fun and participation. (See several good examples on the web.)
- An 'Opportunity Map' can be constructed (or brainstormed) using post-its to show how opportunities can be grouped and grasped.

Design (Co-constructing)
- What should we do?
- What do we need to do to deliver the Dreams?
- Now comes the broad detail. Groups translate the Dreams into plans and 'Provocative Propositions'.
- A design Worksheet can be constructed with columns for:
  - Design elements
  - What we learned in our discovery
  - What our dreams suggest we want

   o Our provocative propositions.

Deploy (or Deliver or Destiny) (Sustaining)
- What will we do?
- Develop the Action Plans. Task groups are usually selected for this.

Good AI practice requires skills to be developed by facilitators in Asking questions, Engaging conversations, Listening, and Eliciting stories

Some managers are 'naturals' in these areas. Most are not. Deliberate Practice is desirable if not essential (that is, repeated practice with constructive feedback from an experienced coach). (See Section 4.2 on The Lean People Trilogy.) Each of these skills would not only be required for AI but would be excellent for many concepts in Lean transformation, whether AI is used or not. All of the concepts discussed in the 'Established Approaches' Chapter would benefit from improved skills in these four (or five) areas above. In particular, the development and practice of asking effective questions is covered in Section 9.10.

Afterthought: The 5D circular sequence has parallels with Checkland's 'Soft Systems Methodology'. SSM uses 'Building a rich picture' (Discover); 'What might be' (Dream); Comparison (Design); 'Feasible desirable changes' (Deploy); and 'Root Definition' (Define). SSM uses various Systems concepts (for instance CATWOE) that may be useful in the AI context. Conversely, AI may be very useful for effective SSM! (See the Systems Chapter: Chapter 5.)

Further Readings.
David L. Cooperrider, Diana Whitney, Jacqueline M Stavros, *The Appreciative Inquiry Handbook*, Berrett-Koehler, 2nd edition, 2018. (This is the 'standard text' from the founders, containing numerous guides and templates)
Sarah Lewis, Jonathan Passmore, Stefan Cantore, *Appreciative Inquiry for Change Management*, Kogan Page, 2009
Joyce Orsini (ed), *The Essential Deming*, McGraw Hill, 2013
Jackie Stavros and Cheri Torres, *Conversations Worth Having: Using Appreciative Inquiry to Fuel Productive and Meaningful Engagement*, Berrett-Koehler, 2018
Diana Whitney and Amanda Trosten-Bloom, *The Power of Appreciative Inquiry*, 2nd ed., Berrett-Koehler, 2010

7.6 Mindfulness

Mindfulness has become a fashionable topic in recent years. Some would regard it with disdain, questioning its relevance in a book on Lean. A fad. We would beg to differ. Of course Positive Psychology and Mindfulness have resulted in many specialist books. Here, we only attempt a brief overview with comments on the relevance to Lean.

Mindfulness also has long roots, going back centuries to Greek (Aristotle) and Eastern philosophers. An important theme in mindfulness is focus on one subject at a time. This in turn relates to the widespread, but often denied, problem of multitasking.

The benefits of Mindfulness – for all, but especially relevant for leaders, are

- Greater emotional intelligence (EI)
- Clearer focus

- Reduced mind wandering
- Improved concentration
- Improved creativity
- Reduced stress
- Improved relationships – personal and professional.

All of these have been shown in several studies, leading companies like Google, Apple and McKinsey to initiate Mindfulness training.

Everyone has a strong tendency for their mind to wander. This is the opposite of Mindfulness. Many believe that one can multitask. Sorry to say, you cannot, or at least you cannot give attention to two tasks at once. But your mind can go into a state of mindlessness, when you are essentially on 'autopilot'. Your mind can and does flip from topic to topic. Distractions, such as phone and e mail abound. Interruptions such as these cause one to lose focus – not only during the interruption itself but the time taken to regain the focus. Mind wandering leads to, for example, losing concentration during a meeting or presentation, not listening attentively, and thinking about what you will say next or shortly rather than giving attention. These are real 'losses' – as severe as the classic Lean 7 waste losses, but are difficult to see. Daniel Gilbert, famous psychology professor at Harvard, estimates lost potentially productive time at over 40%!

What can be done to improve Mindfulness? Try these:

- Discuss with your team on how to increase awareness and decide on what interruptions are allowed and what are not allowed. (This is, or should be, part of 'Respect')
- Set a 'no interruption' time zone.
- Concentrate for a few minutes each day on your breathing (Apple watch may help!)
- Bang a gong and concentrate on the sound until it ceases (An old Zen trick!)
- Answer e mails only once or twice a day.
- Turn off your cell phone during time slots. Inform others of the slots.
- Practise focused listening, perhaps by feeding back what you have heard. (Humility?)
- Establish 'Cues' that trigger the Habit cycle of (say) breathing. (See Section 3.23 on Habits).
- Formal meditation is very effective. Can you find a time slot each day where you can sit (straight back) for a few uninterrupted minutes of focus?
- Moving away from the expectation of a quick or immediate response (to, say, e mails or WhatsApp) could well improve your productivity!

By the way, this is not just at work. Several leading sportsmen use Mindfulness.

It is now known that the human brain can develop throughout its life, not just in the formative years up to the teens. The connections between neurons strengthen with use and pathways are established and widened. The brain seeks out the established pathways first, so the more you do something the more likely you are to do it again. Habits are formed.

Closely related to Mindfulness are attitudes to risk and to uncertainty or probability – both of which have been recognised as increasingly relevant in recent years. Ellen Langer, one of earliest writers on Mindfulness says *"…although work may often be accomplished mindlessly, with a sense of certainty, play is almost always mindful…. In play there is no reason not to take risks….To encourage mindfulness at work, we should make the office a place where ideas may be played with, where questions are encouraged, and where 'an unlucky toss of the dice' does not mean getting fired."* Langer's research has shown how 'the teaching of facts as absolute truth' can lead to mindlessness. For example teaching 'this is a pen' instead of 'this could be a pen' has a direct influence on creativity.

Also closely related to Mindfulness is Positive Outlook – and Appreciative Inquiry. Having a Positive Outlook has also been shown, in numerous studies, to improve creativity, openness, empathy, health. Unfortunately we all have a tendency towards a negativity bias – perhaps a survival legacy. But again, a Positive Outlook can be developed through habit. Neuron paths in the brain are strengthened, so the more one fosters a Positive Outlook the more likely it is to grow. If you are not already doing so, try these:

- Notice and comment on achievement. At a Gemba board, as noted before, comment on the Green areas first particularly those that have changed from Red
- A bias towards generosity rather than criticism. Try to avoid negative judgements.
- Positive Framing: focus on solutions and opportunities rather than problems. (On the day of writing this, one of the authors received a speeding ticket. Bad news or a timely reminder?) A value stream map shows opportunities not problems.
- Positive Priming: Begin with the positive – at meetings, giving feedback, commenting on an A3.

But be warned, councils Seligman, don't use optimism if planning a risky venture, or in any situation where the cost of failure is high. Here, 'mild pessimism' is a virtue. Beware the overconfidence bias, so common in project management. Alvesson and Spicer in *The Stupidity Paradox* agree and criticise the idea that by being optimistic you can succeed in every aspect of your life. Seligman's warning is appropriate. What is needed, Alvesson and Spicer and others maintain, is better critical thinking. See section 8.10 on More Complex Problems.

Finally…Hamlet *"…for there is nothing either good or bad, but thinking makes it so."* (Shakespeare)

Further Readings.
The NHS has excellent and free material on Mindfulness. There many free UTube courses
Mats Alversson and André Spicer, *The Stupidity Paradox*, Profile, 2016
Adam Grant, *Give and Take*, Weidenfeld and Nicholson, 2013
Ellen Langer, *Mindfulness: 25th Anniversary edition*, DeCapo Press, 2014
Martin Seligman, *Learned Optimism*, Nicholas Brearley, 2006
Mark Williams, *Mindfulness*, Piatkus, 2011

Chapter 8
Problems and Problem Solving

This Chapter deals with two crucial aspects of Human Lean: problems and ideas. But 'solving' is often a misnomer because few problems are actually permanently solved but improvement (hopefully) takes place. Problems and Ideas overlap – a perceived problem is the basis for an Idea. Ideas take place every moment, every second, and range across all levels in an organisation.

This Chapter does not get into the detail of the 'how' or the tools of addressing problems. That is left to the numerous excellent texts and videos in the area. This Chapter does address frameworks for problems and decisions. It also addresses Improvement types and categories of Idea management. However, the reader will be guided to appropriate approaches and tools for many situations.

Let us begin with wise words from the great science philosopher Karl Popper: *"Whenever a theory appears to you as the only possible one, take this as a sign that you have neither understood the theory nor the problem which it was intended to solve."*

8.1 Recognising and Seeking-out Problems

First, before we even start to look at problem solving and improvement, problems must be recognised. Without this, it is a fool's paradise. Ohno's statement was *"Having no problems is the biggest problem of all"*. Problems can be real or potential, and the response can be reactive or proactive. We humans have difficulty in saying 'I don't know' and 'I was wrong'. But both of these are the starting point for knowledge, the starting point for improvement. It is about Humility. Beware of 'I knew that'. Research by Kahneman has shown that this statement is often simply not true.

Often real problems tend to be addressed by a short-term focus on limitation rather than with the longer-term aim of improvement. Addressing potential problems aims at prevention, but prevention can have a short-term focus (say a poka-yoke device) or aim at the longer-term elimination of the need for short-term preventive measures (say by product design).

There are overlaps here but in general there are two approaches (I) for improvement and (R) for restoration. Restoration has a short-term, fixed goal but does not necessarily lead to Lean. Ohno's statement was aimed at Improvement, not restoration.

The next question is, of course, 'What is a problem?' This could be…

- Not yet reaching an ideal state: 'True North', 'Perfection', 'Waste free' (I)
- A perceived bottleneck or constraint, preventing progress towards a goal (I)
- A desire to do something or to understand something. (I)
- A deviation from specification (R)
- Something unexpected which causes concern (R)
- Unacceptable variation (R)
- …..

Here, a quote from General George Patton: *"I don't want to get any message saying "I am holding my position." We are not holding a Goddamned thing. Let the Germans do that. We are advancing constantly and we are not interested in holding onto anything, except the enemy's ass."* (Quoted in *Certain to Win* by Chet Richards).

It is worth noting that a 'problem' is not only physical but also conceptual. 'Ohno's Method', as discussed by Nakane and Hall is, 'Through mentoring, Taiichi Ohno developed people by challenging them with provocative questions, stimulating them to improve processes on their own, and then learning to self-manage themselves'. His approach is called Ohno's Method. It is:

1. <u>Mentally</u> force yourself into tight spots. (Underline added)
2. Think hard; systematically observe reality.
3. Generate ideas; find and implement simple, ingenious, low cost solutions.
4. Derive personal pleasure from accomplishing Kaizen
5. Develop all people's capabilities to accomplish steps 1-4.

8.2 Thinking People

Teruyuki Minoura, MD of Global Purchasing at Toyota says *"When production stops everyone is forced to solve the problem immediately. So team members have to think and, through thinking, team members grow and become better team members and people."* TPS, he says, is *"a manufacturing process where he or she alone must decide what needs to be made and how quickly it needs to be made.....It's a basic characteristic of human beings that they develop wisdom from being put under pressure."....and "There can be no successful monozukuri (making thing) without hito-zukuri (making people). To keep coming up with revolutionary new production techniques, we need to develop unique ideas and knowledge by thinking about problems in terms of genchi genbutsu. This means it's necessary to think about how we can develop people who can come up with these ideas."* (From media.toyota.co.uk, 2003)

What we get from this is

- Problems must be brought to the surface and be made clearly visible.
- Some decisions must be made quickly and at the front line.
- Problems are opportunities for improvement, not just restoration
- Problems are a route to developing people.

TPS can be thought of as a problem surfacing system. There are many tools and methods for surfacing. (See the sections below) but the over-riding requirement is a no-fears climate - climate where problems are seen as opportunities.

8.3 Harder or Smarter?

Repenning and Sterman contrasted working harder with working smarter. Harder would imply longer hours, cost cutting, bonus incentives, delayed replacement of equipment, checking and monitoring. Smarter would imply kaizen, innovation, investment, training, and moving towards devolved decision-making. Harder would imply less time spent on improvement, more time spent working. Smarter would imply less time spent working, more time on improvement.

The result is shown in the figure, adapted from the original. The dotted curve shows the possibility of some initial gains from 'low hanging fruit' by working smarter.

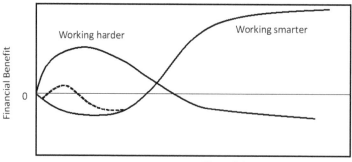

This is a great temptation for leaders: A financial return now or later? Clayton Christensen (see later) believes that 'now' decisions underlie the decline of productivity growth in the West, and that these have resulted from short-term, cost-saving, bonus-driven calculations and ratios rather than from learning and innovation that takes time to work through and carries risk.

Further Readings.
Nelson Repenning and John Sterman, 'Nobody Ever Gets Credit for Fixing Problems that Never Happened: Creating and Sustaining Process Improvement', *California Management Review*, Summer 2001

8.4 Incremental and Breakthrough

A problem condition can be restored to its previous condition or the condition can be improved upon. Improvement categories can be incremental or breakthrough. The two improvement categories should be two faces of the same coin. Both are necessary, neither is sufficient on its own! Thus Juran refers to 'breakthrough' activities, using 'project by project' improvement, to attack 'chronic' underlying quality problems as being different from more obvious problems. Davenport, in the context of business process reengineering, has referred to 'the sequence of continuous alteration' between continuous improvement and more radical breakthroughs by reengineering. And Womack and Jones discuss 'Kaikaku' (also called kaizen-blitz, or rapid improvement events) resulting in large, infrequent gains as being different from kaizen or continuous improvement resulting in frequent but small gains. A traditional industrial engineering idea is that breakthrough or major event improvement activities are not continuous at all, but take place infrequently in response to a major change such as a new product introduction or in response to a problem or 'crisis'. But during the past years, through Kaizen events, we learned that effective breakthrough should be both proactive and frequent. More senior management working across a value stream generally drives breakthrough or Flow kaizen. Incremental or Point Kaizen is led by team leaders, and sometimes by Six Sigma Black Belts working on local issues that have arisen either through value stream analysis (proactive), or from workplace suggestions (reactive).

8.5 Surfacing Problems: Process or Intervention

An organisation can take a passive or an active approach to problems. A passive approach just involves 'wait and see'. If nothing happens – fine. 'If it ain't broke, don't fix it'. If a problem occurs, sort it out. An active organisation – better to call it proactive – tries to identify problems before they occur. This can be done by intervention where a person or manager directs an initiative, or by monitoring a process to give an early indication of impending problems. As an example, take the brakes in your car. You can drive happily until the brake pads wear out and you experience failure – hopefully not fatal. You (or your garage) can check the wear and instigate timely replacement, or your car may have an automatic wear monitoring sensor to give an early warning. From this example, it will be appreciated that pro-active surfacing is not an absolute guarantee against failure, but is widely considered to be wise.

In the same way, in an organisation, problems can be deliberately pro-actively surfaced by management intervention, or surfacing can occur as a result of something happening to the process. Examples are given in the table. Generally, Intervention surfacing is top-down (at least in hierarchical organisations), carried out as a result of a management initiative, believing that there is an opportunity for improvement. Process surfacing generally is bottom-up and is initiated by process drift or something in the process performance that has not met expectations.

Examples are given in the table. (These are lists, not direct comparisons).

Intervention Surfacing	Process Surfacing
Value Stream Mapping	Reliability-centred maintenance
Kaizen Events	Andon / Line Stop
Supply Chain Mapping	Heijunka / Missed schedule
Inventory Withdrawal	Standard work, 5S
Industrial Engineering	Pokayoke and Jidoka
Six Sigma projects	Daily meetings, Q Circles
A3, Kata	Recording failure demand
Operations Research	SPC
Demand / takt time change	Suggestion schemes?

A process surfacing experience: On a group visit to a Toyota plant, a group member from another automotive company asked 'How many Andon stops are there per day?' The answer "Over 1,000!". The response 'You obviously have many problems at Toyota!' The answer "We stop for our problems; others ship their mistakes!")

As a non-manufacturing example of process surfacing, consider the recording of Failure Demand. As noted in Chapter 5 on Systems), John Seddon defines Failure Demand as demand arising through 'not doing something or not doing something right first time'. The opposite of failure demand is value demand – first time demands for service. Many organisations are simply not aware of how much failure demand there is. In one Telecommunications Company failure demand was reaching towards 80% of calls. But, of course, failure demand consumes resources. Repeat phone calls have to be dealt with. So an initial step is to record the frequencies of various types of failure demand. Just listen to customers. The results will astound all who have merely treated all demands equally. Failure demand is a systemic problem that requires elimination not reduction.

The response times to issues that have been surfaced, varies:
- Process surfacing, of course, arises at the process. A process failure (such as Line-stop) demands an immediate response. Some process surfacing (such as unsatisfactory 5S, or a missed schedule) are early-warning indications of developing problems. Here, proactive action is appropriate, but it may take time to resolve and improve. Most of these are addressed by bottom-up (or shop floor) actions at the Gemba. However, there are certainly situations that arise at process level that can only be addressed by more senior management.
- Intervention surfacing may arise internally or externally – based on internal information or analysis, 'gut feel', external events, or on opportunity that has become apparent. The response might range from a tactical pivot to a strategic breakthrough. Response time would range from short- to medium-term but seldom immediate.

8.6 Six Categories of Problems

The earlier sections have outlined Restoration, Process Surfacing, and Intervention Surfacing. Also outlined was the reaction time and type – reactive and proactive. Combining gives six categories. See the Figure. The Figure shows the six types as fitting into boxes, but the boundaries of the boxes overlap.

2. Restore	4. Experimental Kaizen	6. Breakthrough Innovation
1. Fix it Now	3. Short-term Kaizen	5. Directed Improvement

In the Figure, the shading indicates improvement, unshaded indicates restoration.

Rows: Moving from left to right involves a relatively longer response time. More correctly the relative response time is a diagonal from bottom left to top right.
Columns: In each column the lower categories elicit a response from people closer to the gemba, whereas the upper categories involve people at higher organisational levels.

The Six Categories arise from typical situations, elicit typical responses and are treated with typical tools. These are shown in the Table.

Type	Arises from	Typical responses	Typical Tools or Approaches
1	Breakdown	Fix now	Rapid Response
2	Deterioration	Refurbish TPM?	RCM, TPM, SPC
3	Line stop or Defect detection	Team leader, Rapid Response	5 Why, 7 Q-tools, ECRS, Rapid Response, Poka-yoke (Jidoka), TWI, 7 Wastes, Brainstorm, Visual Problems
4	Waste recognition	PDSA, A3, Kata	A3, Kata, 7 Q-Tools, Kipling, ECRS, Six Sigma, TWI, Brainstorm, Sprint and Scrum, Shainin
5	Measures, Change initiatives	Value Stream Mapping	Value Stream Mapping, Kaizen Event, Scamper, Questionstorm, Simulation, O.R., Systems Methodologies, Digital Twin, AI, Data Mining, Value Eng., DOE, 3P, Obeya
6	External threat, opportunity	Product or Process Redesign	TRIZ, DFSS, Lateral Thinking, Design Thinking, Set-based Design, Creativity tools, LAMDA, Lean Startup

Each of the problem types arises from a typical cause, and has a range of approaches to tackling the problem, as given in the table below. The Figure will be used to discuss various concepts in relation to problems, improvement and decisions. But before that, let us be reminded (once again) of George Box's famous statement: "*All models are wrong, but some models are useful.*"

An overview of the Typical Tools listed in the Table above is given in Appendix 1. This gives recommendations for more detailed reading.

The Six Categories are surrounded by a range of typical characteristics and responses. Everyone in the Lean area should be aware of these characteristics and responses. All are discussed in later sections.

- Kahneman's System 1 and System 2. The human brain defaults to so-called System1, but the answers are sometimes wrong.
- Much of Lean is counter-intuitive. For instance, stopping the line when there is a problem.
- The OODA loop and the PDSA cycle. The Deming PDSA cycle may be desirable but is not always feasible.
- Bias.
- Non-linearities, laminar and turbulent flow. This is linked to all of the above points.
- Top-level Decision making.
- The VUCA environment and Cynefin® Model

First however, an overview of several well-known models and typologies, related to the Six Category Framework, is given.

After looking at other models and typologies we will return to the Six Categories in section 8.15. The Six Category Model is a meta concept that includes consideration of sections 8.7 through 8.14.

8.7 Other Problem Typologies

Tame, Wicked and Critical Problems

A *Tame* problem has limited uncertainty and is resolvable by a process such as, in the Lean area, Kata, A3, 5 Why, or even the classic 7 tools of Quality. In the Design area, tools such as TRIZ and set-based design come to mind. A solution is clear. Grint says that such problems are the concern of managers. In Snowden's framework (see later) a Tame problem would fall into the Clear or Complicated domains. Many Lean improvement problems would be classified as Tame.

A *Wicked* problem would fall into Snowden's Complex domain. According to Grint, 'There is no 'stopping point', it is novel, any apparent 'solution' often generates other problems, there is no 'right' or 'wrong' answer but there are better or worse alternatives.' Collaboration is required. Such a problem type must usually be escalated to Leadership rather than remaining with Managers. Sense and respond. The Leader's role would be to ask the right questions rather than to provide answers. Many strategic and directional problems would be classified as Wicked. (Should the company pivot into a new venture? The response to COVID. See the later section on Decision Making and the case of the Cuban Missile Crisis.)

A *Critical* Problem demands an immediate response. An industrial accident has just occurred. A power failure or a fire. If the problem is a small one – a machine breakdown, a line-stop – it can be resolved at a low level, but some need to be immediately escalated to the top. Here the appropriate manager or leader assumes the role of a Commander – decision authority without discussion.

Puzzles and Problems

Some authors distinguish Problems from Puzzles. A puzzle has a definite solution, often technical. Engineers solve puzzles, managers address problems – which usually have strong social or human considerations. Puzzles – such as 'best practice' can easily be transferred between sites. The transfer of solutions to problems, on the other hand, should be treated with considerable caution. Pedler, in discussing Action Learning, criticises the inappropriate use of puzzles in human-oriented situations. This is a good warning to many aspiring Lean managers who think that a solution seen in another business can easily be transferred.

Further Readings.
Keith Grint, Problems, problems, problems: The social construction of 'leadership', *Human Relations*, Vol 58 (11), 2005
Mike Pedler, *Action Learning in Practice*, Gower / Henley Business School, 2014

8.8 Smalley's Four Types of Problems

In Art Smalley's popular book, *Four Types of Problems*, he discusses four types each having appropriate tools. A history of problem solving is included, moving from Pareto, through TWI, the 7 Quality tools, PDCA, and Six Sigma. Smalley's work is strongly influenced by Toyota, where a problem is never 'solved' – but rather a level is reached that opens up yet another opportunity. Many Toyota examples are given. The four types are:

1. Trouble Shooting. (Caused reactive). Fixing problems immediately and returning conditions to normal.
2. Gap from Standard. (Caused reactive). Root cause problem solving for recurring problems.
3. Target Condition. (Created proactive). 'Removing obstacles toward achieving a well-defined vision or new and better standards.' Systematic Kaizen.
4. Open Ended. (Created proactive). 'Open-ended pursuit of a (perhaps) vision or ideal conditions.' Perhaps Type 4 is not considered 'problem solving' but rather innovation.

Generally, Types 2 to 4 are used by ever-higher levels within an organisation.

Types 1 and 2 are 'caused problems' eliciting 'reactive responses'. Types 3 and 4 are 'created problems' eliciting 'proactive responses'. (This is much like the ideas of passive and enforced (surfacing) problems. Types 2 and 3 involve PDCA – or a variant. Types 3 and 4 involve experiments and building on previous experimental outcomes – such as Kata.

Further Readings.
Art Smalley, *Four Types of Problems*, LEI, 2018

8.9 Complexity and Snowden's Cynefin® Framework

The Cynefin® Framework has become widely used, as its originator Dave Snowden says, for *"making sense of the world so that we can act in it."* By 'act in it' means a way for practitioners to apply appropriate approaches and 'stances'. To quote Blignaut; *"being able to locate ourselves...helps us determine the appropriate actions to take, and the methods and tools that are fit for that particular systemic context"*. As such, we hope that it will be useful reference point for Lean practitioners in improvement and decision-making – particularly in a VUCA world. An important point is that context is important – a point made several times in this Chapter and by others such as Art Smalley.

The wide use of the framework is summarised in Dave Snowden's website: www.cognitive-edge.com. This also contains details of several programs, activities and videos.

An early version of Cynefin® appeared in 2003 and later in *Harvard Business Review* in 2007. It has since been modified and adapted. Strictly, the framework should be seen alongside various principles and heuristics, particularly as Snowden sees the framework as work-in-progress. It is useful in "sense-making" or helping to understand why approaches such as Six Sigma, and perhaps Lean, go haywire. Why 'Scientific Management' (Taylorism) works well in some environments but is a disaster in others.

There are four domains in the framework, plus a central 'confused' domain. Some characteristics of the four domains and associated principles are briefly described below together with comments on their relevance for Lean problems and decisions. The domains are defined by the types of constraint – or no constraint in the case of chaotic. To move between domains requires energy. However, the reader should regard what follows as a brief overview and seek out fuller discussions – particularly as the framework is a developing one. The figure shows the Cynefin® framework superimposed with various Lean concepts.

Scott Page uses an excellent landscape analogy, although not directly related to Cynefin®. In the Clear domain there is one clear mountain peak. It is easy to identify. This is similar to FW Taylor's 'one best way'. In the Complicated domain the landscape is rugged. A mountain range with many local peaks. The overall highest peak may be very difficult to find, but advanced analysis techniques (Lean tools?) can get to a good or 'satisficing' solution. In the Complex domain, the landscape 'dances' – there are earthquakes and volcanoes and the highest peak today may not even exist tomorrow.

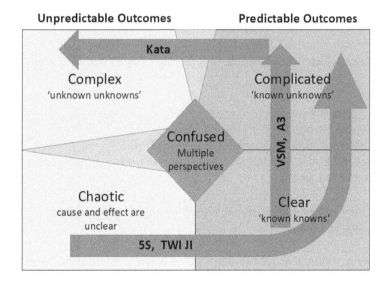

Figure: The Cynefin Framework and Lean Concepts. Adapted from Snowden and friends, 'Cynefin® weaving sense-making into the fabric of our world; and from Graupp, Steward and Parsons, 'Creating an Effective Management System'

The first two domains can be regarded as Reductionist. (The parts can be studied separately; outcomes are predictable and repeatable experiments are possible.) Perhaps also these first two could be thought of as 'scientific' domains and the last two 'artistic' domains.

Snowden and Boone make the important point that most business education is focused on the Clear and Complicated domains, but most leaders today actually work in the other domains.

Clear: (previously 'Simple' or 'Obvious'). This domain has 'known-knowns'. We understand the relationships. The domain of Best Practice. The repeatable scientific experiment is possible and reliable. The sequence is Sense, Categorise, Respond. A single part in an engine. People are regarded as machines. Best or established practice holds sway. Lean: an individual process or workstation.

Complicated. The domain of 'known-unknowns'. We know what we don't know. The domain of the Expert, and 'good practice'. The relationships between the parts are known, but there is uncertainty as to how they work together. Analysis can still be scientific but the many possible interactions between the parts leads to uncertainty. Mathematical modelling possible, but will always be incomplete. Lean: An internal value stream. The sequence is Sense, Analyse, Respond. Judgment and expertise are necessary.

The next two domains fall into the 'Systems' area. Outcomes may not be reproducible.

Complex. Here there are unknown-unknowns. In this domain, solutions can 'emerge' (Snowden and Boone quote Apollo 13 as an example. A solution emerged using the materials at hand in the spacecraft.) The sequence should be Probe, Sense, Respond. In the Complex domain, behaviour is unpredictable. Since the cause-and-effect relationships are uncertain, *experimentation is necessary to see what works*

Note: the phases known-knowns, known-unknowns, unknown-unknowns were made popular by controversial US Secretary of Defence Donald Rumsfeld, who died in July 2021.

Snowden, in his *Harvard Business Review* article, says that the Complex domain has the following characteristics:

- Non-linear interactions
- A large number of interactions
- Dynamic or emergent. Solutions arise rather than imposed
- Hindsight does not lead to foresight, because the wider system constantly changes
- We cannot forecast or predict.

Scott Page says there are four characteristics of Complex systems: Interdependence, Connectedness, Diversity, and Adaptation.

In this Complex domain, non-linear relationships are common but unknown. Here, the best solution found today may not be the best solution tomorrow – because the other players or events may have changed. Because complex systems are in flux, adapting, and changing, this means that something that works today may not work tomorrow, and something that doesn't work today might work tomorrow. This is a problem for scientific method! There is a low probability of very high impact events – what Nassim Taleb calls 'black swans'. For instance, predictions of the financial crisis of 2007 were overlooked by the vast majority of analysts. An optimal solution to a supply chain problem may suddenly become non-optimal, or even poor. Such events are, according to some, becoming the norm. The impact for all organisations, but particularly for the Lean-aspiring, can be huge.

Sonja Blignaut has made the point that uncertainty is now the normal state. We used to think that stability was the normal state. But instability reigns: COVID, Brexit, Trump, Putin, Kim Jong, and Climate change are examples. The more connected we become, the more complexity becomes apparent. She says complexity cannot be tamed, wished away, or simplified. Everything has risk and uncertainty. In this domain mutual consensus is an illusion – at best it is temporary. Also 'alignment' is difficult or impossible - because all relevant players have viewpoints that change.

Blastland offers another perspective which we have found useful. In the Clear and Complicated domains, forecasts and extrapolations are made but treating any small variation from the forecast as 'noise'. But in the complex area, noise dominates and the cone of uncertainty is huge. According to Kahneman, noise may well be more important than bias. Kahneman et al in their book *Noise* tell of two highly skilled insurance underwriters who, given the same information, are asked to suggest suitable insurance premiums. Their answers differed by 55%, not by the 10% that their managers predicted. A forecast elicits a response, so paradoxically as we have more data and better models, noise actually increases.

Chaotic is a mess. Unpredictable. Here there is extreme sensitivity to conditions. One small change, and everything interacts. This is the domain of crisis management. The sequence should be 'Act, Sense, Respond'. To quote Snowden and Boone: *"In the chaotic domain, a leader's immediate job is not to discover patterns but to staunch the bleeding. A leader must first act to establish order, then sense where stability is present and from where it is absent, and then respond by working to transform the situation from chaos to complexity…"* Hence it is the domain of rapid response.

Directions:

To quote Graupp et al, *"There will be a clockwise movement from chaotic to complex to complicated to Clear as control is gradually gained over the situation. However, when attention wanes and entropy sets in, there will be a counter-clockwise drift as standards and practices fall to the wayside or veteran employees leave the organization to be replaced by people unfamiliar with past traditions and culture".* According to the law of entropy, situations will also tend to grow in complexity over time. In addition to this natural drift, one important insight Snowden stresses is that the Clear domain is actually the danger zone because here complacency sets in. People assume that, because conditions are stable, they will remain so indefinitely without their attention or intervention and, if action is needed, the standards and practices that worked in the past will continue…. As Snowden describes it, the border between Clear and Chaotic is not a line but a cliff that is easy to fall off. The real danger, then, is not gravitating counter-clockwise through the domains, but going the other way, clockwise from Clear directly to Chaos. Snowden's advice is to try to stay in the Complicated domain and not let your organization fall into the complacency of Clear.'

Implications for Lean and problem solving: (Speculation!)

- Many Lean and Six Sigma tools are best applicable in the Clear and Complicated domains. Countermeasures are clear.
- Tools such as A3 and Value Stream Mapping are most applicable in the Complicated domain. Basic problem-solving tools such as the 7 Quality Tools work satisfactorily in the Clear domain.
- Kata would seem applicable in Complicated domains, and may work (with caution) in the Complex domain.
- Beware of PDSA in the Complex domain. Experimentation is vital in order to learn, but the 'landscape' may change meaning that experimental results are not necessarily repeatable.
- OODA would seem more applicable than PDSA in the Complex and Chaotic domains. (See below on OODA and PDSA).

- To restore or gain control, 5S and TWI job instruction seem to be appropriate interventions in the Chaotic domain. TWI JM and JR are would be applicable in the Complicated domain.
- An example of the onset of complexity could be the transition from laminar to turbulent flow in a river. Often, a surge will appear suddenly because a critical mass has been reached. Laminar flow is certainly complicated but the flow is predictable. What happens when a sudden change, such as a waterfall occurs? Turbulence! Engineers will be aware that the onset of turbulent flow is predicted by the Reynolds number which is the ratio of inertia force to viscosity (stickiness). Here is some speculation: Could it be that the onset of problems in an organisation (turbulence) occur suddenly as a result of the speed of change and the 'stickiness' of the organisation?
- The Complex domain is the realm of innovative and creative counter-measures. Here Kata type experiments must be conducted as, as shown in several of Mike Rother's diagrams, the path will not be linear but may often double back when some experiments don't work out.
- Finally, to quote Graupp et al, "*Use TWI to get out of and stay out of chaos, and use Kata to gravitate from Complex back to Complicated and avoid the complacency of Simple. If we view the world as being a "complicated" place, then we can see how we must maintain constant vigilance and diligence in order to stay on track to getting to our goals, no matter how strong the temptation may be to fall into a sense of satisfaction with "the way things are." Our sand castle will crumble if we don't fight against the forces of nature that work to bring it down.*"

Solutions?

Scott Page suggests some actions we can take if we find we are in a complex situation. We summarise below. (Note Scott Page is not referring to Snowden's model):

- Experiment. Try it out, but expect to fail quite often. Keep trying. What works this year may not work next year. Sense and respond.
- Diversity. Cognitive diversity or opinion diversity reduces the risk of error and increases the probability of innovation. If we promote only accountants, then there will (probably) be only a short-term, cost-variance, ROI viewpoint. Only HR people: a people viewpoint but nothing on ops, markets, finance. We need a mix, even if the mix means not including some high IQ people. There is no point to a team who agree with everything!
- Measures. "*Tell me how you will measure me, and I'll tell you what I will do*", said Eli Goldratt. Try to think though the second-, or even the third-, order effects. What will be the effect of a measure on people indirectly affected? Example: An Indian state paid for each rat caught. The result: People grew rats!
- Efficiency. Be very wary of 'optimal' efficiency with no buffer. See Queuing, Section 4.8. Although a Lean aim is to reduce buffers, going for zero waste could be a disaster. Your optimal shipping solution could get stuck in the Suez Canal.
- A hypothesis is not always required because of uncertainty and change. Sometimes just exploration is fine – using (perhaps) 'agent-based models' (An ABM uses various autonomous decision makers with different perspectives that interact.)
- Connections. Steven Johnson says the root of almost all innovation is what he calls 'the adjacent possible'. Look in adjacent areas and seek what is possible. The iPhone came out of phone, microprocessor, glass, internet, music, memory chip, haptic, app possibilities, and other technologies.

Here is an important point about the Complex domain: Since there are unknown non-linear relationships, and because the entities and their inter-relationships change, the scientific method is much less reliable. How can one best respond when everything is a moving target? Blastland offers some suggestions, a few of which are commented on below:

- Keep experimenting and adapting. Since we don't know that we don't know, we need to try things out and be prepared to change direction. If possible, do a randomised trial with a control group. To do so is far superior to a single pilot experiment. Is this possible in an operations environment? Challenging! (This is discussed further under PDSA.)
- Triangulate. As in good research design, try more than one path aiming for the same conclusion. Parallel Kata paths?
- Manage for uncertainty. Think ahead as to what can go wrong. (Similar to Gary Klein's 'pre-mortem' concept – see Section 9.5.)

Further Readings.

Michael Blastland, *The Hidden Half,* Atlantic Books, 2019
Patrick Graupp, Steward and Parsons*, Creating an Effective Management System: Integrating Policy Deployment, WI, ad Kata,* CRC Press, 2020
Daniel Kahneman, Oliver Sibony, and Cass Sunstein, *Noise*, Collins, 2021
Scott Page, *The Model Thinker*, Hachette Books, 2018
David Snowden and Mary Boone, 'A Leaders Framework for Decision Making', *Harvard Business Review*, November 2007, pp68-76
David Snowden and friends, *Cynefin – Weaving sense-making into the fabric of the world*, Cognitive Edge, 2021
www.cynefin.io is a developing discussion forum covering many aspects, including Design Principles for managing complexity.
Dave Snowden, Video: www.youtube.com/watch?v=N7oz366X0-8

8.10 More on More Complex and Complicated Problems

Alvesson and Spicer in *The Stupidity Paradox* criticise some for the idea that by being optimistic you can succeed in every aspect of your life. (See Seligman on AI above). What is needed, they and others maintain, is better critical thinking – or 'negative capability' – 'the ability to face up to uncertainty, paradoxes and ambiguities.' They suggest

- *Observe*. Look and listen, including beneath the surface, and avoiding premature problem definition. 'What is going here?'
- *Interpret*. Find out what others think – the perspectives of others – other disciplines, other levels, other players. 'What do the natives think is happening here?'
- *Question*. 'What are the assumptions we are making, and the reasons behind the assumptions?' 'Why are you interested in this?'

Alvesson and Spicer suggest that 9 processes would be useful to engage in critical thinking. Here, we build on their excellent ideas:

- *Reflective routines*. Instead of having ad-hoc Hansei-type sessions, set aside specific regular Reflective sessions. For instance, around 'What have we done this month?'. Also, as per Google, invite outside speakers with provocative viewpoints.
- *Devil's advocates*. Give specific devil's advocate responsibility to some managers. A specific role to challenge groupthink and the conventional. This is suggested by DeBono as one of his '6 Thinking Hats'. A devil's advocate was used by JFK during the Cuban Missile Crisis.

- *Post-mortems*. Build these in, for all cases not just for failures. This is done in routinely in AAR. (See Section 10.20). Don't miss the opportunity to look back, critically – not just the lip service of 'lessons will be learned'. Avoid personal blame – instead look at the system.
- *Pre-mortems*. As suggested by Gary Klein. (See Section 9.5).
- *Newcomers.* Newcomers frequently bring new, fresh ideas. Encourage these to be aired, not suppressed. And the next point…
- *Outsiders.* As stated by Steven Johnson, most innovations stem from 'the adjacent possible' where breakthroughs result from combining with outside concepts (See Sections 4.2 and 8.9). Invite outsiders to come see and solicit their views. One of the authors has experienced being pumped for ideas following visits to, for example, Dell and McLaren.
- *Engage your Critics.* Much has been said in this book about types of bias, wilful blindness and the fundamental attribution error. A way to counter this is to give some credibility to your critics. (Heffernan)
- *Competitions and games.* Alvesson and Spicer suggest 'bullshit bingo' where a prize is given for the biggest meaningless statement, to counter gobbledegook speak so common in management, including Lean.
- *Anti-stupidity task force.* Such as group is tasked with identifying organisational bullshit. This theme is taken up in the section on Bullshit in the Organisation Chapter.

Further Readings.
Mats Alversson and André Spicer, *The Stupidity Paradox*, Profile, 2016
Stella Cottrell, *Critical Thinking Skills: Effective Analysis, Argument and Reflection*, Macmillan, 2017
Margaret Heffernan, *Wilful Blindness*, Simon and Schuster, 2011
Stefan Maidan, *The Systems Thinker: A Practical guide to use Critical Thinking for Changing your Life*, Independent, 2020
Peter Simpson, et al, 'Leadership and negative capability', *Human Relations*, v55n10, pp1209-1226, 2002

8.11 Christensen's Innovation Types

The late and great Clayton Christensen of Harvard Business School postulated four types of innovation. A very brief summary is given together with comments relating to Lean and other concepts in this Chapter, but the reader is urged to consult Christensen's award-winning books.

Efficiency – where existing products are made more efficiently. Cost reduction would be a big factor so Kaizen, but particularly of the flow type, has an important role. Value Stream Mapping would be important. Lean consultants would be very active here. Outsourcing has been an important strategy.

Sustaining – where existing products are improved. Cars and computers are made better. Moore's Law for semiconductors. Lean design, set-based design, Design Thinking are all relevant approaches. The market does not grow as better products replace older versions.

Both these types are probably of the 'known known' type; the next two types are probably of the 'known unknown' type, and are a more of a challenge:

Potential – where new products or services come into the market. TRIZ trends could give an indication of the future. Christensen's concept of seeking out 'The Job to be done', rather than asking customers by market survey, is an important insight for Lean about customer value! Stephen

Johnson's concept of the Adjacent Possible, mentioned in the last section, would be a driver. The iPad.

Disruptive – making products more accessible and affordable using a new approach. Probably not as good, at least initially but surpassing the established players later on. Toyota coming into the US market with the Corona, or Amazon taking on established bookshops in 2000. This often widens the customer base as many new customers take up the opportunity. The Toyota Production System was a disruptor in as far as cars were made 'in half the time, with half the cost, and with far less than half the defects'. Is this still an opportunity for Lean? Probably no longer in manufacturing, but possibly in other fields: Education? Health? Travel? Food?

Further Readings.
Clayton Christensen, Anthony and Roth, *Seeing What's Next*, Harvard Business School Press, 2004.
Clayton Christensen, Hall and Dillon, *Competing Against Luck*, Harvard Business School Press, 2016
Clayton Christensen and Michael Raynor, *The Innovator's Solution*, Harvard Business School Press, 2000

8.12 Ackoff's Four Problem Treatments

The great Systems Thinker Russell Ackoff (see also Chapter 5 on Systems) also had views about four 'problem treatments': Absolving, Resolving, Solving, Dissolving.

- *Absolving* is essentially ignoring – it might go away on its own accord. That sometimes happens. A flood. Excess demand on a facility drops away. A difficult person retires. Customers leave!
- *Resolving* is tackling a problem (often by common sense, and basic tools such as the 7 Quality Tools). This is in line with Herbert Simon's 'satisficing'- not optimising but just doing good enough. Experimentation may play a part.
- *Solving* is more sophisticated. Systems thinking is probably involved. Value stream mapping used but alongside statistics and operations research. Six Sigma including perhaps design of experiments. Optimising within the known parameters. Example: Kaizen improvement activities aiming to make a great car in a great system.
- *Dissolving*. Essentially making the problem go away by design and/or a new way of looking at the problem. System thinking is usually involved. Ackoff talked about Idealized design, beginning with a blank sheet. Assume everything burned down yesterday. One of the techniques that Ackoff uses is a Reference Projection that extrapolates an existing trend assuming no change. As an example, one of the authors used a Reference Projection of the number of cars entering a city centre. The projection showed that in 15 years' time the entire city would have to be converted into a parking lot. Something had to change!

A mundane example from Lean: Instead of solving the Economic Order Quantity problem by an optimal trade-off calculation, Dissolving is to reduce the changeover time to zero.

In his usual wise and witty way, Ackoff said that solving the wrong problem right was worse than solving the right problem wrong. An example using the four treatments: Solving car manufacturing problems might be the aim. But a defect-free, inexpensive car is not really a solution if the result makes transportation increasingly worse. Dissolving, then, would be doing away with cars and reinventing transportation so as to solve the wider problems of pollution, congestion and delay. (Electric flying cars expected by 2030?)

A problem, said Ackoff, has five components: the decision maker; the controllable variables; the uncontrolled variables; constraints; and possible outcomes produced jointly by the decision maker's choice and the uncontrolled variables. The art of problem solving is gaining a solution to all these components <u>as a set</u>, not individually. (One of the author's mothers had these well-known words by her bed: *'God grant me the serenity to accept the things I cannot change, courage to change the things I can, and wisdom to know the difference.'* Ackoff's five?)

By the way, dear reader, if you like this sort of thinking, you will find John Galt's *The Systems Bible*, stimulating and subversive! Guaranteed to provoke your thinking, make you laugh, and annoy anyone with conventional views. (As noted in Chapter 5 on Systems.)

Further Readings.
Russell Ackoff, *The Art of Problem Solving*, Wiley, 1978

8.13 PDSA, DMAIC and OODA

PDSA

The Plan Do Check Act Cycle, or Deming Cycle, has become a standard improvement and learning method in the Lean world. (Here, we will use PDSA, Plan Do Study Act as Deming recommended.) Synonymous with the experimental method, it should be used as an experimental cycle for problem solving to test plans and hypotheses. In that respect, perhaps it better to use Plan Do Study Adjust. Often PDSA is shown as a cycle, but it actually alternates between theory (plan and adjust) and implementation (do and study). Planning is about formulating a proposal, plan or hypothesis. Do is about carrying out the plan. Study is about comparing the outcome with the hypothesis, and then learning any lessons. Adjust is tweaking and re-standardising, ready for the next cycle.
Two points about PDSA
- It requires time to go through the cycle
- It is more suitable for recurring processes
- Scientific method assumes a repeatable experiment. If there is a chaotic or complex situation this may not be the case.

PDSA is eminently suitable for experimental Kaizen problem solving, such as Kata and A3 problem solving, and in re-setting standards.

DMAIC

Define Measure Analyse Improve, Control. The Six Sigma version of PDSA is more specific on measurement which is appropriate for the quantitative nature of Six Sigma. 'Control' may give the impression that the problem is solved rather than a continuing cycle.

There is, however, overlap between PDCA /PDCA and DMAIC, as the following 8 step methodology, based on a Toyota sequence, illustrates. This 8 Step methodology is widely applicable but especially in Types 3, 4 and 5 of the Six Category Classification. Beware, however, showing 8 steps without closing the loop for the next cycle could suggest one-off problem 'solving' rather than continuous improvement.

The left-hand side of an A3 consists of the first 3 steps. Do not move onto the right hand side Step 4 before setting the clear target. It is a common mistake to move too rapidly to Step 4.

So, for example, the initial problem might have been 'the unsatisfactory quality of coffee' from a coffee shop. By Step 3 the clear SMART (specific, measurable, achievable, realistic, timely) target has been set as a problem with cold cappuccino in the afternoon.

Taking time to pin down the problem reflects Einstein's famous statement: *"If I had an hour to solve a problem, I'd spend 55 minutes thinking about the problem and 5 minutes thinking about solutions."*

An important point is not the actual 8 step methodology itself, or A3 or Kata, but how they are used. If the 8 steps, A3 or Kata, are used in a mechanical way they will be of limited benefit. But if they are seen as vehicles to learn, through coaching and mentoring, this enables another dimension to be realised. Culture change becomes possible. As John Shook says, *'It takes two to A3'* – in other words there must be a learner and a mentor. More on this in System 1 and System 2 in a later section.

Feedback should be given by the mentor, preferably as soon as possible. This means that there will probably be several sessions of feedback before Step 3 is finalised. Of course, as with AAR's, criticising the person is not allowed. Focus on the process. (See Section 5.3 on Feedback.)

	Step		
P	1	Clarify the problem	D
		a. Background	
		b. Visualise / Gemba	
		c. Identify the gap	
		d. Contain	
	2	Break down the problem	M
		a. 5W and 1 H	
		b. Process chart	
	3	Target setting (SMART)	
	4	Root cause	A
		a. 5 Why	
		b. 4 M's	
D	5	Countermeasures	I
	6	Execution plan	
S	7	Monitor results	
A	8	Standardise and Share	C

An Experience with PDSA

PDSA was brought home to one of the authors in 1986. (Yes, five years before the word Lean was first used by Womack and Jones). The experience was similar to one told by Steve Spear in Decoding the DNA of the Toyota Production System (*Harvard Business Review*, November 1999). This short story would fit in with the Type 4 problem category.

In 1985, Shingo's book on SMED had just come out. (Shigeo Shingo, *A revolution in Manufacturing: the SMED System*, Productivity, 1985). Companies in South Africa were keen to have SMED applied. Industrial Engineering students undertook a SMED project in a press shop, and achieved a significant changeover time reduction. The management was very pleased, and the author, as student supervisor, 'basked in reflected glory'. Pressings were supplied to Toyota South Africa and a Jishuken facilitator from Toyota attended the student presentation. He asked about how the results had matched up against expectations. 'Well, the expectation was a reduction in changeover time'. But what was the specific aim? No answer. 'I thought that the students were taking a Batchelor of Science Degree. Did they not learn scientific method?' Embarrassment! It transpired that the facilitator was much more interested in what the students had learned than their actual results. PDSA is win, win. Either you confirm your prediction, or you discover aspects that you did not know, but can learn. That is the proper scientific method.

Too often, PDSA is one-off, uni-directional, has no clear prediction, no comparison with prediction, and no learning potential. It is PD not PDSA. If this is the case it may be a project but is not scientific method.

A Service Framework

John Seddon's Vanguard improvement Methodology is a variant, most applicable in service: Overall, the structure is 'Check, Plan, Do'. The stages were briefly described in Chapter 5 on Systems.

Jackson has suggested a classification for 'Systems' problems, dependant on the problem. A more extensive description of these types is given in Chapter 5 on Systems.

Further Readings.
John Bicheno, *The Service Systems Toolbox*, PICSIE, 2012
John Seddon, *Freedom from Command and Control*, Vanguard, 2003

OODA

Observe Orient Decide Act is a sequence devised by Col. John Boyd of USAF drawing on air combat experience. For Boyd, OODA is about agility – meaning the ability to rapidly change orientation in response to what is happening externally – especially in what we have referred to as VUCA times.

OODA is a more rapid, continually adjusting, problem methodology as befits its origins in air combat. By contrast PDSA involves experimental cycles usually of a longer duration – although in the case of a mentor/mentee coaching process both OODA and PDSA would give frequent and rapid feedback. OODA is belatedly but increasingly favoured in dynamic environments and in rapid adjustment cycles such as in agile software and product development. According to Wikipedia, "OODA has become an important concept in litigation, business, law enforcement, and the military.... The cycle is repeated continuously. The aggressive and conscious application of the process gives a business advantage over a competitor who is merely reacting to conditions as they occur or has poor awareness of the situation.... The approach favours agility over raw power in dealing with human opponents in any endeavour."

An important and differentiating point is that a decision is constantly under review and can be changed (or pivoted) 'on the fly' as more or different information becomes available. 'The effects of faster decisions are cumulative' says Reinertsen, so a slower decision cycle is rapidly left behind.

A comparison of PDSA and OODA cycles is shown in the Figure. The PDSA cycle is adapted from Scholtes, and the OODA cycle adapted from Boyd.

In the OODA figure 'Guidance and Control' reflects the philosophy of rapid, local decision making. 'Guidance and Control' would include an understanding of Lean aims and principles ('True North') allowing local initiatives to take place without permissions and approvals up and down the hierarchy. The military equivalent is having clear direction but also clearly understood 'rules of engagement'.

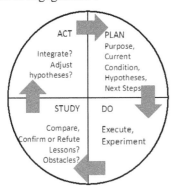 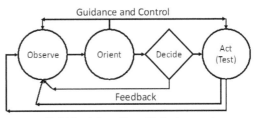

Unfolding interaction with Environment

OODA is sometimes shown as a 4-stage cycle like PDSA, but in fact has feedback loops back to Observe from all three other stages. OODA is an attractive model for 'Fix It Now', Immediate Kaizen and for Directed Improvement. Why? Because OODA is

- A rapid decision process, not a scientific experiment
- Rapid feedback allows adjustment
- Dynamic. The decision evolves as changes take place
- It follows the sequence of how people actually decide in the short term.
- Starting with Observe fits well with the Lean 'Go see' requirement.
- At a strategic level, Observe and Orient nicely implies looking at the developing external situation.

In short, OODA is the opposite of top-down command and control, where analytical models are built and then tested (by which time the 'landscape' may have changed). This was the by-now well-known problem in software development known as the 'Waterfall' method, and why 'sprints' and 'pivoting' have grown in popularity. These latter concepts are fully compatible with OODA.

Boyd was also a fan of WW2 German military thinking – where significant reliance is given to field commanders, indeed to platoon commanders, to make the right decisions as a battle develops, given that they know the broad plan. It is about mutual trust and cohesion. An 'intuitive feel, especially for complex and potentially chaotic situations.' Seize and keep the initiative. Create and exploit opportunities. Strategy is about creating surprise and confusion – an abrupt, unexpected, and disorienting pattern of action (according to Richards).

OODA has been strongly linked with Sun Tsu's 'Art of War' which attempts to out-manoeuvre an opponent before the battle even starts.

Further Readings.
Chet Richards, *Certain to Win: The strategy of John Boyd applied to business*, Xlibris, 2004
Peter Scholtes, *The Leader's Handbook*, McGraw Hill, 1998 (on PDSA)
John Shook, *Managing to Learn*, LEI, 2008 (On A3)
Stefan Thomke and Don Reinertsen, 'Six Myths of Product Development', *Harvard Business Review*, May 2012, pp85-94

8.14 System 1 and System 2

Daniel Kahneman's concept of brain function, known as System 1 and System 2 has become widely accepted in psychology particularly since the publication of his wonderful book *Thinking, Fast and Slow* and his receipt of the Nobel Prize. According to Kahneman, the human brain has two modes of thinking, summarised by us in the table below:

A by-now famous question developed by Shane Frederick of Yale University, is 'A bat and a ball cost $1.10 in total. The bat costs $1.00 more than the ball. How much does the ball cost?' A very high proportion of people (irrespective of education) give the incorrect answer of $0.10. This is System 1 thinking. (We will not give the correct answer. If you got this wrong, use System 2 thinking to get the answer.)

This is illustrative of the danger of using quick-response, intuitive answers. In Lean the correct answer is often counter-intuitive.

System 1 Thinking	System 2 Thinking
Unconscious, automatic, effortless	Conscious, deliberate, effortful
Fast	Slow
Hypothetical	Logical, sceptical
Without self-awareness or control	With self-awareness and control
98% of our thinking	2% of our thinking
Influenced by experiences, emotions, memories	Influenced by facts, logic, evidence
Can be overridden by System 2	Used when System 1 fails
Recognition, perception, orientation	Comparisons, weighting of options
Most think they are using logic but aren't.	
Feels right even if shown to be wrong	
Rough estimates may be OK but not precision.	

According to Kahneman, many of our decisions are made on 'autopilot'. They are habits that bypass conscious decisions. They influence our behaviour without us even realising.

Some problems demand an immediate or short-term response. There is no time to do an analysis, to try experiments or PDCA, or to go through several A3 mentoring cycles. You don't do an A3 if you are being charged by a tiger. So, System 1 responds immediately based on experience (as in OODA). However, System 1 is sometimes wrong – particularly in the case of counterintuitive situations.

Here is a vital point: In a Lean or operations environment, many decisions are made, or have to be made, in the short term. There may not be time for a considered System 2 decision. But there are many counterintuitive beliefs in Lean and operations. Therefore System 1 decisions need to reinforce, not detract from Lean. So the question is, 'how do Lean managers learn the correct System 1 responses? It is possible: Much recent brain research has uncovered *neuroplasticity* – a developing and changing brain – that continues throughout life.

The intuitive beliefs of System 1 thinking in a Lean Environment form a long list. Counter-intuitive System 2 thinking should come to replace wrong System 1 thinking. A list of intuitive and counterintuitive beliefs is given in the Appendix to this chapter.

Psychologists now know that System 2 can train System 1 through habits – deliberate or unconscious – good or bad. As has been said, the more you do something, the more likely you are to do it again. For instance, learning to drive takes real mental effort (System 2) but eventually becomes automatic, subconscious System 1. Habits have power. With repetition they can turn a deliberate time-consuming System 2 decision into an automatic, fast System 1 response. (See Section 3.23 for more on Habits.)

If A3, or Kata, or any other problem response does not feed back into System 1 thinking, then learning will be limited. Lean will progress very slowly, or not at all.

It is important that people at all levels in a Lean-aspiring organisation train their System 1 thinking by reflecting on System 2 experiences, relating them back to education and theory. Without reflection back to education and theory, much experience is wasted. Recall Quality Guru Phil Crosby asking people if they have 25 years' experience or one year 25 times!

There should be a deliberate transfer of counterintuitive knowledge from System 2 (e.g. A3, Kata) back to the System 1 mindset. Reflection and discussion are crucial. (Please refer to the Learning Chapter, particularly the Stages of Learning and The Cone of Experience.) It is important that everyone has a clear concept of the Ideal State or what 'True North' is. Without this, the same mistake may be made over and over again without anyone realising the problem or anyone seeking about a better way.

System 1 tends to jump to conclusions, so Kahneman has adopted WYSIATI – what you see is all there is. This applies to several types of bias – overconfidence, framing, anchoring, sunk cost, and confirmation. We are all subject to many biases. For instance we are more sensitive to loss than to gain. A study showed that surgeons rejected a procedure having a 10% mortality but accepted a procedure with a 90% survival rate. They have the same outcome! It is important that decision makers be aware of the dangers of bias. (Various types of bias are given in Section 9.7)

Kahneman gives 6 modes of interaction between System 1 and System 2, leading to a failure to learn. The modes, with Lean examples, are:

- Approval. Where System 2 approves of a System 1 decision. S1 has decided to reduce batch size and S2 approves.
- Override. S1 decides on a larger batch but S2 knows it is wrong and overrides.
- Neglect. S2 is too busy with other concerns and has no time to examine an S1 decision. An inconsistent batch size decision creeps in.
- Influenced. S2 has overridden S1, but S1 keeps reminding S2. "I told you that a smaller batch would spell trouble."
- Informed. S1 gives feedback to S2 – for or against.
- Solo. S1 just cannot make the decision. Easy to calculate 6x3, but cannot do 37x54 automatically. What will be the implications of a smaller batch on safety stock?

Further Readings.
Daniel Kahneman, *Thinking, Fast and Slow*, Allen Lane, 2011

8.15 The Six Categories of Problems Revisited

We can now bring these concepts together:

Appropriate Responses			Maintenance / Restoration	Improvement	
				Process	Intervention
System 2	PDSA	Proactive	2. Restore	4. Experimental Kaizen	6. Breakthrough Innovation
System 1	OODA	Reactive	1. Fix it Now	3. Short-term Kaizen	5. Directed Improvement
				Kaizen	Kaikaku
			Internal Pull		External Push

The Six Categories are shown in the highlighted box.

In the Figure, we have attempted to link the 6 Types with Responses, with improvement approaches, with incremental (Kaizen) and breakthrough (Kaikaku), and with pull and push. The boundaries between the 6 types are not clear cut, neither are the applicable tools. Responses to problems in each of the Six Categories are best thought of, at least in the first instance, by using the concepts in the corresponding rows and columns.

A central idea is that a 'horses for courses' or situational approach is an appropriate response to problems. As one moves from bottom left (Type 1) to top right (Type 6) complexity increases and with it the necessity to discuss more widely the assumptions and system boundary, and to recognise bias that is implicit in any proposed solution. (This is further discussed in Section 9.4 on Strategic Decisions and avoiding Groupthink.)

8.16 A Comparison of Problem Frameworks

An approximate comparison between frameworks is given in the Table below. Each framework comes from a different perspective or view-of-the-world so they are not strictly comparable. Each offers a valuable insight, so it is hoped that the reader will gain an enhanced appreciation of the general area.

This book	Imai's Flag	Smalley's Four Types	Ackoff's Four Types	Snowden's Cynefin®	Christensen's Innovation
			Absolve	Chaotic	
Fix	Standard -isation	Type 1			
Restore			Resolve		
Now Kaizen	Point Kaizen	Type 2		Clear	
Experiment	Flow Kaizen		Solve	Complicated	Efficiency / Sustaining
Directed Kaizen		Type 3			
Breakthrough	Innovation	Type 4	Dissolve	Complex	Potential / Disruptive

Finally...We end this section on problems with some provocation..

- We live in a world of uncertainty, not certainty. Assuming we will return to a period of non-complex normality could well be an illusion and a forlorn hope.
- The scientific method – breaking down a problem into component parts and studying each, or reductionism is not always applicable.
- Problem 'solving' is often a misnomer except in the case of small often technical situations.

8.17 Ideas, Idea Management and Creativity

Idea generation is one thing. But idea development is another. Most ideas, when first mooted, are half-baked and need tweaking and adaptation to begin to pay off. Hence,

idea management = idea generation + idea development

...and there is often a third aspect: Idea propagation.

An organisation may well need a system for each of these three areas. In all three areas, essential skills for leaders in an idea-driven organisation include; listening, coaching, facilitation, problem solving and leading improvement activities. Personal humility and a genuine respect for people are also pre-requisites.

Unfortunately, in some organisations that we know of, great attention is given to hiring good people, and to fostering their development and to in-house training. But then, alas, the great potential of these people is not realised because of a failure to surface, capture, and develop the wonderful ideas of which these people are capable.

Idea Management is an important part of Problem Solving. An Idea system can work well with all 6 Categories of Problems, but is usually associated with types 3 and 4.

Idea Generation

While all organisations integrate some form of idea or suggestion scheme into their business, the proposition put forward by Alan Robinson and Dean Schroeder in their book *The Idea-Driven Organisation* is that the organisation should be structured and aligned around idea generation. A surprising statistic is that on average 80% of an organisation's performance improvement opportunity resides in front-line ideas, and only 20% in management focused initiatives. The notion that front-line improvements can outperform management initiatives by a factor of 4 to 1 is something that senior management teams find very hard to grasp. So why is this the case?

Idea generation can be push or pull, passive or pro-active. The classic passive type is the suggestion box. Generally, this only works for a while and later attracts cynical comments instead of suggestions. Non-acknowledgement and non-recognition have probably been the major reason for suggestion schemes producing poor results and being abandoned. If accepted, the idea is assigned to an individual or department for implementation which may result in further delay or unenthusiastic 'not-invented-here' attitude. Such systems are bureaucratic, slow and biased towards rejecting ideas. The results do not justify the time, hassle and overhead of running the system.

A passive type that does seem to work is the submission of ideas over the web, calling on the general public. There have been competitions with big prizes. Interestingly there are companies whose business is to develop ideas submitted from external individuals. (So, if your company rejects your idea, try submitting it to an idea company. Revenge could be sweet!)

The pro-active type begins with education on wastes, and a no-fears culture of encouragement. As an example, a company in North-East England set up a workshop with tools and materials to encourage employees to develop poka-yoke devices. The workshop itself was set up following a suggestion. The workshop ran for several years and generated a score of devices that were implemented... (Some companies call this 'The Engineering Sandbox' – an area or workshop where employees can build and try out their ideas.) A famous example is Google's policy of allowing one day per week for employees to develop their own ideas. Google has also developed a 'Jamboard' which is a collaborative digital whiteboard. Other outstanding 'Ideas' companies are Gore-Tex and 3M. (The 3M case is interesting because a subsequent focus towards Six Sigma resulted in a huge decline in ideas from this famous ideas company. This has now been reversed.)

A PiT-Stop event is a Kaizen-event variation where, in 15-minute interviews, employee ideas are solicited. This stems from the '70% Thesis' whereby studies have revealed that, typically, 70% of employees have never submitted a suggestion; 70% can identify a problem but not necessarily a solution; 70% simply work according to their job description; 70% have never been asked for their ideas.

Thomas Edison is reported to have said that the way to have great inventions is to have many inventions. He set up a deliberate methodology for the exhaustive exploration of possibilities. An interesting variant on this was explained to one of the authors by a Toyota manager. He said that the volume of ideas counts. The concept is the pareto-type recognition that most ideas will have little value but a few will have major impact. How to get the 'big ones'? Get them all! Send out the positive message by implementing as many as possible even if they are marginal.

Yuso Yasuda has described the Toyota suggestion scheme or 'Kaizen system'. The scheme is co-ordinated by a 'creative idea suggestion committee' whose chairmanship has included Toyota chairmen (Toyoda and Saito) as well as Taiichi Ohno. Rewards for suggestions are given at Toyota based on a points system. Points are scored for tangible and intangible benefits, and for adaptability, creativity, originality, and effort. The rewards are invariably small amounts, and are not based on a percentage of savings. However, operators value the token reward and the presentation ceremony itself. Note the contrast with typical Western Suggestion Schemes. From the foregoing we learn a few important lessons; (1) Not all improvements will pay, but creating the culture of improvement is more important. (2) Give it time, and expand slowly (3) recognition is important - management cannot always be expected to give personal support, so establish a facilitator or function that can. (4) Do not underestimate potential opposition, (5) React rapidly to suggestions and (6) Give groups the tools and techniques, and the time.

Physical Layout of workspace for ideas could be important. The famous innovation company IDEO has studios where almost everyone can see each other's problems and projects. They use 'Tech boxes' comprising tools, toys, fabrics, objects, and so on - to stimulate cross-fertilization of ideas. Several companies have 'meeting pods'. Colours have been shown to make a difference. Many ideas are generated away from the workplace – on walks, in the bath, in the gym, whilst sleeping. So having an on-site gym, showers, garden, and even a place for a nap, are more than just nice features.

'Doodle for Google', is a web-site and idea competition. Any US-based student can submit a doodle (or sketch) that is judged by a panel with the national winner receiving a $30k scholarship and a $50k package for the school. There are also prizes for finalists.

These and others, of course, tie in well with brainstorming and After Action Reviews – see Section 10.20.

Idea Development

Most ideas require development. Rather than simply overlaying the idea system on an existing management structure, it is necessary to align the entire organisation to support the development and implementation of ideas. Personal, departmental and site goals need to be aligned, according to Robinson and Schroeder. Time and capital should be allocated to implementing ideas - as well as to running the business. Just as with any other performance element, ideas should be integrated into performance appraisals, bonuses and promotion criteria. Some organisations have appointed an 'Idea Facilitator' (or similar title) – full time or part-time.

An organisation can encourage participation in idea development with participation in cell design and layout. Use cardboard mock-ups and flexible 'Crayform' to allow employees to adjust and develop their own workstations. Bottom-up, not top-down imposed!

The visual progression of ideas is vital: A prominent board should display new, in development, and completed ideas. The idea approval process should be frequent and streamlined. A good policy is to insist that all suggestions are acknowledged within 24 hours and evaluated within a week. The reasons for rejected ideas should be carefully explained. Beware of cash for ideas, particularly where a percentage of savings is paid. This can work against team cooperation and cause resentment: in one case known to the authors a £40k pay-out made to an employee for a suggestion considered 'obvious' by CI facilitators set back kaizen efforts for an extended period.

Search the Images section of 'Google Ideas Board' on Google for numerous examples of visual idea boards.

Idea Propagation

In many large organisations, a third element, idea propagation is desirable if the potential of an idea is to be realised. Adaption could be required as an idea is propagated, so loop back to the previous stage.

Yokoten: another strange Japanese word. It means 'horizontal deployment' of ideas, innovations, solutions. But Yokoten has some specific characteristics:

- Not only is the idea logged onto a data base – although that would be a good idea in itself using keywords – but it involves 'go see' for yourself. Why? The richness of an idea is difficult to communicate by text or video. Seeing first-hand and communicating with the source not only clarifies but may lead onto further opportunities, and more, and yet more.
- It is about communicating failures as well as success. 'You only learn through mistakes'. This is a very important aspect – and something that is lost in many organisations. What a waste! Sometimes there is reluctance or fear to admit failure. What a shame! So this is in fact Psychological Safety. But Yokoten encourages failures to be seen in a positive light. Yokoten, in fact, encourages a 'Growth Mindset' – you haven't got there YET. (See Carol Dwek, Section 7.4, and Mistakes, Section 9.9)
- Yokoten should be the final step in a PDSA / PDCA cycle, the final 8th step in an A3, and even the final step in a Kaizen event.

Horizontal deployment in a large multi-site operation is important. You would like to avoid reinventing the wheel. This is not to say that compulsory copying is required – local adaptation must still be allowed. Yokoten may begin with a presentation to other Kaizen groups but a way should be found to cross communicate. Video libraries are becoming more popular, but a follow up visit should be a possibility.

Power and Ideas

A great obstacle to creating an Idea-Driven Organisation is moving away from a top-down, command and control organisation. And away from a silo-organisation. With the symbols of position and power such as offices, remuneration, education being a constant reminder of elevated status, it can be easy for managers to start believing they are superior. This may manifest in dysfunctional behaviours which alienate the very people they are meant to lead and support. Over the past half century there has been much research into how power affects people. Some findings are of particular significance in building the trust and respect required for an organisation to operate an idea system effectively. For example – perhaps slightly exaggerated (but not much):

- Power, says Dan Cable of London Business School, *"can cause leaders to become overly obsessed with outcomes and control, ...thereby ramping up 'people's fear – fear of not hitting targets, fear of losing bonuses, fear of failing – and as a consequence their drive to experiment and learn is stifled."*
- Power reduces a person's ability to consider alternative suggestions.
- Power is often inversely correlated with learning and with humility.
- Power leads to subordinates being viewed as a means to an end, rather than real people.
- People with power have a tendency to listen less carefully and not to acknowledge what others know. They tend to be less open to the perspectives of others, and less accurate in their estimations of the interests and positions of others.
- People with power have a tendency to develop egos and become preoccupied with their own interests, at the expense of everyone else's.

Finally, a story on ideas and incentives:

A short version of a classic story: Tom Sawyer was asked to whitewash a fence. He pretended to do so with gusto. When a steamboat passed, he ignored it and continued to paint. When a friend asked him to go swimming, he continued to paint. 'Why not, Tom?' 'Because I'm having so much fun painting.' 'Say, Tom, let me whitewash a little.' 'Aw no, it's too much fun.' 'Oh, shucks, Tom, I'll give you all of my apple if you let me have a go'. Tom gave up the brush with reluctance in his face... 'the retired artist sat on a barrel in the shade close by, dangled his legs, munched his apple, and planned the slaughter of more innocents. There was no lack of material; boys happened along every little while; they came to jeer, but remained to whitewash.'

Cautions.

- It is important to remember that ideas begin with problems. If employees are not sensitised to see problems, then they won't be thinking about how to solve them.
- Linking monetary rewards to idea generation systems may encourage wrong behaviours and mitigate teamwork.
- Idea systems should be kept as straightforward as possible with localised approval for implementation. Scrap the suggestion box.
- If ideas are not acted upon in a reasonably short period of time, with a minimum of fuss, the flow of new ideas will quickly dry up.
- Systems are required to hold managers accountable for engaging with front-line employees, encouraging their participation and implementing large numbers of their ideas.

Further Readings.
C. M. Axtell, D. J. Holman, K. L. Unsworth, T. D. Wall and P. E. Waterson, *Shop floor innovation: Facilitating the suggestion and implementation of ideas*, Institute of Work Psychology, University of Sheffield, UK
Andy Brophy and John Bicheno, *Innovative Lean*, PICSIE Books, 2010 (This contains details of several Idea Management Systems, and concepts for Idea generation.)
Alan Robinson and Dean Schroeder, *The Idea Driven Organisation*, Berrett-Koehler, 2014
Yuzo Yasuda, *40 Years, 20 Million Ideas,* Productivity, 1990.

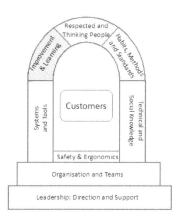

Problem Solving Appendix 1: General Tips and Techniques

There are many sources for more effective problem solving – and some serious research. Here, we select a few of our 'top' concepts and research findings. But see also Ackoff's Four Problem Treatments, earlier in this chapter.

First, in line with Toyota, we like the word 'countermeasure' rather than 'solution'. Virtually no problem is 'solved'. Instead, a countermeasure suggests further opportunities are possible.

Stages: State or define the apparent problem; Break down (use a sequence of trees); Reframe; Analyse; Re-define; seek root causes; hypotheses and testing; select; present and implement; check.

It is useful is to start with lists: 'We want' and 'We don't want'. Simon Dodds, founder of 'Health Care Systems Engineering' has the excellent and powerful concept of beginning with '4N': Nuggets (good current points), Niggles (complaints and aspects that are in the way), Nice-if (what we hope to achieve), and No-Nos (things to be avoided).

The divergent, convergent, divergent, convergent sequence – used in design - is effective. Also known as the Double Diamond (or right brain, left brain, right, left) or the exploration, exploitation sequence. Widen out the area with brainstormed possibilities and lateral thinking; then narrow it down by prioritising. Then, with a new level of detail, repeat the sequence.

Logical Trees (or decision trees) help with disaggregation. A basic tree can be used for how the problem arose: what, why, when, where, who, how. Use Fishbone diagrams. Is and 'is not' trees. Follow the branches for more and more resolution. See mindmapart.com

Verbalisation (talking through with others), drawing it out and active listening all help with clarity. People have different insights which these practices help to surface. When working with others 'bodily feedback' shows subtle encouragement or discouragement. Deliberate practice is required. As with sports, problem capability increases with practice – but not just any practice, deliberate practice is needed. Learning, step by step, from a master, with feedback.

(By the way, on feedback, Daniel Pink in one of his excellent Pinkcasts, suggested that, instead of asking for feedback, ask instead for advice. Why? Because many people feel awkward giving critical feedback but are comfortable and willing to give advice.)

Fixation, Mental set, and Functional fixedness are barriers. See the problem from another perspective. How would someone from another discipline, age group, function, sex, see it? Anthropology? This 'reframing' has long been used by psychologists to shift a client's viewpoint revealing opportunities. This helps with 'lateral thinking' (From the late DeBono's many books) including using random words, and 'Po' thinking. (Say Po not No.) Deliberately take multiple paths, perhaps with a break in-between.

Everyone brings bias to problem solving. As an example, from Davidson and Sternberg, consider this:
1. All living things need water
2. Roses need water
3. Therefore, roses are living things.

Does this follow? If you think that this sequence is valid you are in good company – and wrong! Most of us are biased by what we know. (See the similar sequence at section end.) Can bias be broken? Maybe. First, be aware that everyone filters information and downplays non-supporting evidence. Deliberately include diverse persons.

Incubation, Sleeping on it, Dreaming. The human mind works in the background. Take a break, take a bath, do something different for a while. Feelings of mood or fear have been shown to impact problem solving.

The psychology of problem solving is complex and much remains to be learned. (For an overview see Davidson and Sternberg.) Here are a few pointers:
*   Some believe there are four stages: Preparation and information gathering; Incubation (time away from the problem); Illumination and insight (Aha!); Verification. Experience in each is important.
*   Self-motivation to solve a problem is important. Refer back to earlier sections in Chapter 2 on motivation and Expectancy theory.
*   In quantitative problems, attribution-judgement training helps. Most people are notoriously poor at judging risk, but risk training with feedback improves results.
*   Practice on similar types of problems helps.
*   Mood can make a difference. A sad mood apparently favours detail, whereas a happy mood favours wider creativity.
*   Fixation is a barrier, so deliberate exposure to wider viewpoints helps.
*   Incubation helps with seeing new paths to a solution.
*   An incremental step-by-step process helps with non-routine problems. (People were asked to reflect on how they solved the following problem: A dealer in antique coins got an offer to buy an antique coin with an emperor's head on one side and a date 554 BC on the other. The dealer immediately called the police. Why? Here, few people reported an 'Aha!' experience but most were able to solve the problem with systematic steps). (Solution at section end.)

- Walking whilst problem solving or brainstorming (in groups up to 4 not requiring any writing) has been shown to be effective by a Stanford study. (Which might explain its extensive use amongst Californian IT companies)
- Toys. The famous creative company IDEO has lots of Toys and gadgets lying around. Lateral thinking! (Similar to DeBono's 'Po' word.)

Motivation plays a role in problem solving. Intrinsic – yes. But beware of extrinsic. Sometimes payment by results can make problem solving worse! Daniel Pink in *Drive* discusses this, along with many others. Amazing, because so many incentive plans are built around the extrinsic reward assumption!

Numerous TRIZ concepts can help. TRIZ is probably used more for creativity, but of course there is an overlap with problem solving. TRIZ deals with contradictions, not 'OR' trade-offs but 'AND'. (e.g. strong AND light). The classic 40 principles are provocative ('do it the other way around'- dogs should keep their owners on a tight leash; 'nested doll?', 'self-service?' etc.) but sometimes too remote for an inexperienced problem solver. However, we can vouch for some TRIZ concepts: Ideality (e.g. instead of improving a lawnmower, how about slow growing grass?); The 9 box model: This is a 3x3 grid of boxes. Start with the centre box. Move laterally for past and future. Move up for wider systems, and down for sub-systems. Provocative and stimulating!

Office block	Team area layout	Flex organisation
Desks in rows	Office workstation	Hot desk
Paper records	Desk computer	Cloud

Answers to questions in the Chapter:

The sequence: This similar sequence is correctly invalid.
1. All insects need oxygen
2. Mice need oxygen
3. Therefore, mice are insects.

The Coin: The date of Christ's birth cannot be known 554 years ahead.

Further Readings.

Janet Davidson and Robert Sternberg (eds), *The Psychology of Problem Solving*, Cambridge Univ Press, 2003
Karen Gadd, *TRIZ for Engineers*, Wiley, 2011. (Contains numerous comical sketches and inspiring text.)
Michael Michalko, *Thinkertoys*, 10 Speed Press, 2006
Nonaka, I., H. Takeuchi. 1995. The knowledge-creating company: How Japanese companies create the dynamics of innovation. Oxford University Press, New York.
Roger von Oech, *Expect the Unexpected*, BK, 2002
Ken Watanabe, *Problem Solving 101*, Vermillion, 2009

Problem Solving Appendix 2: A Comparison of Lean and Six Sigma

Area	Lean	Six Sigma
Objectives	Reduce waste Improve value, quality Reduce lead time	Reduce variation Quality: shift distribution inside customer requirements
Frameworks	5 Principles, Lean House, PDSA, Hoshin	DMAIC, SIPOC
Improvement	Many small, everywhere simultaneous, Kaizen, A3, Kata	A small number of larger projects; sometimes $0.25m cut-off.
Typical goals	Quality, Cost, Lead time, Setup, Delivery; Financials often not quantified	Improved Sigma level. Money saving
People involved	Teams led by (sometimes) Sensei. Wide involvement on different levels. All	Master Black belt, Black belts, Green belts. Selective
Time Horizon	Long term, continuous. Also short-term kaizens	Short-term, project-by-project
Tools	Often simple, but may be complicated to integrate	Often complex statistical
Typical early steps	Value stream map	Collect process data
Impact	Can be large, system-wide	A few individual projects may lead to large savings
Problem root causes	Via 5Whys, A3	Via e.g. DOE

Chapter 9
Decisions, Mistakes and Insight

In the previous Chapter, problem types were considered. This Chapter extends 'problems' into the three overlapping areas of Decisions, Mistakes and Insight. We will also briefly examine Design Thinking as a growing way to improve decisions, reduce mistakes, and gain insight.

9.1 Decision Making in General: A Quick Overview

Problems and decisions are faced every day at all levels. They range from the minor (what should I buy for lunch today?) to the strategic (what should be the company's next major venture?). They are all problems in search of solutions. In this chapter we are focused on operations problems concerning cost, quality, delivery and how these issues impact people at work.

Decision making research is vast….

- There is a huge legacy of rational decision making. Operational Research and Industrial Engineering are prime examples, a legacy from Fred Taylor and World War II. Often significant use is made of mathematics and statistics. 'Optimisation' is a goal. Six Sigma, building on statistical foundations, is a more recent development which now appears to be fading. All this is essentially a reductionist approach – a detailed study of parts not wholes.
- In the 1970's Herbert Simon proposed that much decision making was 'bounded rationality'. Not optimisation but 'satisficing' - doing well enough.
- In the last 30 or so years, Rational decision making began to be challenged by psychologists and behavioural economists, notably Kahneman and Tversky, and others such as Daniel Ariely and Richard Thaler. These have become very influential in business and government.
- Since the mid part of last century the realisation has dawned about inter-connectiveness. A challenge to the reductionist approach. Eco-systems. Wholes rather than parts. Hence, Systems Thinking. (Systems Thinking is discussed at some length in Chapter 5.)
- Increasingly a VUCA (volatility, uncertainty, complexity, ambiguity) world has been and is being addressed by more experimentation, greater physical capacity and flexibility such as with robotics and 3D printing, and more sophisticated information – such as data mining and artificial intelligence, and the 'digital twin'.
- In particular, Complexity is particularly relevant. Here the work of Dave Snowden and the Cynefin model is useful, as is the work of Charles Perrow.
- Risk management has also emerged as a major field. Here, the work of Gerd Gigerenzer is of relevance to some Lean managers.

Lean Thinking, with respect to problems and decisions, has progressed alongside these developments. This chapter aims to give an overview, particularly those developments which relate to Lean.

Linear or Exponential?

First, a conceptual viewpoint: In the Eight Models Chapter, Queues (Waiting Lines) were discussed. A classic queue curve is reproduced below. The point was made that the non-linear relationship between queue time and utilization is frequently missed or not fully appreciated, particularly at higher levels of utilization. However, this lack of appreciation is not confined to queues. It is known that humans tend to see positive linear relationships even when there are none. Non-linear relationships tend to be far less appreciated. For example we see a relationship between time spent working and output, between money and happiness, between temperature and comfort, between exercise and health. (And, we often hear 'Size matters!'). In all these cases, many people make the 'more is better' assumption. CO_2 and climate change are nom-linear: a little CO_2 makes little difference but suddenly a little more begins to make a huge difference, at which stage recovery or restoration becomes difficult.

Other phenomena that follow the exponential curve include population growth, the number of microprocessors on a chip (Moore's Law), and the number of internet users.

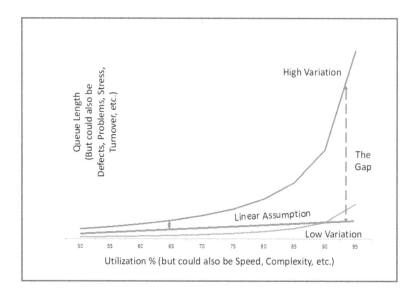

The point is that at low levels of variation (or utilization), a linear assumption is fine. But the gap widens with variation, utilization or time. In the VUCA world (volatility, uncertainty, complexity, and ambiguity) that is increasingly being encountered, a growing gap is ever more likely to be ignored but then to appear suddenly. One example from Lean is the cost of fixing defects against time. The cost of recovery increases exponentially. Toyota at NUMMI got straight onto this through andon, but it had been downplayed for years at the previously-owned GM plant.

The gap is unconscious bias that we all have. The curve represents a significant warning, with implications for how people and organisations are managed. There is an optimal level of human work (and not 'more is better') for innovation, ideas, improvement, quality, team-working, and on and on – and that level is not the maximum. And, as education, customers, society and environment change, so the optimal level changes. (See section 13.6 on Yerkes-Dodson for further discussion.)

In the section on Adoption Curves the phenomenon of diversity and feedback loops was discussed. In short, diversity of opinion can accelerate the onset of a tipping point where the curve seemingly suddenly 'takes off'. In a VUCA world, diversity is much more likely and so also is the likelihood of tipping points being reached.

9.2 Design Thinking and the Double Diamond

The realisation has grown that being truly Lean requires beginning at the design stage. It is often too late when improvement is attempted at the execution stage – too many wastes are already built in. A poorly designed product or service can never fully be compensated for by excellent execution.

Design Thinking is sometimes called 'Human-Centred Design'. Design Thinking is different from operations thinking. Roger Martin explains this well by citing James March (of 'The Behavioural Theory of the Firm' fame) who stated that a firm might engage primarily in *exploration* (seeking new knowledge) or *exploitation* (seeking payoff from existing knowledge or refinement of the knowledge). The former is the realm of Design Thinking, the latter operations thinking. Operations have been the traditional area of Lean Thinking – see for example The Shingo Prize. But the emphasis is now changing. (See Section 10.19 on OODA, and SunTsu's message about winning the war before the battle starts.) Systems Thinking encompasses both areas.

Every system, natural or human-activity, in order to be sustainable, needs to find a balance between exploration and exploitation. Too much exploration does not translate ideas sufficiently into action. (A British phenomenon?) Too much exploitation leads to stagnation. All natural systems evolve – slowly but continuously. The hare and the tortoise. So should organisations.

The British Design Council has for years used the 'Double Diamond' approach to design. This is a two-stage approach. The top diamond is about Discover and Define, the bottom Diamond is about Develop and Deliver. This is roughly equivalent to exploration and exploitation, or to open thinking and closed thinking, to design thinking and operations thinking. Yet another view is that the top diamond is concerned with heuristics and the lower diamond with algorithms. The Double Diamond is shown below.

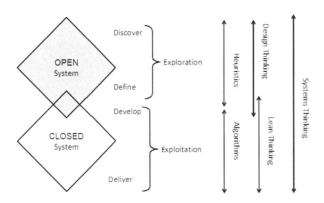

Design Thinking and Lean Thinking both harness the creative skills of employees, but do so in different ways. Design thinking is much more open. There is a blank sheet of paper to begin with. Lean Thinking is about creativity within given parameters – developing ways in which a given product or service can be better made and delivered.

Design thinking cuts through the traditional barriers that frequently exist between industrial design and operations, between R and D and product and service design, between service designers and customers, and between those who design the service and those who deliver the service. Design thinking is therefore a natural extension of Lean Thinking.

Design Thinking is about moving towards 'Experiment First, Then Design' rather than Design then trial. There are great similarities with the Eric Ries' 'Lean Startup'. Design authority Ron

Mascitelli talks about making a wooden table, varnishing it, and then discovering problems with the varnish: far better to test the varnish on a sample of the wood first. Likewise in software or service design, just do enough to test and get feedback. In other words, learn as early as possible.

The Double Diamond has similarities to the problem-solving funnel used within A3 problem solving, and in Value Engineering. The Double Diamond figure shows four stages of improvement. These stages are frequently not uni-directional. Many recursions take place. (Note: In this figure, the diamonds overlap. Some, like Westrick and Cooper, think this is a bad idea and there should be a clear cut between the diamonds. Others disagree.)

- The problem area is **'Discovered'**. This may involve several of the following:
  o Accepting complexity;
  o Visiting the gemba for direct observation;
  o Understanding customer needs and 'The Job to be Done'
  o Defining value and pains for the clients (there may be several);
  o Embracing technology – Web, Smartphone, MOOC, IoT, Zoom, etc.
  o Questioning the system boundary;
  o 'Needfinding' and understanding early adopters.
  o A 'Painstorm' – identifying customer's greatest pain points or a 'Questionstorm'

Other ways in which the top diamond is explored are, for instance:
- Generating alternatives via creative thinking techniques such as 3P, Lateral Thinking;
- Benchmarking;
- Data mining;
- TRIZ: the Ideal Final Result; and 9 box window (system, supersystem, subsystem vs past, present, future); and TRIZ trends
- Keeping options open rather than closing them down too early. This is so called set-based design.
- Or, as Picasso once said, *"Lesser artists borrow; great artists steal"* (!)

- The **Define** stage may involve
  o Homing in on the real issues as in the left side of an A3;
  o Defining the Purpose;
  o Testing prototypes;
  o Demand analysis, including failure demand

- **Develop:** here the defined area is explored, by for instance
  o Lean analysis tools, including mapping;
  o Muri and Mura;
  o Kaizen events;
  o Idea management;
  o A3 analysis;
  o The 7 Quality Tools, 5 Why;
  o Six Sigma tools for variation reduction

- **Deliver:** Methods and tools include
  o Leader standard work;
  o Visual management;
  o 5S;
  o Standard work;
  o Detail waste reduction.

In the Exploitation diamond, Eric Reis discusses four stages: Execution, Behaviour change, Customer impact, and Financial impact. These four stages each require specific attention and are relevant to project teams, business units, and to Corporate.

We may note that:
- Not all problems or situations progress through all four stages, nor should they. Rather, there is evolution from top to bottom as understanding develops and experience is gained.
- For effective design, there is a need to understand current customers, current technology, and current service delivery practice.
- Systems Thinking is highly relevant in the top three areas of discover, define, and develop
- Design thinking is most relevant in the top diamond.
- Both Daniel Pink and Roger Martin discuss 'heuristics' and 'algorithms'. Both make the point that competing on heuristics rather than algorithms is already a necessity for work, especially in the West. A heuristic sets the general course, but allows adaptation. For instance 'keep going up' is a heuristic that will get you to the top of a mountain – if not to the summit, at least to a localised peak. An algorithm is more specific. It provides much more detailed instruction: 'walk 100m, turn right'. An extreme case of an algorithm is computer code. Heuristics are found in the explore stage, algorithms in the develop and deliver stage. They overlap in the refine stage. Heuristics are more applicable in professional services and interactive services. Algorithms are more applicable in transactional service. Pink makes the point that extrinsic motivators MAY be applicable with algorithmic work, but that intrinsic motivators are the only successful type in heuristic work.
- You should only attempt 'algorithmic' control when the system is routine. Parts of some manufacturing jobs are like this, but virtually no service job is completely algorithmic. There are implications here for RPA (Robotic Process Automation).
- Much of lean thinking has been too narrowly defined, being limited to the 'deliver' stage only. This is 'Fake Lean' leading to 'Lean is Mean' accusations, and to a disrespectful use of employees whose opinions are not sought despite their being on the front line.
- Industrialised working and traditional Lean thinking (emphasising a high degree of standard work) is NOT appropriate in open ended, exploratory situations. Design thinking allows variety to be designed into processes.
- There may be different starting and end points. Some situations are clear and can start at the Develop stage. But beware, defining a problem too narrowly may be what the late Russell Ackoff called 'resolving' the problem rather than 'dissolving' it by systems or design thinking. Ackoff also talked about 'solving the wrong problem right'. Other situations may carry the 'solution' too far – reducing the 'solution' to algorithm status (too closely specified work standards?) when a heuristic solution would be more appropriate.

Further Readings.
Michael Lewrick at al, *The Design Thinking Playbook*, Wiley, 2018
Thomas Lockwood (ed), *Design Thinking: Integrating Innovation, Customer Experience, and Brand Value*, Allworth Press, 2010
Darrell Mann, *Hands-on Systematic Innovation*, CREAX, 2002 (On TRIZ)
Roger Martin, *The Design of Business*, Harvard, 2009
Ronald Mascitelli, *Mastering Lean Product Development*, Technology Perspectives, 2011
Eric Reis, *The Lean Startup*, Portfolio, 2012; and *The Startup Way*, Penguin, 2017
Marc Strickdorn et al, *This is Service Design Thinking*, BIS Publishers, 2010
Rob Westrick and Chris Cooper, *Winning by Design*, 2012

9.3 The Rubicon Model of Decision Making

Somewhat similar to the Double Diamond is the Rubicon model. This says that there are 4 phases in a decision: goal setting, planning, action, post action. Each has a different mindset. In the first two we are in deliberation mode. This is open-minded. Once the decision is made, we are in an implementation mode. At this stage it becomes close-minded. Take planning an overseas journey: First there is considerable uncertainty about where and when. But, once destination and time is decided, you book your travel on-line from home. Like Caesar, we have crossed the Rubicon – there is no going back. Or like Cortes who burned his ships when he arrived in America. Think Brexit: opinions, discussion and deliberation. But when 1 January 2021 arrived a whole lot of other concerns become the focus. The stages have different motivations. In the fourth stage one can reflect back to learn, but it is a sunk cost. A sunk cost means that only future costs are relevant. The 'sunk cost fallacy' is where past costs are influential but should not be. General Motors Saturn car project is a classic case. Losses continued to mount even when the project was already a failure.

9.4 Strategic Decisions and Avoiding Groupthink

First, let us appreciate that almost every strategic decision involves bias, uncertainty and risk. This is particularly the case in a VUCA environment. Yet, often, much less attention and time is given to these factors. Decision makers are apt to get into the detail of analyses, be it based on discounted cash flow, financial analysis, operations research, simulation, six sigma, value stream maps, or whatever, whilst failing to question the bias and assumptions of those proposing the change. This process applies at C-level and in middle management. Occasionally, but only occasionally, a decision needs to be taken immediately by a single executive. But most times, a team – be they a company board or a group of managers – should probe bias, uncertainty, and risk. That is their duty, and not to simply agree with the boss or the HiPPO (The Highest Paid Person's Opinion). A pre-mortem or scenarios as discussed in the next section should be the standard. Referring to the six types of problem discussed in Section 8.15, as one moves from type 1 to type 6, the consultation process becomes ever-more important.

The story of President Kennedy (JFK) and Cuba is instructive, based on a book by Irving Janis the originator of the Groupthink concept, and by Michael Roberto.

In 1961 JFK became US President, taking over from Eisenhower. During the preceding years the CIA became increasingly concerned about Castro and Cuba. As a result the CIA trained a group of Cuban exiles in Guatemala. The idea was to stage an invasion to overthrow Castro. On becoming President, JFK was briefed by the CIA on the plan. JFK consulted the Joint Chiefs of Defence Staff who gave tentative approval, subject to some changes. They said the plan could only work if there was sufficient backing from within Cuba. But the pressure was on JFK to act quickly because of weather and from Guatemala. JFK had by this time gathered an impressive Cabinet including Dean Rusk and Robert McNamara. The Cabinet had reservations but felt that they did not have the experience and background of the CIA. JFK felt the same way. No-one expressed open disapproval. The Bay of Pigs invasion went ahead – with disastrous results. There was no general uprising in Cuba. The invaders become bogged down in swamp and were quickly captured. JFK was severely embarrassed and the reputation of the USA was damaged.

Groupthink had occurred. The wise had not spoken up. Peer pressure played a significant role. The people who made the plan were the only ones to give an opinion on its future success. The planners saw only their own viewpoint and convinced each other. Crucially, the exiles themselves were not consulted – they knew about the swamps but were not asked. The apparent consensus was false. A good phrase about Groupthink is 'Going along to get along'. Another is 'Don't rock the boat'. (There is a similar story in the movie 'A Bridge Too Far'.)

JFK took the blame personally and decided to put in place procedures aimed at avoiding another catastrophic decision. He consulted Eisenhower who asked not about the 'who' but about the 'how'. The idea was tested the following year when it became apparent that missile bases were being constructed in Cuba. How to deal with this? The procedures included:

- Two groups were set up, each considering a different course of action. They interchanged detailed position papers. Group members downplayed rank and hierarchy.
- Two overall 'devil's advocates' were appointed - Robert Kennedy and Theo Sorensen. But not JFK. (So as to avoid agreeing with the boss.)
- Meetings were held at a neutral venue.

The Cuban Missile Crisis was peacefully resolved – but a close run thing. Who knows: perhaps the procedures helped avoid nuclear war?

(By the way: The foregoing is a highly over-simplified account of the Cuban Missile Crisis that actually involved several parties on each side, U2 spy-plane incidents, and numerous communications and threats between the USSR and USA. See, for example, Michael Roberto.)

One surprising way of addressing Groupthink, and improving decision making, is simply to adopt periods of silence. Amazon is known to begin all meetings with a period of silence during which time people are expected to reflect and often to read appropriate material. Jeff Bizos also required Amazon managers to bring and to read out written alternatives. The Society of Friends (Quakers) have, for 350 years, used periods of silence whenever dominance or heated discussion arises. Quakers also have no organisational hierarchy, and build in respect and ensure participation by believing that there is 'God in every man'.

A deliberate policy of considering the opposite viewpoint is commendable as a means to not only counter Groupthink, but also to counter confirmation bias.

We are all influenced by others. It is unwise to begin a meeting with the meeting leader calling for everyone's ideas. Groupthink can then set in by not wishing to disagree with other previously-expressed opinions. Far better for the meeting leader to request everyone to write down their views, and then have one person read out all the notes (anonymously) while everyone else stays silent.

Further Readings.
Irving Janis, *Group Think*, (Second edition), Houghton Mifflin, 1982
Michael Roberto, *Why Great Leaders don't take Yes for an Answer*, (Second edition), FT Press, 2013

9.5 Intuition, Complexity and Decisions

Karl Weick famously studied groups who were fighting forest fires in 1949. In one incident, 12 fire-fighters died and 3 survived. A lead fire-fighter, realising that they could not outrun the fire, did something counter-intuitive but also based on calculation. He lit a small fire and lay down in the ashes allowing the fire to sweep over three of them. Those that died were experienced fire-fighters but did not appreciate the changing situation as the fire developed. They used their experience, ran and died. This would seem to be a case of System 2 vs. System 1 thinking, but trust in the leader is also necessary.

In this Chapter we also make the point that intuitive decisions can often be wrong in a Lean environment. Lean Thinking is a paradigm shift from traditional operations thinking, and in such cases counter-intuitive thinking is appropriate. (For example, make a smaller batch.)

Gary Klein, an authority on decision making, also studied intuition – with fire-fighters and nurses. In complex situations, they sometimes have a gut feel that something is wrong even though it is not strictly data based. The point made by Klein is that intuition can save lives even though it is sometimes unfounded. However, intuition must be based on experience together with feedback and communicated. Worth a thought in relation to Deming's 'In God we trust. All others must bring data'. Can Intuition be learned? Yes, says Klein: for instance asking hospital matrons to articulate their thoughts to trainee nurses. The same surely applies to Lean team leaders and workers. Again, a case of System 2 training System 1?

In related situations Weick also studied what he calls High-reliability organisations. These are organisations working in complex, often high-tech, situations but which nevertheless have very low accident rates – air traffic control, some hospitals, nuclear reactors, aircraft carriers. See the right hand side of the Charles Perrow matrix below. Here too counter-intuitive decisions play a part. Successful high-reliability organisations have the following characteristics.

- They are pre-occupied by attention to failures – both big and small. (A point also made by Steve Spear in *Chasing the Rabbit* – one of the best books on improvement.)
- A reluctance to simplify. (Recall the statement 'For every complex problem there is a solution that is clear, simple – and wrong!', said the witty HL Menkin (or Mark Twain – unsure which was first). See also Chapter 14 on Job Safety.
- They do not allow the big picture to minimise the importance of events at the frontline. The frontline may know best.
- Mistakes represent systemic problems. No complex system will be error free. This is also an echo of Deming's 94/6 rule: 94% of problems are due to the system.
- Expertise must be tapped into from all levels. The boss does not have a monopoly on wisdom.

These characteristics, we feel, are not only very much in line with Lean humility but are increasingly relevant in the developing VUCA and high-tech world. Perhaps also, it is to do with using OODA rather than PDSA.

Karl Weick suggests a five step process for leaders in complex, gut-feel, decisions:

- Here's what I think we face.
- Here's what I think we should do.
- Here's why.
- Here's what we should keep our eyes open on.
- Talk to me about my flaws and assumptions.

Is this similar to Kurt Lewin's Force Field Analysis?

Charles Perrow has a famous theory on complexity and accidents. An adaptation of his matrix is shown below. Coupling refers to the amount of slack in the system – if one part fails, how does this affect the whole. Complexity is about the extent of unseen and non-linear interactions.

So, in the Figure below, risk increases towards the top right. Failures in this region can lead to very high cost. Today, there are increasing numbers of Lean-aspiring organisations that work in, or are affected by, complexity and tight coupling. Biotech and international supply chains are examples.

COVID has affected almost everyone. In the years since Perrow first published his classic book in 1984, the book has been criticised for downplaying the human and organisational aspects. But Dekker and Klein offer hope…see below.

		Complexity or Interactions		
		Low / Linear		High/Complex
Coupling	Tight	e.g. Maritime supply chain. Less opportunity for unforeseen interactions	Hospitals	e.g. Chemical plant The danger zone. COVID. Small errors are inevitable and propagate.
			Deepwater Oil spill	
	Loose	e.g. Construction. Predictable problems can be resolved by capacity, inventory or time	Car Assembly	e.g. University unexpected problems but time and flexibility are available

(Figure adapted from Perrow and from Clearfield and Tilcsik, with own positioning.)

Perrow tells the story of going for an interview. (Perhaps a similar sequence has befallen you?). As he sets out…

- The coffee maker has been dropped – and he needs the coffee…
- He locks himself out of the house in his haste…
- But the spare car key was lent to a friend…
- No problem – he can use the neighbour's car – but the neighbour has taken it for repair..
- So take the bus – but there is a bus drivers' strike, and now all taxis are booked…
- So the interview is missed.

So, what caused this?

- Human error (coffee maker)
- System failure (automatic house lock)
- Mechanical failure (neighbour's car)
- Environment (strike)
- Procedures and time allowance (misjudged).

The point that Perrow makes is that complex systems have many points of failure. So although 'redundant pathways' can be created, and will help, it is the knock-on effects that lead to system failure. Major fail-safed but failed examples include Chernobyl, Challenger, 9/11, Deepwater, Titanic, Toyota's brake pedal problem – and more recently, the blocking of the Suez Canal by a supertanker. A 'black swan'-type serious failure results from several events that compound.

Solutions?

- Deliberate design for loose coupling. (See above Table.)
- Attention to detail, but avoiding overlapping responsibilities.
- Poka-yoke devices can help, of course, especially in closed systems, but are just one element in a chain.
- Excess capacity. Kingman's equation (See Section 4.8 on Queues) shows high uncertainty and instability when utilization goes above 85% or 90% - combined with arrival and process variation. Hence, as one moves from bottom left to top right in the above table, one should be increasingly cautious about high utilization.

- Scenario planning.
- Gary Klein, put forward the case for 'Pre-mortems'. This is essentially a brainstorming session pretending, in advance of starting, that the project has already been implemented and has failed. The idea is to make it safe for dissenters who are knowledgeable about the undertaking and worried about its weaknesses to speak up. It is a proactive approach – taking preventive action.
- Sidney Dekker says that it is no longer individual actions and broken components that are at the root of the 'drift into failure', but organisational complexity. Humans should no longer be seen as the cause of trouble – they are the recipients of trouble. Human error is a consequence not a cause. He calls for a re-think in organisation, away from the witch-hunts that seek to pin blame on individuals. (British government – take note!)

Further Reading.

Chris Clearfield and András Tilcsik, *Meltdown: Why our systems fail*, Atlantic, 2018
Sidney Dekker, *Drift into Failure: From hunting broken components to understanding complex systems*, Routledge, 2011
Atul Gawande, *The Checklist Manifesto*, Profile, 2009
Gary Klein, *Seeing What Other's Don't*, Nicholas Brearly, 2013
Gary Klein, 'Performing a Project Premortem', *Harvard Business Review*, Sept 2007
Charles Perrow, *Normal Accidents*, Updated edition, Princeton, 1999 (first was in 1984)
Karl Weick and Kathleen Sutcliffe, *Managing the unexpected*. Jossey-Bass, 2001 (written before Kahneman's *Thinking, Fast and Slow* but, we think, giving credibility to the theory.)

9.6 Dimensions of Performance Improvement: Errors, Insight and Blindness

Gary Klein (see also references above), maintains that there are two components to performance improvement: reducing errors and uncertainty, and increasing 'insight'. Performance Improvement results from BOTH a reduction in errors (mistakes) AND from gaining insight.

Error and uncertainty reduction have become strongly associated with Lean, through variation reduction, A3 problem solving, standard work, SPC, and poka-yoke. Six Sigma's focus is on error and defect reduction. No doubt remains as to the importance of these.

Major reasons for the focus on error reduction have been a realisation of the costs of rework and 'failure demand', the productivity advantages, and the fear of litigation in field defects and of internal accidents. Another major reason is that no-one gets fired for playing it safe.

But, has 'insight' been neglected? Klein explains that intuition – briefly discussed in the last section – is the use of patterns people have already learned, whereas insight is the discovery of new patterns. Insight is concerned with advances, sometimes breakthroughs that result from new and different ways of seeing things. Insight often results from linking different fields – for instance the opportunities of using touch sensitive glass in a smart phone. Sometimes these are 'disruptive technologies' as described by Clayton Christensen. Sometimes they result from direct observation in appreciating customer needs – like a new pram that doesn't get stuck on a kerb or self-cleaning glass.

Klein gives many examples of where insight has been downgraded by increased focus on errors and risk. One example is Six Sigma. Klein quotes an article from *Fortune* that 91% of large companies that adopted Six Sigma failed to keep pace with the S&P 500 index, and from *Business Week* on how Six Sigma has limited creativity at 3M. Another example is the BBC where editorial guidelines ran to 200 pages probably limiting creativity of TV production. Perhaps the fear of an error resulted in the Jimmy Saville child molestation case being suppressed for years. This is not to say that error reduction procedures are a waste. But they need to be balanced against the possibilities of reducing insight. Both error reduction and insight are needed.

Is it obvious that both error reduction and creativity are needed? Perhaps. But the focus in Lean has often been on waste and error reduction rather than on creativity and design. One might argue that in the future state phase of value stream mapping, creativity is involved. Yes, but often it is waste reduction creativity, using standard tools of Lean such as takt time, rather than radical re-design. Could it be that the Toyota limitation is waste reduction rather than creativity – reliable and defect free, but boring? (First in with Prius, but missing out against Tesla.)

Klein believes there are four ways in which insight may be lost:

- Flawed Beliefs, where a wrong or outdated theory remains dominant, and goes unquestioned. (MRP used for scheduling, not only for material requirements? Using ALL of TPS applied in non-repetitive, high variation environments when some is inappropriate?)
- Lack of Experience. Flashes of insight don't just happen, but as Louis Pasteur said, 'Change favours the prepared mind'. Keep learning!
- Passive Stance. It was not that Kodak was unaware of digital photo, in fact they invented it, but old thinking dominated the new.
- Concrete Reasoning. 'Concrete head' was a phrase often used by Dan Jones in early days of Lean.

Comparisons

Klein aligns Kahneman's System 1 concept with the reduction of errors, and System 2 with gaining insight.

Klein's concept also has parallels with Clayton Christensen, saying that too much emphasis has been given to cost-down (Efficiency and Sustaining Innovations), and insufficient to Potential and Disruptive innovation. This is due to the attractiveness of short-term gains through cost reduction against long-term and risky investment in innovation. Driven by stock-exchange expectations, analyst ROI and DCF calculations, and by CEO bonus plans.

Also Klein's concept has parallels with Reg Revans' Action Learning (See Section 10.21 in the Chapter on Positive Psychology). Overlapping both problem solving and decision making, Revans uses the relationship L=P+Q, where L is learning, P is programmed knowledge and Q is questioning insight. He then proposes three necessary systems – alpha, beta and gamma. System alpha focuses on investigating a problem. System beta focuses on solving the problem, and on implementing the solution. System gamma focuses on the learning as experienced by participants, and the gaining of insight. This is also similar to Argyris' 'Double Loop Learning' (See Section 5.5).

Remedies?

As Heffernan says, *"Because we are all biased, and biases are quick and effortless, exhaustion tends to make us prefer the information we know and are comfortable with. We're too tired to do the heavier lifting of examining new or contradictory information, so we fall back on our biases, the opinions and people we already trust."*

Accountants appoint accountants to senior positions. A Six Sigma qualification may focus attention on variation reduction rather than redesign. A TOC mindset will look for the bottleneck rather than the pacemaker. Again, it is Kahneman's System 1 (fast and automatic) and System 2 (slow, considered and deliberate) thinking. All of these work against insight.

Seek the opinion of someone from another field. Tolerate dissent. TRIZ may be a good start. Again, Heffernan: 'What we do know is that hierarchies exacerbate blindness and obedience. That means we need either to tease the obedience out of these organisations or to change their structures.'

Many will have seen the classic Gorilla video. (If you have not, we will not spoil it for you here.) When we are focused on a particular topic, we fail to notice other aspects. This is the efficiency of the human brain at work – we simply cannot notice everything.

Insight results from resolving contradictions as in TRIZ. TRIZ seeks the 'AND' (e.g. low cost AND high quality) and not the trade-off (finding the 'optimal' trade-off between cost and quality). Also, as per Ackoff, seek to dissolve the problem.

Further Readings.

Margaret Heffernan, *Wilful Blindness*, Simon and Schuster, 2012
Gary Klein, *Seeing What Others Don't*, Nicholas Brearley, 2014
Mike Pedler, *Action Learning in Practice*, Gower, 2012
Phil Rosenzweig, *The Halo Effect*, Free Press, 2007
Richard Tetlow, *Denial: Why business leaders fail to look facts in the face – and what to do about it*, Portfolio, 2011

9.7 Mistakes: Bias, Noise and Psychological Safety

We all make mistakes. We would like to prevent mistakes, but what happens when they occur – opportunity or suppression? In the sections below we will discuss both physical and human mistakes, mention (briefly) prevention systems – (that apply mainly in repetitive operations) and ways in which psychological safety can be improved – (this applies to everyone).

Mistakes: Human or System? Too often the 5 Why root cause-finding approach stops at 'human error'. It should not! What caused the human error? Inadequate instruction? (There is the famous TWI job instruction quotation that all who take the 10-hour class must repeat out loud: 'If the worker hasn't learned, the instructor hasn't taught.') Was it poor ergonomics? But today it could just as easily be stress, lack of sleep, or attempted multitasking. These latter reasons have been found to be the major causes of catastrophic failures in aircraft crashes, car crashes, and complex plant failures. And, surprisingly (?) monetary incentives have been shown to lead to poor decisions, lack of teamworking and mistakes. Also, diet (type, too much, too little) and dehydration.

The effective management of mistakes has long been recognised as having a dramatic effect on company performance. An outstanding example was Toyota's entry into the USA with their joint venture with GM at the NUMMI plant in California. Mistakes and rework were endemic when the plant was run by GM. A strong focus that Toyota brought was the reduction of rework through what is now called Psychological Safety – the elimination of the fear of highlighting problems. The lesson is now widely appreciated – including for example the effect on lead time (See Section 4.8 on Queues). Although the advantage of the elimination of rework in the manufacturing process is appreciated, the wider question of the elimination of fear is less appreciated. Fear of surfacing not only defects but mistakes and opportunities in the wider contexts of service, design, software, healthcare, and government represents huge potential. Why? Because fear works directly against the 'bring your brain to work' concept in Lean, and a break from Taylor's concept of the separation of thinkers from doers. Today, everyone's contribution is needed. Psychological safety is the elixir that unlocks empowerment and creativity. (Psychological Safety is discussed below in Section 9.9)

First, however, a mistake is not an accident. An accident is something the timing of which could not have been reasonably expected or planned for. Mitigation is possible. A mistake is an opportunity to improve. It is not only something physical but more importantly is a mistaken attitude, bias, or process that works against the full realisation of brainpower.

Noise Mistakes

Both bias and noise are important sources of mistakes. Bias has attracted much attention, but Kahneman makes the point that 'noise' can be even more significant. Noise is an unaccounted for variation in human judgement, and is always present due to innumerable factors including changes in the 'M's: men (people), material, management, measurement, method, and 'mother nature'. Our brains are extremely noisy says Kahneman. Particularly in a Complex environment significant noise can work against or distort that foundation of scientific method – the repeatable experiment and PDCA.

What can be done about noise? Not much! But we can recognise that it is always present, particularly in Complex environments, and...

- Since computer algorithms are noise and emotion free can they be used to supplement or even replace human judgement? (For example, using AI for diagnosis of a medical condition, recruitment, or even opinion on the state of an organisational transformation.)
- Where possible, measure the extent of noise. This will at least give an indication of the zone of uncertainty. It has long been good practice that a forecast should be two numbers – the number itself and an indication of the uncertainty or standard deviation. In Six Sigma, Measurement System Analysis (MSA) and Gauge repeatability and reproducibility (R&R) are well established. How much variation is there within a process and between similar processes? Sampling should come with a confidence limit. Exams marking and worker assessment should establish how much noise is there between markers. Likewise job between job appointments, and between criminal sentences. Kahneman, Sibony and Sunstein measured the insurance premiums quoted between two underwrites given the same information and found a 55% difference!
- Disaggregate a prediction situation into components, having different degrees of uncertainty. Isolate, then seek to understand, major regions of noise.

Bias mistakes.

Let us accept that we all have biases.

- Confirmation bias. Everyone has this bias. If something we read or hear agrees with our viewpoint, we take it as confirmation and accept it immediately. If it is something we disagree with we give it harsh, critical examination. We tend to pick holes. Interestingly, two people with opposite viewpoints hearing the same evidence tend to have their viewpoints reinforced by selective interpretation. (The Beatles song, 'Nowhere man, please listen /, ….just sees what he wants to see / isn't he a bit like you and me?')
- Cognitive dissonance. When there is an inconsistency between two thoughts or between a thought and a behaviour. When people do something that is inconsistent with their view of themselves, they tend to feel physically uncomfortable. You are the leader in implementing Lean, but you have just authorised the purchase of a fast large machine instead of three smaller slower machines. So, self-justify? (It will be less expensive in the long run. We sometimes need the extra speed. Etc.) You believe in team working. You have an idea that will benefit the team, but don't share it because you would like individual recognition. What to do? Change your ideas about team working? Beware! Self-justification is a mechanism that can get in the way of learning.

Leon Festinger, the originator of the concept, found that the more you invest in a set of beliefs, the more resistant you will be to evidence that suggests that your belief is wrong. This is a finding of huge significance for change and inertia.

Suppose someone you dislike intensely comes up with a really great idea. Dissonance! What do you do? Shoot down the idea by picking on any weak points or do you separate the message from the messenger?

- Context. We are all influenced by context. If you visit a plant that has a strong Lean reputation, all that you see will tend to be favourable, but you are likely to self-justify the unfavourable. Likewise hearing from a high-status person, or from a reputable institution.

- Sunk Cost Bias. Reluctance to abandon projects on which time and money have been spent. Economists will say that previously spent costs are irrelevant. The only consideration is future costs and benefits. The problem here is having to admit that a previous decision was wrong. But was it? At the time it might have been the best course of action, but things have changed, and this should not be seen as negative.

- Framing. How information is presented makes a difference. A loss has more influence than a gain. Two options: (a) A lean implementation has a 10% chance of a gain of $95k but a 90% chance of a loss of $5k. Or (b) a lean implementation will cost $5k and there is a 10% chance of gaining $100k and a 90% chance of zero benefit. Which of these two is better? These are identical, but most people would select the second! (Kahneman, again)

- Overconfidence Bias. In the Established Approaches Chapter, Humility was discussed including the Dunning-Kruger Effect. This is where people, especially those with low ability, tend to over-estimate their ability. Mistakes are the result. In projects, overconfidence is the norm – witness the many projects that overrun on time and budget.

- Availability bias. This is where too much emphasis is placed on the most recent information - or fad! What's the 'latest'? Go do it! A problem is that frequent change of direction does not allow any experiment to be adequately judged. Deming spoke about constancy of purpose, and about common cause and special cause variation.

- Anchoring. Almost unbelievable, but shown by Kahneman to be widespread, this is where people 'consider a particular value for an unknown quantity before estimating that quantity' (Kahneman). So, for instance, the number that comes up when rolling a die before setting an improvement target will (?) influence the target – high or low!

- Primacy bias is the tendency to give preference to the first idea or person; and Affinity bias where we tend to favour people like ourselves.

- Forecasting. Tetlow found that, in the medium term, many professional forecasters are poor. But the few 'super forecasters' are people who get regular feedback (like weather forecasters), usually collaborate, and learn as a result. (See more on forecasting in Section 10.4)

- Cause and Effect. Does regular sex make you look younger, or are the younger looking able to attract partners enabling them to have more regular sex? In 2021 a fair proportion of people are refusing COVID vaccination. They have heard it is dangerous based on previous vaccination evidence. But was the 'evidence' merely a timing coincidence between a jab and the onset of a health problem?

- Fundamental attribution error or FAE. Situations influence decisions. Appearance, reputation, a partial view has undue influence. We tend to think the quizmaster is wise, but he or she is just asking questions and answers that have been researched by others. We tend to think someone with a suit is more educated that someone in an overall. Is the CEO truly wiser than a supervisor? Accents have been shown to have undue influence.

- Not respecting. The objectivity illusion. Becoming increasingly convinced of one's own opinions – but blind to our own prejudices. A famous quote repeated here: Abraham Lincoln said, *'I don't like the man. I must get to know him better'*

Further reading on Bias
Undoubtedly the seminal book on bias is Daniel Kahneman, *Thinking, Fast and Slow*, Allen Lane, 2011
Also Daniel Kahneman, Oliver Sibony, and Cass Sunstein, *Noise*, Collins, 2021

Visual mistakes

- The task or the stream? Gemba walks and 'staple yourself to an order' are established concepts, linked with mapping. Certainly it is better than management by spreadsheet or opinion. But how representative is a single visit and can an order be tracked? Software and Data Mining are partial solutions.
- Go see at the Gemba. It is certainly desirable, if not compulsory, to go see first-hand at the gemba. But just 'go see' may not be adequate. There are many cautions several of which are briefly discussed below. Over 50% of all workers now apparently spend much of the day peering at a computer screen or smartphone. The work is essentially invisible. The over-riding caution is that, having visited the gemba, you then think that you know the full story…
- Office and service work. A partial picture, because much of this type is brain work that cannot be directly observed. (Is the person sleeping or thinking creatively?)
- How to observe creativity? Don't try!
- Timing. What is the best time to go see? Immediately? Hour of the day, day of the week, week of the month? And, for how long should one visit? (One of the authors recalls Prof. Gene Woolsey who insisted that his Masters students literally spend 24/7 to collect representative data.)
- In observing, is work being done more quickly or more slowly than normal? (Work Study rating is supposed to adjust for this, but is an inexact procedure.)
- Detail. It takes skill to observe detail. (One of the authors was amazed at the detail of what Patrick Graupp, TWI Master Trainer, saw in observing a job.) The human brain is a wonderful filtering device – it only remembers the apparently relevant. (Otherwise it would overflow.) We have all seen a bicycle thousands of times. So now, try drawing one in detail.…
- Increasingly, remote working is happening. How to visit the gemba if it is at someone's home? Observing office work? Zoom? Varied work?
- Optical illusions. There are so many traps. See Michael Bach's wonderful web site for over 100 examples, including many interactive illustrations.
- There is the "Rashomon effect" which is the proven unreliability of eyewitness accounts. (Named for four viewers who see the same murder being committed, but the accounts are contradictory, sometimes diametrically opposed.) People see events as they perceive them, or want them to be perceived. Bias? A good reason for seeing first-hand, and if not seen first-hand can the reports be relied upon?
- Gwendolyn Galsworth, doyen of 'visuality', has 2 questions, the answers to which should be on display at (almost) every workplace: What do I need to know? What do I need to share?
-

Memory mistakes

- People think they remember accurately. It is even counted as evidence in court. There is much disturbing evidence that memory is fallible, and can be manipulated.
- 'I always knew that!' Have you ever heard from people who claim to have known about Lean concepts for 30, 40, even 50 years? Perhaps they are correct, but perhaps the concept only became known more recently. There is strong evidence that once a concept becomes

mainstream, or the facts become known, people with former opinions deny them. ('I always knew that Hitler was a bad guy', said millions of Germans.)

Distraction mistakes

- *The invisible Gorilla.* This is the title of a book by Chabris and Simons. A now famous video (https://youtu.be/UtKt8YF7dgQ) shows people passing a ball. You are asked to count the number of passes. A large gorilla walks past but only about half of people see it. Seeing is not the same as looking. Other remarkable findings, leading to possible mistakes, are that, in a group, the first person to speak is likely to be recognised as the leader.
- Multitasking. We all think we can multitask. We can't. Like a computer we can shift from one task to another with rapid frequency – but not as rapidly as a computer. When we do so, mistakes are more frequent and decision making takes longer. Further, if we are distracted from a deep-thinking situation such as design, it takes several minutes to recover back to where we were.

9.8 Prevention Systems

This section relates mainly to mistakes in physical operations.

Poka-yoke
The late Shigeo Shingo developed and classified the poka-yoke concept, particularly in manufacturing. Shingo's book *Zero Quality Control: Source Inspection and the Poka-yoke System* is the classic work. More recently C Martin Hinckley made a significant contribution through his work *Make No Mistake!* 'Poka-yoke' literally means you must prevent (yoke) inadvertent mistakes (poka). (If you don't like the Japanese term, try mistake-proof, fail-safe, but not fool proof – 'fools are so creative!')

A poka-yoke (or mistake-proof) device according to Shingo uses '100% automatic inspection together with warning or stop'. Here, key words are 100% and automatic. Note that a poka-yoke is not a control device like a thermostat or toilet control valve that takes action every time, but rather a device that senses abnormalities and takes action only when an abnormality is identified. Interestingly, a poka-yoke can apparently also mean 'distraction–proofing' in Japanese – with implications for using a mobile phone when driving or e-mail interruptions.

Shingo distinguishes between 'mistakes' (which are inevitable) and 'defects' (which result when a mistake reaches a customer). The aim of poka-yoke is to design devices that prevent mistakes becoming defects. According to Shingo there are two categories – those that warn, and those that prevent or control. There are three types: 'contact', 'fixed value', and 'motion step'. This means that there are six categories, as shown in the figure with service examples.

Poka-yoke Types		
	Control	Warning
Contact	Parking height bars	Shop Entrance Bell
Fixed Value	Pre-dosed medication	Egg tray
Motion Step	Airline lavatory door	Spellcheckers
Adapted from Richard Chase and Douglas Stewart 'Failsafe Service', OMA Conference, 1993		

According to John Grout, areas where poka-yokes should be considered include areas where worker vigilance is required, where mispositioning is likely, where SPC is difficult, where external failure costs dramatically exceed internal failure costs, and in mixed model and production. Shingo says that poka-yoke should be thought of as having both a short action cycle (where immediate shut down or warning is given), but also a long action cycle where the reasons for the defect occurring in the first place are investigated. John Grout makes the useful point that one drawback of poka-yoke devices is that potentially valuable information about process variance may be lost, thereby inhibiting improvement.

Hinckley developed an excellent approach to mistake proofing. He developed a classification scheme comprising 10 common categories: omitted operations, omitted parts, wrong orientation, misaligned, wrong location, wrong part, misadjusted, prohibited action, added part, misread instruction. For each category, various mistake proofing solutions have been developed. Thus, having identified the type of mistake, one can look through the set of possible solutions and adapt or select the most suitable one. See his excellent web site: assuredquality.com

There is a continuum of poka-yokes. Take seatbelts: A weak poka-yoke would require a driver to use a checklist, including fastening a seatbelt before setting off. A slightly stronger version would require any car passenger to go through the checklist with the driver. A medium strength poka-yoke would give an audio or display warning when a seatbelt is not fastened. A strong poka-yoke would prevent the car from starting unless the driver's seatbelt is fastened. The seatbelt example illustrates that the choice of poka-yoke needs to consider both risk and user acceptance.
(BTW: Andon is not a poka-yoke. A poka-yoke requires 100% automatic detection.)

Checklists

A checklist is not a true poka-yoke, but nevertheless is important in reducing mistakes. A checklist is not automatic, relies on human conscientiousness, and often requires a change in culture or attitude to be effective. Note that this is not a question of training or competence but a problem of the human brain just having too much to think of, particularly in stressful situations. (Surgeons are highly trained but occasionally might leave an instrument inside a patient – due to pressure.)

Checklists have received long overdue attention recently due to the work of Atul Gawande's book *The Checklist Manifesto*. Gawande is a Harvard surgeon. The number of errors made in hospitals is truly astounding. From cutting off the wrong limb, to leaving instruments inside a patient, to administering the wrong medicine. Thousands of such cases occur each year in the UK, tens of thousands in USA. Checklists have had remarkable success in reducing such errors, but they require a change in culture – allowing a nurse to go through a checklist for a surgeon (previously a no-no). This is not seen as a reflection of competence, but as a life-saver in a highly stressful, pressurized environment. Gawande points out that checklists have been hundreds of times more cost effective than many new drugs. In fact, new drugs are part of the problem – which one to select? …and is the most effective drug even known to the doctor?
In the UK, 1 in 16 hospital patients get an infection. This situation has led the deputy head of the health service to encourage patients to carry out their own check: ask the nurse or doctor if they have washed their hands!

(By the way, a Checklist should not be used in high-frequency situations, where a poka-yoke (mistake-proof) device is far preferable.)

Of course, checklists have long been used in aircraft, starting with the B-17 bomber in WW II.

There are the three important points:

1. The checklist must not be too long. (Only the 'key points' in TWI terms.) Perhaps 10 points or less. (A case in point was the crash of an airliner taking off from La Guardia, New York.

When the engines failed, the pilot used a checklist but it was too long to complete. Sullenberger nevertheless ditched the aircraft safely in the East River.)

2. The checklist is not a reflection of incompetence, but a recognition that in a focused, stressful situation, important points can be missed. (Recall the 'Invisible Gorilla' experiment above, where many people counting ball throws simply do not see a man in a gorilla suit walking past!)

3. A checklist of a 'do-confirm' or 'read-do' type is best administered by a second person, again not as a reflection of competence but in recognition that the first person may have many simultaneous things on his or her mind. The second person is therefore helping not hindering. In fact, it has been found that in commercial aircraft there is a less likelihood of error when the co-pilot is flying rather than the pilot – because the pilot has so many other things to think about.

Given these characteristics, checklists have a great future in service and manufacturing.

There are links between checklists and TWI. Key points are picked up in TWI Job Instruction.

1. Ask, can each key point be failsafed? If yes, then it would no longer necessarily be a key point.

2. Key points should be audited using the TWI Job Breakdown chart. In complex work, and repetitive manual work this is especially important. Of course, only periodically. Without this, defects and failure demand are inevitable. Not a policeman, but a helper, as above.

3. Note the TWI mantra that not every step has a key point or points. But there are a few critical key points that have to be done correctly. This is NOT the over-standardising of work that some critics of Lean cite as a major drawback.

4. TWI Job Methods, in questioning every step through 'Kipling analysis' (what, why, when, where, how, who) brings out the key points and checklist possibilities.

Single Point Lessons

A useful and widely adopted procedure for combatting repetitive mistakes is the Single Point Lesson. These are found on factory floors and in some service situations (such as fast food). They:

- Focus on one single point or issue where improvement is required.
- Are highly visual – containing the steps, key points, and invariably a diagram or photograph
- Contain content that can be delivered in 15 minutes or less
- Address the main stages of learning – awareness, understanding, competence, ability to train others.

Note: See Section 3.8 on the Training within Industry (TWI) concepts that should be the foundation for Single Point Lessons.

Problem (Trouble shooting) Cards. These are 'what if' cards to cope with relatively rare but important contingencies. (What to do if the chuck breaks..) Most air force pilots are used to the idea of consulting a card in an emergency – so as to avoid potentially disastrous mistakes in a time of great stress and crisis.

The Role of Employees: Poka-yokes and checklists may help in routine situations. Employees themselves are the major route to developing effective poka-yokes and checklists. Note that, as Atul Gawande has discussed in the case of surgeons and nurses, an attitude change may be necessary for the lower status employee to use checklists with higher status employees. The same applies to much quality control. Some employee 'mistakes' can be addressed by creative methods such as asking employees to record the eye colour of customers, thereby (perhaps) ensuring eye contact.

Further Readings.

Christopher Chabris and Daniel Simons, *The Invisible Gorilla: and other ways our intuition deceives us*, Harper, 2011
Amy Edmondson, *The Fearless Organisation*, Wiley, 2019
Gwendolyn Galsworth, *Work that makes sense*, Visual Lean, 2011
Atul Gawande, *The Checklist Manifesto*, Profile Books, 2011
John Grout's *Mistake-Proofing Centre*. www.mistakeproofing.com
Joseph Hallinan, *Why we make mistakes*, Broadway, 2009
C. Martin Hinckley, *Make No Mistake*, Productivity, 2001
David Sibbet, *Visual Meetings*, Wiley, 2010
Carol Tavris and Elliot Aronson, *Mistakes were made but not by me*, Harcourt, 2007

Note: Although not directly about Lean, or about Value Stream Mapping, Amy Herman's, *Visual Intelligence*, HMH, 2016 is in our opinion the best book on actually learning to see, or observe.

9.9 Managing Mistakes and Achieving Psychological Safety

'Drive out fear', said Deming. Absolutely, but not easy! Tavris and Aronson in their superb book, *Mistakes were made but not by us*, say that 'America' (but surely not only America) '*is a mistake-phobic culture, one that links mistakes with incompetence and stupidity. So even when people are aware of having made a mistake, they are often reluctant to admit it, even to themselves, because they take it as evidence that they are a blithering idiot.'.....'*One lamentable consequence of the belief that mistakes equal stupidity is that when people do make a mistake, they don't learn from it.'...Too often we lecture or shout 'what were you thinking?'. *'Such accusations cause already embarrassed victims to withdraw further into themselves and clam up, refusing to tell anyone what they did.'*
There is a famous story of Tom Watson, IBM founder, who said to an employee who had just made a $10m mistake and expected to be fired, *"You must be kidding. I have just invested $10m in your education!"*

This whole area, now called Psychological Safety, has been extensively studied by Amy Edmondson of Harvard Business School. Psychological Safety is the lack of fear that bringing bad news to the boss will be treated positively not negatively. As she explains, Psychological Safety is *"People are not hindered by interpersonal fear"* and where *"they fear holding back their full participation more than they fear sharing a potentially sensitive, threatening or wrong idea."* So people realise that their job may be lost due to economic or company competitiveness, but are not threatened through highlighting defects and mistakes.

In her book, *The Fearless Organisation*, Edmondson quotes three case studies - Volkswagen, Wells Fargo bank, and Nokia phones – where a culture of fear worked against the transmission of bad news. In the case of VW, a domineering boss encouraged an elaborate scheme to defraud regulators by the development of software that allowed diesel emission regulations to be bypassed. (The engines passed static testing, but failed in roadgoing conditions.) The eventual outcome for the company saw a third of its market value vanish.

Motivation by threat such as 'I want a 30% increase in sales or you will all be looking for another job' are not only incompatible with Lean continuous improvement but ultimately highly dangerous. Edmondson believes that many managers believe that motivation by fear is effective, but in fact it ensures *"that (the) creativity, good process, and passion needed to accomplish challenging goals in knowledge-intensive workplaces"* is eliminated. Dramatically, during the 8-year Iran/Iraq war, Saddam Husain's field commanders were afraid of reporting reversals on pain of execution leading to a major loss in Basra. Literally, 'Don't shoot the messenger!'

There is the saying that bad news does not travel upwards. So Psychological Safety is more than 'speaking truth to power'. It is actively encouraging truth to be spoken to power.

Improving Psychological Safety

Deming spoke about driving out fear. But how to do this? Here we draw on the excellent work of Amy Edmondson for inspiration. Briefly, active work is required for all of the following:

- Purpose. What, exactly, is the expected response with respect to mistakes, accidents, and safety?
- Structure. What needs to be reported and what doesn't? Ease and speed of communicating mistakes.
- Understanding, responding and not over-reacting, to mistakes that are predictable, preventable, complex, and an 'intelligent mistake'. Classify those that one can learn from, and those that need to be fixed. Standards that need to be followed, and standards that can be questioned. The time frames for expected responses require consideration.
- Personal security. Attitudes to mistakes and to being wrong.
- Behaviour. Clarify the types of behaviour that will always be supported, and the types of 'mistakes' that will get you fired. (e.g. Sexist remarks). Whistleblowing policy?
- Active listening
- Questions (See Section 9.10 on Questions)
- Discouraging and surfacing workarounds. (A workaround may gain 'brownie points' but they result in problems and mistakes being overlooked – or, worse, encouraged.)
- Being Humble. See Ed Schein's excellent book, *Humble Inquiry*, and the section on Humility.
- Overcoming the 'Sounds of Silence' (to quote Simon and Garfunkel). Methods include round-robin speaking opportunity at meetings, and direct asking.
- Voice. The choice of words used in an organisation with respect to mistakes is influential to actions. Words need to be consistent and unambiguous within the organisation. A mistake or an error? A failure or an accident? A stoppage or an opportunity? A setback. A deviation or a defect? A nuisance and a 'screw-up'?
- Appreciation and acknowledgement of mistakes that have been surfaced.

The columns below show some possible situations where fear or psychological safety issues may arise, and a range of possible responses. Note that these are simply lists, and not a one-on-one appropriate response to each situation. Of course, most organisations already have policies and procedures for many of these situations, but the question is – does the response, or anticipated response, encourage psychological safety and 'drive out fear'? It would be most desirable to have an appropriate default response to each listed situation.

Situations	Possible responses
Cost reduction opportunity	Silence
Customer interaction	Criticism
Value stream opportunity	Sanction
Policy unclear	Immediate response
Colleague error	Delayed response
Waste removal opportunity	Support
Work standards not followed	Thank
Ignore customer request	Log the occurrence
Customer dissatisfaction	Support
Customer suggestion	Listen
Design effect	Notify line manager
Design specification error	Coach
Design opportunity	Notify Lean office
Inappropriate behaviour	Notify CEO
Ergonomic issues	Notify HR
Injury	Celebrate
Lateness	Tolerate in emergency
Assembly defect	Root cause?
Software coding error	Root cause?
Whistleblowing	
Etc. etc.	

9.10 Questions and Questioning

A 'questioning culture' is closely associated with both problems and decisions. The '5 Why's', 'Root cause problem solving', 'Go to the Gemba', TWI, 'Idea management', and the 'Kipling's 5 Honest Mean', 'Socratic Method' are all established concepts. Detail on these can be found in numerous texts on Lean. All these are good, when used effectively. But asking the right questions, and actually establishing a questioning culture remains a challenge. As Deming once said, 'If you do not know how to ask the right question, you discover nothing.'

Begin with the question: 'Why is so much Lean training delivered in a classroom setting where participants must sit passively and listen?' Those same participants are then expected to return to the workplace and begin questioning!

There have been great advances in learning, retention, and questioning in recent years. See Chapter 10 on Learning. Here we explore some relevant considerations from the field of Questioning.

For any organisation, questioning is vital. In a fast-changing world, expertise cannot reside only at the top. We all need to be more childlike, asking questions to find out, to learn, but also to challenge.

Warren Berger points out that, increasingly, answers are less important than questions. Many answers are to be found on the internet, in data bases, libraries, with experts, and with your people if you can only ask the right question. It was not always like this, but many managers still have the outdated mindset that, somehow, they must have all the answers. Schools, unfortunately, remain bastions of uni-directional instruction, and re-gurgitation during tests. That won't do in a Lean and changing environment. Levitt and Dubner say that three of the most powerful words a manager can use are 'I don't know'. Many times, managers don't actually know, but simply guess or put forward their opinion in areas outside of their expertise, thus stifling creativity and innovation. But, of course, questions need to be followed by action.

From Michael Marquardt in *Leading with Questions:*

"I thought a managers' job was to provide answers, to provide solutions…. But I came to realize how disempowering this is, and how much more effective I could be by posing the question back to the person with the problem…It is much more effective to provide the opportunity for them to solve their own problems."

And from Steven Covey: *"Seek first to understand, before seeking to be understood"*

And from Bertrand Russell: *"It is a healthy thing now and then to hang a question mark on things you have long taken for granted."*

A few pointers:

- Drive out fear, said Deming. Without this, a questioning culture cannot begin. Such a culture cannot be achieved by edict, only by demonstration. To repeat, Deming also spoke about the 94/6 rule (94% of problems lie with the process; only about 6% with the people.) So, questioning should not begin with a people witch-hunt.
- Not only learning from mistakes and failures, but also Learn from successes! Ask what went <u>right</u>?
- 'God gave you two ears and one mouth'.
- The higher your position the less you should give your opinion and the more you should ask and listen.
- Don't monopolise the conversation. Have round robin sessions that give everyone a chance.
- Open questions rather than closed questions. Remember, that many KPI's are answers to closed questions – How much? How many? On target? – rather than encouraging open questions using Why? Or How? (asked with genuine humility).

Instead of giving a PowerPoint presentation on the 7 Wastes or Kanban, try the following questions or provocations in a training program:

- Is one piece flow a bad idea? Why or why not?
- How should you calculate the correct batch size / size of a supermarket / number of kanbans?
- Determining a bottleneck can be dangerous.
- Is waste sometimes good? Is failure?
- 'Respect is horse shit' (Seddon)
- Why use Hoshin? (Is there an alternative?)
- Could TPS be dangerous to you, to shareholders, to suppliers?
- Why are women vastly underrepresented in manufacturing management?
- What are the benefits of doing Lean? What are the pre-requisites?
- Is Lean is a con? It is really about cutting jobs. Toyota uses a lot of temps.
- Standard work means less thinking.

The Right Question Institute have designed a 'better way' to gain from questioning. This is an excellent free source! Here we adapt from their ideas and expand:

- Leaders design the Question Focus. "We have a great opportunity to design this new layout. We know the product, and the required volume, but apart from that there is a blank sheet."
- Operators write down the questions. No prompting from the leaders, and no discussion. "Can it be done sideways?", "Can it be done on one level?", "Why in that room?", "Why in that order",
- Operators improve their questions. "How many people will be required?", "What would be the easiest sequence?"
- Operators prioritise their questions. Perhaps: Sequence, Orientation, Shape, People
- Operators and Leaders decide on the next steps. Maybe "How are we going to do a trial on this proposal"?
- Reflection

Questions can be *Clarifying*, for instance:

- Please explain to me… (but be careful here to avoid sounding like an accusation)
- How so?
- What happens if….
- Could you tell me more about that?
- Why do you think that is?

… or *Process*, for instance

- What do you think would be a better way to…?
- What is preventing better flow from taking place?
- What's your reaction to that suggestion?
- How would that affect you?
- Could we make this process 100% fool-proof?

….or on *Solutions*, for instance

- In this situation, what are you most pleased with and what are you least pleased with?
- What would happen then?
- How could we reduce the queues?
- What could be done about that?

Poor Questions are *Closed* or *Aggressive*. For instance:

- Why are you behind schedule?
- Why? (asked aggressively or without listening to the answers)
- Who is not keeping up?
- Don't you know the rules? (or Don't you know better?)
- Or, any question that is asked to illustrate the cleverness or superiority of the asker.

Spear and Bowen suggest that their Four Rules of Rules of TPS are not learned by instruction, but by questioning. (The rules are standardisation, clear communication, removing barriers to flow, and scientific method). The rules are not formally stated but are absorbed by indirect questioning over time. The manager is a teacher, not a 'boss'. And Socratic teaching is highly effective. Challenging questions involve going to Gemba and asking, with humility:

- How do you do this work?
- How do you know that you are doing it correctly?
- How do you know that the outcome is defect free?
- What do you do if you have a problem?

We would add a few:

- Who do you communicate with?
- How do you know what to do next?
- Do you do this in the same way as others?
- What do you think are the options?
- Could you elaborate? (or, Could you develop that idea?)
- What would that enable us to do?
- What things would need to happen for that to take place?

In fact, it is learning by the ongoing use of (Kipling's) 'six honest serving men' – who taught me all I knew; their names are what and why and when; and how and where and who.' This Socratic Method encourages operators to think, question and learn. Persistent asking of the questions allows decentralisation to evolve.

Keep in mind that 'it is not the quality of the answers that distinguishes a Lean expert, but the quality of the questions' (source unknown), and as Yogi Berra said, "*Don't tell me the answer, just explain the question.*"

Further Readings.

Warren Berger, *A More Beautiful Question*, Bloomsbury, 2014
Steven Covey, 7 Habits of Highly Effective People, Simon and Schuster, 2020.
Steven Levitt and Stephen Dubner, *Think like a Freak*, Allen Lane, 2014
Michael Marquardt, *Leading with Questions*, Jossey Bass, 2005
Steven Spear and Bowen, 'Decoding the DNA of the Toyota Production System', *Harvard Business Review*, Sept-Oct 1999, pp. 97-106
Right Question Institute: https://rightquestion.org

Appendix 1 on Problems: System 1 and System 2: Counterintuitive Thinking

Decision area	Typical System 1, Intuitive Thinking (often wrong in a Lean environment)	Counterintuitive System 2 Thinking (usually correct)
Batch Size	Big is good	Small. Batch size of 1?
EOQ thinking	Tradeoff calculation	Reduce changeover time
Utilization	100% is good	Beware above 85%
Rework	Fix at end	Fix at source
Mistakes	Blame	Opportunity
Line stop	A No No; Fear of censure.	Surface the problem; Thanks
Push and Pull	Push is preferable	Pull is better
Knowledge	The boss knows best	Go to Gemba
Decisions	Top down	..and bottom-up; diverse opinions considered
Analysis	On paper	At the Gemba
People	High IQ best	Mixed teams
The Plan	Stick with it	Be flexible
Idle time	Bad	Time to think and improve
Machines	Big, fast, sophisticated	Small and simple
Shared resources	Are efficient	Dedicated lines
Automation	Good, early	After waste removal
Product development	Right first time	Fail early, fail fast
Layout	Functional, Fixed	Cells, value stream, Flexible
Process Variation	Ignore non linear effects	Allow for but question
Arrival variation	Accept	Influence
Bottlenecks	At high utilization	..but blocking and starving
Projects	The critical path	The critical chain
Image	We are best	Lots to learn
Customer knowledge	By survey	By Gemba experience
WIP Inventory	Good, necessary	Minimise
Investments	On cost basis	..and Leadtime
Overhead	Allocated by labour hours	Boxed
Product cost and price	Price = Cost plus	Begin with target price
Sunk costs	Considered	Irrelevant
Budgets	Essential, variances	Guidance, Flexible
Cost centres	Functional	Value stream
Buffers	Inventory buffers necessary	Three types: time, inventory, capacity: reduce all.

Appendix 2 on Problems: Brief Explanation of Tools for Problems and Decisions

Tool or Method	Brief Explanation	Further reading
Rapid Response	When a problem occurs, siren or lights. Team immediately gathers	
RCM	Reliability Centred Maintenance. Prediction by vibration, sound, wear	Moubray, *RCM*
TPM	Total Productive Maintenance. May use 8 steps	McCarthy and Rich, *Lean TPM*
SPC	Statistical Process Control for detecting out of control conditions	Wheeler, *Understanding Variation*
5 Why	Ask again until root cause is revealed	Bicheno, *The Lean Toolbox* (LTB)
7 Q-tools	Process map, Pareto, Fishbone, Histogram, Run, Correlation, Check Sheets	Bicheno, *Six Sigma and the Quality Toolbox* (SSQT)
Pokayoke	Failsafe devices	Hinckley, *Make No Mistake*
ECRS	Eliminate, Combine, Rearrange, Simplify	Kato, *Toyota Kaizen Methods*
Kipling	What, Why, When, Where, How, Who. Linked with ECRS and TWI	Bicheno, LTB
TWI	Job Instruction, Job Methods, Job Relations	Graupp and Wrona, *The TWI Workbook*
Six Sigma	Large range of statistical tools, using DMAIC	Gitlow & Levine, *Six Sigma for Greenbelts*
Brainstorm	Open ended generate ideas from a team	Bicheno, SSQT
Visual Problems	A range of tools for Looking, seeing, imagining, showing	Roam, *Unfolding the Napkin*
Kata	Move to the next target condition with coaching	Rother, *Toyota Kata*
A3	Toyota ordered 8 step method with mentoring	Shook, *Managing to Learn*
Sprint	Short duration sub project esp. in IT	Knapp, *Sprint*
Scrum	Team-based IT method	Sutherland, *SCRUM*
Shainin	Find the root RED X. Many tools but observation is crucial	Bhote & Bhote, *World Class quality* (2nd ed)
Value Stream Mapping	Standard Lean process analysis	Rother and Shook, *Learning to See*
Kaizen Event	Team based 5-day focus on an area	Bicheno, LTB
SCAMPER	Substitute, combine, adapt, magnify or minimise, put to other use, eliminate, rearrange	Dyer, *The Innovator's DNA*
Questionstorm	As for Brainstorm except generate questions	Dyer, *The Innovator's DNA*
Simulation	Computer or physical. Several computer simulation languages available	Ciaburro, *Hands-on Simulation Modelling*

O.R.	Operations Research: mathematical and statistical tools for optimisation. Minimise or maximise subject to constraints	Hillier, *Introduction to Operations Research*
Systems Methodologies	'Hard' e.g. system dynamics, 'Soft' e.g. Soft Systems Methodology. Vanguard method	Dennis Sherwood, *Seeing the Wood for the Trees*; Checkland, *Systems Thinking*. Seddon.
Digital twin	Computer model of the factory	W. Kühn, *Handbook of Digital Enterprise Systems*
AI	Artificial Intelligence. Machine learning.	Daniel Susskind, *A World without work*
Value Eng	Break down a product or part and can it be improved or cost less	Bytheway, *FAST Creativity and Innovation*
DOE	Design of Experiments. Several variables examined simultaneously	Gitlow and Levine, *Six Sigma*
3P	Production Preparation Process	Coletta, *The Lean 3P Advantage*
Set-based Design	Keep the design options open as late as possible	Morgan and Liker, *Designing the Future*
Obeya	Big Room for coordinating NPD	Allen Ward, *Lean Product Development*
TRIZ	Someone, somewhere has looked at a similar problem usually in a different field	Darrell Mann, *Hands-on Systematic Innovation*
Lateral Thinking	One of several methods so think differently about a solution	DeBono, *Lateral Thinking*
Creativity Tools	Many in addition to Lateral Thinking	Michalko, *Thinkertoys*
Design Thinking	Go to the Gemba, multi-discipline. Redesign the 'Job to be done'	Lockwood, *Design Thinking*
LAMDA	Look Ask Model Discuss Act, for new product introduction	Ward and Kennedy, *Product Development for Lean*
Lean Startup	Minimal viable product; fail fast	Reis, *The Lean Startup*

Chapter 10
Learning

In this Chapter, we discuss general learning principles and frameworks. The Chapter is concerned primarily with Individual and Team learning. There is however vast material on Organisational Learning, much of it overlapping with Systems Thinking and Change. For example there is the well-known theory on Single and Double Loop Learning discussed by Chris Argyris. Some of these concepts are discussed in the Systems chapter. (Section 5.5.). In other words it is not just Learning, but also Learning how to learn.

Once it was fine for only an individual to learn – alone. Those days are long past. Today, individual learning remains crucial, but so too is team learning and organisational learning.

10.1 Why learn?

"The only secret to Toyota is its attitude towards learning." - Isao Yoshino, speaking at European Lean Educator Conference, Braga, Portugal, 2018

…and, from Heathcote and Powell in The Lean Post: *"Lean is about learning. Learning to find real problems, learning to face the limits of our current knowledge in light of these problems, learning to frame the gaps as learning challenges, and finally, learning to form and share actionable solutions. As such, lean is really about learning-to-learn."*

…and, from George Davidson (retired Manufacturing Director at Toyota South Africa) *"The aim of the Toyota Production System is to create thinking people"*. (Or, as otherwise said, TPS is a *Thinking People System*.)

…and, from H. Thomas Johnson *"…what management is all about in Toyota, where learning is the work and the work is learning."*

…and from David Novak (CEO and author of the huge bestseller *Taking People With You*, who believes that *"…being an avid learner is the single biggest thing that separates a good leader from a great one."*

…and, From Reg Revans (originator of the Action Learning approach), *"In any epoch of rapid change, those organizations unable to adapt are soon in trouble. Adaption is achieved only by learning."*

And, of course, in a VUCA world, continuous learning and continuous adapting is essential. (VUCA for volatility, uncertainty, complexity and ambiguity is not a new acronym – it is from 1987 – but is increasingly relevant today.)

It is said that Toyota grows people then builds cars. VS Mahesh, former HR director at Tata Hotels, talked about 'the corporation as a nursery for human growth'.

So…It is not just 'learning' – it is thirsting to learn, continuing to learn, self-learning, team learning, organisational learning, helping others to learn, daily learning, the habit of learning, and learning how to learn.

Learning is the essence of continuous improvement. It is *rate* of learning that is important. A range of companies might make (say) cars but it is the rate of learning that widens the gap. The gap widens in both cost and revenue, resulting from learning to improve quality and productivity that ultimately stem from people. Toyota is reported to say that 'we build people first, then cars'. Note that it is everyone, not just managers and engineers. Work smarter, not harder.

Almost every manager subscribes to a 'learning organisation', but the how and the what, are not necessarily clear. Indeed, the why is not necessarily clear either.

A learning organisation stems from a myriad of practices that are discussed throughout this book. Examples include Gemba walks, A3 problem solving and mentoring, the Kata methodology, Ideas, and 'Hansei' reflection. Learning is also closely related to experimentation, especially controlled experimentation. These are the subjects of other sections in the book.

10.2 Lean is Continuous Learning

In a Lean organisation: *mistakes are seen as opportunities to improve*, not as something that needs to be monitored and punished. There is no-blame game if something goes wrong. People are not rewarded for how few mistakes they make, but on how well they improve the process when mistakes have occurred. The ability to continuously learn is the real competitive advantage.

Taiichi Ohno believed in developing managers by the Socratic Method – by asking tough questions rather than giving answers. If you give the answer the person does not learn as much, and is less committed, compared with thinking it out him or herself. It can be frustrating to not be told 'the answers' – a particular shock to people who have gone through years of formal education by passive sitting and listening and then cramming for exams. This is much like a top-down system that imposes the detailed (Lean?) tools, makes decisions and sets KPIs without consultation. It is a form of arrogance, and not surprising that the learning rate is low. Contrast this with the practice of Hoshin Kanri or Policy Deployment, whereby top management sets the strategic direction (the 'what' and the 'why') but evolves the detail level by level in a process of consultation (the how). Decisions are taken locally, only migrating upwards in exceptional circumstances. This is much like the human body's management system.

10.3 Push and Pull in Learning

Lean practitioners are familiar with push and pull in material flow. Push and Pull also applies in Learning. There is a spectrum from push to pull, as shown in the Table below. TWI and other methods recommend a Training Matrix where learners and managers can see the progression of skills acquisition. At Toyota this progression is essentially pull-based, and the complete list would take several years to work through. Many employees will never progress through the entire list simply because higher level skills are not appropriate.

It is not the case that push is bad and pull is good. In Lean there is a strong tendency to favour pull, but some push education can open up wider perspectives. As an example, one of the authors was with an ex-student (now a consultant) in a welding fabrication shop. The consultant immediately recognised that the sequence of welds was similar to the classic Operations Research 'Travelling Salesman' problem. Analysis and subsequent implementation eliminated a bottleneck, saved the purchase of another machine, and resulted in significant additional throughput. None of the company managers, many of whom had years of experience in Lean, realised the opportunity. Moral: You can't pull detail on concepts you don't know about!

(Of course, this is linked with the fundamental belief of TRIZ: that someone, somewhere, has solved a similar problem – usually in a different context.)

Type	Examples	Comment
Push	Classroom-only: Six Sigma theory and Lean theory. Lean course with applications Books Video-based courses Conferences Video with interaction	Inefficient and wasteful. But some necessary for wider appreciation. Theory-based.
to	Leader standard work TWI Problem-based learning Kaizen events Coaching Mentoring Action-learning	
Pull	A3	More effective, but a risk of not being aware of wider possibilities. More expensive. Problem-based.

10.4 Pre-Requisites for Learning

Lean Thinking is not a permanent capability – without Lean Learning there can be no effective Lean Thinking. There are three inter-related, and challenging, personal pre-requisites:

- *Humility*. An awareness that no-one, however exalted, knows all the answers. Indeed, much learning comes from the front line. There is a joy in discovering that one was wrong. Saying 'I don't know' and 'I was wrong' don't undermine status but are an indication of willingness to learn. The more one strives for Lean, the more one realizes how little one knows, and how much there is yet to learn. Learning begins with humility. Ego is a barrier to learning. No humility means no learning. It is recognition of skills that others have that you do not yet have. These skills need to be drawn out for the benefit of all. Look out for pseudo 'respect' – for example, asking for ideas but then not allowing time for their consideration. (Respect should not be confused with 'being nice'.) Leaders should understand that not having all the answers isn't the problem. The real problem is when the leader isn't aware that he or she doesn't have all the answers. (This is System 1 and System 2 – see also Chapter 8, Problems and Problem Solving).

- *Listening*. Listening is a skill that takes a lifetime to master. It includes genuine interest, warmth, rapport, and reflection. It also takes time and patience. As West Churchman said, *"The systems approach begins when you first see the world through the eyes of another"*. He might have been speaking about Lean learning.
  Two thoughts: The African word 'Ubuntu' – a person becomes a person through other people; and Covey's 5th habit *"Seek first to understand, then to be understood"*.

- *Awareness of bias*. We all have biases. But seek to understand one's own biases. We have come across several 'blinkered' – or tunnel vision – managers who find it hard to cease old concepts as a pre-requisite to gaining Lean benefits. (We are not immune to this ourselves!) Recall Lewin's three stages of change: 'Unfreezing, change, refreezing' (although refreezing should now be chilling rather than refreezing.) Recall also the classic quote from

John Maynard Keynes that could equally apply to Lean, 'Practical men who believe themselves to be quite exempt from any intellectual influence, are usually the slaves of some defunct economist.'

There are also Organisational pre-requisites for learning.

It is quite possible that whilst individuals and teams may have learned, the organisation in which they work has not learned or adapted. The late David Garvin of Harvard Business School used three categories of pre-requisites for organisational learning. Here we add our thoughts to the categories.

1. *A Supportive Learning environment*:

o   Time for reflection (or Hansei as used in Lean). This can be created or built-in. For example, after a kaizen event, or any improvement project, allow a reflection period for participants to think about what went right and not so right. What can be learned? Reflection is part of an AAR (After Action Review). See below. Steve Spear (see Section 3.15) made a point of discussing the proper way to do Plan Do Check Act, by insisting on using the experimental method properly.) Don't just tackle a project, but instead Set a hypothesis, test or carry out, check back against the hypothesis, reflect and develop conclusions. These conclusions are win-win: either you win by confirmation, or you win by learning what you did not know.
o   Toleration of mistakes. Mistakes should not be punished – far better to regard a mistake or defect as an opportunity. 'Drive out Fear,' said Deming. At the 2020 Shakir F1 Grand Prix, the Mercedes Team made what Team Principal Toto Wolff called a 'colossal f--- up' in the pit-stop that cost George Russell victory in his first GP with Mercedes. But there was no blame. Instead Mercedes engineer Shovlin said *"It looked like we don't know what we are doing, but the issue all comes down to this root cause where we lost a key message at a key time, We found this smoking gun, now we just need to go through the logs of how everything was working and once we have got a complete understanding of that and we have filled in some of the blanks that we are not certain of at the moment, we can then find a solution in time for [the next race in] Abu Dhabi."*
Don't give up! James Dyson, explains that it took 5126 attempts to develop his vacuum cleaner.
o   Deliberate feedback. Without deliberate feedback, repetition is ineffective – a point made by Anders Eriksson in his book *Peak*. Eriksson gives the principles of deliberate feedback summarised here as questions: (a) Does it push people to get outside their comfort zone and attempt to do things that are not easy for them? (b) Does it offer immediate feedback on what can be done to improve?; (c) Have those who developed the best approach so far been identified?; (d) Is the practice and repetition designed to develop the particular skills of the experts? And, we should add, feedback should be specific, not general.

2. *Learning Practices and Processes*:

o   Knowledge sharing. How is the best knowledge to be shared? We know of several companies that have a data base of ideas and best practices that is routinely updated and available to be shared using key words. First stage in a kaizen is to look at what we already know somewhere in the company. It means giving 'brownie points' for those who contribute to the data base.
o   Formal and Informal training and coaching. See also below. Company policies to send and sponsor staff on courses, conferences, seminars. Some have book and journal reading groups. (There is the old story about 'What happens if you train a person and he leaves? Or 'What happens if you don't train and he stays?'). Importantly not all training is directly related to the person's job. Dell, Google, and Apple are just a few of the companies where

employees can take a wide range of courses. Stephen Johnson, famous innovation writer, talks about 'the adjacent possible' where (all?) innovation breakthroughs originate from adapted external ideas and technologies. Anyone for flower arranging?

o Formal benchmarking. Process benchmarking and Product benchmarking.

o External visits. Several companies send their front-line employees to visit customers. This is fairly common in medical-related organisations: Novo Nordisk and Johnson and Johnson are examples. A powerful motivating force in addition to learning what customers value.

o Experience. How to capture experience and how to prevent valuable experience and knowledge walking out the door when someone leaves or retires. Some companies known to the authors use experience 'black books' (or similar technology) where lessons are written down. Updating Standard Work, of course, is part of this process.

o Action Learning. See below. A very effective peer teaching and learning methodology.

o Experimentation. The 'gold standard' today is the randomised trial, or A/B test. Or even better the (blind) randomised trial. A pure randomised trial involves a randomly selected experimental group and a control group. This is much better than the widespread use of correlation studies that are subject to a large number of unknown external factors. Web related companies such as Google carry out hundreds of experiments every week – judging the effectiveness of one web page design against another. Randomised trials are the standard in healthcare but remain underused in operations. Why? Often not easy to do, but there are opportunities where, for example, there are parallel assembly lines or dozens of people working in a service centre.

o Machine learning. Set a computer algorithm free and let it learn by itself. Beginning to be widely used in diagnosis, forecasting, advertising, and service. The future.

o Consultants (?) Tetlow has amusingly shown that in the medium term the best expert forecasters are no better than taxi-drivers! Nevertheless some Delphi techniques have shown promise. The most successful 'super-forecasters' are those who change their mind as a situation develops, says Tetlow. (John Maynard Keynes, father of Keynesian macroeconomics, is reported to have said, *"When the facts change, I change my mind. What do you do, Sir?"* and *"The difficulty lies not so much in developing new ideas as in escaping from old ones."*) Good forecasters rely on a variety of sources and often collaborate. The best forecasters are not necessarily the most academically qualified or the most senior, which means that acceptance of their forecasts can threaten the organisational hierarchy. To identify and encourage the 'super forecasters' the UK Government has set up a forecasting tournament called 'Cosmic Bazaar'. About 40 questions are live at any time. This is used by over 1200 forecasters who are ranked by accuracy of their forecasts. In the USA, Tetlock has set up a similar 'Good Judgement Project'.

A fascinating website on forecasting is https://www.gjopen.com/challenges

Many interesting forecasts such as 'Before 1 January 2025, how many major automakers will debut a flying passenger vehicle?'. You too can make a forecast!

3. *Leading Learning*

o Encouragement not punishment, for challenging ideas.

o Downplay the HiPPO. The Highest Paid Person's Opinion. A great barrier to learning where HiPPO's are allowed to be dominant.

o The Progress Principle. Teresa Amabile of Harvard Business School suggests that 'small wins', where progress is recognised, is the most powerful force for motivation. (See The People Trilogy Section 4.2) Amabile says that there are two broad factors, Nourishers and Catalysts. Catalysts include respect and recognition, encouragement, emotional support, and affiliation and camaraderie. Nourishers include clear, meaningful goals, autonomy, sufficient resources, help with the work, open idea flow, and sufficient time (but not too much). (The Catalyst analogy has also been used by Jonah Berger (in his book *The Catalyst*) to facilitate change.

Finally, in this section, a word from Lilian Gilbreth, who said in 1921 "Teaching under Scientific Management trains the senses' – all of his senses are possible." (hear, see, vibration, smell). And "with the training of the senses the possibility of increased efficiency increases".

Further Readings.
Teresa Amabile and Steven Kramer, *The Progress Principle*, Harvard Business School, 2011
James Dyson, *Invention: A life,* Simon and Schuster, 2021
Anders Eriksson, *Peak*, Bodley Head, 2016
David Garvin, *Learning in Action*, Harvard, 2000
L.M. Gilbreth, *The Psychology of Management*, New York, 1921
Richard Nisbett, *Mindset*, Penguin, 2015
Philip Tetlock and Dan Gardner, *Superforecasting*, RH Books, 2015

10.5   70:20:10 Learning and Training

70:20:10 is a time-split reference guideline used by some training and consulting organisations. The underlying philosophy accords with Lean's 'Learning Whilst Doing' philosophy.

The thesis, apparently based on research, states that approximately

70% of learning comes from job-related assignments

20% of learning comes from developmental relationships

10% of learning comes from formal courses

It is a popular notion, and meshes well with hands-on learning experiences, employee engagement, devolved decision-making, and problem-based coaching and mentoring as should happen with good A3 and Kata activities.

Coursework should not be stand-alone, but should act as an amplifier to the other 90%. It is certainly true that the benefits of much formal training are lost if there is no follow through of application. As such the ratio is an aspirational goal.

The 70% of time is made up from problem solving, challenging tasks, and (in accordance with Lean) from reflection (Hansei).

The 20% of development time would include several activities discussed at some length in this book including Action Learning, After-action reviews (AARs), and Feedback. In particular, the next section on ShuHaRi is relevant.

Of course, the 70:20:10 guideline split is certainly not applicable for all disciplines. It has also been criticised as insufficiently researched, and does not reflect more modern training methods such as on-line video and augmented reality (AR). Nevertheless it does encompass the established lean concepts of learning-whilst-doing, mentoring, and being not too heavily classroom based.

The problem would seem to be that there are often insufficient mentors or coaches for the 70% and 20% categories. As a result learning is too slow and there is too much reliance on the 10% (ineffective?) category. The lesson is that the 70:20:10 guideline cannot simply be adopted at short notice, but is a provocative challenge to traditional training and education, and a reminder that training should be continuous. Toyota's small span of control for team leaders is an indication of what would be needed.

Further Readings.
Download from www.702010institute.com

10.6 ShuHaRi

Some organisations known to the authors of this book also use the Japanese Martial Arts ShuHaRi learning stages. ShuHaRi is also the framework for learning at Toyota.

The stages are:

Shu: learning from a master. This could also be 'follow the rules'. This stage closely follows TWI training:

- PRESENT: tell, show and illustrate one key point at a time;
- do it again stressing key points;
- do it again stressing reasons for key points
- TRY OUT: have the person do the job, and correct errors
- Repeat with explaining each important step
- Repeat with explaining each key point
- Repeat with explaining reasons for each key point.

This sounds repetitive. It is! But it builds a thorough understanding of the job. This stage is really about mastering technique, as would be required in many sports, cooking, and music. There are close similarities with Deliberate Practice as described by Anders Ericsson. (See below.)

Ha: The master still keeps tabs on the learner to make sure the steps are being carried out correctly. As the learner becomes proficient, he or she may learn from other masters and begin to integrate those wider learnings. This could also imply adapting the rules. The master may now begin to adopt more of a Socratic approach – management by asking questions instead of telling. (See Section 3.14 on the Socratic approach.) A small number of Western companies carry out Shu and Ri – the latter by auditing the process. It is interesting that sport stars throughout their careers – for example in tennis – still retain a coach to essentially continue with the Shu and Ha stages. It is not unknown for some CEOs to use understudies.

Ri: Now, at least, the person is no longer a learner but can develop own practices, and teach others.

Note that this is a philosophy of developing yourself before leading others. 'Developing yourself' may include taking an external degree or course, but the main development takes place within the organisation.

ShuHaRi is not confined to shop-floor work. Many disciplines can learn the same way: engineers, designers, accountants, and logistics. HR? Managers also go through these stages, but many would have come up through the ranks and would already be familiar with the thoroughness of the process.

Steve Spear's well-known Harvard case study Jack Smith A, B, and C tells of how a new senior manager recruited into Toyota progressed though similar stages, taking several months to reach the Ri stage. ShuHaRi is not mentioned specifically but the learning process was similar. In the West, many apprentices essentially follow similar steps, although not necessarily as detailed. ShuHaRi is also reminiscent of Lewin's "Unfreeze, change, re-freeze." Similarities with The Dreyfus Model are also apparent.

10.7 The Stages of Learning

Learning progresses through 7 stages: The 7 'A's of Learning. In each stage there are 'Friends' or concepts that assist the stage, and 'Enemies' – concepts that can set the stage back. The stages are presented in the Table below.

Stages:	'Friends'	'Enemies'
Avoidance	-	Bias, Fear
Awareness	Curiosity, Sharers, Media, Conferences, Evidence, Exposure, Customers	Silos, Time, Cost, Disbelief, Openness
Acquiring	Benchmarking, Media, Gemba,	Overload (Muri), Lack of support
Accepting (Interpreting)	Evidence, Evidence-based, Measures, Experiences, Sharing	False information and measures, Contradictions, Bias
Applying	Kaizen activities, Lean tools, Quality tools, being coached, PDCA, Gemba	Piecemeal, No models and false models, Punishment not reward, Fear of failure,
Adopting	Habits, Team activities, People, Being mentored, Leader standard work, Clear goals and a 'true north', Mindset	Deming's 4 SoPK (variation, systems thinking, scientific method, psychology (motivation), accounting? Positional threats, Lack of incentives
Adept (Becoming)	Practice, Feedback, Mentoring, Coaching others	Lack of 'Friends'

The Waste of Forgetting what was learned.

This waste results from simply letting knowledge disappear. It applies particularly in Design and Innovation, but also in many professional fields. So, experience and knowledge that is gained when, for example, new products are designed, made, introduced, and marketed is not recorded and is simply forgotten about next time around. Such knowledge has to be re-discovered all over again. 'Learning the hard way' is so silly when it already has been learned. Even if knowledge is re-used but not recorded, but instead is kept in the head of the person, there is the significant danger that it will be lost when that person leaves. This waste is similar to the waste of untapped human potential, but concerns knowledge and experience that the company has already used and paid for. So, have a procedure for recording lessons learned – even if this is as simple as a 'little black book'. Insist that it be done. Also include a "lessons learned" step in every project management and problem-solving process. (This is also known as Yokoten – see under Idea Management, Section 8.17)

Questioning and Learning

Questioning and Learning are closely related for both the learner and the teacher.

An ability for good questioning is a skill that every Lean manager should aspire to.

Questioning was discussed at some length in the Chapter on Decisions, and will not be repeated here.

10.8 General Points on Learning Methods

Research on learning over the past few decades has revealed several important points – and myths! Every manager concerned with training and developing their people (and is there anyone in Lean who does not have this concern?) should understand the basic lessons that follow. This is based on material by Brown et al, by Bush and Watson, and by Carey.

(But first, think for a moment about your most memorable learning experience - about any topic – including Lean – ....)

- Repetition: By itself, repetition is fairly useless – despite it being encouraged in schools. (Re-read to remember, especially if repeated immediately, is weak). (To repeat an earlier section, the Quality Guru Phil Crosby used to ask if people had 25 years' experience or 1 year 25 times?). But repetition with guided or deliberate repetition is better; And varied repetition (with guidance) is best of all. (Varied repetition is tasks ABCABC rather than big batch AAA…In other words mixed model scheduling!)
- Allowing mistakes to be quickly discussed and corrected is very effective. (As in A3 mentoring.) Systems that encourage the hiding of mistakes can be disastrous. (So, 'Thank you for pulling the Andon cord.') (See Section 9.9 on Psychological Safety.)
- Self-quizzing is very effective. ('What did I learn yesterday?') Consciously retrieve what was learned. An instructor, or team leader should always include this, by asking members. Even better, if it can be done, is a short administered quiz on past material.
- Arrogance is a barrier. To help overcome this, ask an early question(s) where the correct answer is a surprise or not known.
- Small chunks of material are better than large chunks. One small single topic at a time.
- Spacing out sessions is better. (On this, recall the classic TWI instruction '10-hour class': 5 daily sessions of 2 hours, not 1 of 10 hours).
- Arrangement. Try to avoid managers and supervisors sitting in with operators. If this cannot be avoided, physically separate the levels, and then address the operators not the managers.
- Taking a break (as, for example, spreading material into the next day) actually improves memory. Tapering off only begins after 3 or 4 days. Not just a break every hour, but spread the material over days.
- Interleaving, whereby you deliberately break off from a problem you are stuck on, do something different, then return, has been shown to be very effective.
- Posing questions at the beginning of a session is more effective than just leaping into giving a training session. Learners make the connection, particularly if they got the answer wrong or did not know the answer.
- Discussion amongst the group. Encourage. Ask and the stay silent.
- Effortful learning is more effective. The more one has to struggle with a topic, the greater the learning. Fast learning is an illusion. Easier and faster is not better. Counterintuitive?
- Sequence is important. Build up knowledge gradually, with a future path seen where possible. Recall the last session's material or lessons learned.
- Playing background music with lyrics generally leads to a fall-off in performance. Music without lyrics has less effect.
- Reciting is effective. Why does TWI JI training require participants to say out loud 'If the worker hasn't learned the instructor hasn't taught,'?)
- Relating material back to own experience is better. (Do you work better on a hot or a cold day? Sitting or standing? What were the circumstances when you made a mistake?).
- Images are better than text. (The authors of this book should take note!)

- Mindset is important. A growth mindset rather than a fixed mindset. (See Section 7.4 on Mindset and Carol Dwek. Dwek's research clearly shows that a Growth Mindset can be developed.) Parents (and managers) who view failure as a positive opportunity encourage a growth mindset in kids (and learners).
- Remembering: Things learned when an external event occurs have greater retention. (You will probably remember where you were during an England football or rugby match; you will probably remember points from your first kaizen event.)
- Forgetting: The famous Ebbinghaus curve (from 1870s) showing memory retention against time has been re-thought. It probably only applies to abstract things. In fact, your brain is an excellent filtering device continually sorting the relevant from the irrelevant. There is now the 'Theory of Disuse' whereby memory fades with disuse and relevance. (Relax, forgetting is not necessarily a sign of dementia, it is a sign that your brain is working well!).
- Memory is fallible, and can be conditioned by subsequent experiences. (Some very worrying research on people giving evidence in court.)
- Humour improves memory if it is relevant.
- Unfinished jobs or projects remain in the memory, and get mulled over. Completed jobs are deleted or fade away. Kurt Lewin discovered this. (See Section 4.5 on Lewin.)
- People remember better when the same material is put forward in different environments.
- The habit of reflecting on one's experiences leads to increased learning and retention. (Hansei?)
- Anecdotes and case studies can be useful. But better when there is interest or reasons why. TWI job instruction gives reasons for key points – this is necessary for retention.
- Fitting material into a wider context helps understanding and retention. (Not just, for example, kanban but why kanban? And techniques associated with moving towards 'True North'.)
- Having a goal in mind heightens your perceptions of relevant, related things. Writing a book on human Lean; reducing changeover on a particular machine; planning a holiday to Botswana – all of these will sensitise you to events and material that would otherwise be ignored.
- Encourage scepticism and inquiry. Encourage self-interrogation. This is humility. 'We don't really know all the answers. Yet? 'Why so?')
- There is a 'familiarity trap' – feeling that you know something so don't need to practise. (This is why Toyota and others audit Standard Work.)
- Watching somebody doing a task gives greater confidence that they can do it, but this is not translated into actually doing the task. (TWI job instruction training begins by showing the fallacy of 'showing alone' and 'telling alone'.)
- There is a self-fulfilling prophesy (or Pygmalion effect) also demonstrated by Kahneman and Tversky. Instructors who think they are dealing with a good group get good results from the group, and vice versa. (Tested with Israeli army recruits, and many others.)
- Sleep is essential to learning because the brain reorganises and rearranges.
- Incubation is effective ('sleep on it') where a problem has been struggled with. This could be 5 minutes, 20 minutes, or overnight – or longer for complex issues. Take a short break for one-off less complex problems. But wait overnight for complex, messy or strategic decisions. (The Quaker church has no hierarchy. Decisions are by agreement. Not everyone has to agree but where there is disagreement a short period of silence is used.)
- End a training session (face-to-face or Zoom) with individual Action Plans. Participants should compile a list of what they will do and share with others before the session ends.
- Hold an AAR (After Action Review) if possible. What was intended, what was actually done, what was good, what could be better next time. No personal criticism.

Further Readings.
Peter Brown, Henry Roediger, Mark McDaniel, *Make it Stick: The Science of Successful Learning*, Belknap Harvard, 2014
Bradley Busch and Edward Watson, *The Science of Learning: 77 Studies that Every Teacher Needs to Know,* Routledge, 2019
Benedict Carey, *How We Learn: The surprizing truth about when, where and why it happens*, Macmillan, 2014

10.9 Matching Existing Skills with Learning Materials

In any training there should be a match between the learners' existing skills or competence and the material that is being presented. There are three situations, given below. Please check which situation applies, perhaps by questioning or test. Don't assume! (Refer also to the Mager and Pipe flowchart in Section 4.4)

- The learner has low skills but the presented material is too complex or advanced: Here the learner will become frustrated, concerned, stressed – and de-motivated. A waste!
- The opposite: The learner has high existing skills but the material is familiar or low level. Here the learner will feel bored and annoyed. A waste! Some learners could become subversive to others. However a good instructor could make good use of the learner's existing skills to enhance the experience of others. Today there is widespread experience of Lean – good and bad. Make good use if it!
- There is a match. Here the learner should feel engaged and motivated.

This is similar to Mihály Csíkszentmihályi's (MC's) FLOW Concept and diagram discussed in Section 7.3

10.10 Learning Theories and Andragogy

(Andragogy is a label for the art and science of teaching that is relevant to adults. By contrast 'pedagogy' is the approach used for kids.)

There are several authorities on andragogy, but here we will briefly give an overview of the theories of Malcolm Knowles. Knowles has 5 Assumptions and 4 Principles, The Assumptions are, as a person matures, he or she…

- …moves from dependency towards self-directed; so Learners should later be given several options or methods for learning and be involved in course design.
- …accumulates a growing reservoir of experience that is a valuable resource; so focus on application – doing rather than knowing.
- …becomes increasingly oriented towards developmental tasks – self learning.
- …becomes increasingly oriented towards immediacy of application; so don't 'dump' material. Adult learning is problem-centred rather than content-oriented. (We hope that does not apply to this book – feel free to skip irrelevant material!)
- …has motivations that are increasingly internal; so material should point the way in which a learner could benefit.

These fit-in well, or should fit-in well, with the best Lean learning approaches – TWI, Kata, A3. There are also implications for effective management, Design thinking, Teams, and Projects (such as SCRUM in Agile software development).

If you are in a Lean-learning situation, do take a look on the web for material under the "Flipped Classroom" concept that incorporates learning principles. This material has exploded in the COVID crisis. Although focused on schoolkid learning it has much relevance to adults including Lean learners. See for instance: https://www.youtube.com/watch?v=qdKzSq_t8k8

10.11 The SAMR Model

SAMR (Substitution, Augmentation, Modification, and Redefinition) is a hierarchical model created by Dr. Ruben Puentedura showing 4 levels of increasing sophistication of educational technology.

SAMR will be increasingly relevant in Lean learning as books make room for videos, PowerPoint, apps and tweets, Zoom, and augmented reality (AR). COVID has accelerated the progression up the levels.
The SAMR levels, with examples, follow from lowest to highest. In the lowest two levels, technology acts as an enhancement; in the higher two levels transformation is made possible. Any Lean training or learning should endeavour to move up the levels in the model. They are:

Substitution: a direct tool substitute: from paper based value stream maps to VSM mapping software; computer word processing; substitute lectures on Lean course with video.
Augmentation: a direct tool substitute with functional substitute: moving to interactive whiteboards for mapping; word processing with grammar and spell checks; a course includes videos and computer-based answer polling
Modification: allowing significant task substitution: adding simulation modelling to a VSM; embedded videos and hyperlinks; course includes live links with international authorities.
Redefinition: the creation of new tasks, previously inconceivable: the digital twin with IoT data capture; computer interaction between readers of the same book and with authors and experts; course includes augmented reality (AR) visits, virtual reality (VR).

Further Readings.
Please see the web for the many diagrams and examples on SAMR.

10.12 Murdoch's Inquiry Cycle

Kath Murdoch, an Australian educational expert, developed the 6 stage Inquiry Cycle. This has large relevance for Lean learners, problem solvers, designers, as well as those involved in Appreciative Inquiry (See Section 7.5). The Stages, (that don't necessarily need to be followed in strict sequence) and some questions are…

- Tuning-in: what do you know about this? What do I need to know? How do I know that I know?
- Finding-out: where might I go to find out? what resources are available? What are my questions?
- Sorting-out: how can I sort the material? How is it connected to what I already know?
- Going further: What information do I need to share? Have I considered different points of view? How can I plan to show the connections?
- Making conclusions: What do I know and understand about the main questions? What am I going to do with what I have learned? What would I do differently?
- Taking action: How can what I have learned help me? How am I going to use what I have learned? How will it affect others?

What a wonderful sequence and set of questions! You can and should use this in many Lean interventions and projects. Please refer to the web for more inspiration from the model.

Comparing Murdoch's Cycle with the A3 stages and PDSA

A3 Steps	PDSA	Murdoch Inquiry
Clarification (background, the problem, containment)	Study	Tune-in
Breakdown (5 whys, process map)		Finding-out, Sorting-out
Target Setting		Going further
Cause Analysis (M's)	Plan	Making conclusions
Countermeasures		
Execution	Do	Taking action
Monitoring	Study	And Making conclusions
Standardise	Act	

Further Readings.
https://www.kathmurdoch.com.au

10.13 Bloom's Taxonomy and the Dreyfus Skill Acquisition Model

Next, two widely-used learning models are briefly discussed. There are similarities, but the Bloom Taxonomy appears to be more widely used in formal education, and the Dreyfus model for adult Skills. Dreyfus has been used in Mike Rother's work on Kata.

Bloom's Taxonomy

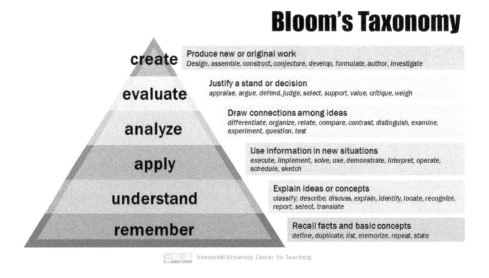

Bloom's Taxonomy is a widely used framework to arrange and classify educational learning goals. First put forward by in 1956 by Benjamin Bloom, the framework has been modified several times. A taxonomy is simply a hierarchy of processes. To master any level, the level below must first be mastered. In other words, the steps shown are progressive As such, it is a useful reference for educators including in the Lean area to set learning goals. All Lean trainers would benefit from familiarity with Bloom's Taxonomy. The figure above is from Vanderbilt University Center for Teaching, from which a large amount of teaching and learning aids are available.

Today there are a set of three 'Levels' models – for knowledge based, for emotion-based and for action-based (or physical psychomotor) skills.

The appropriate learning goal, of course, would depend upon the function in the organisation and the required skills

There are typical questions that would apply to each level in the model. For example:

- Knowledge (remembering: define, repeat, recall): What is SMED?
- Comprehension (understanding: describe, explain): What are the stages of SMED?
- Application (transferring: compare, demonstrate): What information would you need to collect for a SMED project?
- Analysis (relating: distinguish, explain): What is the relationship between SMED and batch size?
- Synthesis (creating: arrange, develop, design): How would you prioritise if you had several SMED project possibilities?
- Evaluation (judging: assess, critique): How would you test the effectiveness of a SMED project?

The Dreyfus Model

The five stage Dreyfus Model of adult skill proficiency was developed for the US Air Force in 1980. To quote from the original report *"the student normally passes through five developmental stages which we designate novice, competence, proficiency, expertise and mastery. We argue, based on analysis of careful descriptions of skill acquisition, that as the student becomes skilled, he depends less on abstract principles and more on concrete experience."* And later *"we argue that skill in its minimal form is produced by following abstract formal rules, but that only experience with concrete cases can account for higher levels of performance.... A detailed understanding of the stages through which skilful performance develops is essential if one is to design training programs and training materials to facilitate the acquisition of high-order skills. In any such endeavour, it is essential to identify at each stage what capacities the performer has acquired and which more sophisticated capacity he is then in a position to attain."* As students progress they depend less on theory and principles, and more on their experience. They also get to view the environment in which they are working differently.

Note that the model refers to skill, not to the person. ('Mastery' was later changed to Expert.)

There are also 'four binary qualities'. Each of these progresses from Novice to Expert as follows:

- Recollection – from non-situational to situational (i.e. ability to adapt to the specific situation)
- Recognition – from decomposed to holistic (i.e. towards a more 'systems' viewpoint)
- Decision – from analytical to intuitive (i.e. becoming more automatic or from Kahneman's System 2 to System 1)
- Awareness – from monitoring to absorbed (perhaps from KPI to Gemba?)

As with Bloom's Taxonomy (and Maslow's hierarchy) the Dreyfus Model is often represented as a triangle or pyramid to show the successive acquisition of skills building on one another. Here we use a table with our own Lean-related comment.

In Dreyfus and Dreyfus' book *Mind over Machine*, the authors say that the five successive stages can be used as a framework for judging machine intelligence and artificial intelligence. As such, The Dreyfus model has become popular in the Agile software community.

Stage	Characteristics	Lean related
Novice	Rule based; no judgement	Follows standard work.
Advanced Beginner	Limited situational perception; aspects treated separately	An early awareness of the value stream but still independent
Competent	Coping with multiple activities, some appreciation of how actions relate to others. Deliberate planning and formulating routines	Developing a value stream viewpoint. Beginning to adjust standard work. Early PDCA?
Proficient	Holistic view; Prioritises; Perceives deviations	Systems view. Problem solving skills developing. Kata coach?
Expert	Transcends reliance on rules; Has vision; Uses analytical approaches	'True North' viewpoint leading to adaption. Full PDCA.

Further Readings.

Lorin Anderson, David Krathwohl, (eds) *A taxonomy for learning, teaching, and assessing: a revision of Bloom's taxonomy of educational objectives,* Longman, 2001

Stuart Dreyfus and Hubert Dreyfus, *A Five Stage Model of the Mental Activities Involved in Directed Skill Acquisition*, University of California, Berkeley, 1980. Available as a free download on pdf.

en.wikipeda.org/dreyfus

10.14 Listening

At this stage, following Bloom's Taxonomy, it is useful to take a diversion to refer to an absolutely essential skill for any Lean-aspiring person, at any level: Listening!

Listening is the first stage for change. Listen and understand first, and only then decide an appropriate change or persuasion strategy – rational, emotional, hard or soft.

Let us recall The Beatles, who sang…
> *Nowhere Man*
> *Please listen..*
> *You don't know what you're missin...'*
> *... The world is at your command...)*

Great! ..and
> *"When people talk, listen completely"*, said Earnest Hemmingway

..and
> *"We have two ears and one mouth, so we should listen more than we say."* Zeno of Citium, Greek Philosopher; and *'It's better to bite your tongue than to eat your words.'* Frank Sonnenberg.

..and more

"You can make more friends in two months by becoming interested in other people than you can in two years by trying to get other people interested in you."

Dale Carnegie, *How to Win Friends and Influence People*

We quote here from Richard Mullender, retired British Police Officer and hostage negotiator from *The Listening Institute:*

"Good listening is not 'nodding your head and eye contact.' A good listener is always looking for facts, emotions, and indications of values. In negotiations, the aim is to ascertain what the other side is trying to achieve. When you talk you are not listening. In negotiations, every time you share an opinion, you are giving out information. By keeping quiet, a good listener gains an edge."

(The Listening Institute. https://listeninginstitute.com, gives courses on negotiation and listening, covering, for example, mindset, echoing, values, mirroring priorities, bargaining.)

When you do speak, check with the other person. For instance, 'So as I understand it, what you are saying is. ....' Let the other person know that you are listening, not by nodding, but by summarising, recapping, paraphrasing, commenting. But all briefly.

Also, avoid distractions. Switch off your phone. In another HBR study participants paired with distracted listeners felt more anxious than those who received full attention. Many people don't give full attention. Rather, they are always preparing their own story, response, argument, or rebuttal – or thinking about looking at their iPhone....

This brings us directly onto an old (1946, but revised in the 1960's) but widely used model that relates to Learning sources: Edgar Dale's 'Cone of Experience'. See the figure below. Quite salutary, including for the readers and writers of this book!

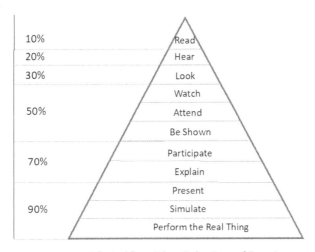

Adapted from Edger Dale, *Cone of Experience*

By the way, we disagree about Hearing, if it is related to a catchy song!

10.15 Learning Approaches: Kagan and Oakley

The Kagan Cooperative Learning Approach

Dr. Spencer Kagan has developed a range of learning methods for schoolchildren. However, his 5 Basic Structures can be used with effect in wider adult situations. Of course, as for school kids, they are engaging and participative. Students work together to learn. They can and have been used to great effect in Lean group training. The five are, briefly:

- Rally Robin: In pairs, students alternate oral responses: e.g. What wastes can be seen?
- Timed Pair Share: After a training session, in pairs, students take turns in stating what they have learned.
- Round Robin: In teams, students respond orally to questions. Brainstorming?
- Rally Coach: In pairs, one suggests a solution while the other listens and coaches. Then change around.
- Stand up, Hand up, Pair up: Get the class moving around. The instructor poses a question and the student's stand, and pair to discuss.

Fun and stimulating!
Web site: www.Kaganonline.com

Barbara Oakley's Mindshift

Barbara Oakley is an Engineering Professor who has developed a raft of methods designed to help engineering students overcome problems with Math and Science. Her learning methods are now more widely used. But here are her excellent books and an explanatory video. We are big fans!

Further Readings.
Barbara Oakley, *A Mind for Numbers*, Tarcher Pedigree, 2014
Barbara Oakley, *Mindshift*, Tarcher Pedigree, 2017
Web: https://youtu.be/vd2dtkMINIw

10.16 Learning Curves

There are several versions of Learning Curve. Most (all?) are empirically observed phenomena rather than scientific theories. These show the relationship between (typically) productivity or time taken to do a job and the cycles performed. Confusingly, some people talk of a 'steep learning curve' (meaning that the task is difficult to master) whilst others talk of the learning curve (meaning that it becomes easier with time or experience).

The Experience Curve is not a 'law' but was first observed in the aircraft industry and became a major strategy tool used by the Boston Consulting Group (BCG). There is an equation for the Experience Curve:

$$P_n = P_1 n^{(\log_2 b)}$$

Where P_n is the time or cost for the nth unit; P_1 is the time for the first unit; b for the learning (or experience) parameter – for 90% learning (or experience) b would be 0.9. It is to do with the effect of each doubling of the cumulative number of units, with the unit time or cost falling exponentially. So, for a 90% rate, if the first unit took 100 hours; 2nd would take 90; 4th 81 (i.e 90*0.9); 8th 72.9; 16th 65.6; 32nd 59, etc. This means more learning / practice cycles are less and less effective. There are diminishing returns. On the other hand, there could be a significant 'first mover advantage' because costs could be translated into prices and into market share. This was the BCG strategy. Today, the concept of the first mover advantage has suffered – a second mover that improves, and continues to improve, on the first concept – or design - will often win. Take Apple: Not the first mover on a cell phone, but by linking in with music and apps, it become the clear winner. But now Samsung is on the warpath.

Why does the experience curve happen? Many reasons including CI, standardisation, economies of scale, product re-design, and supplier costs. Of course, an experience rate will not just happen; it needs to be pursued. There is a risk of just presuming an experience rate translated into cost reduction. The cost of producing the Ford Model T followed an experience curve very accurately from 1908 to 1926, but then ran into customer acceptance problems. The Douglas Aircraft Corporation was forced into a merger with McDonnell Corporation mainly due to pricing problems based on the assumption of continuing experience rates. A warning that CI needs to be continuous!

S Curves

Another type of Learning Curve is the S curve, apparently quite widely experienced in Lean. Used for Improvement or Acceptance, or participation or Ideas or Savings. Here, there is slow start, followed by steep growth followed by slowing growth, followed by minimal growth.

S curves are often associated with product life cycle or innovation. Darryl Mann, of TRIZ fame, sees much innovation, including Lean, following a series of overlapping S curves. The new S curve starts below the former one, but overtakes it.

In the mid 1960's the Olympic record for the high jump was progressing slowly. The dominant approach was the 'Western Roll'. Enter Dick Fosbury with a radically new approach, initially scorned by his coach. But persistence won out and the 'Fosbury Flop' triumphed in the 1968 Olympics. From that moment other approaches were instantly outdated. The Western Roll could be improved upon continuously, but will never again win gold.

So it is with Lean: Kaizen and Breakthrough (or Kaikaku) need to work together. Breakthroughs often come from outside. As Steven Johnson has pointed out in *Where Good Ideas Come From*, they almost invariably involve 'the adjacent possible'. Innovations are imported from adjacent areas. So Henry Ford used ideas from cattle slaughter disassembly, from 'scientific methods' and from the electric motor that enabled high consistency of parts and movement. Toyota built on Ford, but added ideas from the loom, from Juran's quality ideas and Deming's teaching, and from American supermarkets and trams.

Within each big S-curve there are little s curves – smaller innovations that accumulate through time. These are necessary, but not sufficient. Without the occasional breakthrough, Lean will invariably stagnate.

A great danger in Lean, as in other fields, is Groupthink. (See earlier Section.) Lean people always talking to Lean people. Always taking only one company as the role model. As Harvard Business School professor Clayton Christensen has shown, 'disruptive' innovations classically come from the outside and are seen as irrelevant until they improve and cross the customer acceptance line to become 'good enough'. Perhaps the future of Lean lies with frugal innovations from India, from additive manufacturing, AI, from service concepts, from Anthropology or from participative flatter organisations.

Indeed, Joseph Schumpeter's 'Creative Destruction' never ends.

A Warning!

Some consultancies still make great use of Learning Curve theory. But there are dangers. The late David Garvin of Harvard Business School pointed out the fallacy of believing that 'learning curves are universal sources of competitive advantage'. According to Garvin, misguided views are 'Labour learning is the primary engine driving improvement' (many factors are involved),

'Learning rates are uniform across products, processes, industries', 'learning curves are stable', and 'knowledge gained through experience is easily retained'.

Further Readings.
William Abernathy and Kenneth Wayne, 'Limits of the Learning Curve', *HBR*, Sept 1974
David Garvin, *Learning in Action*, Harvard, 2000
Darrell Mann, *Hands-on Systematic Innovation*, IFR, 2009

10.17 Deliberate Practice

Deliberate Practice is different from just repetitive practice. To part-repeat an earlier section, (The Lean Trilogy Model in the Eight Models Chapter), there are four questions:

- Have those who developed the best approach so far been identified? (or, 'Find a good teacher')
- Identify what it is that makes them superior. This may involve close observation, close questioning, perhaps video. One call centre known to the authors recorded and analysed what it was that operators having the greatest level of customer satisfaction actually said. Communicating these sometimes very minor phrases to all had dramatic results.
- Engage. Does it push people to get outside their comfort zone and attempt to do things that are not easy for them?
- Does it offer immediate feedback on what can be done to improve? (why is it that successful pop groups, such as The Beatles, spent hundreds of hours in live clubs?)
- Keep going. Plateaus of performance are common, according to Eriksson. It is not a smooth upward curve! Surely a lesson for all Lean transformations!
- Is the practice and repetition designed to develop the particular skills of the experts?

Many readers will be familiar with Malcolm Gladwell's '10,000 hour rule for mastery' as put forward in his book *Outliers*. Discouraging! But this only applies to super-performers, such as Olympic winners, in very specialised situations. So there is hope for us all! (See also Section 4.2)

Further Readings.
Anders Eriksson, *Peak*, Bodley Head, 2016

10.18 Learning on the Job, the OODA Loop and After Action Reviews (AAR)

Many readers will be familiar with the movie Top Gun starring Tom Cruise. Both Anders Eriksson and David Garvin have delved into the fascinating and important background story of the development of effective learnings– for Lean and for more wider use.

The story goes like this: During the Vietnam War there were many aerial dogfights between the North Vietnamese pilots and pilots from the US Navy and US Air Force. The Americans had superior aircraft, such as the F4 Phantom but the Vietnamese, with older MiGs, did comparatively well almost matching the US kill ratio. Then there was a truce in air operations to encourage the Vietnamese to begin peace negotiations. The US Navy and USAF took the opportunity to enhance pilot training but took different paths. Both used classroom-based instruction followed by flying experience. The USAF used its best pilots to train new pilots by flying instruction. The US Navy established the Top Gun school and undertook flying instruction by simulating actual combat with experienced pilots role-playing North Vietnamese pilots. Of course, the 'Vietnamese' usually won. All simulated combats were recorded by video and voice, and played back and analysed after each 'combat'. Thus, between the US Navy and USAF a good experiment with a control group was set up. When the air war resumed, the difference in kill ratio was dramatic. The Top Gun methodology eventually became standard practice in the USAF.

One can relate this story back to Lean learning-by-doing such as TWI, and to the Dreyfus model. *Deliberate* practice, involving detailed observation and coaching and feedback (not just practice by repetition) is required. A method of review such as After Action Reviews (AAR) that uses data-based scientific method is effective. PDCA or Plan Do Study Act (PDSA) is one such method. The USAF and RAF teach a related method – the OODA Loop. OODA and After Action Reviews (AAR) are discussed below.

As Mike Rother says in *The Toyota Kata Practice Guide*, 'Not training leading to doing, but doing and training together.'

10.19 OODA

OODA stands for Observe, Orient, Decide, Act. It is a fast-learning cycle. OODA is considered superior to PDSA where fast decisions are required. It was developed by Colonel John Boyd, USAF during the Korean War. The side that can move through the cycles fastest is likely to win. By moving rapidly through the OODA cycle, the opposition is de-stabilised. Don Reinertsen is an enthusiastic advocate of OODA in Lean Product Development, especially in situations where fast, lateral communication in changing conditions, is required – as opposed to up and down a project management hierarchy. OODA has continual feedback to the Orient stage, unlike PDCA.

The OODA and PDSA methods are discussed in greater detail in the Problem Solving Chapter. (See 8.13 PDSA, DMAIC and OODA.)

10.20 After Action Reviews (AAR)

The characteristics of AAR's are:

- Done routinely
- A good facilitator (not the leader), who follows the rules below.
- Done immediately after the action, or as soon as possible thereafter.
- Use objective data only. What was the aim, and what exactly was done?
- Participation: As far as possible all should attend, including all managers. Of course, there are practical group size limitations. A dozen people?
- Status and hierarchy are downplayed. Subordinates should feel free to express views without threat. (Psychological safety).
- Start by asking the team members (NOT the leader) the questions below. But…
- No personal criticism is allowed. *What* happened, not *who*.
- Leaders should be willing to admit that mistakes were made.
- An opportunity for all to reflect and then to learn, via a learning cycle.
- A time limit. 30 minutes (or less) ? The late David Garvin of Harvard Business School suggests time is spent approximately; What did we set out to do and What actually happened: (together 25%); Why did it happen that way (25%); What should be done next time / What would be better (50%)
- Garvin's studies reveal that AARs fail when not following the above characteristics or rules, with a big issue being the willingness of seniors to admit that they got it wrong.

The great similarity between PDCA and AAR will be apparent.e

Further Readings.
Anders Eriksson, *Peak*, Bodley Head, 2016
David Garvin, *Learning in Action*, Harvard, 2000
Donald Reinertsen, *The Principles of Product Development Flow*, Celeritas, 2009

10.21 Action Learning

Action Learning is not an 'or' concept for Lean learning but an 'and' concept. In other words it can be very effectively employed with many or all of the learning approaches from push to pull as listed in the earlier sections, and with most of the models described above.

One of the authors has used Action Learning with great effect in several contexts. For instance, in introducing pull systems, managers from the shop floor, quality, purchasing, and logistics meet regularly to discuss, share, criticise, and mutually learn. In Healthcare, people from along a patient pathway meet to share learning on lead-time reduction. In both cases, other learnings and tools were employed simultaneously – for instance mapping, demand management and queuing theory, A3, bottleneck concepts as well as short formal lecture sessions (with participation and readings). It is a mystery why Action Learning has not been more widely adopted in Lean-aspiring organisations. On the other hand, several organisations are undoubtedly doing their own version without actually knowing it!

To quote Seddon: *"Systems thinking is only truly learned by doing, by action learning: it is only by doing that managers can unlearn."*

A central theme is that learners learn best in action settings where they interact with others and learn by doing, combining theory and developing solutions on the job. At the Gemba, not in the classroom! Reflection plays a central role, as does the testing of hypotheses. Great advantages are the simplicity of the approach and its acceptance by participants. For learning, it is effective because it is a learning-by-doing, pull-based, approach.

Action learning is focused on work-related problems, often of a 'wicked' nature where trade-offs must be made, and where there is no one-optimal solution. Technical problems are less suitable, although engineers and designers can use the essential features to share knowledge rather than to solve a particular problem. (A 'wicked' problem is difficult to solve because there is no clear definition, knowledge is incomplete, there are many opinions, often conflicting, and the 'problem' links with several other problems. Wicked problems are discussed in the chapters on Decision Making and Problem Solving.)

Action Learning has a long history but over the past two decades has emerged as a significant intervention or transformation theory and practice. It is used to our knowledge by several organisations in the Lean/Systems/Six Sigma world.

The story starts with Reg Revans who worked with several leading academics at Cambridge University in the 1940s. The group of colleagues – later to be called a 'project set' - work and share mutual constructive criticism, reflect on progress and encourage re-interpretation of hypotheses. Revans applied the approach in the British Coal Board achieving remarkable productivity gains, before establishing International Management Centres (in Buckingham just a stone's throw from the publisher of this book).

Revans stated that: *"There can be no learning without action and no (sober and deliberate) action without learning."* Revans formulated his action learning concept around the formula $L=P+Q$, where L stands for learning, P for programmed knowledge and Q for questioning insight.

Basically, the method is:

- 'Sets' of up to (say) 8 people are established. The criteria are that they have a common problem and have a willingness to share knowledge and experience, to mutually advise, challenge and constructively criticise so as to support one another. They have a willingness to learn from one another in a spirit of humility.
- The set will be focused on a particular project or concern. The project duration has a fixed period – say 6 months – and is not open-ended. Managerial support is vital.
- Members of a set are usually on approximately the same level in the organisation. It would be unusual for a manager and her subordinate to be in the same set.
- The sets meet regularly. Once per week would be less usual, once a month more common – but depending on urgency and complexity.
- The set discuss and formulate hypotheses that are tested between meetings by 'actions'. In other words, 'experiments', trials, or pilots are usual. Set members talk about a 'stimulus' (something that has provoked a particular action) and a 'response'. A response may be by reaction (or no reaction!), exploration, and feedback.
- Feedback about actions is important and given at the next meeting. Did it go as planned; why or why not?
- Between meetings other learnings may well take place – a mapping exercise, a formal course, a benchmarking visit, a conference.
- Reflection is vital. What was learned? Hypotheses are accepted or rejected.
- Learning can take place on what has been discovered about the problem or area – for the organisation, for the individual set member, and for the learning process itself. (See below on Kata.)
- It is common to have a facilitator (or 'set adviser') for a set. Some sets do not have a facilitator, but a skilled facilitator, experienced in Action Learning, is a big advantage. Pedler believes that any Action Learning trainer must be a line manager. (The further readings at the end of this section are recommended particularly for facilitators but also for set members.)
- In some larger projects or transformations there may be a two-level process. For instance, in a large Lean change program there may be, on a first level, a multi-discipline set – say one each from Operations, Accounting, Logistics and Marketing. On the second level the sets are specialised, drawing on members from the particular topic area. One member from each second level set would attend meetings of the first level set.

An interesting point, and challenge, is that the adoption of Action Learning moves an organisation towards more of a participative culture and away from a top-down command and control culture.

Readers will notice some similarity with Mike Rother's Toyota Kata approach – at least as far as 'the challenge', defining the next target condition, experiments to reach the next target condition, as well as the coach. The five Kata questions have great similarity, but are more specific. (See Section 3.12 on Toyota Kata). Toyota Kata uses an 'Improvement Kata' and a 'Coaching Kata'.

In a thoughtful review, Heathcote and Powell, state in 'Towards a Learning Kata':

"The teacher-manager can steer the inquiry process. The truth is improvement routines and resultant optimization are never enough, by posing thoughtful questions to the learner, which often unearths shared unknowns. Controlling managers, on the other hand, coax learners towards their own thinking, sometimes using Toyota Kata as the vehicle. Control-managers get what they want, and the learner believes it was their creation, but, in reality, thought-potential and creativity were unwittingly muzzled. The ultimate learning experience is suppressed.

They warn,

Make no mistake, the mechanistic nature of the improvement and coaching kata promises to cultivate problem-solving skill and an indispensable scientific mindset. It presents learning moments with each failure or each gap closed. Yet it falls short of transitioning the mature student to personal mastery and self-awareness – enabling them to think through situations more challenging than the familiar. Critically, the learning process must become "about the self".

Further Readings.
Lynne Butler and Nigel Leach, *Action Learning for Change; A practical guide for managers*, Management Books, 2011
Rose Heathcote and Daryl Powell, 'Improve Continuously by Mastering the Lean Kata', Lean.org / *Lean Post*, December 9, 2020
Mike Pedler and Christine Abbott, *Facilitating Action Learning: A Practitioner's Guide*, Open University Press, 2013
Reg Revans, *Developing effective managers: A new approach to business education, Praeger, 1971*
Reg Revans, *The ABC of Action Learning*, Routledge, 2011

10.22 Lean in Higher Education

This book is not focused on Lean education and improvement at colleges and universities, but the following are some examples.

For 15 years one of the authors of this book, John, was Course Director of the MSc in Lean first at Lean Enterprise Research Centre (Cardiff University) (LERC was started by Dan Jones) and later at The University of Buckingham. The other author, Noel, was a student on the course. The 2-year, part time executive course involved 8 one-week modules and a dissertation. All students were practitioners. Seven of the modules were held on-site at factory locations involving a blend of lectures and hands-on exercises. A range of international speakers took part. Close coaching meant that only about 15 students per cohort could attend. There was much in common with the Action Learning approach discussed in this chapter and with TWI. Covid brought the course to an end, but a Masters in Lean Leadership under Rose Heathcote is planned at Buckingham.

An innovation that has begun on several Lean-related courses has been a 'Lean Lab' where students get hands-on practice on a full-scale plant simulation. Examples are at Dortmund University, Germany, Mandela University South Africa, and Coventry University England.

Bob Emiliani has been a long-time innovator in university Lean education. His 'Evolution in Lean Teaching', in *International Journal. of Productivity and Performance*, 2016 summarises the many innovative ways that this professor has used in teaching business and engineering students. Of significance is a 'pull' methodology whereby students have open ended assignments and pull from the professor. (Available as a pdf from bobemiliani.com)

William Balzar, *Lean Higher Education: Increasing the value and performance of university processes,* (Second edition), Routledge, 2020. This book is a survey of several universities that have used Lean principles in improving courses and administration. A main focus is on Rapid Improvement Events (Kaizen Events).

10.23 Action Plans…

After EVERY significant learning event, such as completing a mentored A3 series, a Kata or Kaizen event, after a TWI 10-hour class, or after an Action Learning sequence, an Action Plan should be developed. (And perhaps captured as part of Yokoten – see Section 8.17 under Idea Propagation.)

Developing and verbally stating (or writing) an Action Plan has been shown to be highly effective for memorising and commitment. The idea is to create a habit. There are five steps:

State (out loud, or write down)

1. I need to remember to….(e.g. check the process is in control)
2. Because …(e.g. the process can become unstable when…)
3. So, I will ….(e.g. check the current queue buffer length, and notify…)
4. My plan (or action) may fail because of… (e.g. I get involved with…)
5. To help my plan (or action) to succeed, I will get into the habit of…. (Whenever the schedule mix changes, I will check the queue, notify upstream and the team if necessary.)

Or, if more suitable

1. I am most at risk of….(e.g. failing to discuss ideas with my team)
2. Because I….(e.g. I often feel pressured for time)
3. To reduce the risk, I will….(e.g. put 'ideas' on the agenda of every team meeting)
4. My plan (or action) may fail because (e.g. there are sometimes more urgent matters.)
5. To help my plan (or action) to succeed, I will get into the habit of….(e.g. asking a team member to always remind us about possible ideas at the team meeting, if I forget.)

Chapter 11
Leadership

"We say at Toyota that every leader is a teacher developing the next generation of leaders. This is their most important job." Akio Toyoda, CEO Toyota

And two from Mary Parker Follett
'The great leader is he who is able to integrate the experience of all and use it for a common purpose.' (From *Dynamic Administration, The collected papers of Mary Parker Follett*, 1941)
'Leadership is not defined by the exercise of power but by the capacity to increase the sense of power among those led. The most essential work of the leader is to create more leaders.' (From *The Creative Experience*, 1924)

Of course Leadership is a huge industry in itself, with thousands of books and hundreds of courses offered by universities, consultants, adventurers, 'gurus', sport stars, and, let's face it, con men. There is no barrier to entry for such people. All promise great results with unique insights. So considerable caution is called for.

It is not our goal to join in with this great continuing debate. For our purposes we will adopt the nuanced definition put forward by Woods and West (2020) which we believe best represents the challenges which business leaders of the 21st century face, *"Leadership is the process of influencing others to understand and agree about what needs to be done and how to do it, and the process of facilitating individual and collective efforts to accomplish shared objectives"*

A good place to begin in discussing leadership is General Stanley McChrystal's magisterial book *Leaders: Myth and Reality*. After reviewing the careers of 18 famous leaders, McChrystal debunks what he calls Three Myths of Leadership. First, the 'Formulaic Myth' which is to do with having a checklist of characteristics. Leadership is intensely contextual. 'Leadership is dynamic, and must be modulated from situation to situation'. Second, the 'Attribution Myth' whereby leadership is a process directed by the leader. Here, says McChrystal we: *"overstate the influence of the leader, and neglect that the real agency in leadership is bound up in a system of followers."* The third myth is the 'Results Myth'. Here it is results that are important. In fact, leadership is *"as much in what leaders symbolise as what they accomplish"*. Instead of seeing leadership as a top-down force focused on results gained through followers and context, rather leadership is an emergent property in a dynamic system of context and followers, 'fuelled by more than just results' and including identity, purpose, and future potential.

Debunking these myths about leadership helps overcome many of the 'superman' characteristics that a leader, Lean or otherwise, is expected to have or to learn from much of the leadership industry.

Of course, there is a difference between a leader as a person, and the process of leadership. Both are important, but are partly independent. Many great potential leaders have been frustrated by the process or 'the system'. Ask many Prime Ministers or Presidents. Traits are about the person. Processes are discussed throughout this book.

11.1 Managers and Leaders

But what about managers? Are managers' leaders, and are leaders managers? Simple definitions are: Manager: a person who has control and responsibility for ensuring that work is being performed as planned. Leader: somebody who creates an inspiring vision and motivates others to work towards it.

Of course, today it is not 'sexy' to be a manager. Many, at all levels, would like to be leaders or 'thought leaders'. But managers and administrators are vital. Don't underestimate their role.

A more nuanced contrast is offered in the following table.

The Manager	The Leader
Predominantly looks internally. Best if the manager looks at the full internal value stream.	Predominantly looks externally. Takes a systems view, end-to-end.
Commands and Controls: *This is what I want you to do and this is how I want you to do it.*	Inspires and Energises: *This is what I believe is required. I encourage you to think and discuss.*
Has Objectives: *Stick to the plans at all costs.*	Has a Vision: *Anything is possible if we put our hearts and minds towards it.*
Creates more Followers: *People are there to do the job we hired them for.*	Creates more Leaders: *I want to develop people who can replace me.*
Accepts the Status Quo: *If it's not broken, don't fix it.*	Challenges the Status Quo: *There's always a better way, let's find it.*
Managers love stability: *If we follow the process, we'll get the expected result.*	Leaders thrive on uncertainty: *In uncertainly lies great opportunity.*
Plans the Details: *I have a plan for everybody, everything, every day.*	Sets the Direction: *We all know the goal. Now let's work out how to achieve it together.*
Makes Proposals	Makes Decisions
Identifies Problems: *This is going to set us back, fix it fast.*	Recognises Opportunities: *Things go wrong, that's life. Now let's figure out how to stop it ever happening again.*
Communicates: *The target today was 20,000 units we produced 22,000. Well done*	Motivates: *Sets appropriate targets in the light of circumstances and developments.*
Does Things Right: *Rules are there for a reason. We have to follow the rules.*	Does the Right Thing: *The rules aren't always right. Reviews and sets appropriate rules*
Change is done to people: *Improvement activities are driven by leaders and subject matter experts.*	Change is done with people. *You [employees] are the real experts. Our job is to give you the tools to improve your work.*

We are great long-term fans of Frei and Morris. Their book *Unleashed* captures much of the above and is in line with Lean. They content that…

- The real work of Leadership is not, or at least should not be, about the person – how smart, how far-seeing, whether loved or feared. 'It is not about you – it is about how effective you are at unleashing other people.'
- Beware of relying too much on your main strengths. Instead identify what you do well for others and what you do not do so well.

- Leaders learn most when they are challenged. Be prepared to take one step backward in order to move several steps forward.
- Decision making should be prioritized. Ask yourself "Is this a decision I have to make, or could it be made just as well, by others?"

Researchers charting the evolution of leadership have identified five main areas of focus. These are, the trait, behaviour, contingency, dyadic and charismatic / transformational theories. Trait theory is one of the earliest leadership theories and is based on the idea that some people are born with certain traits which enable them to become successful leaders. Giving rise to the old adage "Leaders are born, not made". However 20th century researchers found that leaders' and followers traits were very similar. In fact, what differentiated leaders from followers was circumstantial. The behavioural approach takes the view that leadership is something which can be learned and developed. It proposes that there are certain behaviours which if adopted by leaders will increase their chances of being successful. It also educates leaders about the need to be self-aware of their behaviours and to recognise how they affect those around them. Contingency theory suggests the leader's effectiveness is contingent upon how his or her leadership style matches the situation – being most effective when the style of leadership fits with the situation. This differs from situational leadership which proposed that leaders must be able to adapt to a given situation and act accordingly. Dyadic leadership theory focuses on the relationships between leaders and their followers and the level of reciprocity (Exchange of benefits) within those relationships.

We will now discus some of the most prevalent leadership styles in more detail before looking at what makes an effective Lean Leader.

Further Readings.

Francis Frei and Anne Morris, *Unleashed; The unapologetic Leader's Guide to Empowering Everyone around yo*u, Harvard Business School Press, 2020

11.2 Transformational Leadership

Transformational leadership is a leadership style, built on trust, which inspires people to achieve organisational goals, but also enables them to develop and achieve their full potential. Transformational leaders are engaging, have empathy and are often seen as being excellent mentors and role models. They create a culture where creative thinking is aligned with the values, beliefs and objectives of the organisation, and individuals are openly recognised for their contributions. Transformational leaders set high expectation and can lead people to achieve things that they would never before have seen of as being possible. Bernard Bass (1985) characterised transformational leadership as having four main elements, commonly known as the four I's which are outlined in the table below.

Transformational leadership is without doubt the form of leadership which employees most require in these very uncertain times. The principles of loyalty and trust are universal and timeless. When transformational leaders focus and care about their people's needs and development, they are rewarded with increased levels of performance and discretionary effort

Idealised Influence	Walks the walk. Sets high moral and ethical standards. Provides a sense of belonging. Highly respected and viewed as a role model.
Inspirational Motivation	Ability to create a future vision that inspires and engages others in its pursuit. Outlines expectations clearly, always demonstrates personal commitment, optimism & enthusiasm.
Individualised Consideration	The degree to which the leader really understands their people. Their concerns, talents and ambitions. Creates opportunities and provides one-to-one coaching and mentoring to enable growth & fulfilment.
Individualised Stimulation	Encourages people to challenge the status quo and act independently. Involves people in making decisions and solving problems which directly affect them.

11.3 Transactional Leadership

As the name implies, transactional leaders emphasize the transaction or exchange that takes place among leaders and their sub-ordinates. The pull of extrinsic rewards and the fear of reprimand are used to motivate employees to achieve goals and objectives. Transactional leadership is based on the following assumptions;

- People favour structure and like having rules to follow
- Workers are motivated by rewards and penalties
- The primary function of subordinates is to follow the leader's instructions
- Workers require careful monitoring to ensure that performance expectations are met

Transactional leadership works well in ensuring consistency in organizations where structure and scalability is important such as production assembly lines and call centres. Here the work is likely to be standardised and repetitive, and expectations regarding rewards and penalties understood and agreed. In a similar vein, most sales jobs and senior leadership positions use commissions or bonuses as a type of transactional leadership method. Transactional leadership is not the right fit for organizations or functions where initiative, discretionary effort, personal growth and change are required. This is particularly the case in creative fields such as advertising or marketing where professionals need the flexibility to come up with ideas, slogans or pitches for their product. Applying transactional leadership in these environments is more likely to reduce morale, rather than motivate individuals.

11.4 Situational Leadership®

Situational leadership is about adopting leadership style to the context of the situation at hand. The situational leadership® model was developed by Paul Hersey and Ken Blanchard. The model proposes that there is no-one-size-fits-all pre-eminent leadership style, but rather a case of the required leadership style being dependant on many factors including the skill levels and maturity of the team members, and the task at hand.

In response to each situation leaders adopt any one of four primary leadership styles. For example, when managing team members with low maturity and skill levels, the leader uses a commanding (Telling) style i.e. he tells the team what to do and how to do it. As the team matures, the leaders will start to interact with the team members and engage them in the task at hand (Selling). At the next level (Participating), the leader withdraws further allowing the team to start developing their ideas and making some decisions themselves. At the highest level (Delegating), the team has the skill and confidence to complete the task with minimum involvement from the leader.

Note: What applies to a team could also apply to an individual.

Leadership Styles	Maturity Levels	Most suitable for / when
S1 Telling: leader provides close supervision and guidance. Very directive, communicates exactly what everyone's roles are and what exactly is required.	D1	Enthusiastic beginners Inexperienced teams Pressure / crisis situations
S2 Selling: leader explains ideas and strategies to engage and motive team members.	D2	Low commitment Low confidence Coaching opportunity
S3 Participating: leader seeks input from team, shares own expertise and facilitates team to organise the work for themselves	D3	Team has a high level of competency but varying commitment
S4 Delegating: with main responsibilities passed on the team, the leader's role is to monitor team progress at predetermined intervals	D4	Team are confident, motivated and skilled. Work is very routine

A major advantage of the model is that it takes into account the various levels of development which employees go through in their work and facilitates both the employee and the leader in meeting their needs. It's also a relatively simple concept for leaders to grasp, all that is required is the ability to access a given situation and adjust to it. Successful application of the model is dependent on the leader's ability to judge an employee's maturity level. Leaders unable to do this effectively may provide a style of leadership that does not suit a particular situation, employee or team. This is also the added risk of the leader causing confusion among employees as they constantly switch between styles.

In summary the situational leadership® model emphasises the need for leaders to have flexibility so that they can adapt according to the needs of their sub-ordinates. It is important to remember the best style will always depend on the situation, the task to be performed and the team performing it.

11.5 Lean Leadership

A lean transformation requires a completely different approach to how the people with responsibility for running organisations interact with their employees. Successful lean leaders understand that employee engagement is a contact sport. If you are not interested in people at a personal level, rather than just at a work level, then you, as a leader are never going to get the best out of them. Experience has shown that while the best lean tools and systems can be taught, unless embraced by employees they will be ineffective. This is where the real challenge lies.

It would be wrong to assume that all people are resistant to change. Change is a fundamental part of life that we all experience. We frequently change jobs, cars, houses, holidays and sometimes even partners. (William Bridges suggests that, whilst we all make such changes, a 'transition' is different – requiring an ending, a neutral zone, and only then a new beginning. Not dissimilar to Kurt Lewin's unfreeze, change, refreeze!).

What people do resist however is change being imposed or forced on them. It is not unusual when we visit organisations to hear the management team express with great frustration how their employees are refusing to co-operate with change initiatives vital to the future of the organisation, *"Don't they understand this plant could close if we cannot improve productivity?"* However, when we speak to employees on the floor, we find them just as frustrated *"We want this plant to be successful, our family's futures are tied up here. If only management would listen to us, we could show them where to save millions."* We have even seen cases where a toxic environment with management focusing on showing who is boss, has unfortunately resulted is plant closure and redundancies. Similar comments are to be found in service organisations.

A celebrated Harvard Business School case study by Steven Spear (2004) details how Toyota prepare an externally recruited senior leader to adopt to working at Toyota. The subject of the case, Jack Smith, is a former plant manager with an MBA and MSc, and worked at one of the America's big three automobile manufacturers. As a training case study the class is asked how Smith should be inducted. Many members in a training class suggest that Smith first be shown around the organisation, visiting various functions and perhaps attending an induction day. In fact, Smith was immediately assigned to work, over the next 12 weeks, with 19 assembly operators, to assist in improving productivity. Using direct observation, and weekly coaching sessions from his Sensei, Smith, along with the wider team implemented over 100 ergonomic, manual-handling and machine availability improvements. Smith learns that operators have many good ideas that he missed despite his experience and education – learning trust, humility, and respect by experience. Next for Smith was a trip to a Toyota engine plant in Japan where he was assigned with a colleague to work alongside a non-English speaking operator to identify and implement 50 improvements over three days. Spear makes the point that this intensive hands-on training instils four key Lean Leadership insights:

1. There is no substitute for direct observation
2. All improvement opportunities should be structured as experiments
3. Workers and managers should be encouraged to experiment as much as possible
4. The managers role is to coach others how to problem solve.

The Jack Smith case closely follows the ShuHaRi steps that were discussed in the Learning chapter. ShuHaRi is the framework for learning at Toyota. It is not just learning a task, but also learning to lead. Namely:

- Learning from a master (Shu)
- The master keeps tabs on the learner (Ha)
- The person is no longer a learner, but can now teach others. (Ri)

Note that this is a philosophy of developing yourself before leading others. 'Developing yourself' may include taking an external degree or course, but the main development takes place within the organisation…and is reminiscent of the quote from Akio Toyoda, CEO Toyota given at the head of this chapter.

11.6 Values and Behaviours of Lean Leaders.

In a study to identify the values and behaviours of successful lean leaders, van Dun found that they focused their efforts on building a relationship with the person, rather than the actual task itself. Examples of this relations-oriented behaviour include;

Relations-oriented behaviour	Examples
Active listening	*"Paraphrasing to show understanding, using nonverbal cues which show understanding such as nodding, eye contact"*
Agreeing	*"Exactly, I see where you going with this"*
Encouraging	*"Brilliant progress, I can start to see some results already"*
Giving positive feedback	*"I like you're the way you're thinking"*
Co-operating	*"This is an area where I have some experience, let's make time to look at it together"*
Socialising	*"Any vacation plans for the summer, I've promised the family I'll bring them to Disneyland, if they pass their exams"*

The results of the study confirm just how important it is for lean leaders to establish trust with individual employees and build a psychologically safe environment where they become active participants in continuous improvement <u>before</u> launching a lean program. The authors have seen many well-resourced lean programs fail simply because consideration on its impact on the employees concerned hadn't been thought through.

It is not surprising therefore to see when it comes to listing the requirements for successful Lean Leadership that our focus is very much on the human aspects of change management.

11.7 Characteristics of Lean Leaders

- Knowledge and experience of lean tools, systems, and principles
- Visionary – the ability to develop, articulate and communicate a vision for the future.
- Impatient – a natural tendency towards change and inventiveness
- Influencer – uses a high level of personal impact to motivate others to join in creating a culture of change
- Growth mind-set – a relentless desire for acquiring new knowledge and skills
- Empathy – understands that change is difficult for lots of people
- Optimism – the ability to bounce back from disappointment and see new opportunities
- Coach & Mentor – a genuine desire to help others achieve their full potential
- Finisher – the ability, determination and resilience to bring projects to completion

While the list outlined above may be seen as being idealistic and sets an expectation which may be difficult to achieve, we find it very difficult to eliminate any of these elements. This is reflected in the fact that a common trait of the most capable lean leaders we have crossed paths with in our careers is that they all considered themselves to be 'a work-in-progress'. See Chapter 15 – every great leader has led a great team! A leader simply cannot do it alone.

Beware. Take note of McChrystal's myths and Frei and Morris' comments at the beginning of the chapter. Alvesson and Spicer point out the danger of assuming the leader will have all these characteristics. 'Cultish' organisations, they say, are built on a strong differentiation between leaders and followers with those in subordinate positions 'pushed to refrain from thinking outside of the box' – 'their leader has the big picture and knows best'. Danger! (See Decisions Chapter.)

Amy Edmondson, a HBS colleague of Frei, suggests that leaders should begin by encouraging their people to become more curious, passionate, and empathic. Curiosity motivates and stimulates people to learn, solve problems and innovate at work. Passion adds meaning and a greater sense of purpose that drives effort and builds momentum. Empathy allows to understand and appreciate other people's perspectives. Her advice for leaders is to model these behaviours, and get into the habit of asking sincere questions that will elicit important insights into why people hold competing viewpoints. The power of this approach in creating a culture of trust, transparency and psychological safety that enables organisations to learn from failure is wonderfully explained in a HBR article titled 'Fixing a Weak Safety Culture in General Motors'.

Further Readings.
B.M. Bass, 'Does the transactional-transformational leadership paradigm transcend organizational and national boundaries?' *American Psychologist*, 52(2), 130-139, 1997
B.M. Bass, *Leadership and performance beyond expectations*, New York: Free Press, 1985
William Bridges, *Managing Transitions*, Nicholas Brearley, 2011
Desirée Van Dun, Jeff N. Hicks, and Celeste PM Wilderom. "Values and behaviors of effective lean managers: Mixed-methods exploratory research." *European Management Journal* 35, no. 2, 174-186, 2017
Amy Edmondson, The Three Pillars of a Teaming Culture, *HBR*, Dec 2013
Amy Edmondson, Fixing a Weak Safety Culture in General Motors, *HBR*, Mar. 2014
Francis Frei and Anne Morris, *Unleashed; The unapologetic Leader's Guide to Empowering Everyone around yo*u, Harvard Business School Press, 2020
Paul Hersey, Kenneth H. Blanchard, and Dewey E. Johnson. *Management of Organizational Behavior*. Vol. 9. Upper Saddle River, NJ: Prentice Hall, 2007.
Jeffrey Liker and Gary Convis, *The Toyota Way to Lean Leadership*, McGraw Hill, 2012
Stanley McChrystal, J. Eggers and J. Mangone, J. *Leaders: Myth and reality*, New York, NY: Penguin, 2018
Steven Spear and Kent Bowen, 'Decoding the DNA of the Toyota Production System', *Harvard Business Review*, Sept/Oct 1999
Steven Spear and C Purrington, *Jack Smith (A): Career Launch at Toyota*, Harvard Case Study. 2004
S. Woods and M. West, *The Psychology of Work and Organisations*, South-Western Cengage Learning, 2010

11.8 Goleman's Six Leadership Styles

Why is emotional intelligence so important for leaders? As stated earlier in this chapter, it is leaders who play an important role in setting the tone and creating the culture of their organization. Regardless of their technical prowess, leaders who are lacking in emotional intelligence are likely to exhibit behaviours which will disengage employees. This dis-engagement will result in a reduction in discretionary effort, job satisfaction and overall contribution to the organisation. Emotional intelligence can help leaders build stronger relationships, succeed at work, and achieve career and personal goals, it can also help leaders to connect with their feelings, turn intention into action, and make informed decisions about what's important to them. Goleman established a direct link between measurable business results and emotional intelligence. According to his research, the most competent leaders all presented a high degree of emotional intelligence. Goleman identified six leadership styles each of which has a different impact on an individual, team and organisation. Similar to the situational leadership model outlined earlier, there is not a right or wrong leadership style. It is a case of matching the right style to a particular situation. The six Goleman Leadership Styles are as follows:

Coercive Style: This is a compliance approach characterised by the phrase "Do what I tell you." While this style may be suitable for crisis situations, once the crisis is over, it is likely to have a very negative impact on the organisation.

Authoritative Style: This is very much a commanding style used by visionary leaders to unite and rally people towards a common goal by saying "Come with me". It is a positive style best suited to reinvigorate an organisation that has lost its mojo and lead them in a new direction.

Affinitive Style: Characterised by the phrase "People come first" this style is used by leaders to break down functional silos, strengthen relationships and build harmony. Helps to motivate teams through stressful situations.

Democratic Style: This approach is used by leaders when they need to get buy-in and build consensus ("What do you think?") This is particularly effective when leaders need to tap into subordinates deep well of expertise and tacit knowledge to inform decision making. The main disadvantage of the democratic approach is the time required to reach consensus.

Pacesetting Style: When quick results are required, leaders who possess the requisite skill-set, step in and set a high performance standard for others to follow ("Do as I do, now"). If used too frequently, there is a risk of de-motivating the team and preventing them from developing their own expertise and leadership.

Coaching Style: This style focuses more on personal development than on immediate work-related tasks. Typically the leader will suggest a personal development opportunity with the employee with the catch phrase "try this". This style works best with employees who recognise their weak points, are ambitious and receptive to coaching. It does however demand patience from both parties as setbacks may occur during the coaching process.

The ability of a leader to switch between styles as situations and contexts dictate, is an important skill. While some leaders will naturally be empathetic, the good news for leaders is that emotional intelligence is a skill which can be learned and honed.

For further thoughts on Emotional Intelligence, please refer to Section 6.6

11.9 Halos, Delusions and other Warnings

Getting the right people is a perennial theme in Lean. Jim Collins in *Good to Great*, studied various successful transformations and believes that their leaders did not do so by setting a new vision and a new strategy. A famous quote is *"...first get the right people on the bus, the wrong people off the bus, and the right people in the right seats – and then figure out where to drive it"*. *Good to Great*, identified characteristics of Great companies (and Leaders). The secret of the 11 companies having lasting excellence lay in 'level 5 leadership'. Unfortunately years later, in several instances, performance declined, and two companies went bankrupt, with basically the same leadership characteristics. Incidentally, a similar fate befell Peters and Waterman's *In Search of Excellence* two decades earlier. This should be a significant warning about leadership secrets.

The book *The Halo Effect* gives a devastating criticism of *Good to Great*, as being overly simplistic. Nevertheless, there are certainly problem people and people who have great influence.

Phil Rosenzweig in his stimulating and provocative book, *The Halo Effect*, discusses Nine 'Delusions'. For each, Rosenzweig amusingly illustrates instances where the delusion is found to be false. First, the Halo Effect itself is the tendency to see all good and no evil in a leader or organisation. (Toyota: a superb organisation, and a Lean icon, but also having its share of failures – Formula 1, the floor mat problem, inventory turn performance, and possibly 'missing the boat' with electric vehicles.) Such failures always elicit a 'but' response. Of course, this is confirmation bias – the problem being that defensiveness or blindness can lead to a failure to learn. The truly great company and leader acknowledges failures and seeks to improve – as indeed CEO Toyoda did to the US government about floor mats.

A great drawback of believing in the leadership abilities of particular individuals is the fundamental attribution error. Here the characteristics of the leader is overvalued whilst the influence of the situation is undervalued. So there is widespread belief that most problems can ultimately be solved by leadership or have, at their root, a failure in leadership.

Other delusions include 'the wrong end of the stick' – a focused strategy causes results, but could results cause a focused strategy to be identified. (What about failures of focused strategies?). Absolute performance is attributed to the leader but may simply be the result of favourable circumstances. Single explanations: results are the outcome of numerous factors, but a single factor (or leader) is given credit – or discredit. Lasting success – almost all high performing companies suffer periods of relatively moderate results – but the leader is given the blame. (Fire the coach is common with football clubs.)

(BTW: Look back on the earlier section 4.1 describing Deming's Red Bead Game. Could this apply to leaders?)

Further Readings.
Bob Emiliani, Lean behaviors, *Management Decision*, 36 (1998), pp. 615–631
Phil Rosenzweig, *The Halo Effect:... and the eight other business delusions that deceive managers*, Simon and Schuster, 2014

11.10 The GLOBE Studies and Anthropology

GLOBE is a 'unique large-scale study of cultural practices, leadership ideals, and generalized and interpersonal trust in more than 160 countries in collaboration with more than 500 researchers.' The GLOBE study provides scores on six dimensions — charismatic/value-based/performance-based, team-oriented, humane-oriented, participative, autonomous, and self-protective.

A working definition of *leadership* that reflected the diverse viewpoints held by the GLOBE researchers emerged: *the ability of an individual to influence, motivate, and enable others to contribute toward the effectiveness and success of the organizations of which they are members.* Note that this is a definition of organizational leadership, not leadership in general.
The findings are very briefly summarised in the table. The full story is given in books and monographs, some of which are available at https://globeproject.com/results/clusters/

It is interesting that Latin America figures strongly in Shingo Prize recipients, and the region also figured prominently in best brewery assessments carried out by the SAB Miller group.

A related aspect: Hofstede proposed the PDI (Power Distance Index) as a means of measuring acceptance of power. Generally, Western people are far less accepting of authority and more willing to challenge, than Eastern people. The implications for Lean concepts are profound.

Region	Characteristics of Outstanding Leaders
Latin America	Highest on team oriented. Highly charismatic, visionary, team-oriented but only moderately participative.
Anglo (UK, USA, Australia, Ireland, South Africa)	Highest on Charismatic. Creates a desirable and realistic vision. Able to provide inspiration, vision, and encouragement of high performance while creating outstanding teams. It is important for leaders in this cluster to value freedom, delegate responsibility, and include all relevant parties in the decision-making process.
Confucian (China, Japan, South Korea, Taiwan)	While participative leadership is valued, it's score is among the lowest of all culture clusters. The Humane-Oriented Leadership is higher than most other clusters as is Autonomous and Self-Protective Leadership.
Germanic (Austria, Germany, Netherlands)	Charismatic who believe in participative leadership but also support independent thinking. They would hesitate to engage in self-protective behaviour such as being self-centred and particularly being conscious of status.
Latin Europe (France, Israel, Italy, Portugal)	Moderately charismatic, team-oriented and participative but not particularly caring and giving or acting in an independent manner.

Note that there would seem to be overlaps and contradictions with some Anthropological studies of organisations. Briody, Trotter and Meerwarth studied cultures across manufacturing organisations and found many issues that should be far more widely appreciated than appears to be the case at present. For instance, there is often cultural misunderstanding between teams within the same ethnic group but from different locations and backgrounds. People make assumptions about, for instance, 'Germans' and 'Americans' but rather than these groupings it was the cultures that developed at various sites that was significant. People from different sites can use the same word with different understanding but because the word is so commonly used it is not realised that there is a difference. Japanese terms add to the misunderstanding. In any case, the groupings may themselves be misleading because, particularly in multinationals, groups are almost invariably multi-cultural.

In a Six Sigma study, multi-vari charts track variation within a process and between processes. But the multi-vari concept does not appear to have made headway with culture or understanding differences within a site and between similar sites. Management often assumes there are no differences. This can be disastrous for a Lean transformation. Two examples:

At a plant visited by one of the authors the word 'Mokita' was written surreptitiously in large letters on a wall one night. It was taken as a prank by managers and ignored. However, Mokita is a word from a language called Kivila in Papua New Guinea. A good translation is, "the truth we all know but agree not to talk about.". Eventually it transpired that, at the plant, there were undisclosed political and racial viewpoints setting groups apart that effectively prevented value stream co-operation. It took many months of failure before managers began to enquire about their cultural assumptions.

A second example is the (in) famous exchange between Lord Robens of the National Coal Board and a Welsh miner in the 1960's. Lord Robins (mindset probably to do with productivity, cost, and profit): 'Why do you come to work for only four days per week instead of the expected five?' The miner: 'Because I can't quite make out on the money I earn in three days per week.' (!). A bonus scheme here would certainly prove counterproductive!

The Lord Robens story is an illustration of what is called 'Weltanschauung' (or world view) in some 'systems' studies. In a good Systems study an attempt is made to understand the viewpoints of stakeholders who may influence the outcome of the study.

Always remember that much of the Lean literature, indeed much of this book, is written from a WEIRD perspective – Western, Educated, Individualistic, Rich, and Democratic perspective. Moreover, much of the Lean literature is also written by Generation X people (born before 1975) instead of by millennials. Generation X tend to be much more respectful of authority, science, and sequential thinking. And, if that were not enough, many psychological studies are carried out with Western students rather than with employees. The conclusions may simply not apply! Beware! (The authors of this book are Generation X. Sorry!)

Further Readings.
Elizabeth Briody, R. Trotter and T. Meerwarth, *Transforming Culture*, Palgrave, 2011
Robert J. House, Paul J. Hanges, S. Antonio Ruiz-Quintanilla, Peter W. Dorfman, Mansour Javidan, Marcus Dickson, and About 170 GLOBE Country Co-Investigators to be listed by name and institution, *CULTURAL INFLUENCES ON LEADERSHIP AND ORGANIZATIONS: PROJECT GLOBE.* Monograph.

11.11 Leadership Failure

Instead of success, consider the reasons for leadership failure. The Center for Creative Leadership (CCL) has done just this. They call this 'derailing'. The traits that predict leadership derailing are given below.

- Emotional instability – an inability to handle pressure
- Defensiveness
- Lack of integrity
- Less developed interpersonal skills
- Technical and cognitive skill. Confusingly this trait shows up both as a positive and a negative factor. It seems to be that some technically highly skilled people get promoted to leadership positions where they are unsuited. The Peter Principle?

Another reason for leaders not being successful is that they don't take enough responsibility for helping others to succeed. Leaders must decide which is their priority: being successful, or making the team successful. The authors have yet to discover a successful team which didn't have a successful team leader. Yet, very often leaders are too inward focused with their energies concentrated on their goals and fears, rather than the team they lead. Frei and Morris outline ten warning signs for leaders concerned that they are becoming too focused on themselves to the detriment of team development.

1. Unconcerned about what other people are experiencing
2. Don't value other people opinions very highly
3. Conversations with co-workers are mainly focused on the leader
4. Increasingly preoccupied with own weaknesses and limitations
5. Being around strong, successful colleagues starting to make the leader feel inadequate
6. Constantly lurching from crisis to crisis

7. Optimism for a better future is diminishing
8. Work has become tedious and boring
9. Feeling increasing powerless to influence events
10. Energy is primarily focused on leader's goals and desires

Further Readings.
The Center for Creative Leadership www.ccl.org
Francis Frei and Anne Morris, *Unleashed; The Unapologetic Leader's Guide to Empowering Everyone around you*, Harvard Business School Press, 2020
Jeffrey Liker and Convis, *The Toyota Way to Lean Leadership*, McGraw Hill, 2012
Web site: www.hofstede-insights.com

11.12 The Big Five Revisited.

The 'Big Five' (OCEAN) personality traits were discussed in the Psychology Chapter. (Section 6.3). The Big Five Model is widely accepted by organisations and academics to be an accurate measurement of personality and has been the predominant system in use over the past decade. Of course, OCEAN has relevance to leadership effectiveness. Several studies on the relationship between leader effectiveness and the OCEAN traits have been carried out, albeit that that there is no one definition of leader effectiveness. However, broad conclusions are as follows:

- **O**penness: fairly strongly positively correlated with leader effectiveness. Openness to ideas seems important.
- **C**onscientiousness: weakly positively correlated with leader effectiveness. Competence not quite as important as openness or extroversion.
- **E**xtroversion: positively correlated with leader effectiveness. But beware of the 'loud mouth' and don't forget the quiet introvert who can be effective in problem solving.
- **A**greeableness: not correlated with leader effectiveness. The agreeable but ineffective friend?
- **N**euroticism: negatively correlated with leader effectiveness. Unsurprisingly, anxiety, depression, and anger don't sit comfortably with leader effectiveness.

However, these conclusions are very general, and not situation specific.

11.13 Influence

Many people in the Lean world will have to influence others. Influence is required almost every day – in almost every human interaction – not just when some change or transformation is being attempted. It is as well, therefore, to know of some of the basics. Like many sections in this book, the material is by no means comprehensive. But to ignore Influence theory in any Lean transformation is simply naïve.

Influence theory uses 4 components:

1. Agent. The person who is trying to influence others. Caildini and others suggest that 'liking' and affiliation are most successful. Physical attractiveness and perceived trustworthiness make a difference. As does eye contact. You tend to like someone who has a similar background, similar age, supports the same football team, shares birthdays, has an appealing sense of humour, or is a well-recognised expert or personality. So it is worth finding out, and emphasizing similarities, with the..

2. Target. The person or persons that the Agent is trying to influence. There is likely to be more impact where the needs are clearer, and where people's views are listened to and respected. (See Lewin's Force-Field Diagram: simple and effective! Section 4.5). Some nationalities are by nature more receptive than others. (The authors have found marked differences even within the U.K. and certainly internationally.)

3. Tactics. Listen. Encourage participation. Share information. Sometimes it takes time for people to 'buy-in'. Slow can be fast. But see 'Engagement' Section 7.2. Also see Section 4.7 on the 'Adoption Curve'.

4. Context. Make urgency, risk and need clear. People are strongly influenced by peers. Identity with the groups' perceived beliefs has a big influence on the person. (Hence adverts saying that 90% of adults don't litter, speed, talk in the cinema, etc. are much more effective than just saying, for instance, 'Don't litter'. The famous and surprising Solomon Ash studies showed how a high proportion of people would agree with three or more (planted) others about line lengths even when the lengths were clearly wrong. The 'shocking' Stanley Milgram experiments on 'Obedience to Authority' showed how a high proportion of people were prepared to administer electric shocks to others when they believed that it was OK to do so when being encouraged by a person with apparent authority or credibility.

Cialdini is the world's greatest authority on Influence. He makes many, many points. Some are:

- His 6 Concepts of Influence:
  o 'Reciprocation' (The 'norm of reciprocity'. Meaningful and customised giving advice, information or help and not just one-way taking (See also Adam Grant's book *Give and Take));*
  o Liking (see above);
  o Social proof (doing what is right – morally and socially);
  o Authority (the status of the Agent – has he or she got credibility? This includes appearance.)
  o Scarcity (craving what we can't get enough of, and aversion to loss. Loss is more influential than gain. (Kahneman also wrote on this – see Section 8.14 on System 1 and 2);
  o Consistency (a consistent message – not 'people are our best asset' followed shortly by redundancies. Deming spoke of 'Constancy of purpose'.)

- Timing is important. When to send a message. 'Never let a crisis go to waste.'

- Cialdini discusses pre-suation. It is how we set the stage for the message to come that is vital to grab attention or to switch people off. Pre-warning of difficulties that may result in changes ahead is good policy. Saying or doing just the right thing before we begin – perhaps commenting on a local football team success, or helping a person in a wheelchair instead of ignoring him.

- Association. The attitude of who is sending the message and when, and the attitude of the group receiving the message – including timing in relation to wider events. Does the Agent know the current feelings of the Target group? ("We are worried because of a closure of a sister plant".) What do the Target group think of themselves? ("Who the heck do you think you are to presume about us?") The association with relevant situations, and case studies, is powerful. Some Lean learners find playing a Lean game with Lego fun and useful; some find it insulting.

- Mimicry has been widely found to be influential. It is an unconscious human trait to mimic others in close contact. Confidence, happiness, worry, and so on, are often subconsciously transferred.

Here we consider a sample of findings on Influence that we consider to be of particular relevance to Lean and Lean Transformation:

Information: We now live in an information-rich society. Almost anyone can publish their views on the web. Some blogs 'take off' and become widely accepted, whether true or false. Of course, this applies in the Lean and Agile world also. Sorting the wheat from the chaff is a challenge. And, did you know that Google tailors searches to what they know about you? (Try it with a friend!)

Likewise, Trying to *Scare* people into change is not very effective. 'We have a burning platform'. Forget it! (We humans tend to freeze with a threat. Imagine you come across a cobra on a walk. What do you do?) Sticks are less effective than carrots. A recent case in point: COVID has encouraged the washing of hands for 20 seconds after the toilet. Do it or else risk both yourself and others! Does that work? Visit a motorway service station and observe: over 80% wash their hands for less than 6 seconds. But a hospital trial that measured length of wash and displayed the percentage of 20 second washes, led to a reversal – over 80% did then wash hands properly.

And another hand-wash true story: A US hospital chain found that only 20% of nurses had washed their hands before tending a patient in bed. Fire, threaten, or educate? But first investigate. Sanitiser stations were found to be located at the far ends of corridors. So if nurses were responding to an urgent patient call, they would not have time to visit the sanitiser. The solution: Locate sanitisers at each bedside. The percentage of pre-patient hand washes rose to nearly 100%.

…and *Pay Attention!* Do you listen to the safety announcement on an airplane? If delivered with more fun or variety, such as on SouthWest or Virgin, the attention and retention level rockets. And emphasize the positive not the negative. 'We want you to enjoy your holiday' not 'Listen or you may die.'

Stickiness: Once a person has decided on a particular course, it is difficult to change their mind – however 'rational' the argument may be. Some of the great findings in Behavioural Economics (for instance, Kahneman, Thaler, Sunstein) show that people are not driven entirely by the rational and logical, but the emotions play a significant part. Not what was said, but who said it. This is also confirmation bias – people put more weight on information that supports their previous view, and less weight on information that contradicts or undermines. We tend to ignore evidence that shows we might be wrong. A solution to this, is not direct contradiction but to seek common ground. For instance, there may be a fear that Lean will lead to job loss. Instead of direct contradiction, explain that Lean opens opportunity for growth.

Shadowing is powerful. If you feel stressed, so will your audience. Saying 'calm down' is not as effective as displaying that you are relaxed. (Amazing and amusing experiments of a few people standing in a street looking up. Soon there will be many doing likewise.)

Advertising and Signs. Be careful, it may backfire. For instance, in American national parks putting up signs saying that rock paintings should not be removed because they represent heritage, resulted in more rock paintings being removed.

Defaults. Let's face it – many people just can't be bothered to change. Many studies throughout the world have shown that human organ donation agreement, or charity donations, saving deductions increase dramatically when they are made the default. Inform us if you don't want to instead of inform us if you want it to happen. There are many non-Lean built-in defaults: Examples are ERP systems (weekly batch size bucket?), not requiring feedback, limited time for speaking to customers, not informing of changes that affect people – on and on. Can these negative defaults be made positive by building in positive defaults – small batch size, requiring feedback, allowing time?

Letting Go. 'Take down that picture of your family! It is against regulations'. Silly rules, red-tape and bureaucracy destroy motivation and commitment. Beware of the corporate policeman. Studies show that allowing limited choice leads to happier and healthier workers, students, kids, and shoppers. (But too much choice can overwhelm – there is a famous jam selection study: a mid-range of selection choice maximises sales; too wide a selection or too small a selection results in fewer sales.)

Incentives. A well-known story concerns a fine being imposed on Israeli parents for picking up kids late from school. The result: More pick-ups were late! ('The school can pay to look after my kids'.) Could it be that payment for ideas results in fewer ideas? One of the authors of this book was once associated with an organisation that was very strict on punctuality. After long service, employees were given a watch! (You know what you can do with that watch!)

Over-confidence, under-confidence and risk. There are interesting studies of over-confident sportspeople and teams who under-perform, while underdogs take risks and often triumph. There are huge lessons for successful companies who deny they are threatened by the 'little guys'. Arrogance. The Lean mantra of Humility is not always easy.

Influence and Reciprocity

Regardless of where a leader sits in the organisation, a critical factor in determining whether or not they will be successful is their ability to interact socially with others within the organisation. This is particularly the case with those over whom they have no direct authority.

Reciprocity and social exchange, which we introduced earlier in this book (Refer to Section 2.7) outlines how the development of human relationships is based on an internalised effort versus reward analysis carried out by each individual. Put simply, reciprocation is the process by which an individual who receives a benefit feels obliged to return the favour. In an ideal world everyone who receives a favour or benefit would return it. Alas, the 'norm of reciprocity' is not always the norm.

In one of our favourite books *Give and Take*, Adam Grant identifies three types of people who lie at different points along the reciprocity scale.

- Takers – these people are only interested in what's in it for them. They are highly competitive, take full credit when things go well and hang out others when they don't. Their main interest in others has only to do with how much they can advance their own agenda. Takers are the opposite of the kind of Lean leader we have discussed in this book. Humility and respect are lacking.
- Givers – not abundantly found in the workplace these peoples' instinct is to help others regardless of payback. They willingly share their experience, knowledge and ideas with others.
- Matchers – these people put great emphasis on making sure that the rules of exchange are maintained. They prefer to give and receive in equal measure.

Studies have indicated that while the attitudes and actions of Takers may yield some success, the bridges they have burned and the people they have trampled on, ultimately prove to be career limiting. On the other hand, while it will take Givers longer to achieve their career goals, the network of trust and goodwill built up along the way will help to consolidate their reputation and continued success. The good guys finish first – eventually!

In summary
- Takers can be so concerned about being exploited that they miss out on making valuable connections. Takers inhibit teamwork, initiative and creativity in the people they manage.
- As Takers acquire greater power, they care less and less about how they are viewed by their subordinates.
- Givers have to be careful that they are not taken advantage of. They radiate energy and enthusiasm but are in danger of burnout until they learn to say no.
- A Matcher's cautious approach is likely to result in having smaller networks.

A short story to conclude:
An old woman was irritated by noisy youths. She invited them in and said she liked their noise and would pay them $1 each if they came back each day. They agreed. The second day she said she could only afford 50 cents. The third day 25 cents. The fourth 10 cents. At this point, the youths said it was not worth their while coming back....

Further Readings.
Jonah Berger, *Invisible Influence*, Simon and Schuster, 2016
Robert Cialdini, *Influence*, 5th edition, Allyn and Bacon, 2009
Robert Cialdini, *Pre-suation*, RH Books, 2016
Adam Grant, *Give and Take*, Allen Lane, 2013
Adam Grant, *Think Again*, WH Allen, 2021
Daniel Kahneman, *Thinking, Fast and Slow*, Allen Lane, 2011
Tali Sharot, *The Influential Mind*, Little Brown, 2017

Chapter 12
Teams

Teams are ubiquitous. Unlike the vast majority of managerial concepts, teams have been a foundation of organisation (and society!) since pre-historic times. Today, teams remain at the core of how work is accomplished in organisations. Senior leadership teams run companies, design teams design, project teams implement, and problem-solving teams improve processes and quality. All of these types are evolving.

However, in many organisations, the term 'team' is a misnomer, used to identify groups of employees who happen to work together or report to the same manager. These are groups or '*Pseudo*' teams. Real teams comprise 2 or more (Typically 8 to 15) members who:
- Work closely towards a shared goal or objective.
- Are interdependent.
- Interact regularly and effectively to share information pertinent to achieving a goal or task.
- Have an organisational identity.

A team is not a team unless co-ordination between members takes place. An effective team requires an awareness of the inter-connections between the roles of team members.

Teams outperform individuals because;
- They can apply their complementary skills and experience to overcome problems as they arise.
- When people work together, synergy develops, and the team becomes much more than the sum of their individual parts.
- Performing in teams brings a social dimension to the work environment. People make friends, learn from each other, and have more fun.

Amy Edmondson of HBS uses the word *Teaming* to describe the way much modern work takes place – not in a linear fashion, but rather as a process of dynamic collaboration 'occurring in constantly shifting configurations'. In such VUCA circumstances, as she says, *"Just as the engine of growth in the Industrial Revolution was standardization, with workers as labouring bodies confined to execute the 'one best way' to get almost any task done, growth today is driven by ideas and ingenuity."* This has been a long-term trend in Lean manufacturing, especially TPS, but the relevance of this statement is even more pertinent with Agile and service operations.

Referring to the OCEAN personality traits (see Psychology Chapter 6) that make for good team players, Openness, Conscientiousness, and Agreeableness are all positive indicators. Extroverts need special attention so as not to dominate the team, whilst Introverts need encouragement to speak-up as do any that are hesitant to contribute. *"Drive out fear"* said Deming, but Edmondson's research has shown that many are still fearful. Again, a team leader has to demonstrate over an extended period that fear is unfounded. Neuroticism can be a problem. From a Lean perspective the ability to reflect and to experiment is highly desirable – perhaps using After Action Reviews or Kata (See Sections 10.20 and 3.12). A willingness to collaborate is important. In all of these, a team leader has an important role, so an awareness of the traits of team members is desirable. Belbin, for instance, showed that a diverse team is more effective than a non-diverse team all having high IQ.

Amy Edmondson, in her excellent book *Teaming*, devotes an entire chapter to overcoming inter-personal problems and barriers to effective 'teaming'.

12.1 Team Types

Teams come in many forms. Many teams are simply grouped around a particular objective or discipline with little thought given as to form, function, autonomy or decision making. However, for team effectiveness it is important to select the most appropriate form that matches the objective, task, and required flexibility with the skills, capabilities, and aspirations of team members.

In the early days of what we now call Lean, Henry Ford's assembly teams operated with close supervision, strict work standards and limited decision making. Ford also kept tabs on workers' sobriety, but was able to get away with such arrangements by paying higher wages. This form may be acceptable in very rare situations today. But todays' work force is altogether better educated and more demanding in terms of aspiration, participation and autonomy. Customers also are increasingly more demanding. As we move further towards a VUCA environment, and with increased information technology and AI, so the choice of team type will become ever more important. Today we hear about teams that are functional, cross-functional, project, high-performance, self-managed, self-organised, self-directed, agile, virtual and, no-doubt, other types. All types have pros and cons. The choice is not straightforward but important.

Characteristic	Traditional	Functional (or Discipline)	High - Performance	Self-directed
Decisions	Issued	From function	Have a say	Participative
Structure	Hierarchy	Hierarchy	Flat hierarchy	Flat
Responsibility	The task	The function	Shared	The outcome
Team Management	Supervisor - appointed	An appointed head	Team leader – from within	Shared or elected
Standards	Rigid	Functional	Tight	Adaptive
Size	<20?	<30?	6-8?	6-15?
Quality	The task	Professional	Kaizen	Customer
Ideas	Top down	From the discipline	Facilitated at the Gemba	Participative
Improvement	Static	Member suggested	PDCA and Leader S-Wk	Everyone's concern
Movement	Restricted	By Seniority	Rotation	Flexible
Training	Single task	Within the discipline	Progressive	Fully Cross-trained
Attitude	The present	Professional	Tomorrow	The future
Advantages				
	Efficient? Easy to scale up. Wage sensitivity	Functional expertise, Stimulating, Professional freedom	Efficient, Less waste, High quality	Flexibility, Participation, Commitment, Low absenteeism
Cautions				
	High turnover, Boring, Recruitment difficulties	Loyalty to profession or trade rather than to the organisation?	Demanding? Recruitment? Burnout? Relies on good team leader	Training costs and time. Responsibility not capable or wanted.

In selecting an appropriate team type it is useful to consider the types of team as a spectrum. In the table above, we contrast typical traditional, functional, high-performance and self-directed types. The table is developed from concepts by Amy Edmondson and by Frederic Laloux.

Beginning on the left are traditional teams. These are to be found in less-sophisticated manufacturers and service organisations. Common in retail and hospitality. Certainly, the scope for a continuous improvement culture is limited.

As one moves across the table from left to right:

- Management involvement decreases, and member initiative increases. 'Command and Control' decreases.
- Trust in the team members by management needs to increase, or else management will not be prepared to delegate.
- The types of operation shift from routine towards varied. Job descriptions shift from tight to loose.
- Uncertainty and variety increase.
- A cognitive (opinion) diversity increase in the people in the team is desirable.
- The required speed of learning and adaptation generally increases.
- A gradual shift in the proportion of teams in each category is taking place, as people become more educated, more demanding.

This shift in requirements and team characteristics should play a role in considering the most appropriate team type.

Functional teams are related to a department or profession – for example an accounting team, a marketing team or a research team. Silos can be a significant drawback. A university department would be a typical example. Hospitals have strong discipline-oriented functions. This type of team certainly has scope for good Lean Thinking. Design teams are a special case because they are often multi-disciplinary with good Lean functional teams having a strong orientation to both customers and to technology. A classic problem is to keep in touch with both technology and customers. A brief description of Toyota design practice is given in a section below.

High-performance teams may be found amongst leading manufacturers, and in world-class sports teams such as Formula 1 motor-racing teams. They comprise goal focused individuals with specialised expertise and complementary skills who collaborate and innovate to deliver consistently superior results. Here, continuous improvement is part of the culture. The team is highly motivated, trained and focused. Standards are strict and high but also need continual modification. A brief description of Toyota teams is given later in this chapter. Writing in *The Times*, Matthew Syed described high performing teams like Mercedes Formula 1 and Liverpool F.C. as being cauldrons of continuous improvement. Here standards are set very high, team members understand and accept that it is the collective, rather than the individual which matters most and hold each other accountable through robust honest conversations. Another characteristic of HPWT's is a willingness to be ruthless when the situation requires it. This was notably demonstrated by Manchester United Manager Alex Ferguson when Jaap Stam, David Beckham and Roy Keane, all once deemed irreplaceable, were quickly moved on when their performance was threatening to damage team solidarity.

The self-directed type is shown towards the right side of the table. This type is labelled self-directed but here there are several hybrids – virtual, agile, cross-functional and self-managed. The boundary between high-performance teams and these various types is somewhat grey – reflecting the evolution. It would generally be a mistake to leap directly into full SDWTs. There would seem to be a strong emergence amongst software developers, but also amongst companies such as P&G

and GE both of which claim significant advantages. A self-directed work team (SDWT) is not only motivated, trained, and focused but also has significant self-decision-making responsibility. Do not align self-direction with formal education. For example many construction teams and maintenance teams have to have self-direction capability.

The border between High-performance and Self-directed is shown as dotted, to indicate that that there is a spectrum between them. A fully-developed SDWT is rare and requires several stages of transition or development.

An issue with SDWTs is the possible conflict between top-down strategy and self-direction. The boundaries of self-direction and the overall strategic requirements need clarification, something that a good OKR measurement system can resolve, together with good visuality, good reflection, and good reflection (or 'retrospectives') shared with senior management.

As discussed in the Organisation Chapter there are even more radical types emerging that may be an indication of the future. Examples are Haier (in China), Buurtzorg (in Holland), and Semco (in Brazil).

Excitingly, for the first time in history, artificial intelligence (AI) is just beginning to introduce non-human 'members', capable of 'thinking' and advising, into teams. (Do you believe that? If not, read Harari's book *Homo Deus*, Chapter on 'The Great Decoupling')

Increasingly, and accelerating as a result of the Covid pandemic, virtual teams are to be found amongst all types except those that require physical contact. Organisational policies vary with respect to working from home – some optional, others not. Indications are that up to half of office workers will work from home, full or part time.

The members of some teams, for example in a hospital, may not know each other well but still need to cooperate well in order to deliver an effective outcome. The process, as in a hospital may have many possible branches so the decision points and necessary information needs to be known by all members and appreciated upstream. So merely selecting staff (however well qualified) and hoping they will cooperate is simply not adequate.

In all these types the characteristics of good jobs are relevant. Please refer to the Job Characteristics Model in Section 4.3

Of course, in a Lean-aspiring organisation, several of these types may be found simultaneously. Perhaps Functional among management, High-performance in operations, Self-directed in Design and R & D.

Degrees of 'Lean thinking' may be found in each of the team types. Some, for instance Bob Emiliani, would claim that traditional teams are 'Fake Lean' – paying more attention to Lean tools and less to people aspects.

Further Readings.
Amy Edmondson, *Teaming: How Organisations Learn, Innovate and Compete in the Knowledge Economy*, Jossey Bass, 2012

12.2 How Team's Develop

In 1965 Bruce Tuckman published his 4 stage "Forming, Storming, Norming, Performing" model to explain the process which most teams go through to become high performing. Tuckman later modified the model to include a fifth stage "Adjourning" This model is still relevant today especially as an overview of what to expect with new teams. Tuchman's model has similarities with Hersey and Blanchard's Situational Leadership® model.

Forming	When a new team is first formed, members will be unsure of the team's goals and might also be apprehensive and harbour concerns about how they will gel as a team. This is quite a natural response and doesn't take away from the fact that they are glad to be on the team. Individual members lack clarity about their roles and responsibilities. Some members may test the leader and the system. Leader Focus: Provide direction as quickly as possible. Set project milestones and assist team members to set personal goals.
Storming	Conflict or friction is likely for a number of reasons; (1) Members start to assert themselves within the team. (2) People begin to reveal their true selves. (3) Lack of clarity or perceived favouritism around roles and responsibilities (4) Frustration at lack of progress. Leader Focus: Establish clear roles and responsibilities. Seek input from team members. Watch out for any simmering tensions between members and address them quickly.
Norming	Team members are starting to resolve their differences, appreciate each other's strengths and respect the leader's authority. Team involved in decision making. Leader Focus: Encourage the team to take increased responsibility for organising the work.
Performing	Team are now confident and motivated towards a shared objective. They perform to their full potential with minimum supervision. Minor disagreements occur and are resolved by the team themselves. Leader Focus: Increase engagement by delegating more tasks and responsibilities.
Adjourning	With the project now finished, the team disbands. This can be a difficult time for some team members who find it difficult to separate from people they have formed close bonds with. This is despite the fact that most of the friendships and alliances that have been created will remain. Rather appropriately, this stage is sometimes known as the "Mourning Phase" Leader Focus: Celebrate success, encourage the team to share learnings and personal growth from the project.

The Tuckman stages of Forming, Storming, Norming, Performing are classic, *but...*

- It takes time to reach the performing stage and often there is a drop-off in productivity during the early stages.
- It is said that high turnover amongst team members (say above 40% per annum) can prevent a team from ever reaching the performing stage. High performance and Self-directed teams may not be possible, unless wages, culture, communication or other impediments are addressed first.

Unquestionably, the VUCA world has spawned a need for a new type of team. A team that brings together employees from various divisions and disciplines, along with subject matter experts and external stakeholders, for a specific purpose, over a relatively short time span, after which they will be disbanded. Edmondson has coined the term "Teaming" to describe this new development where teams are created for situations that are complex, the path to success is uncertain and is likely to require many changes along the way. In other words, situations where the traditional team structure will not work satisfactorily.

Teaming requires leaders to adopt both a best practice approach to project management and a team leadership style that will foster collaboration in a newly formed team. A divergence of views-and the prospect of some conflict is to be expected. Managing a teaming project involves three phases:

Phase 1, Scoping: The leader investigates the challenge or goal and determines what expertise is required, identifies executive sponsors and plans the team members roles and responsibilities.

Phase 2, Structuring: Creating an infrastructure which enables the team to function quickly and efficiently. This is likely to involve the temporary deployment of team members as well as establishing an effective communication system.

Phase 3, Sorting: One of the most difficult aspects of managing remote multi-disciplinary teams is achieving the consensus required to move the project forward and overcome bottlenecks when they appear. Edmondson suggests that leaders should specify review points where individuals or sub-groups should get together, to share progress, identify and anticipate problems, and agree a co-ordinated path forward.

Because working together will have allowed them time to bond, establish trust, and get to know each other's strengths and weakness, well-established teams have a distinct advantage over ad hoc teams (Think the *A Team* versus *The Dirty Dozen*). This is particularly the case when differences of opinions arise. Teaming is more dynamic than in traditional stable teams. In a rapidly changing environment, time (And time-zones) might not allow for full stakeholder input. There is also the need to balance getting enough information (Some people never have enough) to make an informed decision, when pressure is being applied to make an early decision. All of which have the potential to damage team effectiveness. The challenge for leaders is to get team members to understand each other's individual perspective and the value it brings to the team.

Based on Dutch experience, van Amelsvoort and Scholtes identified four phases in the transition to SDWT. In the Figure below we build on their work, adding our own experiences. Today, many teams are moving towards self-direction, but this is not to suggest that it is appropriate or desirable to move all the way towards self-direction.

Transitioning to SDWTs

Responsibility	Manager			Team and Team Leader
Stage	Bundling	Early High-Performance	Developed High Performance	SDWT
Characteristic	Excitement but hesitant	Roles understood Some storming	More independent. Value stream focus	Responsible, Cohesive
Team Leader Role	Appointed	Elected? Regular team meetings	Elected. Performance responsibility	Rotational or shared
Team Members	Orientation. Early cross-train	Participative C.I. Early rotation	Early decisions Self work rotation	Participative decisions
Coach Role	Build vision	Facilitation	Occasional Support	Monitoring
Psychological Safety	Increasing			
Changes	Large, infrequent Static			Small, frequent Dynamic
Learning and Training	Before the Job			Is part of the Job

Note the similarities and differences with the Kaizen Flag in the section on Kaizen in the Established Practices Chapter.

It would be dangerous to attempt to move directly into SDWTs. Evolution is required – perhaps taking 6 months or more through each of the stages. An in-depth review, where team members are encouraged to voice their opinions and suggestions about the team working procedures (not the tasks) should take place at similar intervals. In fact, few teams are fully developed SDWTs because of their own abilities or willingness, or because of management reluctance to allow the team to go the full way.

As an organisation moves towards self-direction, this must be accompanied by learning. (See below.) We like the phrase from Amy Edmondson 'Cycle Out' rather than 'Roll Out'. The former suggests many learning cycles, the latter gives the impression that all the answers are known and it is just a question of extending the concept.

Once a team starts to manage their own the work, management's focus has to shift towards creating and nurturing an environment where SDWT's can flourish. This involves four key requirements:

a)   Providing clear, aligned and inspiring direction.
b)   Setting clear, safe boundaries that will enable the SDWT to take ownership.
c)   Working with the team to develop a healthy culture which reflects the team's values and behaviours. (See Charter, below)
d)   Confidence in to handing over responsibility for many roles to the team

12.3 Leading Teams: Participation and Conflict

The Lean Leader role is discussed in Chapter 11. However, front-line team leaders more than any other leadership group face the greatest challenge. While in theory, their boss is their line manager, in practice they also must answer and coordinate with functional managers from other departments such as quality, safety, and H.R. Uniquely front-line leaders have to communicate (on behalf of themselves and sometimes their team) upwards, downwards and horizontally. A key requirement is their ability to filter the message (going up or down) while ensuring the central message gets through. Positive lean requires an investment in the training and development of all stakeholders, but particularly those like the front-line leaders who have such a wide reach.

Teams are like jigsaws with no two pieces the same. What binds them is a common objective. The leader engages and motivates his or her team in a variety of ways, for example using visual management boards, recognition systems, daily meetings, and 'town halls'. Getting the best from individual employees requires the leader to adopt a subtle personal approach. While team members share a common team goal, each of them will be unique in their life experiences, capabilities, expectations, and career ambitions. Most of this information they will likely keep to themselves. Sometimes, team members may project outwards a different viewpoint than they truly believe - possibly caused by peer pressure or a desire to fit in with the group. (Refer also to the Fundamental Attribution Error, discussed in Section 3.1 Respect.)

Leaders must fight the battle for the hearts and minds of their people both as individuals and as members of a team. Most leaders are comfortable about doing this at the team level but maximising individual member's contribution is different. As stated elsewhere in this book, employee engagement is a contact sport. Leaders must know their employees, not just as workers, but as people, if they are to get the "best" out of them. By best, we mean employees get the opportunity to achieve their full potential and realise their ambitions, while also contributing meaningfully to the organisation. We would advocate that all team leaders should have a one-to-one meeting with each of their direct reports at least once a month. These sessions should not be mini performance reviews, rather a pulse check to gauge worker's satisfaction and provide the opportunity to escalate issues or concerns privately. It also provides a great coaching opportunity for the leader to help the team members to utilise their skills and resources to carry out their work more efficiently. Ideally, these meetings should also be about building trust and moving the working relationship to a higher level.

One of the great problems with participation is – no participation. Silence! Why silence? A big reason is fear. Humans have a built-in tendency to avoid danger and conflict – at least until a certain threshold is reached. It is safer to run away from a potential threat, snake or boss, than to stand and address it. So, why risk the possibility of future loss of position when it is easier just to shut up. ('Let them get on with it. They don't listen to me anyway. They'll learn the hard way.') But silence means the loss of many possibilities and ideas.

Research, for example by Edmondson, shows that effective speaking up can be encouraged with…

- An expectation of speaking up that must be communicated. Letting people know that speaking up is expected.
- Demonstration. When speaking up does occur acknowledgement or thanks is given. Action is taken, not ignored.
- Techniques such as a round robin sequence to collect opinions in a meeting.
- Being aware of introverts who may be reluctant to speak but often have good thoughts.
- Say 'I don't know'.
- Technology has a role. One company in the engineering field maintenance area uses WhatsApp for reminders and encourages members to submit short videos on their experiences.

Adam Grant discusses two types of conflict: Task and Relationship. Although dealing with conflicting opinions is time-consuming it is very useful for feedback. Grant's idea is to separate tasks from relationships. High performing groups spend lots of time on task conflict, but keep relationships or personality out of the equation.

Task disagreement can be very healthy – a great source of innovation. Some of the most innovative groups argue extensively over tasks – new products, web design, improvement. Some of top performing rock bands in recent decades had numerous disagreements. The Beatles, Bee Gees, Fleetwood Mac – often argued over who was to be the lead singer and about lyrics. Numerous fall-outs occurred but, if anything, this led to the emergence of great songs. (Fleetwood Mac's *Sara* is an outstanding example.) By contrast, low performing groups are the reverse – tackling personalities rather than tasks.

In an earlier section, the TWI Job Relations guidelines and the Mager and Pipe Flowchart were discussed. Both of these are very useful for both teams and individuals.

Note: Several other sections of the book are applicable to the management of Teams. These sections include: Coaching, Problem Solving, Gemba management, Kata, Meetings, The Eight Models Chapter (especially TWI and Mager and Pipe), and Organisation. (See Section 4.4)

Further Readings.
Amy Edmondson, *The Fearless Organisation*, Wiley, 2019
Adam Grant, *Think Again*, WH Allen, 2012

12.4 Behaviours and Teams

Have you ever considered why organisations put such enormous efforts into identifying and removing waste from their business processes, while failing abysmally to address poor intra and interpersonal relationships which are present within their teams and groups? These poor behaviours can fracture communication lines, damage trust and working relationships and destabilise the working environment. Does this affect the organisations overall performance and bottom line? Reflect on two scenarios. In the first scenario, you are part of a small team tasked with solving an urgent problem. However some team members bring to the situation some differences of opinions and personality clashes from the past. These legacy issues are manifested in key information not being willingly shared and cliques being formed. Morale, engagement, satisfaction and trust are the casualties of this unhealthy working environment. In the second scenario team members bring no baggage to the situation. Working on the project is enjoyable, members openly share opinions and ideas in a trusting environment and make swift progress. One of America's most renowned management thinkers Steven Covey highlights the importance of interpersonal relationships within organisations; *"Work gets done with and through people. Organisations are made up of an infinite number of connections. Where trust is lacking it takes longer and costs a lot more to get things done."* Matthew Syed believes that trust is THE essential element that explains the difference between successful and less-successful societies.

Emiliani uses the term "fat behaviours" for those behaviours which do not add any value and should therefore be eliminated. Emiliani suggests applying the five lean principles to address this problem:

1. Specify Value – from an interpersonal relationship perspective specifying value is understanding what the people we interact with, expect and need.
2. Identify the Value Stream – the behaviours that add value & those that don't.
3. Map the Value Stream – this is about finding out why people behave as they do and is typically influenced by the role and the work they perform. This helps to better understand things from their perspective.
4. Establish Pull – Once we begin to eliminate fat behaviours that are causing frustration and inhibiting progress, our purpose will be clearer, people will become more engaged and momentum will increase.
5. Pursue Perfection – in a behavioural context this means a constant focus on creating a trusting and transparent organisation.

Further Readings.
Steven M. Covey, *The Speed of Trust*, Simon and Schuster, 2006
Bob Emiliani, Lean behaviors, *Management Decision*, 36 (1998), pp. 615–631
Matthew Syed, Trust is key in the fight against Covid, *Sunday Times*, 11th October 2020

12.5 Team Charter and Framing

Writing a Team Charter (or Contract or Map) is a most useful exercise for more developed teams. Amy Edmondson refers to 'Framing', with her research indicating Framing as the essential differentiator for performance and learning.

A Charter or Frame sets out the essential beliefs and assumptions about a team and its role in the organisation. This may be written down – which is a good discipline – or at the very least discussed by senior leaders and team leaders in a group setting. Not a top-down issue but developed with group or team leaders, and perhaps with the team. It needs to cover the boundaries of responsibility. A 'Team Canvas' has become a more popular type, and whole books have been written on this. A Canvas may cover, for example, responsibilities, necessary collaboration, decision making, learning, roles, meetings, information flow, resources – physical and financial, and health and safety.

The Charter should reflect the genuine beliefs and aspirations for the team or project, not some superficial statement such as 'people are our greatest asset' (shortly to be followed by actions that disprove this). The development of the Charter or Frame should reflect current opportunities for learning and the needs of the wider organisation.

Developing a Charter is even more important for remote teams. This and a range of other useful tools for teams are given in the further readings.

Further Readings.
Stefano Mastrogiacomo and Alexander Osterwalder, *High-Impact Tools for Teams*, Wiley, 2021
Alexander Osterwalder and Yves Pigneur, *Business Model Generation*, Wiley, 2010

12.6 Team Learning

Learning has been discussed numerous times in this book. It is particularly relevant as teams develop – moving from learning before the task, to learning during the task. This is a major change in mindset that can be facilitated by Kata activities. Move away from top-down 'we-know-best' towards building in learning with using the viewpoint that we don't know all the answers so we need to learn together. Two-way communication, allowing time, surfacing and sharing problems, and humility are all part of the game.

PDSA is certainly appropriate, but on a team level rather than an individual level. Remember to study the process as well as the outcomes. Since rapid learning is the aim, 'fail early, fail waste' is the mindset. Failure is not waste if learning happens. Feedback from, for example, TrustPilot surveys could be effective provided follow-up action is taken, particularly from complaints.

Deliberate learning is particularly appropriate in team situations. There are several ways to facilitate learning: Randomised trial, with a study group of customers and a control group the methodology used by Google, Microsoft and many others. Simulation could be considered – there are several types: computer modelling simulation, low-cost prototyping, simulation games, and full-scale simulation.

Case Studies of Team Types

High Performance Teams: Toyota

The Toyota model is centred on ensuring that all teams doing value-added work (Assembly, painting etc.) are fully supported. To outsiders, Toyota's Team leader to team member ratio target of 1 to 4 or 5 seems extraordinarily low. However, when we look at just how highly standardised the team member role is, we begin to understand the requirement for such a low leader to member ratio. This was illustrated by one of the authors during a visit to the Toyota Deeside Plant in Wales. While observing an assembly team member using a power tool to locate and tighten bolts in the engine block, he noticed one bolt falling to the ground. Surprised when the team member didn't pick up the fallen bolt, he inquired with the tour guide who informed him that the team member standard work did not allow time to pick up fallen bolts. This would be done by the team leader doing their rounds. The team member's role is to perform manual jobs to standard and to surface any problems that prevent this using the Andon cord.

The prime role of team leaders is to ensure that their line is running smoothly and producing quality parts. Key to this is their immediate response to Andon alerts. In the second edition of *The Toyota Way* Jeffrey Liker outlines how Team Leaders at Toyota's Burnaston plant in the United Kingdom have 40 core roles defined (Team members have 21). Some of these responsibilities include Andon response, safety, problem solving, team meeting and kaizen. Such is the importance placed on the advanced team leader role that 17 weeks of structured learning are given covering problem solving, leading improvement activities and coaching. The 17 weeks would take several years to complete, on a need, coach, test, verify cycle.

Uddevalla and Suru: A Challenge

A radical alternative to conventional short-cycle assembly teams was Volvo car's experiences at their Uddevalla plant. Here instead of having one long assembly line with cycle times of under 60 seconds, 40 small teams operating in parallel build finished cars. Cycle times ranged from 1.5 to 3.5 hours. Berggren identified four key features from the Swedish experience, which he believes could lay the foundations for the development of competitive humanistic manufacturing.

1. Moving away from short time, highly repetitive work elements towards a more holistic assembly type work. Instead of individual workers making a single piece of the jigsaw, why not have a team of workers making the full jigsaw? As well as helping to create a more social environment, this would also make the work more meaningful and reduce the physical strain on the workers.

2. Taking a much broader view of how ergonomics should shape the working environment. Workplace design, methods and tools should capture the needs of all workers, regardless of sex, size, or strength.

3. Replacing rigid work systems, including a reliance on overtime, with a much more flexible model that will appeal to workers not traditionally associated with car manufacturing.

4. Greater engagement with worker representatives, including recognising that unions are key stakeholders with legitimate rights to advocate for their members.

Another alternative to the Toyota approach is the Seru Manufacturing System which evolved out of Japan during the 1990's in response to a reduction in customer demand and increased product variation. The big reasons are capacity flexibility and operator involvement, rather than cost efficiency. (See Section 13.2 below on Cell Layout and Seru production.).

Seru, the Uddevalla case, and indeed several similar participative team types, pose challenges that are developing as employee demands shift towards participation and away from a willingness to work under Tayloristic principles of labour efficiency to the detriment of motivation and job satisfaction. In mid 2021, *The Economist* reported that, almost worldwide, job vacancies were at near all-time high levels whilst simultaneously unemployment levels were moderate to high. This is a developing challenge to traditional economics and to employers. When considering Berggren's proposed model, one should consider that there have been several studies that established a link between reduced work cycles and employees' increased levels of job anxiety, depression, and other health issues. A common theme across these studies is that as work becomes more intensified, it reduces workers' job decision latitude, which increases worker stress. This is not surprising, as discussed elsewhere in this book (See Yerkes-Dodson in Section 13.6). People are social animals and work is a multifaceted activity that engages humans on many levels. We all need interaction with other people, we need to use our brains, and we definitely need to be more than just one small cog in a large complex machine.

Rotating jobs and sharing responsibilities can result in highly productive multi-skilled teams, who identify and solve problems early and work well together to improve efficiencies. Changing the layout from the traditional long assembly lines towards U shaped cells with small teams, usually around 5 and rarely more than 10, help facilitate this paradigm shift. U shaped cells help to make the working environment more social, improve communications, and facilitates job rotation and teamwork.

We believe there are several reasons why these approaches are not being widely adopted. They go against established lean principles such as one-piece flow. Some cells are likely to require more inventory than assembly lines with associated increases in material handling and space. Greater investment in versatility training is also a requirement. Then there is the issue of managerial control. In a positive lean environment, the front-line leader is a coach, focused on helping the team to grow and become self-sufficient in managing and improving their own work. Unfortunately there is limited opportunity for this type of leader where there are highly standardised tasks and work cycles of under a minute – and made untenable when there are command-and-control managers in charge.

The fact that teams tend towards developing their own work norms creates a dilemma for many organisations of how to get lower performing teams up to the level of the high performing teams. The authors experience is that nobody minds working hard provided everybody is working hard. What really frustrates, disappoints and ultimately dis-engages team members are situations where perhaps half of the team are doing most of the work, while the other half are taking it easy. ('Social loafing'). Management meanwhile are content because the work is being done, albeit not fairly. When team members raise their frustration with their manager, they are told, 'sort it out yourselves'. This is clear abdication by managers of their responsibilities. A related problem particular to teamwork is some members occasionally taking their foot off the pedal, confident in the knowledge that others will work harder to pick up the slack. These are situations we regularly come across, even at companies who consider themselves to be at or close to world class.

Some of these problems however can be prevented, without losing the benefits of teamwork, provided the work is properly organised and controlled. Line-balance-charts, job rotation schedules should be posted. The recruitment process should include the use of personality profiling to exclude those people unsuitable for working in a team environment. Indeed Ford and Toyota actively warn prospective employees about tough work conditions. Daily start of shift huddles set the agenda, while short-interval-tracking visually display performance against target. Any cultural differences need to be understood.

Team Cautions

- Set expectations by making team and individual tasks transparent.
- Use daily team meetings to review team performance.
- Introduce a weekly or bi-weekly one-to-one meeting to engage and motivate team members individually.
- Team effectiveness depends on both task work and teamwork. Investment in teamwork training is essential.

Further Readings.

P. Van Amelsvoort, and J. Benders, Team time: a model for developing self-directed work teams. *International Journal of operations and Production Management*, 1996
www.edelman.com/trust,2021-trust-barometer
Christian Berggren, NUMMI vs Uddevalla, *Sloan Management Review*, Dec 1994
Blanchard and Johnson, *The New One Minute Manager*, 2019
Amy Edmondson, Teamwork on the Fly, *Harvard Business Review*, April 2012
Amy Edmondson, Wicked Problem Solvers, *Harvard Business Review*, June 2016
Amy Edmondson, *Teaming*, Jossey Bass, 2012
Anders Ericsson, *Peak*, Bodley Head, 2016
Thomas Gilovich and Lee Ross, *The Wisest One in the Room*, OneWorld, 2016
Adam Grant, *Think Again*, WH Allen, 2012
Jeffrey Liker, *The Toyota Way*, Second edition, McGraw Hill, 2021
Richard Schonberger, The Human (HR) Side of Lean, *Target*, Fourth Issue 2009
Peter Scholtes, *The Team Handbook*, Oriel Incorporated, 1996
Stephen Woods and Michael West, *The Psychology of Work and Organisations*, South-Western Cengage Learning, 2010

Design Teams

Design teams face several challenges: how to remain customer focused, how to reconcile professional standards and opportunities with company requirements, how to stay technically up to date whilst delivering on time, how to interface with other disciplines, and others. Here we offer some team practices as used by Toyota, IDEO, and others.

A design team for a complex product will usually contain several sub-teams. At Toyota the overall team leader or Chief engineer is not a project manager in the conventional administrator sense but, as Ward calls them, Entrepreneurial System Designers (ESD). Moreover, they are experienced ENGINEERS, not managers. Their task is both holistic (integrating all parts) and end-to-end (from need to use). Thus if an ESD project manager brings a product to market on time but the product itself fails in the market, then she has failed. These chief engineers have only a small staff but work through functional managers using their influence, reputation and considerable experience to avoid the many delays so common in traditional product development. Functional managers are responsible for developing 'towering expertise' in their own teams – maybe for engines, suspension, or controls. They bring state-of-the-art solutions into new products. Functional staff are as much researchers as designers, so they enjoy high status and professional development in their own area. In new product development they work for their functional engineer, not for the chief engineer. The latter needs to negotiate for their time but be concerned with integration.

Several techniques are used. Set based design uses 'sets' of options for the various system elements, and these are gradually narrowed down as the design clarifies using 'Concept Screening'. Possible 'solution sets' are explored in parallel, but once a particular solution is decided upon it is frozen unless a change is absolutely necessary. This is similar to the Lean concept of postponement. Starting with sets may sound wasteful but unused designs are book-shelved for future use. Trade-off curves, for example strength against thickness allow rapid selection of alternatives. Check sheets encourage the recording of experiences systematically as a project proceeds. Rotation. Good new product development rotates staff from design to manufacturing engineering. Concurrency is to work concurrently on stages rather than 'over the wall'. So, while car design is proceeding, engineering and die production also proceed. Project levelling: The Heijunka concept is used to plan and track in small increments. Project flow: Avoiding hold-ups by critical resources whilst waiting for other stages is an important role for the chief designer's team. A leaf can be taken from Lean Construction where the 'Last Planner' methodology aims to do just this by developing checklists for other functions before critical activities are due to start.

Visibility: The good Lean principle of visual management is even more important in product development. Toyota uses an 'Obeya' (Big Room) for each new product where all activities and progress is shown on charts. Problems are highlighted in daily, short, stand-up meetings. Increasingly, ideas from Agile and SCRUM software design are found – for instance, the use of kanban cards for parcels of work. Front loading: The later in the design process a problem is fixed, the more expensive it becomes. Front-loading aims to address this by pulling key decisions forward, whist retaining set-based flexibility.

LAMDA is the product developer's version of PDCA. Look, Ask, Model, Discuss, and Act. (Notice this – much time on finding out from understanding customer's needs, and modelling and discussing alternatives, before starting actual design work.)

IDEO is the famous design consultancy based in California. They use Design Thinking. This cuts through the traditional barriers that frequently exist between industrial design and operations, between R&D and product and service design, between service designers and customers, and between those that design the service and those that deliver the service. Design thinking is therefore a natural extension of Lean Thinking. It is about moving towards 'Experiment First, then Design' rather than Design then Trial. There are great similarities with the Eric Ries' 'Lean Startup'. 'Fail early, fail often' is not a waste in Design and R&D. Design authority Ron Mascitelli talks about making a wooden table, varnishing it, and then discovering problems with the varnish: far better to test the varnish on a sample of the wood first. Likewise in software or service design, just do enough to test and get feedback. In other words, learning!

Rapid, low-cost, Prototyping and experimentation have become the norm amongst design teams. Michael Schrage proposes the '5X5' team: A diverse team of 5 people have 5 days to come up with 5 low-cost experiments that require less than 5 weeks to run. This forces ingenuity to resolve great issues of vision, problems, and disagreements.

Further Readings.
There is a huge literature on Design, Design Thinking, and Startup. A few of our favourites are
Tim Brown, *Change by Design*, Harper, 2009
David Butler and Linda Tischler, *Design to Grow*, Portfolio Penguin, 2016
Ronald Mascitelli, *The Lean Design Guidebook*, Technology Perspectives, 2004
Eric Reis, *The Startup Way*, Portfolio Penguin, 2017
Michael Schrage, *The Innovator's Hypothesis*, MIT Press, 2014

Chapter 13
Organisations: Change and Challenge

13.1 Introduction

The importance of human aspects of Lean have been spoken about for the best part of half a century. The word 'Lean' in its productivity context arose in 1990 with the book *The Machine that Changed the World*. But the concepts were already in place in some Western companies a decade before. Both Robert Hall and Richard Schonberger in the 1980's discussed the importance of people in what would later become known as Lean. Ohno's legacy goes back even further.

However, whilst human aspects of Lean have long been advocated, organisational aspects have had far less attention. The focus has been on individuals, teams, team leaders, and leaders rather than on the organisation arrangements in which they operate. Tools, coaching, problem solving, and 'Culture' have also enjoyed attention. But it is the organisation within which all of these take place that is the focus of this chapter.

Today, according to Kahneman, Harari and others, millennials – the new work force – predominantly seek work-life balance. Happiness is important. No longer live-to-work, or even work-to-live, but today's young workforce is willing to trade-off money for happiness. The aim is not to produce; it is to be happy. Anthropologists now think that it is less about 'survival of the fittest' than it is about 'survival of the happiest' that has had a major impact on human development. This has profound, and growing, implications for society and for Lean organisation in particular.

In 1995, one of the authors, was proudly shown a work cell that had had been kaizened several times with the aim of eliminating the 7 wastes. His reaction was one of horror! The 1915 Ford Assembly line taken to the nth degree! This surely cannot be the future of Lean. The 8th waste was ignored. Of 'head, heart, hands, health, habitat', head and heart did not exist.

Let us set the wider picture.

Despite much discussion on 'empowerment, 'respect', 'humility', and 'engagement', many front-line people and others have, over the past decades, had a relatively thin time. Consider:

- The salary gap had widened. In 2020 the US Economic Policy Institute reports that since 1978 CEO compensation has grown by over 900%, whilst typical worker compensation has grown by only 12%
- Productivity and hourly pay. Susskind points out that for decades prior to the mid 1970's, across 24 countries, productivity and hourly pay were tightly coupled. But since then they have sharply diverged. In real terms, productivity has more than doubled, but hourly wages have barely grown.
- Cuts. Often, when times are tight, the first people to go have been 'directs'. It is usually the easiest work to understand. There is the old cartoon – with more than an element of truth – where, in response to a need to reduce cost, a group from HR, accounting, health and safety, PR, IT, and Security gather around a front-line worker and decide he has to go.
- Gig working has created large numbers of self-employed workers whose total take-home pay has decreased but which has allowed corporations to cut costs and force work-hour flexibility. Not all corporations have acted ethically.

- Monitoring of front-line staff. Monitoring of key-strokes, monitoring of call centre call durations, pick monitoring in warehouses and distribution centres. *The Times* reported in April 2021 that in the UK, during the pandemic, 24% of home workers were monitored by video, audio or key strokes. Amazon workers are apparently monitored by hand-held scanner.
- With many the viewpoint has developed that 'Lean is mean', and that 'job cuts' are really what Lean is about. Lean practitioners deny this, but the evidence does not always support practitioner opinion.
- Outsourcing. Many work categories have been affected, including Lean kaizen.
- Off shoring. Loss of front-line work but also production engineering and industrial engineering skills. The consequences are a communication distancing between senior management and front line, and a separation between design and operations. In the service industry a cost saving in wages has frequently been shown to be more than offset by an increase in failure demand and rework, resulting on some cases to re-shoring.
- Competition from Low wage regions – not just blue collar but some white collar and increasingly professional.
- Automation and robotics, Robotic Process Automation (RPA), and Artificial Intelligence (AI). See below. (13.4; 13.10; 14.1)

Bureaucracy, but 'red tape' in particular, has been and remains widespread in organisations in general but also, disappointingly, in Lean-aspiring organisations. We believe, that after half a century, organisations are evolving towards what we believe can be called Organisational Lean. Is a workers 'golden age' (as *The Economist* calls it) dawning? 'The future is bright', says *The Economist's* Callum Williams.

There are encouraging trends, and the pandemic has accelerated positive change. The pandemic had a devastating impact on employment, mainly amongst the low-skilled and frontline workers who were not able to work from home. But recovery has been remarkable, at least in macro terms.

- Gallup reports a slow but steady growth in job satisfaction and job recognition, each rising by around 10% over the past 20 years.
- For some decades, alternative forms of organisation and working have slowly developed. This has been given greater impetus by the pandemic, not least because some of the fears about home-working and more flexible working have been shown to be exaggerated. Emerging forms of organisation are discussed in a section below.
- During the pandemic, several studies, as quoted in *The Economist*, reported increases in transparency, communication, and engagement. On communication, coffee-machine communication has not been possible so articulation and clarity of work roles has had to follow.
- A predicted fall-off in productivity, despite far less supervision, has not materialised – and in some cases has improved.
- Apparently, the average worker in several countries has expressed a preference for home-working two or three days a week. Whilst some organisations insist that workers return to the office full time, other organisations are adopting flexible working arrangements.
- Zoom and Microsoft Teams meetings have forced clarity in meetings as well as reducing time.
- Many managers have had to reassess their style: less over-the-shoulder checking, greater participation and more trust.

All of these outcomes, and together with the growing expectation for work-life balance, are forcing a re-think in organisation.

Further Readings.

Yuval Harari, *Homo Deus – A brief History of Tomorrow*, Vintage, 2016. (The first three chapters, at least, should be read by all Lean-aspiring leaders.)

13.2 Trends towards an emerging Lean organisation

Two significant trends in operations – found in manufacturing, service, non-profits, some governments– are the demand for flexibility and the demand for greater employee participation. Both are best seen as spectrums.

Process Flexibility is being driven by greater product variety and shorter life cycles. Employee flexibility goes from closely specified jobs to multi-skilled roles. Standard work would go from strict, adhered to standards to adaptive, minimal standards with only key points being specified.

Employee participation is being driven by employee education, unwillingness to do repetitive work, and demands for a greater say in own work. The spectrum goes from Command to Participative. Organisation is relevant here – from multi-layered hierarchies and silos to flat organisation. Generally, there are more 'staff' and overhead functions at the 'Command' end. As one moves from Command to Participation, there is wider involvement in improvement, in problem solving and, later, in decisions. Engagement increases – from little to significant.

Refer to the figure. The trends along both these dimensions drive a vector moving towards the top right – participative and flexible. Note that there are less-feasible regions at top left and bottom right.

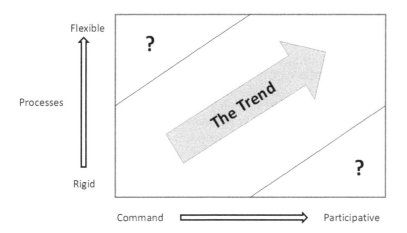

Reasons for the emerging Lean organisation.

Whilst all of the following are obvious and clearly visible, there is inertia in most established organisations adequately to respond to the changes.

- First, let us note that the classic hierarchical organisational pyramid, with supporting 'silos' is a relatively recent human invention, not 'God given'. It is likely to change and evolve. Likewise, the 'back office' concept is very recent. Richard Chase introduced the back-office concept in HBR in 1978, separating routine and non-routine work.
- Ever since Henry Ford's time, or even before Ford, overhead functions (and back-office functions) have grown significantly faster than front-line functions.

- The focus of Lean has been predominantly on front-line activity (in manufacturing, service, and government). Overhead functions have had far less attention. Publications on 'office lean' are almost exclusively to do with repetitive work.
- Manager growth: Hamel and Zanini report that since 1983 the number of managers, supervisors, and administrators in the U.S. workforce has grown by more than 100%, while the number of people in all other occupations has increased by just 44%
- The workforce has changed and is changing. 'Millennials' have greater expectations and demands than their parents. The average worker is much better educated than when Lean first emerged.
- Technology continues to drive change, and this is accelerating with artificial intelligence, the internet, and the cloud. The impact of AI is just beginning but will be significant.
- Product life cycles are shortening - meaning that jobs change more frequently and flexibility and re-training is required.

Together, these reasons are heralding a new generation of Lean. It is exciting. It is inevitable.

13.3 Bureaucracy, The Pyramid and the Sandcastle

The pyramid structure is the legacy of Max Weber and bureaucracy. It may be argued that Bureaucracy was, for decades, a suitable form of organization where there was a relatively stable environment, less educated workers, a shortage of supply over demand, and less demanding customers.

"On October 5, 1841, two Western Railroad passenger trains collided somewhere between Worchester, Massachusetts and Albany, New York, killing a conductor and a passenger and injuring seventeen passengers. That disaster marked the beginning of a new management era." These words open Peter Scholtes classic book on leadership. (Scholtes was a friend and colleague of Deming.) Scholtes explains that the term "management" was unknown 300 years ago. As business grew and became geographically dispersed in the 1800's, a way to run these businesses had to be found. But there were no models outside the church and the military, so investigators into the disaster looked to the Prussian army for a model. And there they found the classic organization chart. It was revolutionary. But is it becoming less relevant? And, in particular, how relevant is it for the future Lean enterprise?

Further Readings.
Peter Scholtes, *The Leaders Handbook*, McGraw Hill, 1998.
Gary Hamel and Michele Zanini, *The End of Bureaucracy*, Harvard Business Review, Nov/Dec 2018

The Sandcastle

As a way of transitioning away from the classic organisation chart, we here consider the Sandcastle. The analogy of a sandcastle to has been used to describe organisations and their environment, usually in non-Lean contexts. But it is also a useful analogy in a Lean context. Of course, the analogy assumes a sandcastle being built on a beach – an unstable foundation.

- The castle is built from many small elements.
- It is a delicate structure. It requires continual rebuilding. Left alone, it will gradually disintegrate.

- It can easily be swept away by wind, rain and tides. There is no such thing as the sustainable sandcastle. (Sustainable from a longevity point of view.)
- Wind happens frequently; tides happen regularly, and occasionally it rains. These are analogous to changes that will almost certainly occur. Some can be accurately predicted – tides. Wind will happen continually. Rain occasionally. One cannot predict, but one can prepare. Like a scout – be prepared!
- Some protection can be given – windshields and moats – but these are limited in the face of wider forces. But most important is continual maintenance.
- Wind 'chips away' continually. Such ignored erosion is similar to managers 'taking their eye off the ball'. What happens is similar to what happens in organisations – small changes, then sudden collapse of a major part.
- The moisture of the sand is analogous to education and training. If dry, the castle will be difficult to build. Some moisture is required. Some light watering is necessary after building. But too much can destroy – or will be wasted.
- Location and timing are important. Don't build when threatened by the tide.
- Incremental building. Many sandcastles are built on the beach in a piecemeal fashion. Likewise in operations – bits are added and subtracted. Can a unified plan be maintained, or will it end up as a mess?
- There is the Sandpile model developed by statistician George Box (he of 'all models are wrong but some models are useful.') Here grains of sand are added one at a time. Most of the time, nothing happens. But very, very occasionally adding just one more grain leads to an avalanche. This is when the angle of repose is exceeded. This is a warning. Just as with the Queueing Model we can get caught out when a tipping point is reached. Just one more order, or just one more customer, just one more part shortage or one more machine breakdown, can throw the system into chaos. The point is that numerous knock-on effects may then happen. When exactly this might happen is hard to predict – but we can prepare. (Please see the Tipping Point section in the section on Diffusion in the Eight Models Chapter, and Sections 8.9 and 9.1)

Organisation Size and Improvement

In an intriguing article in *Nature* journal, Adams et al showed that people systematically default to searching for additive transformations, and consequently overlook subtractive transformations, particularly when they are under 'cognitive load'. Across eight experiments, participants were asked to improve artefacts, essays, sports venues, and universities. Defaulting to searches for additive changes may be one reason that people struggle to reduce overburdened schedules, institutional red tape and damaging effects on the planet·

So, speculation! This intriguing research showed that when faced with a requirement to improve, people were much more likely (often about 80%) to add to an artifact than to subtract from it. This has, we believe, significant implications for Lean design but also (perhaps) for Continuous Improvement and Organisation growth. Certainly, in the authors' experience in several organisations, when a new manager or CEO sought to improve the offering the person chose the expansion route – for example adding 'customer affairs', 'PR', 'help desks', 'student welfare', 'mindfulness' functions, 'leisure', and so on rather than simplifying, streamlining, or improving direct access.

Further Readings.
G.S. Adams, B.A. Converse, A.H. Hales, *et al.*, 2021, 'People systematically overlook subtractive changes', *Nature* 592, 258–261. https://doi.org/10.1038/s41586-021-03380-y

13.4 Pyramids or Streams?

The evolution of organisation types, from military to agile, has been the subject of numerous studies for centuries. Organisation studies have been concerned, amongst others, with structure, bureaucracy, span of control, information flows and reporting. We have found a recent comparison of organisation types by Laloux to be particularly relevant.

However, although organisations have been widely studied, specific studies of Lean organisations are much more limited.

Here, we will take the view that it is useful to study Lean and Agile enterprises as combinations of value streams. An enterprise will very commonly consist of several types of organisational value streams. For instance there may be a design value steam with members having a loose, open structure, a repetitive manufacturing value stream with a Toyota-like manufacturing philosophy, and a service value steam adhering to an open-systems approach. Even very well-established Lean enterprises will have several types of value stream.

In the table, four types of value stream organisation are compared. These types are perhaps extremes usually with some minor overlap with other types.

- The Tools Type. These value streams have approached Lean with a focus on tools, but thus far playing down the people aspects. Bob Emiliani would label this type 'Fake Lean'. This type is the direct legacy of Fred Taylor, Ford, and Scientific Management. It can yield positive gains, at least for a while. The classic Lean tools of changeover reduction, 5S, basic kanban, together with a fairly strict following of work standards would be found. Can it be sustained? Often the results will fall short of expectation.
- The Repetitive Type. The most common manufacturing type of value stream, although very often not applied to its full potential. Reasons are many – very often due to a failure of leadership - as outlined in this book. The Repetitive Type is also to found in some 'back office' situations where there is minimal customer contact, a limited range of variety of work, and creativity is limited. Robotic Process Automation (RPA) is found in such value streams. Fast food and supermarket checkout are of this type.
- The Service Type. A relative newcomer to Lean organisation. Many service organisations. Here, office, better call centres, field service,
- The Evolutionary Type. Although many design groups have been using similar approaches for decades, an exciting development over the past two decades has been the slow emergence of similar concepts being applied in a range of organisations in service, health and manufacturing. In 2016 Thomas Friedman said, 'The best jobs in the future are what I call STEMpathy jobs – jobs that blend Science, Technology, Engineering, and Math with human empathy.' Fred Laloux sees an evolution in organisation – Red, Amber, Orange, Green and finally to the just-emerging 'Teal' type. Detailed characteristics of each are given in Laloux's breakthrough book. Brief descriptions of some Green and Teal organisations (such as Haier and Buurtzorg) are given in Section 13.9 below. The 'Open Book Management' movement begun by Jack Stack are a hybrid, which seem to be growing steadily. (For convenience, the Green and Teal types are called 'Evolutionary' in this section.)

Characteristic	Value Stream Type			
	Tools	Repetitive	Service	Evolutionary
Purpose	Profit /ROI	People	Customers	Product, Future
Focus	Waste	Flow	Satisfaction	System success
Classic Area	Assembly	Assembly	Front line	Design
Division of labour	Narrow, Highly specialised	Limited range of tasks	Limited range of tasks	Wide, shared tasks
Viewpoint	One best way	Several best ways	Limited flexibility	Exploratory
People	As machines	Bring brain to work	As resources	As individuals
Environment	Stable	Fairly stable	Fairly variable	Variable
Management	Command and Control	Transactional	Transformational	Self-directed
Decisions	Top down	Top down and bottom up	Participative	Decentralised
Managers Role	Instruct	Coach	Assist	Small
People	Individual	Teams	Teams	Teaming
Info flow	Upstream	Up and down	Up and down	Horizontal
Hierarchy	Pyramid	Flat pyramid	Inverted pyramid	None / very flat
Functions	Specialist	Expanded specialist	Specialist to generalist	Shared amongst team
Improvement	Experts	Expected by front line	Front line with managers	Everyone
Improvement cycle	None	PDCA	PDCA?	OODA / LAMDA
Mapping	VSM	Follow the object	Follow the customer	Data mining?
Learning	Taught then apply	Primarily at the Gemba	Whilst doing	Whilst doing
Method	Scientific	Scientific	Sense and Respond	Experiment
Motivation	Extrinsic	Extrinsic and Intrinsic	Extrinsic and Intrinsic	Intrinsic
Failure	Bad news	Opportunity	Fix	Expected. Fail fast.
Communication	Reporting	Gemba meetings	Team Meetings	Integral, always
Standards	Instructed	Learn	Adapt	Few
Measures	Monitored	As triggers	As triggers	Outcomes
Variation	Destroys value	Destroys value	May destroy	Adds value
Task sequence	Sequential	Sequential	Not sequential	Not sequential
Queues	Visible	Usually visible	Not visible	Usually not visible
Performance Reviews	By manager	Manager and team leader	Manager and team leader	By peers
Rewards	Individual, bonus	Team and individual	Team and individual	Team

It is not the case that any of the four types of value stream organisations can be applied successfully in any situation. A particular type may be unsuitable or even disastrous in a particular situation. For instance, we have seen:

- the Repetitive type unsuccessfully applied in hospitals and universities.
- the use of transactional mapping and tools in some office environments that have very little repetitive work, often attempting to 'force fit' manufacturing mapping in other environments.
- numerous cases of the Tools type not working well or even failing. However, the Tools type has been seen to work quite well early on during a Lean transformation, and appears to work satisfactorily in some cultures. (Some regions, not necessarily countries, seem more tolerant of command and control. This can change with time and with the local economy.)
- the Evolutionary type unsuccessfully applied in the same company where it has worked well in a different country

It is the case that the most suitable type is certainly situation specific – in fact, rather than being specifically selected, a particular type often evolves out of company and management culture and out of economic circumstance.

Please note that the four types above are not all-inclusive. There are many non-Lean, or beginner-Lean, enterprises that remain traditional or bureaucratic, and where none of the above types can be found except perhaps in pockets that have developed their own way of working.

Moreover, as will be explained below, not only can several types of organisational value stream be found within an enterprise, but each organisational value stream type should be thought of as falling somewhere along a spectrum of development or evolution – from beginner to advanced.

- For the Repetitive Type, Toyota's assembly lines have developed over half a century to todays' participative value streams incorporating all aspects of the 'House of Lean' as discussed in Chapter 1. Developed Repetitive value steams would incorporate most of the Established Approaches described in Chapter 3.
- Service Value stream organisations are evolving rapidly towards system thinking and Agile. Forward-thinking service value streams would incorporate some features of Seddon's Check Methodology as described in the Systems Chapter (Chapter 5).
- The Evolutionary Type of value stream organisation is possibly the oldest type of value stream organisation in as far as designers and innovators have been using what we would now regard as Lean for hundreds of years. At the same time, the Evolutionary type has examples of the newest, most radical types of organisation to emerge in recent years. These types herald a way into the future for many enterprises and, we believe, will gradually subsume the other types. We will focus on this type below.

Please note: The four types of Value Stream should not be confused with Laloux's Organisation Types.

Further Readings.
Frederick Laloux, *Reinventing Organizations*, Nelson Parker, 2014

13.5 Parkinson's Law, Overload and Underload.

In 1958, Northcote Parkinson, in a humorous book on the Civil Service, proposed his famous law: 'Work expands so as to fill the time available for completion'. Of course, this is in everyone's experience. When a new employee starts work, it takes some days to learn the job. Thereafter the new employee settles in to (say) a 9 to 5 job. The job takes the full working time – but no slack and no extra. Leave is somehow often accommodated without extra resources. A tribute to a brilliant manager who arranges capacity to the minute! Or is it a case of elastic work? Parkinson humorously (but unfortunately true to life) describes how managers justify taking on extra staff thereby enhancing their own status and leading to yet more staff on support functions such as HR and accounting. Parkinson calculated (he even gave a formula!) that staff accumulate at an average rate of 5.75% per year. That is doubling every 14 years! A board meeting size also grows in size, eventually leaving behind the five key members who actually make the key decisions before the meeting. Meeting layout is important. The table length will decide the meeting length but with issues being actually decided by the centre bloc. And 'the Law of Triviality' whereby, in a finance committee, 'the time spent on any item of the agenda will be in inverse proportion to the sum involved'. Undue time is spent on trivia (but things that board members understand) against a short time on big spending proposals the technical details of which aren't really understood by most board members. Discussion is limited because of a fear of appearing ignorant amongst peers.

'Big fleas have little fleas on their backs to bite 'em, and little fleas have lesser fleas and so ad infinitum'.

In a remarkable 1978 book Leslie Chapman described the tendency towards non-deliberate over-manning in the civil service. Expansion goes unopposed, but 'cuts' are fiercely resisted by managers and unions. If anything goes wrong (safety, service failures, delays) 'the cuts' are blamed. So, play it safe. It can be career limiting to risk health and safety, so additional resources in this area are seldom called into question. This is not to decry health and safety, but when does necessary health and safety become excessive?

All this is fun, but casual observation attests to the accuracy. It represents a great opportunity in an area that any collection of writings, or conferences, in the Lean area will show to have been largely overlooked.

Parkinson's Law, and Chapman, seems also to apply to inventory and to space. If there is space available, we fill it with inventory (or books, or junk!). If you have excess inventory, you may get a warning, but delivery failure risks your job. So, the response is to keep that inventory!

Mullainathan and Shafir have also explored both underload and overload. Underload is procrastination and 'fat'. Like Parkinson or Yerkes-Dodson. (See next section). We tend to focus more effectively as deadlines approach. When a deadline is far off, we tend to 'juggle' several tasks. We are easily diverted. Several studies (for instance by Speier) show that when interrupted, especially when doing high level mental work, it takes time to regain previous productivity levels – typically 10 or 15 minutes. Similarly Steven Covey spoke about a 2 x 2 matrix of important and urgent. A common tendency is to work on activities that are urgent but not important, whilst giving lower priority to non-urgent but important tasks. Goldratt talked about the 'student syndrome' where, if excess time is available, we tend to take the slack time upfront, and then have to work especially hard if any delay occurs. Levitt and Dubner quote research (and common experience) that productivity or effort tends to increase where there are realistic targets that are under the control of the user. Mullainathan and Shafir say that 'focus' improves with time pressure – the less critical is cut out and productivity improves. During the Falklands war the liner Canberra had to be refitted for troops. The estimate was that it would take 3 months. They were given a week, and made a satisfactory conversion. Of course, there are limits to this. A well-known phrase is *'if you want a piece of work to be completed, give it to a busy person'*.

A particular challenge is that, with excess time, juggling or work expansion takes place. Some workers slow down. Others don't sit idly by, but instead engage in extra, mainly non-urgent or 'bells and whistles' work. They feel busy look busy and are busy. Of course, they are convinced of their own value – such is confirmation bias. (The human tendency to give attention and justification to everything that supports their position; criticise anything does not.) With the best of intentions, they take on extra work on their own initiative. Some initiatives pay off, but other work simply disappears.

In one case where one of the authors worked, the highly regarded HR department set up data bases, did surveys, organised events, prepared notices, set up a newsletter, and arranged visits. All good things, but all call on the time of time-limited others who are involved with direct value adding activities. In another case, as part of a Lean project, all the activities and reports undertaken within an accounting department were listed. The chief accountant had no knowledge of some of these activities and reports.

But others may genuinely be overloaded. According to Mullainathan and Shafir, when work overload occurs work-arounds begin. Unrealistic, imposed, targets (including 'stretch' targets that are literally sucked out of the air) are often the cause. Some activities are left less than fully completed ('borrowing') in order to complete the task by the target time. Other activities are skipped ('tunnelled'). Yet another problem is over-specialisation or standardisation. The danger is that work (or worse, customers) is passed from section to section because workers see their roles too narrowly. The focus is on meeting targets not solving customer problems. But, of course, all of these often result in excessive time, defects, rework, or to use the Seddon term, 'failure demand' (Repeat demand occurring due to not doing something or not doing something completely.) Productivity is destroyed by failure demand, so overload and unrealistic targets are worse than self-defeating!

Today, many people 'multitask'. We all think we can multitask, but numerous studies show how multitasking reduces concentration or productivity. When driving and nearing your destination, do you switch off the radio? This is really the difference between what Kahneman terms 'System1' (automatic) and 'System 2' (deliberate) thinking. Margaret Heffernan says, 'Humans do not have enough mental capacity to do all the things we think we can do. As attentional load increases, attentional capacity gradually diminishes.'

Further Readings.
Leslie Chapman, *Your Disobedient Servant*, Penguin, 1978
Steven Levitt and Stephen Dubner, *Think Like a Freak*, Allen Lane, 2014
Sendhil Mullainathan and Eldar Shafir, *Scarcity*, Allen Lane, 2013
C. Northcote Parkinson, *Parkinson's Law or The Pursuit of Progress*, John Murray, 1958

13.6 Stress, Overload, the Yerkes-Dodson Law, and What to do

The growth of people employed in non-routine work, particularly in overhead functions that are justified on the basis of gut feel, is perhaps the greatest cause of 'fat' in organisations. Why does this happen?

It is relatively easy to calculate the required number of people working in repetitive operations where a physical product is involved. The methods and formulas are known. (A brief summary is given in the Appendix to this Chapter.) But uncertainty begins as one moves further from the front line. There is also uncertainty in service, where for instance call centre operators deal with elastic-duration customer requests. In project management, cost and time overruns persist despite advances in project planning. Witness the Scottish parliament building – three years late and costing £400 million – 10 or more times the original estimate and double the revised estimate.

To add to the uncertainty, in operations management there is often an implicit assumption that the rate of work is independent of load. For instance, the standard time for a job – whether in manufacturing or service – remains constant irrespective of time pressures or work pressures. This is incorrect, as shown by old and by recent research. For Lean, and particularly in office and service operations, the implications are important.

As long ago as 1908, the Yerkes-Dodson law, as it became known, proposed a relationship between performance and 'arousal' (!) – or stress or workload. This is an arch-shaped parabola, with performance falling off below and above a certain level. Above a certain level the pressure of work leads to errors and work skipping. Below the optimal level workers slow down, lose concentration, and again become more careless. Decision making suffers at high workload and at low workload. Moreover later research, summarised by Neiss, suggests that with complex tasks the optimal level of workload shifts downwards. In other words, in complex tasks work 'overload' begins at a lower level. Neiss notes that the effect has been widely observed.

The Goldilocks Effect is named after the Children's fairy tale. Goldilocks comes across three pots of porridge in the bear's house. One is too hot, one is too small, one is just right. An easy-to-understand concept but with important implications. 'Goldilocks' has been used in many fields – medicine, biology, economics and psychology. Playing sport against a beginner or against an Olympic winner is not much fun, but is fun when the opposition is 'just right'.

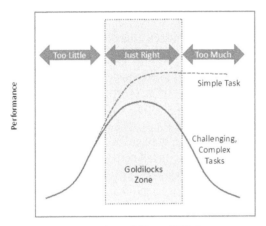

Yerkes-Dodson can also be aligned with Muda, Muri, Mura – particularly Muri (overload). (Please refer to Section 4.8 on Queues.) Muri leads on to personal stress but also, through utilization, onto several types of Muda, and to increasing lead time.

Henry Ford, back in 1926, caused managerial dismay when he adopted a 40 hour work week – five days of 8 hours, against six days of 12 hours. But the outcome was an increase in productivity and a decrease in worker turnover. Many studies have since been undertaken concerning increases in workload. Typically there is a short-term gain in output, but a long-term decline. Unfortunately some managers gain recognition and bonus from the short-term results, leaving successors to pick up the pieces. Overload also cuts down the possibility for improvement. These effects have been modelled by Repenning and Sterman. (See Section 8.3 for detail.)

Toyota understands much of this. Muri is overload. As pointed out by Pound and Spearman, the Toyota system works well because, amongst other things, overcapacity or effective overcapacity is built in with time buffers between shifts, a low worker to team leader ratio, and balancing lines to perhaps 90% of takt time. For instance, the Andon system simply would not be possible if there was not a second to spare. Kaizen could not be practised with excessive time pressures. Time is needed to listen. Of course, some notable companies deliberately encourage extra time. Google famously allowed 20% of time to tackle 'what if' questions, and W.L.Gore allows 10% of time for independent projects and does not have job titles. The hugely successful on-line retailer Zappos does not have work standards for their call centre operators who are expected to stay on a call for as long as it takes.

Readers will recognise similarities with the section on Kingman's equation. This also shows how, at utilization rates approaching 100%, queues ('lines' in USA) or delays explode exponentially. So, overload begins at less than 100% utilization. The culprit in Kingman's equation is variation. According to Kingman's equation, variation makes little difference at low levels of utilization, but really bites at high utilization. Of course, at low utilization productivity is low. At low levels of utilization, 'juggling' or 'soldiering' (Fred Taylor), or 'work expansion' (Parkinson's Law) takes place. At high utilization or overload, queues, rework, and failure demand result. Conceptually, then, there is an optimal level of work load.

Both underload and overload are undesirable, but hard to detect. But how to combat underload and overload? We don't know, but some suggestions:

- Nudge. Deliberately limit the space for storage in office, plant and warehouse. Don't allow cc e-mails. Have no-meeting times. Hold stand-up meetings.
- Listing of tasks. Only listed and displayed tasks may be performed. Only listed and displayed reports may be produced. Everyone to show their activity planning on a visual board.
- Limit multi-tasking. For instance, in design a maximum of (say) three projects at a time.
- Focus on purpose. Tasks that do not relate directly to customer purpose should be reviewed regularly by internal customers. New staff are only taken on after review.
- Standard work: An essential in artefact manufacture, but be very careful in service work not to create failure demand with pressurised standard times. The most productive call centres' prime requirement is customer purpose, not meeting standard times. Standardising a sequence may well be beneficial in service, but standardising detail activity may lead to problems.
- Allow sufficient time and authority to complete customer tasks. This means opening up job specifications and widening standard work to cover the key points.
- Flex resources. Encourage flexible working between functions, so that people can move according to load from function to function – material handing to cell, office to call centre, warehouse to delivery. Office areas have lights to indicate 'do not disturb' and 'doing non purpose' work.
- Time buffers. Allow time for variation and improvement. Do not balance lines to 100% takt or 100% utilization. Allow time between shifts for catch up.

Further Readings.

Steven Levitt and Stephen Dubner, *Think Like a Freak*, Allen Lane, 2014
Rob Neiss, 'Reconceptualizing arousal: psychobiological states in motor performance', *Psychological Bulletin*, 3, p. 345, 1988
Ed Pound, Jeffrey Bell, Mark Spearman, *Factory Physics for Managers*, McGraw Hill, 2014
Repenning and Sterman, 'Nobody ever gets credit for fixing problems that never happened', *California Management Review*, Summer 2001, pp. 64 – 88
John Seddon, *Freedom from Command and Control*, Vanguard, 2003

13.7 Layout: Assembly Line, Cells and Seru Production

The assembly Line has been a feature of Lean and its predecessors for over a hundred years ever since Henry Ford set up the Highland Park plant. Car assembly line working was, in turn, allegedly learned from cattle dis-assembly in Chicago. Assembly line working is well suited to high volume repetitive work. The concept is of a conveyor belt with parts being delivered to the line on a just-in-time basis. Flow is possible where there is minimal or no changeover at any stage. Changeover time, however, meant producing in batches which would work against the continuous flow concept – so changeover reduction became an early lean initiative. Ford began to squeeze waste out of the line – a quest that continues today in all assembly lines. Some automotive plants aim to have 2 hours-worth of parts, or less, on the line. 'Lean' has consistently aimed at the elimination of buffers. (There may be feeder lines or cells flowing into the main line, controlled by pull systems. A supermarket is a more extensive buffer, used when there is a variety of parts that can be pulled in a non-sequential order.)

A Toyota assembly line is seldom straight – because S shapes are more compact and facilitate communication between sections. Importantly the line is broken into segments with an inventory buffer between segments. This allows the Andon system to work. If a worker experiences a problem, he or she can pull the Andon cord to summon immediate help. If the problem is not resolved within the takt time, the line will stop. The Andon system thus brings worker empowerment to the line – a radical departure from Henry Ford's concept. In addition to the Andon cord, an overheard display board shows production progress, time lost, and problem stations. Music and lights are sometimes used as signalling systems.

Toyota also operates a limited flexible time arrangement, where workers are expected to stay at work in order to complete the schedule. This helps near-perfect schedule attainment.

A full assembly line can be very efficient for high volume, limited variety, production, but often is expensive to set up, with purpose designed equipment, automation and robots.

A limitation with the assembly line is boredom, combined with rigorous physical requirements. A repetitive process carried out every minute is physically tough. Job rotation can help, as can team leader support, job rotation, and involvement in improvement activities. Balancing the line – allocating the work between workstations – can be done by workers themselves rather than by industrial engineers. (Bucket Brigade line balance is described in the Appendix.) Nevertheless, plants worldwide now increasingly experience retention and recruitment problems. The drive towards automation, today combined with AI and vision systems, is relentless. Schonberger, in 2009, found that job rotation varied from excellent hourly rotation to a poor 'at least every 10 days'. He described how external monitoring of operator performance can be detrimental and suggested monitoring a cell as a whole leaving the team to sort-out individual performance differences.

What happens if there is a variety of parts, demand uncertainty, and where large investment means that a full assembly line cannot be justified? Enter the cell or Seru concept.

Cellular production has long been established. In the 1970's Group Technology (G.T.) – a part classification and coding methodology – became established with the aim of identifying families of parts that could be made in a single cell. In March 1983 Hewlett Packard produced their Stockless Production video (still available on U tube) which, apart from showing a skit on pull, also showed a cell at HP together with team problem solving. Boeing has been using Chaku Chaku (literally load-load) cells since the mid 1990's.

A cell is often U shaped (although S shape is also found) and has all the machines necessary to make a family of parts, located right next to each other. Central ideas are low-cost, flexible machines, one piece flow, and pokayoke (or Jidoka) checks. At low demand, one worker can work in the cell. As demand increases more workers are added until, at peak production, there is one worker per machine.

Toyota-type assembly lines were not considered economic or suitable for the low-cost, flexible requirements and short product-life requirements of Sony and Canon. With fluctuating demand and changing products, assembly line cost inefficiencies become apparent. A cell is not only lower capital cost, but can be easily dismantled and reconfigured. A significant physical difference is the replacement of traditional lengthy (sometimes conveyor-driven) assembly lines with much smaller one-piece-flow cells (with human movement of parts) and allowing operators to move easily from one cell to another. A cell can work with various numbers of operators depending on demand.

In the 1990's, Sony and Canon began their cell implementation, calling it Seru Production. A central idea is the supporting socio-technical aspect of team working. Gradually this has extended to self-managing teams to include devolved decision-making, scheduling, materials management, and packaging. As well as offering greater flexibility, Seru cells also deliver significant energy savings.

Both Sony and Canon have realised huge cost-savings in inventory, machines, floor space, lead-time and people by changing to a Seru system. To quote from Yin et al: 'Seru is differentiated by its singular focus on responsiveness as a strategy, with efficiency gains as a secondary priority…. Rather than explaining Seru as a combination of lean and agile approaches, understanding its effectiveness requires that we explore the trade-off between responsiveness and efficiency that Seru illustrates.'

We conclude this section with the words of Richard Schonberger, *"For many kinds of production work, one of lean's central practices, organisation into work cells, has remarkable implications. Unless squelched by restrictive management, intense peer pressure tends to bring out the best attributes of each cell associate. Cell teams come to value member differences, some with task proficiency, others skilful as innovators, or communicators, and so forth. Cell members come to be perceptive of what makes the unit function well. Some conventional management devices such as performance appraisals become better handled through peer pressure and teammate savvy."*

Schonberger maintains that, in Western companies, 'blockages' from accounting and marketing often result in higher inventories, preventing the full potential of cells to be realised

Further Readings.
Richard Schonberger, The Human (HR) side of Lean, *Target,* Fourth Issue, 2009
Yong Yin, Kathryn Stecke, Morgan Swink, Ikou Kaku, 'Lessons from Seru production on manufacturing competitively in a high cost environment, *Journal of Operations Management,* 49-51, pp 67-76, 2017

13.8 Transitioning to the Future Lean Organisation

The move from Command to Participative is not easy or fast. But as discussed it is a relentless pressure that many organisations face, or will soon face. There are several dimensions as shown in the Figure below. Frederic Laloux talks about a paradigm shift along Red, Amber, Orange, Green, and finally emerging Teal organisations. (The essential characteristics of each are given in a table in his book, page 36). The evolution has taken place over hundreds or thousands of years, but accelerating since the industrial revolution. This is not to say that all organisations evolve together. There remain Red (gangs), Amber (many government agencies), Orange (some multinationals), and Green (culture-driven such as SouthWest Airlines or Ritz-Carlton Hotels.)

Some of the developing characteristics trending towards the new generation of Lean organisation are shown in the Figure.

Trending towards True Lean	
Us and them	Just Us
Tall (Vertical)	Flat (Horizontal)
Functions	Teams
Specialisation	Participative
Leader managed	Self managed
Machine	Living system
Plan and optimise	Sense and respond
Economies of scale	Economies of time
Experts 'solve' problems	Improve together
Short term	Medium or Long Term
Exploit natural resources	Conserve natural resources
Strong external criteria	Largely internal criteria

This is an organisational transition not an individual change. Within any organisation there will be people with different viewpoints, from command to participative. It is the organisational centre of gravity that shifts. Not everyone will be happy with a transition. Doris Day sung of 'Ready, Willing and Able' – all three need a green light.

Organisations – actual and typical are shown in the Figure below. A particular organisation may vary significantly along both dimensions from that shown. It is also the case that within many medium and large organisations, both the degree of participation and the flexibility of processes varies considerably depending on function. In the figure below, typically, HR, R&D, and Design groups are to be found towards the top right, Accounting and IT in the centre, and Operations towards the bottom left. There are pressures from all these groups to move upwards and to the right.

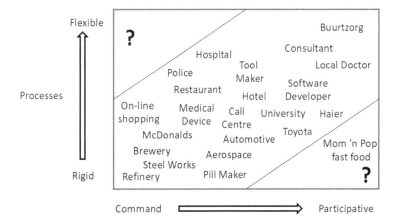

We may note that Toyota is placed mid-way along the trend. Although Toyota has made huge progress in participation and 'respect', the very complex challenge of making a car means that processes cannot be as flexible as (say) in a hotel. Thus Toyota is shown as being more participative but also more rigid with respect to processes compared with the average (say) hotel. On the other hand, a volume manufacturer like Haier (with their team-based structure and flat hierarchy) may point the way to the future.

We believe that a transition in Lean is developing. It is already here in some innovative organisations. The future Lean organisation will be flatter, more flexible, more participative.

13.9 The Emerging Organisation

Alternatives to the traditional pyramid-type bureaucracy have been slowly emerging over the past two decades, but the numbers of organisations with innovative structures seem to have picked up recently. The classic exponential curve appears to in operation – like Kingman's Queue curve the numbers are barely recognisable in early years but soon become significant.

We believe these different models of organisation represent nothing less than a new generation of Lean – with dramatically less hierarchy, greater participation, devolved authority, and much more agility. Steep pyramid bureaucracy was appropriate – and beneficial – in an age where sellers had the power, customers were less demanding, competition was less international, employees were less demanding about empowerment and information was much less widespread. All that has changed.

Here we consider just some of the exciting pioneer organisation innovations.

We are not suggesting that moving towards more democratic, participative organisation is easy. The risks and barriers are great, for example the raising of capital – made more challenging by a management whose privileged position is threatened. A significant barrier is achieving a reasonable degree of financial literacy, and an ability to identify and respond to changes in key performance variables. There are several alternatives from participation without direct financial incentive to a bonus scheme to stock options (ESOP) to full ownership. A spectrum of possibilities.

We recognise that participative organisations such as those described below face two significant barriers:
- They may be seen as a threat to established hierarchy, authority and privilege.
- When an organisation can make more money by transfer pricing, circular goods movement, tax reduction by various means including international accounting, who would bother with participative organisation particularly if such have to be made more transparent?

Koen de Boer of Semco Institute makes a useful point to begin: There is a difference between self-management and self-direction. Self-managing means that the team or value stream are responsible for achieving an objective as set by the wider organisation. Management makes the strategic decisions. 'The teams are responsible, but management remains accountable.' Self-directed means that the team has freedom to set their own goals and are able to make strategic decisions. 'Teams are responsible as well as accountable.'

Here we briefly mention some organisations and approaches that we consider to be pointers towards the Lean organisation of the future. But first, we will take a step back some 350 years..

Pirates

Pirates (yes, Pirates like Blackbeard) had, surprisingly for some, a highly democratic, participative form of organisation. We are not talking about Somali pirates or Roman pirates but about the Golden Age of Piracy between 1690 and 1725.

We are not suggesting that a Lean-aspiring organisation should adopt a pirate form of organisation. We *are* suggesting that several pirate concepts from 300 years ago are relevant for todays and tomorrows Lean-aspiring organisations.

As Steve Jobs said, 'I'd rather be a pirate, than join the navy.'

Piracy was so successful that many sailors, some of whom had been press-ganged into the Royal Navy and suffered lashing, defected to pirate groups. Pirates fostered a fearsome reputation, but this was a deliberate sham because they did not really want to risk their lives or their ship in a battle. Ammunition was expensive, as were ship repairs. Instead, when the black flag was shown, crews knew that if they surrendered, they would be fairly treated if they acknowledged the authority of the pirates. Some features of pirate life – which was very Lean – were:

- All participated in major decisions. The only time that the captain could give unilateral commands was during a battle. At other times the captain might propose a course of action which was discussed and voted on.
- A captain was elected and could, and often was, replaced. This was the norm but would be considered mutiny, punishable by death, in the Royal Navy.
- A captain was elected for his (or sometimes her) skills, not through a separate system of promotion where the first step on the exclusive ladder was based on position in society.
- Almost no hierarchy. A captain, a mate (for sailing and logistics) and the crew.
- 'Staff' functions performed by teams. Including training.
- All volunteers. Free to leave anytime.
- Information available to all. Nothing 'confidential'.
- Spoils were shared equally. By consensus the captain would typically receive three shares and the mate two shares. Everyone else had one share, equally distributed.
- Pirates established insurance compensation scheme for any crew member wounded or killed during battle. (This was hundreds of years before any national scheme.)
- The crew included a few women who were treated the same as male crew and received the same share. The crew were typically highly diverse in race, nationality and age.
- Everyone was free to put forward ideas, and were listened to.
- Self-discipline. No lashing. But punishment for untidy conditions, non-clean weapons, or offences against women crew. Such punishment was decided by the crew, not by the captain.

Eventually, pirate society became such a significant threat to British, Spanish, and Portuguese trade that it had to be destroyed. It is said that another reason was that pirate society had become a threat to the establishment in those countries and was increasingly attractive to crewmen from those countries.

Further Readings.
Sam Allende, *Be More Pirate*, Portfolio, 2018

Open Book Management

Open Book Management (OBM) provides one answer to the question 'How can we get all employees to think and act like owners?'. The movement had a boost when Jack Stack took Springfield Remanufacturing Company out of International Harvester bankruptcy in the early 1980's and began his open book approach. In 1992 Stack wrote the book *The Great Game of Business* to explain the approach. Since then The Great Game of Business® is an organisation that holds regular conferences and training events attended by scores of enthusiastic organisations. Jim Collins said of the 20th anniversary edition of the book 'Inspired and inspiring, a classic.' It is called a game because it game-on competing with other companies. Like a game, there are rules, players, a field, an objective.

In OBM almost everyone is a pseudo management accountant, and knows all the 'financials' pertaining to his or her cell and upwards, and sometimes about the entire organisation. They have 'business literacy'. People know each other's' salaries, material and machine costs, marketing and selling costs and prices, inventory and production volumes. Very likely there is profit sharing. They know the debt situation, and the threat of default.

As authors, we have had the opportunity to attend meetings in Open Book Management organisations. It is impressive. Periodically (the period varies) an accountant or manager displays the financials and other data and seeks comment from all in the cell or value stream. By 'all' is meant all. It is like a boardroom discussion. Very often, excellent ideas are discussed relating to strategy, costs, products, and initiatives. Of course, it is a challenge to get people to change their mindset from employee to owner. Some do not like or want such a dramatic change. They leave.

OBM has its critics – saying that too much time is spent on meetings and in educating employees to understand and appreciate the financials, rather than on (say) Lean tools and problem solving. Others are concerned with confidentiality. The response, however, is that people manage their own financial affairs outside of work, and family data is kept confidential. 'People are treated as grown-ups'. One member of an OBM organisation expressed the view that the Lean mantra of 'respect' is simply a 'con' when there is so much secrecy.

An OBM organisation still has hierarchy and functions, and is not as flat as the organisations mentioned below.

"When the bottom rises, the top rises also", says Jack Stack.

Further Readings.
Jack Stack, *The Great Game of Business: 20th anniversary edition*, Crown Business, 2013
Jack Stack, *A Stake in the Outcome*, Currency Doubleday, 2002
John Schuster, et al, *The Power of Open Book Management*, Wiley, 1996
And see https://www.greatgame.com

Case Studies: Towards Future Lean

Some actual organisations, considered by us to be at leading edge of 'Future Lean' will now be briefly described. There are several sources that describe all the organisations below in much greater detail than given here. See further reading at end of section.

Buurtzorg

Buurtzorg is a home nursing organisation started in the Netherlands in 2006. The aim is to deliver a low cost, high quality, personalised service. The organisation has grown rapidly to around 1000 teams with 14,000 nurses supporting around 100,000 people. The teams are self-organised, self-managed, nurse-lead. Buurtzorg has expanded its concept internationally. Remarkably for an organisation this size, the head-office is tiny – less than 100 people. Customer satisfaction is very high, staff turnover is very low, and costs have been estimated at less than half that of state-run or commercial nursing services. The organisation was founded not for profit, but by a male nurse who simply sought to offer a good social service free of unnecessary bureaucracy. As the founder says 'My assumption was that most (of the overhead work) does not need to be done.' (!)

Buurtzorg does not consider itself a Lean organisation, but is truly Lean.

Each team is, in effect, a mini-business tending perhaps 60 patients, some in terminal decline. The nurse teams assess the situation, decide what needs to be done, draft the care plan, schedule the work, carry out the work, and then self-assess their own performance and effectiveness – they are self-accountable. Team members hire colleagues, and do their own purchasing. Any disputes have to be handled by the team. There are specific job roles and these are spread throughout the team. It is a holistic view, based on trust. that allows time spent with patients to be maximised. 'In a hierarchical organisation people tell others what to do, but if you tell yourself what to do you reduce stress.'

For financial compensation, the founder gets only twice what regular nurses get. He is not the CEO but simply a facilitator.

Further Readings. Both the following have extensive material on Buurtzorg.
Frederick Laloux, *Reinventing Organizations*, Nelson Parker, 2014
Joost Minaar and Pim De Morree, *Corporate Rebels*, Corporate Rebels Nederland, 2019

Haier.

Haier, headquarterd in China, is the world's largest white goods appliance manufacturer (and service distributor) with over 75,000 employees. (GE Appliances became majority-owned by Haier in 2016). Haier is the domestic appliance leader using the Internet of Things (IoT). In fact, the internet is a good analogy to the organisation. 'Every employee as an entrepreneur' and 'Zero distance between employees and users are two main drivers. (Thoughts that are not a million miles from Toyota.) Haier has divided itself into over 4,000 loosely connected microenterprises, each with 10 to 15 members and with little central direction, except for broad targets. In that respect, it is very similar to Buurtzorg, but split into three types – essentially for established, new business, and future business. Each type has support enterprises. The microenterprises sell to the open market and also internally – no compulsion to use uncompetitive internal suppliers. The microenterprises, together with external organisations and experts, also collaborate so as to offer package deals of support to customers, and for technical problems. Hamel and Zanini describe Haier as 'a start-up factory'. In that respect Haier mimics, simultaneously, thousands of start-ups as described by Eric Reis. With such distributed innovation, continuing momentum seems assured.

The organisation is probably best seen as a set of concentric circles – certainly not as an organisational pyramid with tiers of managers. The individual microenterprises have huge flexibility. The innovative style has taken decades to evolve – but then so did Toyota.

Taken as a whole, the many working aspects of Haier organisation are complex and described in more detail in the books by Gary Hamel and Michele Zanini, and by Joost Minaar and Pim De Morree.

Further Readings.

Zhang Ruinin, *Raising Haier*, Harvard Business Review, February 2007 (About early days and gaining commitment.)
Gary Hamel and Michele Zanini, *Humanocracy*, Harvard Business Review Press, 2020. (Chapter 5 is all about Haier.)
Joost Minaar and Pim De Morree, *Corporate Rebels*, Corporate Rebels Nederland, 2019

Semco

A participative innovator was Ricardo Semler who inherited Semco from his father and began a quiet revolution, as described in his books *Maverick*, *The Seven Day Weekend*, and in *Harvard Business Review*. We have been fortunate to hear him in person. Semler's *Top 10 Myths about Democratic Management* is available as a free download. The 10 Myths, we believe, represent a significant challenge and opportunity to contemporary Lean and Agile organisation and thinking – in all sectors. Please take 20 minutes to listen to Semler on U Tube.

Semler says that Semco has three values - democracy, profit sharing or 'aligned self-interest', and common sense – that work together with each dependent on the other two. These three remain as the logo for the Semco Institute. On participation, Semler maintains that there are four obstacles: size, hierarchy, lack of motivation, and ignorance. So all policies and actions counter these. Size is countered by encouraging employees to create their own mini-businesses. Hierarchy is countered by showing concentric circles instead of org-chart pyramids. Motivation comes from within by relying on common sense rather than written rules and regulations. Self-managed cells discourage ignorance.

At Semco almost everyone participates in major decisions. People set their own salaries! (But everyone knows what everyone else earns, so responsibility is maintained.) There is very little hierarchy. Self-control takes place in teams. Employees are encouraged to create their own businesses and become Semco suppliers. Semco has been a very successful enterprise for more than 30 years following Semler's philosophy. As such it is a case study showing that absence of command and control is not only possible but very profitable. Our take on Semler's points follow:

- People can work together on their own – in fact they do just this in their private lives all the time
- Self-control is possible. If treated as adults, with respect, they don't have to be controlled. They won't 'goof off'.
- This type of organisation is not limited to small companies – as Semco illustrates. Self-managed groups can multiply without limit.
- The concepts are even more applicable to the emerging workforce of the future.
- The system will continually re-invent itself. People adapt, so why is a company needed to do the adaptation?
- If people have a say about their own salaries, they will not take advantage. Fear is misplaced. In fact it cuts out an enormous amount of bureaucracy.
- Democratic management certainly works with Lean and Agile. (We would go further, saying that it is the future of Lean and Agile!)
- Trust your employees. But really trust them. Investors will follow.

- Move into democratic management in stages or pilots.
- Participative decision making is not a long process. Once decided, buy-in is rapid and smooth.

Today the Semco Institute advises companies throughout the world.

Further Readings.
Ricardo Semler, Managing without Managers, *Harvard Business Review*, Sept/Oct 1989
https://semcostyle.com/

Mondragon

The Mondragon Corporation was started in 1956 by 5 engineers in the Basque region of Spain. It is now a collection of 96 co-operatives, employing 81k people. There is a central co-ordinating function but the co-operatives are essentially separate businesses including 64 industrial, 14 R&D, 8 schools and a university. The various co-operatives do not compete with one another, but certainly compete internationally with outsiders. One co-operative makes cars.

80% of Mondragon Employees ('Members') are owners with the initial investment contribution being € 15k. All members have equal voting rights, and participate in main strategic decisions at least once per year. Day-to-day decisions are made by local managers. All gross profits are distributed as follows:
- 15% to 40% for restructuring – including capital investment.
- 14% for cooperative funds (7% investment; 7% aid for community and wider.)

Then, net profits are distributed
- 10% for education
- 60% for reserves
- 30% to workers: for Members this goes to their capital which may be taken on retirement or retained. Non-members receive their share in cash.

The four founding basics of Mondragon are:
- Dignity – men and women have equal status, and enjoy respect as co-owners. There is a 1:6 compensation ratio between the highest and lowest paid. (In Spain as a whole the ratio is 1:79 – in some countries it exceeds 500.)
- Solidarity. This includes responsibility with the region. No-one is fired for economic reasons.
- Work. Members are workers and owners. No shareholders.
- Education. A commitment. The cooperative supports 8 of its own schools and the Mondragon University – mainly technical.

See
https://www.youtube.com/watch?v=8hEs1bfMAfE

Google / Alphabet

Google does have a conventional org chart (in fact they sell org chart software!) but it has many innovations.

- Any employee can freely access all internal information except for sensitive user data or company finances. All code, project documents, even a colleague's calendar, are available.
- Employees are expected to ask tough questions at weekly company-wide town-hall meetings with the founders, called TGIF, for "Thank God It's Friday" (now held on

Thursdays to allow Googlers around the world to participate without having to get up on Saturday morning).

- The workplace is meant to be playful; hence the playground-like offices, ping-pong tables and the like.
- Originators Sergey Brin and Larry Page used the idea of letting people follow their passions. Google employees were allowed to spend 20% of their time working on what they thought would most benefit the firm, even if that often led to them working 120%. They also often set their own quarterly goals.
- Recruiting and promotion are similar to academia. Candidates are graded like PhD students and decisions about who should move up the corporate ladder are taken by a committee of peers from across the company, rather than individual managers, who sometimes may promote people they like rather than those who would do the best job.
- Google / Alphabet also use Objectives and Key Results (OKRs). See the section on Hoshin and OKRs (Section 3.13). Today, the innovations of CEO Sundar Pichai has taken Google / Alphabet to new highs.

Further Readings.

Gary Hamel and Michele Zanini, *Humanocracy*, Harvard Business Review Press, 2020.
http://panmore.com/google-organizational-structure-organizational-culture
https://www.bbc.co.uk/iplayer/episode/m000xwll/amol-rajan-interviews-sundar-pichai

Other cases

FAVI is a French Foundry, organised into teams or 'mini-businesses' with outstanding delivery, quality and cos. A first-tier automotive supplier, with minimal central planning and scheduling. Team representatives meet and decide their own schedules and resources. Salespeople report directly to the teams. There is no executive team. For detail see Laloux.

Morning Star is now the largest tomato processor in the world, supplying 40% of tomatoes sold in US stores. No managers, no job titles. Colleagues are organised into business units that follow the process. 'Colleagues' have many roles, following the tomato growing and processing season. 'Human beings should not use force or coercion against others, and people should keep to their commitments.' And 'Everything is based on request and response' – not command and control. For detail, see Laloux, and Hamel and Zanini, and Minaar and De Morree.

Laloux on u-Tube: https://www.youtube.com/watch?v=2GlG_ESETgo

Summarising from the Case Studies

- The case studies cover a wide range of business types: manufacturing and service, large and small. After years of gestation, self-direction and participation are emerging as a viable alternative to hierarchy.
- There is no single structure for participative organisations. Laloux gives three generic types: Parallel (as with Buurtzorg), Individual contracting (following stages as with Morning Star), and Nested (teams with different functions – for example Rand D, IT, manufacturing – as with Haier.)
- All the cases do seem to have a strong belief in people, similar to McGregor's Theory X any (Discussed in Section 2.4). A transition from believing that workers ae lazy, only after the money, self-interested, untrustworthy, need to be told, are like interchangeable machine parts – to being creative, accountable, wanting to contribute.

- Self-direction and participation is not for all. People must be able and willing. For a variety of reasons, some people are happy with hierarchy, and being controlled and told. Hence people must self-select and be carefully selected.
- Opposition from entrenched groups can be expected - for instance, some managers and supervisors, and some from PR, HR, and accounting.
- The transition to self-management is a challenge. It seems the way to go is not a 'big bang' but rather emergence on a team-by-team basis. See Samantha Slade.
- The huge growth in overhead functions will inevitably reverse, due to a combination of AI, self-direction, cost, and flexibility.

Further Readings.
Gary Hamel and Michele Zanini, *The End of Bureaucracy*, Harvard Business Review, Nov/Dec 2018
Gary Hamel and Michele Zanini, *Humanocracy*, Harvard Business Review Press, 2020
Frederick Laloux, *Reinventing Organizations*, Nelson Parker, 2014
Joost Minaar and Pim De Morree, *Corporate Rebels*, Corporate Rebels Nederland, 2019
Samantha Slade, *Going Horizontal*, Berrett-Koehler, 2018 (A 'how-to' book rather than case studies)

13.10 Jobs, Skills, and Automation

When discussing people and organisation, managers and economists have long been used to thinking in terms of 'jobs' and 'skills'. An MIT group has suggested that these are misleading terms with today's technology and organisations. A 'job' suggests a uniform indivisible activity. But many people today undertake a variety of tasks during their work. Likewise 'skilled' has been associated with a level of education. Today it is more appropriate to think in terms of *tasks* and whether the task is *routine* or not. Automation was once thought of as affecting low skilled jobs. No longer. With smart phones, Internet of Things, AI, RPA, and automation in general, very many 'jobs' and 'skills', and tasks at all levels, are affected.

With a list of tasks, the impact of automation can be thought of whether each task could be:
- Augmented – for example using AI, data mining, CAD to enhance the capability of the person. AI as a compliment force is discussed in the next section.
- Automated – for example using RPA, or robots in general, to reduce routine or mundane tasks, (but nevertheless necessary) thereby freeing the person to be more creative or to interact better with customers. Here, Customer Journey Maps may be particularly relevant. The long-established Toyota guideline of taking waste out before automating is relevant. (You don't want to automate waste activity.)
- Abandoned. Is the task value-adding? Here value stream maps would be useful.

This shift, away from jobs and skills towards tasks and degree of repetition, is helpful in Lean environments, particularly when automation is being considered.

Automation as Substitute or Compliment, and AI

It is useful to separate the effects of all types of automation into a substitute force or a compliment (augmented) force. Yes, automation can be used to substitute or replace tasks, but it can also be used to compliment or enhance human tasks.

The substitute force – replacing workers with automation - has had most attention in the popular press, but it is the compliment force that is most relevant to Lean organisation. Susskind gives three effects of the compliment forces of automation. *The Productivity effect* uses automation to enhance productivity – for example CAD systems, computer assisted biopsies, or automatic document scanning. Algorithmic stock trading has not always been positive. *The Bigger Pie effect* enhances or opens-up new task possibilities. As people become richer there is increased demand for goods and services many of which involve automation. On-line education is a prime example. (Education has been unchanged for centuries until recently – a lecturer talking to a small group.) Likewise conferences. Blockchain promises a revolution in purchasing and supply. On-line booking for travel or delivery are further examples. Thirdly, there is the *Changing-Pie effect* whereby massive shifts in employment take place – farming to factory to service – mainly driven by automation and energy.

All three of the compliment forces are already having, and will continue to have, profound influence on Lean working.

In particular, AI (artificial intelligence) when combined with IoT (the internet of things) and automation are very likely to have a big influence. Until recently AI was limited to computers, then came the cloud, and now AI is being built-in to IoT devices. Cars are an expanding example. In factories the Digital Twin concept is just beginning, but think of AI-based real-time scheduling that could influence pull system, takt time, inventory level and TPM thinking. And physical tools – for home, health, hospital, hospitality. All this is made more powerful through Metcalf's Law: the effectiveness is proportional to n^2 where n is the number of linked devices. (Metcalf's Law is not new: think of the telephone network.)

Further Readings.
Special Report, 'The Future of Work', *The Economist*, April 10th, 2021
Daniel Susskind, *A World Without Work*, Allen Lane, 2020

13.11 Overcoming Organisational Defences

The late Chris Argyris, Emeritus Professor at Harvard and famous for his theory of single and double loop learning, discusses what he calls 'traps' that work against learning and change. Ironically, a trap works strongest just when learning and change are most needed. A trap is something that shuts down or limits discussion and conversations, amongst others and ourselves – all in the interest of making progress. According to Argyris most of us have two theories of action – one that we actually use and one that we espouse. Argyris calls these Model I and Model II, respectively.

Model I is used to protect the self against disruptive change. It is used whenever we face threatening or embarrassing situations. The objectives are to stay in control, to win and not loose, and to supress negative feeling and behave rationally. With Model II we 'seek testable information, create informed choice, and monitor to detect and correct error.' Argyris says that his research has revealed that few people actually use a Model II theory-in-use, but most have a Model I theory-in-use despite espousing Model II. We think we are creating trust, empowerment, openness, engagement but we erect hidden traps or barriers such as discouragement to speak up, censorship by having topics that are off-limits, blame, fear, closed monitoring and reporting, and communication barriers. Some issues are made non-discussable.

Argyris maintains that without addressing the underlying hidden traps of Model I, change will not be successful. In fact, excessive exhortation suggests a lack of trust in the commitment to change. Jack Welch is quoted as an example. Welch genuinely believed in implementing ideas that nourished the voice and dignity of every person. But then Welch's leadership actions openly challenged, criticized, and embarrassed people if he believed that in doing so they would be motivated.

Argyris maintains that attention to organisational culture is misplaced because it is the underlying theories-in-use that are fundamental. Culture is a by-product of people's behaviour in the organisation, and lies on top of Model I or Model II. (This is consistent with the JCM: Section 4.3)

Appreciative Inquiry is suggested as a way of surfacing the models-in-use. Why? – because by focusing on the positive, it surfaces Model I theory-in-use. So too is direct listening to conversations, and subsequent analysis and feedback. This involves documenting 'what I thought and felt but did not say' side-by-side with 'what we actually said and did'. Surveys, on the other hand, are relatively useless because there is a difference between the respondents' theory-in-use and that which is espoused.

While organisations across the world see increasing employee morale, satisfaction and loyalty as essential to creating a successful efficient business, it could in fact be impeding overall organisational performance. The reason for this lies in the conflict between maintaining a culture of truth and openness but without damaging morale, satisfaction and loyalty. This has particular significance for those tasked with introducing change. How to deal with this paradox is outlined by Chris Argyris in his book *Overcoming Organisational Defenses.*

The proposition is that despite having strong capable leaders, within organisations there exist certain organisational defences which discourage learning and knowledge creation, leading to mediocre organisational performance. This results in leaders creating and maintaining (through their own choice) a working environment and associated business practices, which are contrary to what they publicly advocate. Argyris suggests the reason why individuals and organisations decide to act in ways contrary to their own interests and expressed beliefs is 'defensive reasoning'. Defensive reasoning includes:

- Blaming the system (government?, economy?) rather than learning lessons.
- Organisational inertia in response to new and threatening ideas. Just ignore the treat or pay lip service to it without taking action. 'It will go away in due course.'
- Defensive routines that delay or kill change initiatives.
- 'Fancy footwork' such as (a) Seeking out faults with the organisation but not accepting responsibility for fixing them, (b) Emphasising the negative while minimising the positive, and (c) Advocating values and beliefs that are not implementable but acting as if they are.

A way to reduce the organisational defensive cycle is to not simply deal with the tactics themselves but to go deeper and question why these tactics were tolerated by the people concerned. (Fear? Time? Groupthink? Etc.) Exercise systems thinking, and deal not merely with the individual tactics or events, but ascertain the systemic problems that permit such errors and events to occur. This would often involve moving away from single-loop learning to double loop learning. (Refer to Section 5.5, on Argyris.)

Further Readings.
Chris Argyris, *Organisational Traps: Leadership, Culture, Organizational Design*, Oxford Univ Press, 2010.
Chris Argyris, *Overcoming Organisational Defenses,* Oxford Univ Press, 1990

13.12 Organisation Transformation

Transforming an Organisation is one of the most challenging tasks a Leader can face. This statement is misleading because it may give the impression of a 'big bang' methodology. Whole organisation change is rare, and usually comes about by numerous local changes at cell, functional or departmental level.

In their wonderful book *Transforming Culture*, Briody, Trotter and Meerwarth discuss, from an Anthropological viewpoint, how the significant change at General Motors Corporation took place between approximately the mid 1980's and 2010. During this period GM moved from a dominant market leader to bankruptcy and then to re-emergence. Productivity moved from well below Japanese levels to more recent near-parity. As an Anthropologist, Briody was an observer of culture and cultural change, not a consultant or manager.

Briody, Trotter and Meerwarth use a bridge model to explain the transformation. The bridge shows moving from 'the old way' to the 'ideal culture' using cultural problem solving and enablers to overcome the obstacles. Detailed discussion is given, and we believe the book is an unrecognised 'gem'.

Here we will adopt a more familiar model similar to Value Stream Mapping, moving from Current State to Future State. See the Figure.

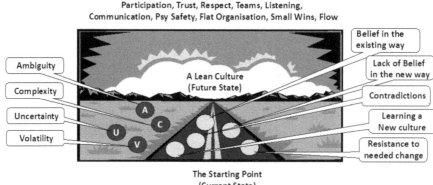

The Figure shows the challenge of transforming a part, or even a whole, organisation from a Current State to a desired Lean Culture. The road has no end, and there are obstacles or boulders along the route and external VUCA boulders rolling towards to road. A particular organisation, or part of an organisation, may be lucky enough not to have all the Current State characteristics as shown, but the actual current state characteristics should certainly be identified. The Shingo Prize may be helpful here, as would 'The Toyota Way' Principles.

Along the road various significant boulders will be encountered. These include
- Overcoming belief in the existing way. 'We have always done it that way', and 'If it's not broke, why fix it?'

- Lack of belief in the new way – both technical and social. 'Kanban is too risky', 'We are not in automotive', 'Sharing is dangerous and time consuming', 'Look at Toyota's failures', 'Lean is Mean', and not least a threat to position and authority.
- Contradictions include mixed messages. 'People are our best asset' – followed by layoffs, Reserved parking, manager bonus, ideas are ignored, no time allowed for improvement. Reward, recognition and payment need to align with the future state. Measures are critical: 'Tell me how you will measure me (or the team) and I'll tell you what I (or we) will do.'
- Learning a new culture cannot be done in a classroom but requires long term commitment. (Toyota sent hundreds of Japanese to work at NUMMI for months, and hundreds of Americans visited Toyota Japan. See the Jack Smith case, Section 10.6)
- Resistance to needed change. Even Henry Ford resisted changing the Model T. Clayton Christensen's brilliant work on disruption is a warning (See Section 8.11)

The enablers of change include many of the concepts outlined in this book: Leader standard work, A3 problem solving, Kata, Habits, Nudge, as well as Engagement methodologies. Demonstrating humility and respect are fundamental.

Further reading
Elizabeth Briody, Robert Trotter and Tracy Meerwarth, *Transforming Culture: Crating and Sustaining a Better Manufacturing Organisation*, Palgrave Macmillan, 2010

13.13 'Bullshit' and the Lean Organisation

Bullshit (BS) has always been present, but more serious discussion of BS has escalated in recent years with the publication of books and articles.

An alternative word to BS is 'Stupidity' – used by Alvesson and Spicer. There is overlap here with functional stupidity being 'the inclination to reduce one's scope of thinking and focus only the narrow technical aspects of the job'. It is about the widespread tendency to avoid deep thinking, about not questioning, not using educational potential. People learn to 'not rock the boat' and believe in an unquestioning way that their 'company pursues excellence'. The paradox spoken about by Alvesson and Spicer is that despite increasing requirements for higher levels of education for jobs, such education is too often not used or is too narrowly used.

BS and Stupidity has seldom been linked to Lean, but surely the identification and reduction of both should be a prime concern for Lean practitioners. Here we will generally stay with the words BS, recognising the overlap with stupidity.

BS comes in various categories:
- BS jobs
- BS in data and measures
- BS in media – including publications, writings, and the web
- BS and Red Tape in Bureaucracy

'There is so much bullshit. Everyone knows this. Each of us contributes his share.' With this, Harry Frankfurt opens his little book *On Bullshit*. BS, says, Frankfurt, is not lying. Rather, it is about deceptive misrepresentation – of speech or action.

Two true stories:

During the week that this section was written, it was widely reported that a group of Italian workers had been discovered drawing salary for 10 years without actually going to work. In one case a 'worker' would clock in, in his underpants, and then return to bed.

In an organisation familiar to one of the authors, a newly appointed C-suite executive insisted that he needed a PA. This was a new appointment, and a PA was duly appointed. In a short period the PA, with encouragement from the executive, took various initiatives including, amongst others, expanding the web site, carrying out internal surveys (that were time-consuming for hard-pressed employees), upgrading the office, introducing a newsletter, proposing selective re-branding, assembling new data from internal and external sources, and appointing consultants to help with these initiatives. For all of this, great praise was lavished. Soon, the PA said she was overwhelmed and an assistant to her was appointed. Within days the assistant was 'fully occupied.' (A case of Parkinson's Law: 'work expands to fill the time available'?). Interesting, however, was that an improvement initiative, instigated by the same C-suite executive, looked only at front-line streams, resulting in redundancies....

BS Jobs

The late left-wing professor David Graeber focused on BS jobs, defining a BS job as 'a form of paid employment that is so completely pointless, unnecessary, or pernicious that even the employee cannot justify its existence even though, as part of the conditions of employment, the employee feels obliged to pretend this is not the case.'(page 9).

Graeber claims that many thousands of workers – predominantly female and middle-class – have self-identified as having a BS job. For instance, his research reveals that some nurses spend as much as 80% of their time on paperwork and meetings, whereas bricklayers are largely unaffected. (So there are partly BS jobs, mostly BS jobs, and purely and entirely BS jobs.). Many, however, do not self-identify but, instead self-justify the essential BS nature of their work.

Please note: Graeber's studies produced much reaction. Some follow up studies disagreed with his percentages of BS jobs and his survey methods.

The proportion of time spent on admin (containing significant BS) has grown steadily, especially among professional, managerial, sales and service workers. This is one explanation why office technology (PCs, e-mail, web, numerous types of software, etc.) has thus far made little impact on productivity. Alvesson and Spicer point out that at most UK universities, the administrative staff far outnumbers the academic staff, despite the admin load on academics actually increasing. Graeber concedes, following the earlier section on tasks instead of jobs, that many jobs are broken down into some tasks that fit with his definition of BS and other tasks that are necessary or worthwhile.

The 2019 US State of Enterprise Work Report for office workers gives their 'best guess estimate' for the percentage of time taken up during a week as 44% performing primary duties and 10% attending useful or productive meetings. E mails and administration account for a further 26%, and other (including interruptions and wasteful meetings) the remaining 20%. Of course these are estimates across many types of job, so wide variation is likely. Nevertheless the opportunity seems vast.

Graeber gives outsourcing as a significant reason for the growth of BS jobs. For example, (and similar has happened to one of the authors), hanging a whiteboard in an office may require notifying maintenance, who in turn contact the maintenance company, that arranges an inspection visit, orders the whiteboard, receives it and checks it into stock, and then schedules a workman together with travel, insurance, health and safety checks and, using scheduling software, followed by the task itself. All this with numerous e mails to arrange suitable times, parking, confirmations, and invoicing – to say nothing of setting up the contract in the first place, involving staff from both the office organisation and the contractor. Once, this could have been done in-house, same day, with one phone call. (Another example is the pothole story discussed in the Systems chapter.)

Graeber identifies five varieties of BS jobs: (Here, although broadly agreeing with Graeber we think it is better to use the word tasks rather than jobs):

- 'Flunkies' – tasks that exist primarily to make someone else look or feel important. Examples might be (some) survey cold-callers, receptionists, gatekeepers, HR assistant, personal assistant.
- 'Goons' – these have an aggressive element, such as (some) lobbyists, telemarketers, corporate lawyers, pension advisers. Scam telephone threats.
- 'Duct Tapers' – tasks that exist to fix problems that have arisen from a source within the organisation, or who merely transcribe forms from one source to another.
- 'Box Tickers' – auditors and administrators who fill out documents, regulations and checks, and prepare reports, that essentially almost no-one reads. 'Cover your backside'.
- 'Taskmasters' – allocating and or monitoring people when there is essentially no need to do so. Supervising people who don't need supervision. The opposite of Flunkies – these are unnecessary superiors rather than unnecessary subordinates.

According to Graeber, a major reason for BS jobs is that many people simply need the money and are prepared to put up with jobs that they know, after a little reflection, are simply BS. Graeber's (controversial) solution is a system of Universal Basic Income that would free many who are locked into BS jobs to do worthwhile things that benefit society: social, environmental, creative, educational, experimental. We would suggest other remedies as adopted by some organisations discussed earlier in this chapter..

BS in statistics and measures

For years there has been much BS data, statistics and measures that mislead – some deliberate, some innocent. A classic work on this is Joel Best's *Damned Lies and Statistics* (2001) – a cautionary work that every manager, Lean included, would be wise to be aware of. But in the intervening two decades the extent of statistical BS has exploded. With 'Big Data' and 'Data Mining' this problem has worsened. All this is a huge topic of course, and here we will offer just a few pointers. Bergstom and West have a good framework built around the classic systems model:

- Inputs:
  - How, when, where, was the data collected?
  - Are meanings or definitions clear?
  - Is the data valid for my circumstances? (similar industry, system?)
  - Who collected the data and was there a hidden agenda?
- Process:
  - Has a control group been used? (This is one of the only ways to reduce contamination of results caused by changing circumstances.)
  - Is there a confidence interval? (A forecast should always be two numbers: the forecast itself and a measure of deviation.)
  - Reliability and validity. (Would the same result be obtained by others? Does it measure what it is supposed to measure?)
  - Has any data been changed? (Filtered? Adjusted?). Why?
  - Has learning been involved in developing the measure?

- Output:
    - How presented? (Huge material here, including two all-time classics, Edward Tufte's 'Visual Explanations', Graphics Press, 1997, and Howard Wainer's 'Graphic Discovery', Princeton, 2005)

- Goodhart's Law.

  'When a measure becomes a target, it ceases to be a good measure.' Examples abound. Here is one from Lean: Inventory Turns. Quite a good measure for Lean particularly when trends are examined. BUT, when used as a target, can it be gamed? Yes! Run down the inventory before the annual stock take. Years ago one of the authors found collaboration: Keep my inventory in your warehouse in the weeks before my annual stock take, and I will pay you a bonus. As soon as marks are awarded to students, gaming begins by both students and teachers. And similarly, marks or points are awarded for suppliers, for the Shingo Prize, for CO_2 output (ask VW). The list goes on and on. The result? Chase the points not the objective. Beware.

- Formulas.
  Beware! A Lean example: Overall Equipment Effectiveness (OEE) used by many. OEE is availability x efficiency x quality. But, this assumes all three factors are of equal importance. They are not! Also the common target of 85% depends on the industry. Availability is Availability is made up of MTTR (mean time to repair) and MTBF (mean time between failures). The formula is: Availability = MTBF / (MTBF + MTTR). Thus we can have two machines with the same availability but very different breakdown intervals and repair times! And, how much variation: Two similar OEEs but with different variation!
  Every formula should be checked for what engineers and scientists call 'dimensions'. In other words, don't mix parts of a formula with different dimensions – for instance multiplying 'quality', 'lead time', 'customer satisfaction' and 'waste'. Meaningless!

- Percentages.
  Your Lead time has been reduced by 40% as a result of Lean. From what base? Is it 40% compared to the original figure or the final figure? Is it the weighted average of all products? Please check for consistency using Little's Law. (See Appendix to Organisation Chapter.)

BS in media

Frankfurt explains that BS is unavoidable whenever circumstances require someone to talk without knowing what he is talking about…whenever a person's obligations or opportunities to speak about some topic exceed his knowledge of the facts that are relevant to that topic.' This is an interesting warning in as far as Lean is an ever-expanding field of endeavour – so we should all be on the lookout for doubtful talk.

BS and Red Tape in Bureaucracy

Very many organisations have silly red tape arrangements. 'Pain points'. Typically, junior and middle-level employees are aware of these because they experience them frequently but senior executives are blissfully unaware. Customers are often aware of service shortcomings but long experience has taught them that it is too much trouble to report shortcomings. Sometimes red tape and duplication is picked up as part of a Lean or waste study but often it endures for lengthy periods. Some examples…

- Travel rules. Mode of travel and travel times.
- Expense claims. Checkers are notoriously pernickety and slow.
- Parking arrangements. Spaces are available but cannot be used.
- Compulsory meetings, and some compulsory training
- Software approval processes
- Approved buying procedures for small or urgent supplies
- Preparation of reports that are not read
- And, for customers: navigating some web sites, delivery times, customer waiting while desk staff are visibly unoccupied, no information on delays, the official or doctor's time is more important, visa applications, automated check-in or check-out that goes wrong but no response is available, Packaging: cannot open, wasteful, instructions too small to be read. And not forgetting officious 'control-freaks'.

Martin Lindstrom, in *The Ministry of Common Sense* amusingly describes many such incidents. Japanese examples are given in *The Blue-eyed Salaryman*. (Be thankful you don't work there!)

The point is that all such red tape, for employees and customers, have distrust at the root. A lack of respect. The message that is sent out is clear to employees....

What to do?
- Pretend you are a customer. Go through the whole process end-to-end. Particularly important for senior managers. Mystery shopping is a variant. Managers working on the front line at regular intervals is another.
- No special rules for senior managers. They too should feel the pain. The days of the 'Zil Lane' (car lanes reserved for Soviet up-and-ups) should be a thing of the past.
- Customer Journey mapping will help. Including 'moments of truth', (a concept from Jan Carlsson of SAS from the 1980's), 'magic moments' and 'misery moments'. See *The Service Systems Toolbox.*
- Lindstrom (a top consultant) suggests setting up a 'Ministry of Common Sense' with one or two full time staff reporting to a senior level. Independent action is mandated, and how-to advice is given. Essential for any larger organisation?
- This 'Ministry' concept is not new. In the 1970's Leslie Chapman was a civil servant employed by the UK government to tackle what we have called BS. His amusing book *Your Disobedient Servant* tells of how his team removed signs, parking, sold off inventory, destroyed warehouses (any empty space always fills!), and much else. A tonic! Needed today!
- Stop devising slogans that are endlessly trotted out, irrespective of context. (Deming also spoke about this tendency in his 14 points.)
- Warren Buffet said, '(Organisations') get the reputation they deserve.' So don't try to plaster it over with fancy (and expensive) PR campaigns.
- Failure demand is a good indication of BS that affects customers – where a customer repeatedly comes for unsatisfied service. See the Systems section of this book and *The Service Systems Toolbox.*
- Encourage employees to keep notes and take photos of BS or pain-points. Then have a regular (twice-yearly?) series of meetings chaired by a senior manager – a 'go-getter' not a 'naysayer'. Notes should also be kept of corporate gobbledygook. (An annual prize?)
- Consider flat-rate expense claims. £x per night; £y car travel per month. If there were only self-claim or flat-rate forms – what would be the saving, and the risk? Or take it one step further like Semco: employees set their own expenses.

Further Readings.

Mats Alvesson and André Spicer, *The Stupidity Paradox*, Profile Books, 2016

Carl Bergstrom and Jevlin West, *Calling Bullshit*, Allen Lane, 2020

John Bicheno, *The Service Systems Toolbox*. PICSIE Books, 2012

Evan Davis, *Post Truth: Peak bullshit and what we can do about it*, Abacus, 2017

Harry Frankfurt, *On Bullshit*, Princeton University Press, 2005

David Graeber, *Bullshit Jobs* – A theory, Allen Lane, 2018

Martin Lindstrom, *The Ministry of Common Sense: How to eliminate bureaucratic red tape, bad excuses and corporate bullshit*, John Murray Learning, 2021

13.14 Engineering Analogies: Newton's Laws, Stress-strain, and Bridges

Newton

Of course, Newton was not a change psychologist (although he probably was a Lean Thinker) but his laws of physics are remarkably useful in a Change context.

First Law: Objects at rest remain at rest and objects in motion remain in motion in a straight line unless acted on by an unbalanced force. People: Will not change or change direction unless they have to. There is inertia. A force (not to say 'forced change') is required. The force, or effort, has to be sufficient to overcome resistance.

Second Law: Force equals mass time acceleration. People: The greater the mass (or numbers) the greater the force that is required. And the faster the change, the greater the force required. Acceleration is not just speed (or velocity) – it is the change in speed per unit time.

Third Law: For every action there is an equal and opposite reaction. People: A manager should expect a reaction to a change proposal in direct proportion to the amount of change that is proposed. Smaller changes will be easier than larger change.

Newton's Law of Universal Gravitation: Every particle attracts every other particle in the universe with a force that is directly proportional to the product of their masses and inversely proportional to the square of the distance between them. People: The further people are apart the smaller the force between them. Distance squared, not just distance. A small body (organisation) will find it hard to resist a large body (organisation). A tipping point when the mass of opinion becomes irresistible, and when the mass is nearby.

Load, Stress, and Strain

As a force (or tension load) is applied to a section of steel, stress increases and strain (elongation) increases. This occurs in stages. First there is a linear elastic stage where stress is proportional to strain. (Young's modulus). With more force, a yield point is reached. Up to this point the steel will completely recover – it can return to its initial state. Beyond the yield point, plastic deformation and strain hardening begins. Now the steel will no longer return to its original state. With further force, eventually the ultimate tensile strength is reached. No further stress is possible. Further elongation (distortion) occurs and eventually the steel breaks.

Similarly as load (orders or work) increases so the stress and strain on the facility and people increases. In this first stage, people will work happily and flexibly. But with increasing load eventually a point is reached where, quite suddenly, people feel they can no longer cope. Trust is lost and people will never return to their initial state. Service deteriorates and people become less willing, and hardened. Eventually performance declines (See Yerkes-Dodson) and a complete breakdown in goodwill occurs, including work-stoppages.

Bridge Development – a Parallel with Lean

Bridges have developed over centuries using compression (push) or tension (pull) or both. An analogy with inventory, waste, and efficiency is given below.

Type	Description	Tension /. Compression	Typical Span	Inventory analogy	Comment
Slab	Block of stone as a beam	Both. Weak in tension	3-4 m	Non Scientific	Inefficient. Wasteful
Arch	Brick / stone with keystone	Compression	12m	EOQ inventory	Push, more efficient
Iron Bridge	Brittle iron framework	Weak tension, compression	20m	EOQ + ROP	Early attempt at calculation
Reinforced Concrete (RC)	Steel and concrete beam, using bending moment calc.	Steel for tension, concrete for compression	50m	MRP. Bill of material calculation.	Push and Pull, but heavy. Wasteful push?
Pre-stressed concrete (or RC Arch)	Steel and concrete, pre-prepared	As for RC	100m	MRP + TOC / DDMRP	As for RC but less wasteful
Truss	Steel framework	Both. Efficient	250m	Integrated pull & push	Relies on calculation
Suspension Bridge	Cables from towers	Pure tension	1500m	Integrated elegance	Pure pull No waste
Composite Bridge	Panels. No steel, concrete	Both. (Made by printer)	30m ?	Recycle, Reconfigure	Agile, the future?

Note: Bridge Span (Not Span of Control) is a measure of efficiency. The inverse of lead-time?

The analogy continues: Initially inventory control is easy but later becomes complicated and sophisticated calculation or tools are required. Some think that tools are easy but people are the real issue. But the analogy is that, later, tools are not easy. The bridge will fall down if there is insufficient understanding of appropriate tools.

Appendix to Organisation Chapter

Little's Law, Capacity, Wait times, and Distributing Work.

Little's Law is a deceptively simple formula that is, nevertheless, very robust and independent of time distributions and variation. It is:

$$L = \lambda \, W$$

Where (using a health example)
- L is average number of patients in the system; λ is average arrival (or throughput rate); W is average time in the <u>system. </u>(System time includes queue time and process time)
- (Note: L could also be inventory or jobs)

For example
- Patients arrive at average rate 10 per hour, and stay an average of 0.5 hour, then L= 10*0.5 = 2 patients.

Another example
- If we found that on average there were 2 customers in the system, and $\lambda = 10$, then W = L / λ = 2/10 = 0.2 hour or 12 minutes.

The Gantt Chart

Is a useful way to calculate and to show capacity and utilization. Dr. Simon Dodds (Surgeon) makes extensive use of Gantt charts in hospital settings and in his excellent FISH course (Foundations of Improvement Science in Healthcare.)

Example

Patients are expected to arrive at the following minutes: 0, 20, 40, 50, 75, 85, 95, 105
Check in and prep is 10 minutes
Operation time is 15 minutes
5 minutes to clean up Operation room

Given this data, What is:
- Total time to complete all 8 patients?
- Number of chairs to be provided in waiting room?
- Average time spent in the system?

These can easily and clearly be shown using a Gantt chart, as shown. Note also that the average time spent in the system can be calculated using Little's Law.

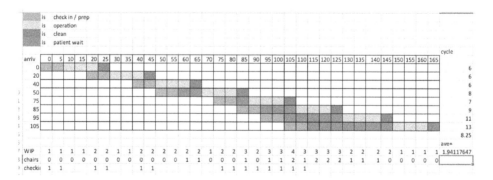

Number of Operators required in a cell.

(A calculation performed by Industrial Engineers – but better would be to allow the cell operators to determine this themselves.)

The basic formula for the number of operators in a cell is:

(Sum of all direct operations times) / (takt time x 0.85)
…and why 0.85? Because there should be some slack in the system to allow for variation. (See section on Queues in Eight Models chapter.)
So if the sum of all task times is 480 seconds, takt time is 60 seconds; then
No of operators required = 480 / (60 * 0.85) = 9.41 operators.
Some would round this up to 10; others would hope that learning occurs and would round down to 9 operators.

Bucket Brigade Line Balancing

Traditional Line balancing requires that all operation times are known. This generally means stopwatch timing or video. This is a disadvantage – unreliable, subject to 'gaming', and no accounting for different operator work rates. Good traditional line balancing should be done for several rates.

Bucket Brigade line balancing requires NO timing, or external analyst. It balances automatically, coping with changes in work content, operator variability and demand.
Bucket Brigade automatically limits accumulation of WIP as well as increasing productivity. It copes easily with changes such as operators going off to the toilet, and with job rotation.
The method is often more efficient than traditional line balancing because time is used better by, for instance, not requiring exactly the same work activities in each work cycle.
There is none of the working faster or working slower deceptions found with traditional timed work balancing. Rather, operators sort themselves out. Group dynamics tends to sort out slower or faster workers, but if not, it does not matter. Motivation should be better.
Possible downsides are monitoring difficulties, and traceability.

First, make an estimate of the number of operators required in the cell. Assume there are 7 separate operations (1 to 7) to complete the work in the cell. A piece (job) moves through the 7 operations in sequence.

Assume, for this example, that three are estimated. This can be adjusted at any time. The more operators, the greater will be the throughput.

- Tell the operators to work at normal, relaxed speed. All operators should be familiar with the work required. (This is a possible drawback of the method.)
- Three operators line up in front of the first three operations
- Operator 1 starts work at Operation 1. Operator 1 passes the piece to Operator 2 who carries out Operation 2 and passes the piece to Operator 3.
- Operator 3 completes Operation 3, then moves downstream to Operation 4, then 5, then 6, and so on until the last Operation is complete and the finished piece (job) is deposited in the Finished Product area. Operator 3 then walks upstream – not to the beginning of the line, but upstream - passing Operations 7, 6, 5, etc until Operator 3 meets Operator 2

- When Operator 1 hands the piece to Operator 2, Operator 1 returns to the beginning of the Line and starts making a new piece (job)
- Operator 1 hands Operator 2 the second piece. Operator 2 does Operation 2 but then proceeds downstream carrying out Operations 3, 4, etc., until Operator 2 meets Operator 3 walking back upstream.
- Operator 2 then hands the part-completed piece to Operator 3. Operator 2 then turns around and walks upstream towards Operator 1. (So, Operator 2 does not complete all operations.)
- Operator 3 takes the piece from Operator 2, turns around, and moves downstream completing all Operations until the job is complete. Then, once again, Operator 3 walks upstream until she meets Operator 2 moving downstream.
- When Operator 1 handed the second piece to Operator 2, Operator 1 once again returns to the start (Operation 1) and begins the third piece (job). This time, however, Operator 2 is likely to be busy further downstream. So, Operator 1 then works downstream doing Operations 2, 3 etc until Operator 1 meets Operator 2 walking upstream. Operator 1 hands the part-made piece to Operator 2. Operator 2 turns around proceeds downstream. Operator 1 walks back to the beginning of the line and starts making the fourth piece (job).
- Now the pattern of work is becoming established. Operator 1 works downstream until meeting Operator 2. Operator 2 works downstream until she meets Operator 3. When meetings (or job completion in the case of Operator 3) take place, Operators turn around and walk upstream, until they meet the earlier Operator working downstream, or in the case of Operator 1, when she starts a new piece (job).
- Eventually balance occurs. The work becomes automatically distributed between the Operators, although not every cycle will be the same. For instance, Operator 1 may sometimes do Operations 1, 2 and 3 – and sometimes only Operations 1 and 2.
- COMMUNICATE! This is a very important point on flexibility of working. Operators should talk to one another about work progress.

Further Readings.

John Bicheno, *The Lean Games and Simulations Book*, PICSIE, 2017
Simon Dodds, FISH course, www.saasoft.co.uk
Wallace Hopp, *Supply Chain Science*, McGraw Hill, 2008

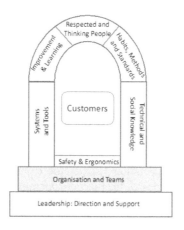

Chapter 14
Ergonomics (Human Factors), 5S and Job Safety

14.1 Ergonomics

"Ergonomics (or human factors) is the scientific discipline concerned with understanding the interactions among humans and other elements of a system, and the profession that applies theory, principles, data and methods to design, in order to optimize human well-being and overall system performance.." (Dul and Weerdmeester, 2008, p.1)

Although 'human factors' is a preferred term by many, 'ergonomics' will be used here since the majority of sections in this book are 'human factors' in the widest sense.

Let us begin with a reminder of the 3 'M's of TPS: Muda, Mura, Muri. Muda (waste) has received huge attention with the classic 7 or 8 wastes. One of the 7 – motion – is directly relevant to ergonomics. Mura (variation) has received attention often through discussion of standard work. The reduction of variation has been an important aim of Six Sigma. Muri (overburden, overload, stress) has received the least attention of the three. But, in TPS, the 'M's are regarded as a trilogy. Ergonomics or "human factors" engineering is a discipline in its own right which pays specific attention to Muri, Mura, and Muda – probably in that order although they are words that would seldom appear in Ergonomics literature. Several seminal texts on Lean make no mention of ergonomics (indeed some make no mention of mura and muri), even though it is considered fundamental to quality and productivity – not only in labour-intensive operations.

Ergonomics is sometimes an afterthought in the design of a Lean workplace, but doing so can mean an opportunity lost to create working conditions that can have a major impact on morale, motivation, employee turnover, ideas, and quality and productivity in general. As Churchill said, 'We shape our buildings; therafter they shape us.' Today, there is increased awareness of the wisdom of this statement – the unseen effects of poor ergonomics – often lasting for years.

It is noteworthy that when Elton Mayo began work at the Hawthorne Works of Western Electric in 1927, a study on the relationships between egonomics and productivity was already in progress, most famously between illumination intensity and worker output, and in relay assembly. Although (as noted in Chapter 2) many of the studies were flawed the 'Hawthorne Effect' (as it became known) highlighted the importance of managerial attention and interest. Effectively, the Hawthone studies were a significant nail in the coffin of Taylorism. Thus, 'Gemba', 'Respect' and Ergonomics are, and should be, closely related.

Ergonomics is usually split into three areas: Physical, Cognitive and Organisational. The table below gives a boad outline of the various factors. It is not the place here to detail all the aspects, but merely to provide a listing, or reminder, of factors that affect human wellbeing at work, productivity and quality. At a minimum, every workplace and layout designer In Lean should consult one of the many texts in the ergonomics area. Even better would be to use the services of a professional Ergonomist, or Occupational Health professional. A walk through of offices and factory spaces with such a person can be a sobering experience, revealing a host of opportunity, unseen by the non-professional. However, 'people are more commited to solutions they have helped to design than to carrying out 'expert' advice'. (Kurt Lewin)

The integration of Egonomics with 'Lean is Green' is an opportunity that is only just opening up.

Area	Factor		Lean Comment
Physical	Posture	Neck	Home, office & plant. Possible sources of muscular skeletal disorders (MSD)
		Shoulders	
		Hands	
		Forearms	
		Back	
		Feet	
		Eye strain	
	Movement	Lifting / Weight	Motion wastes and Cells. Standing may be of benefit.
		Distance	
	Environmental	Noise	All require careful ergonomic design and are essential for the modern workplace. TWI Job Safety
		Light	
		Vibration	
		Temperature	
		Slip and Trip	
		Space	
Cognitive	Psychosocial	Psycho Strain	Yerkes Dodson
		Job Stress	
		Mental Load	
Organisational	Information	Standards	TWI Job Instruction
		Controls	Visual
		Communications	Stand up meeting
	Work Design	Repetition	Mixed model
		Duration	More than 1 min.
		Job Rotation	Every 2 hours?
		Time pressure	85% of takt
		Rest and Recovery	Team areas
	Managerial	Supervisor Support	TWI JR, Feedback
		Co-worker Support	Skills matrix
		Job Autonomy	TWI JM, Ideas
		Participation	Kaizen,
		Decision making	Thinking worker
		Job satisfaction	Respect, Involvement
		Task identification	End product

If professional help is not available, several ergonomics assessment tools are readily available, often free. Do not neglect! (See, for example 'Humantech' BRIEF Assessment, and web sites.) Many good Lean companies have their own internal standards – for example Toyota and Johnson and Johnson.

Health and Safety legislation and advice covers several aspects in all the areas, but such legislation should be considered a minimum standard, not necessarily the desirable. Examples: Health and safty at work regulations, Manual handling regs, Stress risk asssesment, Shift work, Packing machinery, Display screen equipment standards.

And, not least, workers and operators themselves are a considerable source of good ergonomic advise and comment. Listen. Take note of the unofficial appearance of cushions, footrests, props of various sorts, rests, and added reminders and notes.

It is unfortunate that some managers continue to see Lean as a cost reduction initiative. In such circumstances the ergonomic implications may be negative, including increased risk of muscular skeletal disorders (MSD), stress, and work intensification, which may be combined with high repetition, and low autonomy and participation. Work standards are fixed. Such factors have been shown to impact worker turnover, absenteeism, and quality and productivity issues.

On the other hand, Lean can and should be seen as symbiotic with ergonomics – increasing autonomy, participation and teamworking, combined with job enrichment and engagement – through, for example, participation in kaizen and problem solving. Try to incorporate specific ergonomic considerations in all such activities. Good Lean should involve less human effort employing well designed ergonomic workplaces – in short, the elimination of 'muri'.

The Ageing Challenge, Diversity and Automation

In OECD countries there has been an increase in the average age of the workforce and an increase in diversity of the workforce. A third factor is the change in required cognitive and physical abilities resulting from automation and robotics, AI, RPA, and other decision-support tools. Increasing automation will result in a shift in the nature of work – from operator to maintenance person in manufacturing and logistics, and towards interpretation and integration in the office. Together, these factors mean that ergonomics or human-factors, must feature much more prominently in both service and manufacturing contexts. And, amongst millennials in OECD countries, there is increasing reluctance to do repetitive work, particularly short cycle. To cap it all, there is the emerging challenge of home-working brought about by COVID, transport costs, and 'green'.

14.2 5S

The goals of ergonomics and 5S align perfectly; to improve worker safety and productivity. 5S is a five stage program often mistakenly seen as just a housekeeping exercise, but it is much more than this. The system aims at putting everything where it belongs, removing excess material and tools and keeping the workplace clean and tidy. This makes it easier for people to do their jobs without wasting time or risking injury. The main benefits of 5S include increased efficiency (through the elimination of the 7 lean wastes), a safer working environment, a reduction in the space required to perform the work and increased worker satisfaction. 5S has a direct impact on quality Almost everyone works better in a cleaner, tidier environment – and this affects mindset, pride, and attitude. The classic 5S's are: Seiri, Seiton, Seiso, Seiketsu, Shitsuke. Most commonly these are translated into:

Step 1 Sort – This involves reviewing all the tools, equipment, parts and materials in the work area. Those that are no longer necessary are removed and those that are are only required periodically are relocated.

Step 2 Set in Order – Next, all the tools, equipment, and parts and materials that have been identified as needed regularly are now organised in a logical way that facilitates the flow of work and increases employee efficiency. As the old adage goes "*A place for everything and everything in its place*"

Step 3 Shine – This step is about ensuring the workplace and equipment is restored back to its optimum condition. Regular check procedures, and ongoing clean-up and sweeping are put in place – not for the cleaners but for the workers themselves. Total productive maintenance activities (TPM) may be necessary. Visual management concepts are essential.

Step 4 Standardise – To maintain the new standard a set of rules and procedures for the first three S's are required. This includes an agreed understanding of where all items are located, safety procedures, 5S task assignment and the frequency with which they are carried out. It is important that these procedures are agreed, not imposed. Once agreed they are posted in the area so that they become part of the daily work.

Step 5 Sustain – As with any lean initiative there is a danger that, over time things may revert back to where they were before. This is why the sustain element is critical. Sustain is about ingraining 5S into the organisation's culture. Team leaders have a vital role. Regular audits are common. Some 5S programme expect improvement, not only maintenance.

An alternative name for 5S is CANDO: Clean-up, Arrange, Neatness, Discipline, Ongoing Improvement. Some companies add a sixth S – SAFETY. However, a good 5S program should stress safety as an aspect of each of the five stages. It may confuse to list safety separately. Safety procedures and standards should also be developed, maintained and audited as part of the programme. The removal of unsafe conditions should certainly be integral to 5S.

When designing a 5S program it is important that consideration is given both to the people and the actual work area itself. An overzealous 5S campaign where desks are taped off and labelled for staplers, keyboard and phone, risks making 5S, and worse where 5S is linked with Lean, open for ridicule. Some readers might recall a 2007 5S implementation at HM Revenue and Customs (HMRC), a UK civil service department which made headlines in the U.K. press. According to the Daily Telegraph , the programme was so far reaching that one member of staff was asked whether a banana was 'active' or 'inactive' - in other words whether it was going to be eaten immediately, which was acceptable, or whether it was for later, which would mean the fruit would have to be cleared from the desk!

5S is best done as 'pull' not 'push' In other words as a solution to a problem, not as something nice to do or as an unconnected project. Examples of initiatives where a 5S focus would be particularly advantageous include scrap reduction, health and safety, SMED, and process improvement projects. Employee participation in area re-layout is an opportunity not to be missed.

Many organisations link their 5S program with incentives to generate interest, recognise early adopters and sustain improvements. Incentives may include company t shirts, meal vouchers or a trophy awarded to the monthly winner. At their best these incentive programs can create healthy competition and bring an element of fun into the workplace. We have seen examples where the employee with the untidiest office is presented with his or her own personalised set of cleaning products. In another, any items left out of place are taken and deposited in a manager's office from where they must be collected by the operator. No comment is made. Good practice is prominently to display a league table of the various areas with the results of the 5S audits. Members of the judging panel are usually drawn from the senior management team. This demonstrates commitment to the program, and ensures that managers act as 5S role models.

Hirano suggests a host of 5S activities, carried out at various frequencies: Amongst others:
- A 5S month, once a year (?), to re-energise efforts.
- 5S days, one to four per month including evaluations.
- 5S seminars by outside experts – with lots of photos.
- 5S visits to leading outside companies to capture best practice.
- 5S patrols, following a set route.
- 5S model workplaces (this has become popular in NHS hospitals).
- 5S competitions, award ceremonies, and displays.
- 5 minute 5S each day (This is usually at the end of the day / shift to ensure the work area is left in showroom condition).

Thus 5S is much more than a housekeeping program. A clean organised workplace (factory floor or office) is representative of a positive work culture. It can lift morale, instil pride and confidence, while also setting expectations for what is acceptable now and in the future.

Cautions

- The real productivity and quality benefit of 5S are in the later S's, particularly standardisation, not the relatively easy-to-do first two.
- Failure to address the fifth S sustain will result in the program having to be re-energised.
- While it is acceptable that 5S may start as a project or initiative, in order for it to be properly sustained it has to become fully ingrained in the culture. A habit.
- If the workplace is untidy, begin with a 'tidy up' program, coupled with Safety. Don't launch straight into 5S program, particularly one that is over zealous.

14.3 Job Safety

Job Safety (JS) is an additional TWI program that focuses on health and safety in the workplace. JS was developed in Japan and added to the original TWI trilogy of job instruction, job methods, and job relations. JS emphasizes that the relationship between the supervisor and the employee plays a central role in a safe and responsible workplace - working together to 'break the chain' of causal factors where an unsafe act may eventually lead to a fatality.

The progression from unsafe act to fatality is shown by the Heinrich-Bird safety pyramid. This classic (1930s) study postulated Heinrich's ratios of 600 near misses to 30 minor injuries to 10 serious injuries, to 1 fatality. What follows from this is an iceberg sequence of leading indicators and the necessity for early reporting and hazard removal. Subsequent research has disputed much of the original findings, showing that the ratios vary hugely by industry and, importantly, that the root causes of serious injury are often very different from the causes of minor injury. Nevertheless, Heinrich-Bird continues to be a useful starting point for any safety program.

Steve Spear, in his classic book on CI, described how Alcoa's focus on accident reporting – right up to CEO level – not only drastically cut injuries and fatalities, but was a foundation for their Lean initiative.

TWI Job safety considers three critical factors: Physical Conditions, Personal Conditions and Cultural Conditions. All three contribute to safety and risk reduction in the workplace.

- Physical links in the chain include the facility, equipment, workplace floor plan and traffic, lighting, signage, clothing and protective gear – and the risks they may present.

- Personal conditions involve knowledge, skills, abilities, emotions, supervisor-worker relationships, behaviours, routines, and personal health. Psychological safety.

- Cultural links are institutional in nature and involve policies, leadership attitudes, risk management procedures and related organizational behaviours and attitudes.

Additional information on Job Safety can be found on these excellent websites.
https://www.twi-trainingwithinindustry.com/job-safety
https://www.twi-institute.com/job-safety/
www.risk engineering.org

Further Readings.

P. Arezes, J. Dinis-Carvalho, and A.C. Alves, 2010. Threats and Opportunities for Workplace Ergonomics in Lean Environments, *Proc EurOM*.

R. Carter, A. Danford, D. Howcroft, R. Richardson, A. Smith, and P. Taylor, 2012, March. Inactive banana time: lean production and the degradation of work in the UK civil service. In *30th International Labour Process Conference, 27th March, Stockholm*.

T.Y. Choi, and J.K. Liker, 1992. Institutional conformity and technology implementation: A process model of ergonomics dissemination. *Journal of Engineering and Technology Management* 9, pp. 155-195.

J. Dul, and B. Weerdmeester, 2008. *Ergonomics for beginners*. Boca Raton: CRC.

E. Grandjean, 1969. *Fitting the task to the man*. 3rd ed. London: Taylor and Francis

Humantech, ed., (2009). *Applied Industrial Ergonomics*. 4th ed. Ann Arbor.

Hiroyuki Hirano, *5S for Operators*, Routledge, 1996

Johnson, M. C. 1996. Ergonomics in the manufacturing environment. *Production and Inventory Management Journal* 37(2), pp. 80-82.

Kroemer, K. and Grandjean, E. (1997). *Fitting the task to the human*. London: Taylor and Francis.

T. Sakthi Nagaraj and R. Jeyapaul, (2020) 'An empirical investigation on association between human factors, ergonomics and lean manufacturing', *Production Planning and Control*, Published online: https://doi.org/10.1080/09537287.2020.1810815

Fabio Sgarbossa et al, Human Factors in production and logistics systems of the future, *Annual Reviews in Control*, Vol 49, 295-305, 2020. https://doi.org/10.1016/j.arcontrol.2020.04.007.

Steven Spear, *Chasing the Rabbit*, McGraw Hill, 2009. (A later edition is titled *The Excellence Edge*.)

Chapter 15
It's up to You

Throughout this book there is emphasis on respect, humility, and the dangers and problems with bias, the halo effect, and groupthink. There is also the relevance of different situations and of VUCA. All of these have significant implications for Lean leaders – not only the CEO but also value stream leaders, functional leaders as well as anyone involved with decisions and motivation. The point is that all the desirable characteristics of Lean leadership listed in Section 11.7 are unlikely to be found in any single individual. The 'Great Man' theory seldom applies - if it ever has - in a Lean or Agile organisation. All is not lost, however…

Today's Lean Leader can take several actions to improve his or her decision making and effectiveness, through good team interaction.

The following suggestions stem from a wide range of topics discussed in the book….

- Be honest with yourself. Are you mainly Theory X or Theory Y.? (See Section 2.4)
- Are you being heard? Are you listening? (Chapter 3)
- Something did not work out as planned. Was a person blamed or was the situation or system the cause? (See Section 3.1)
- Today experts are found at all levels in an organisation. Take time to listen. (See Section 3.4). This is also Respect and Humility (See Section 3.1 and 3.2)
- So you think you know the story. But could it be that you are in the 'Mount Stupid' region? (See Section 3.2)
- If possible, go to the gemba and see first-hand. (See Section 3.3)
- When last did you have a meaningful conversation with a front-line employee? (See Section 3.5)
- A principal role of consultants and middle managers is to challenge and to make one think. If they are merely agreeing and filtering……(See Section 3.18)
- Don't be rushed or pressurised. Sleep on it overnight. (Kahneman System 1 and System 2). (See Sections 3.19 and 8.14)
- When you walk the floor, is the status easy to see? (See Section 3.22)
- Are good habits being cultivated or destroyed by you? (See Section 3.23)
- Split decision making into two - As Eisenhower said before D-Day 'Plans are useless; Planning is everything'. And Mike Tyson said 'Everyone has a plan until they get punched in the mouth' (See Section 4.2)
- Can a series of small changes be made instead of a big change? (See Section 4.2)
- Do you acknowledge and encourage small wins? (See Section 4.2)
- Beware of prioritising a "biggest bang for your buck" approach when selecting projects as this may send out a message that C.I. is just about cost reduction. (See Section 4.2)
- Remember C.I. is about improvement rather than perfection. (See Section 4.2)
- Remember Fred Taylor who separated thinking from doing. Does Taylor still have an influence? (See Section 4.3)
- Is performance punishing – or non-performance rewarding? (See Section 4.4)
- Use Kurt Lewin's Force Field Analysis diagram (See Section 4.5)
- Avoid inappropriate analogies. Is it valid? Is the company you are quoting in the same business, similar volume, similar complexity? (See Section 4.7)
- Consider variation. Many situations in Lean are non-linear and have variation, so a simple average might not suffice. (See Muda, Muri, Mura and Deming Red Bead (Section 4.8))
- What about feedback? Note that a value steam map has no feedback loop! 'Systems bite back'. (See Section 5.3)

- The concept of the 'system boundary' is powerful. Who and what is considered inside and outside? (See Section 5.4)
- Culture: What are the fundamental beliefs of the group? Do they have the same values and objectives as the people who will actually make the decision? (See Section 5.5)
- Who will be the victims and the beneficiaries of the change? (See Section 5.5)
- Failure demand? (Not just total demand!) (See Section 5.7)
- Have you ignored the introverts? (See Section 6.3)
- A diverse group is often more effective. (See Section 6.5)
- Consensus is good – sometimes. This is the 'Wisdom of Crowds' (See Section 6.8). But the 'crowd' is not always correct. Are they independent? Do they have specific expertise?
- Cultivate that mindset! Can a person not do it, or not do it YET? (See Section 7.4)
- Be careful about blame. There is always something to learn. (See Section 7.5)
- In the complex domain, the repeatable experiment may not work. This has implications for Kata, PDCA, and A3 problem solving (See Section 8.9)
- Have you considered the second-order effects of a measure? (See section 8.10, page 164)
- What are your smaller competitors doing – in technology, people, and products? (See Section 8.11)
- In any proposed change, PDCA or PDSA: What is the hypothesis? (See Section 8.13)
- The book suggests six categories of problems, each with their own problem 'solving' characteristics. (See Section 8.15)
- Implemented ideas are an important indicator of organisational health. What is the status? (See Section 8.17)
- Ensure that at least one alternative is surfaced and discussed. (See Section 9.4)
- Appoint a person to act as 'Devil's Advocate' (See Section 9.4)
- Your intuition may be useful, but only in situations where there is specific similarity with previous experience, including feedback. (See Section 9.5)
- Conduct a 'pre-mortem' as suggested by Gary Klein (See Section 9.5)
- Improve psychological safety – critics and proposers of alternative ideas are not penalised, or afraid. (See Section 9.7)
- Mistakes are often positive. (See Section 9.7 to 9.9)
- Are you coaching your successor? (Chapter 10)
- Do After Action Reviews as a matter of course. (See Section 10.18)
- Don't let the senior person speak first when alternatives are considered. Beware at meetings of the 'information cascade' where prior speakers have undue influence. This is also the Solomon Ash experiment. (See Section 11.3)
- When last did you have a meaningful conversation with a customer? (See Section 13.10)
- What privileges, bonuses, and rules apply to only a limited few? (See Section 13.12)
- Confidentiality is often an over-used, unnecessary excuse. It undermines trust...(See Section 13.9)

Now, it up to you. Best wishes!

Index

Concepts

People

Human Lean

Lightning Source UK Ltd.
Milton Keynes UK
UKHW030649011121
393187UK00005B/222

9 780956 830784